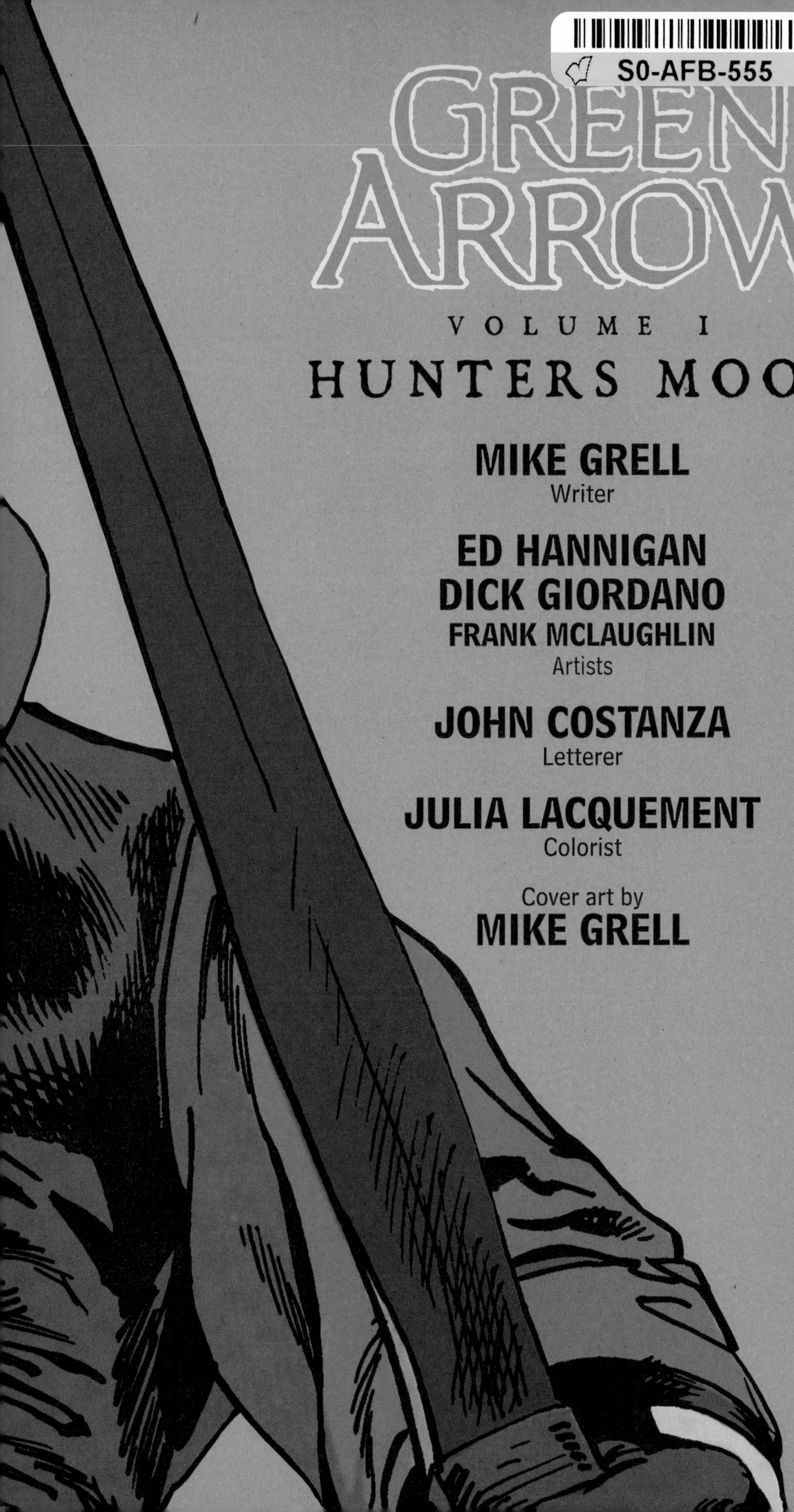

GREEN ARROW

VOLUME I

HUNTERS MOON

MIKE GRELL
Writer

ED HANNIGAN
DICK GIORDANO
FRANK MCLAUGHLIN
Artists

JOHN COSTANZA
Letterer

JULIA LACQUEMENT
Colorist

Cover art by
MIKE GRELL

Mike Gold Editor – Original Series
Rowena Yow Editor
Robbin Brosterman Design Director – Books
Damian Ryland Publication Design

Bob Harras Senior VP – Editor-in-Chief, DC Comics

Diane Nelson President
Dan DiDio and Jim Lee Co-Publishers
Geoff Johns Chief Creative Officer
John Rood Executive VP – Sales, Marketing & Business Development
Amy Genkins Senior VP – Business & Legal Affairs
Nairi Gardiner Senior VP – Finance
Jeff Boison VP – Publishing Planning
Mark Chiarello VP – Art Direction & Design
John Cunningham VP – Marketing
Terri Cunningham VP – Editorial Administration
Alison Gill Senior VP – Manufacturing & Operations
Hank Kanalz Senior VP – Vertigo & Integrated Publishing
Jay Kogan VP – Business & Legal Affairs, Publishing
Jack Mahan VP – Business Affairs, Talent
Nick Napolitano VP – Manufacturing Administration
Sue Pohja VP – Book Sales
Courtney Simmons Senior VP – Publicity
Bob Wayne Senior VP – Sales

GREEN ARROW VOLUME 1: HUNTERS MOON

DC Comics, 1700 Broadway, New York, NY 10019
A Warner Bros. Entertainment Company.
Printed by RR Donnelley, Salem, VA, USA. 10/25/13. First Printing.
ISBN: 978-1-4012-4326-5

Library of Congress Cataloging-in-Publication Data

Grell, Mike, author.
  Green Arrow. Volume 1, Hunters Moon / Mike Grell, Ed Hannigan, Dick Giordano.
    pages cm
  Summary: "In these cult favorite stories from the 1980s, Green Arrow hunts down
a child killer, races to find a lost biological weapon before Chinese spies can find
it, and tackles a rash of violence against gays. These stories, written by Mike Grell,
repositioned Green Arrow as an inner city crusader for justice who deals not only with
super-villains but also with street level crime. Collects the 1988 GREEN ARROW #1-
6"-- Provided by publisher.
  ISBN 978-1-4012-4326-5 (pbk.)
1. Graphic novels. I. Hannigan, Edward, illustrator. II. Giordano, Dick, illustrator. III.
Title. IV. Title: Hunters Moon.
  PN6728.G725G75 2013
  741.5'973–dc23
                                    2013031440

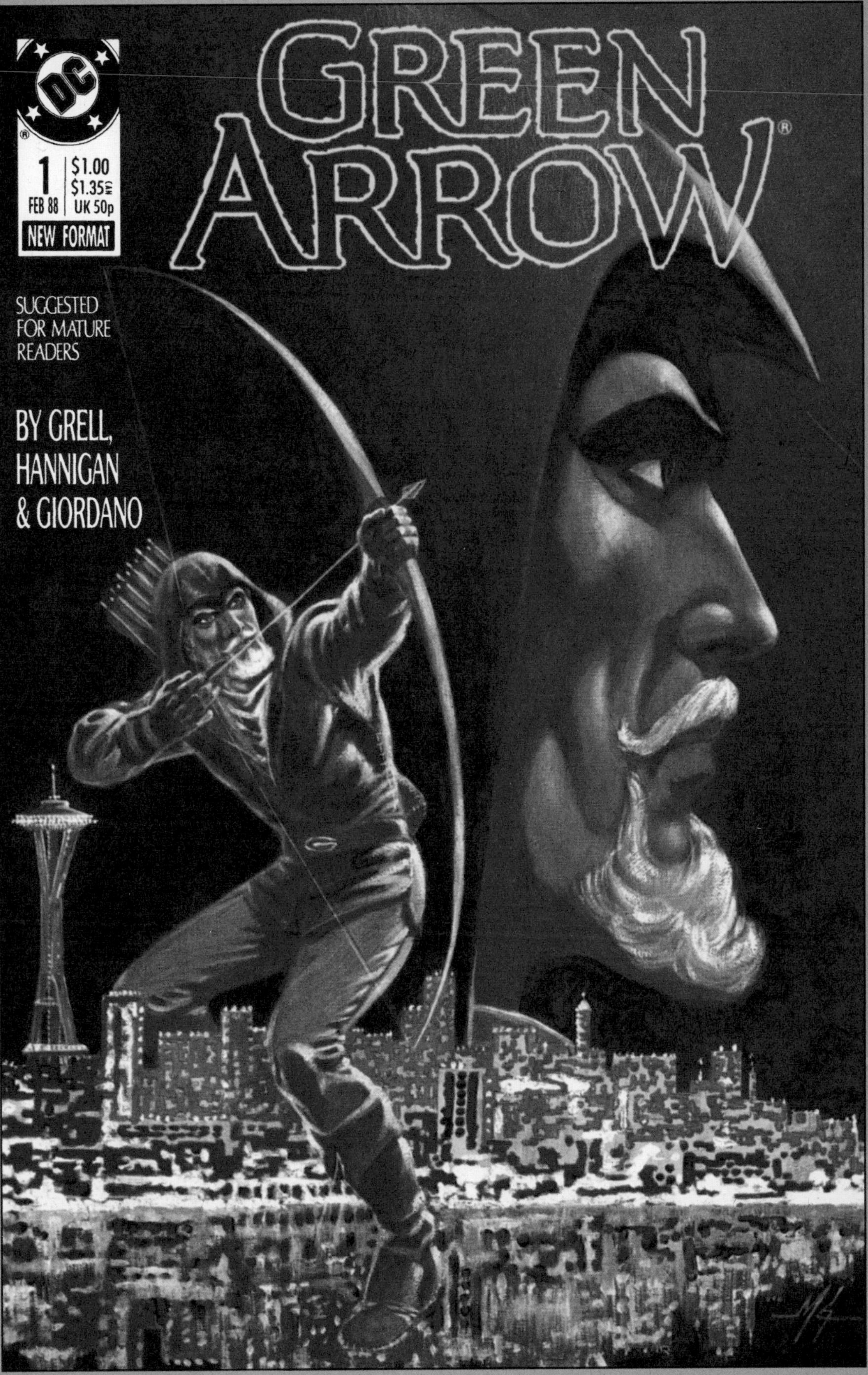

GREEN ARROW

1
FEB 88
NEW FORMAT

$1.00
$1.35 CAN
UK 50p

SUGGESTED
FOR MATURE
READERS

BY GRELL,
HANNIGAN
& GIORDANO

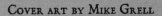

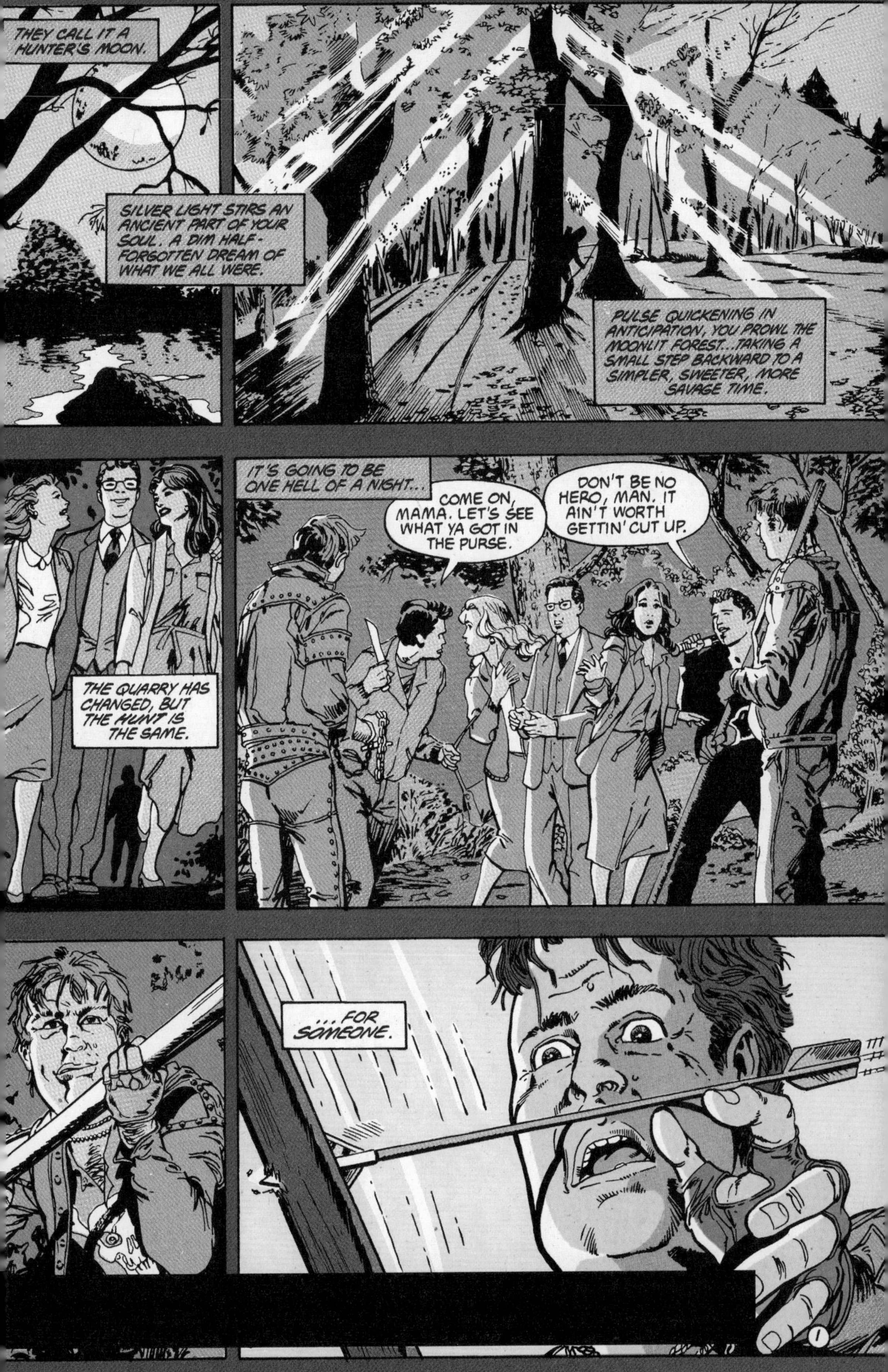
THEY CALL IT A HUNTER'S MOON.
SILVER LIGHT STIRS AN ANCIENT PART OF YOUR SOUL. A DIM HALF-FORGOTTEN DREAM OF WHAT WE ALL WERE.
PULSE QUICKENING IN ANTICIPATION, YOU PROWL THE MOONLIT FOREST...TAKING A SMALL STEP BACKWARD TO A SIMPLER, SWEETER, MORE SAVAGE TIME.
THE QUARRY HAS CHANGED, BUT THE HUNT IS THE SAME.
IT'S GOING TO BE ONE HELL OF A NIGHT...
COME ON, MAMA. LET'S SEE WHAT YA GOT IN THE PURSE.
DON'T BE NO HERO, MAN. IT AIN'T WORTH GETTIN' CUT UP.
...FOR SOMEONE.
[redacted]

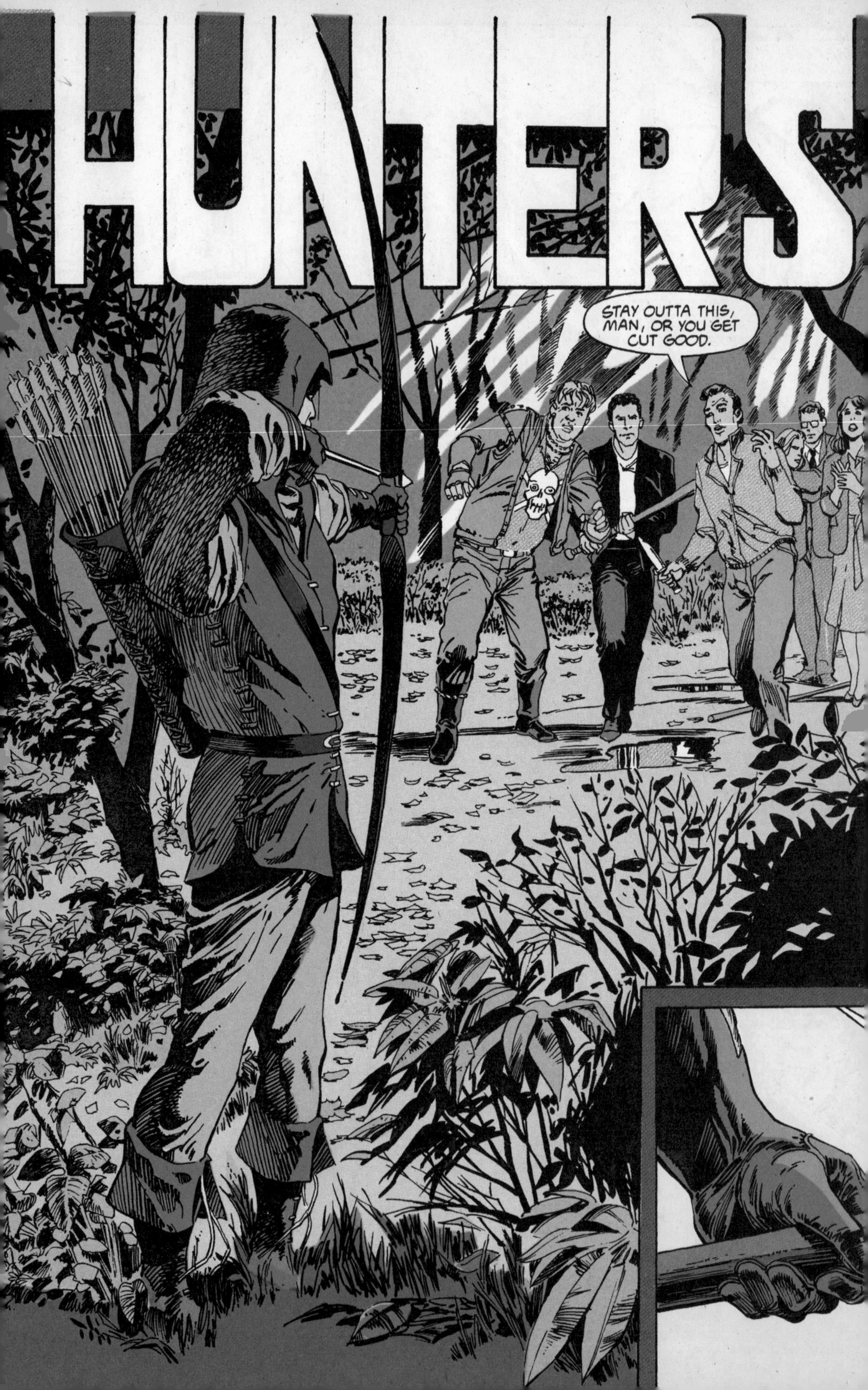
HUNTERS
STAY OUTTA THIS, MAN, OR YOU GET CUT GOOD.

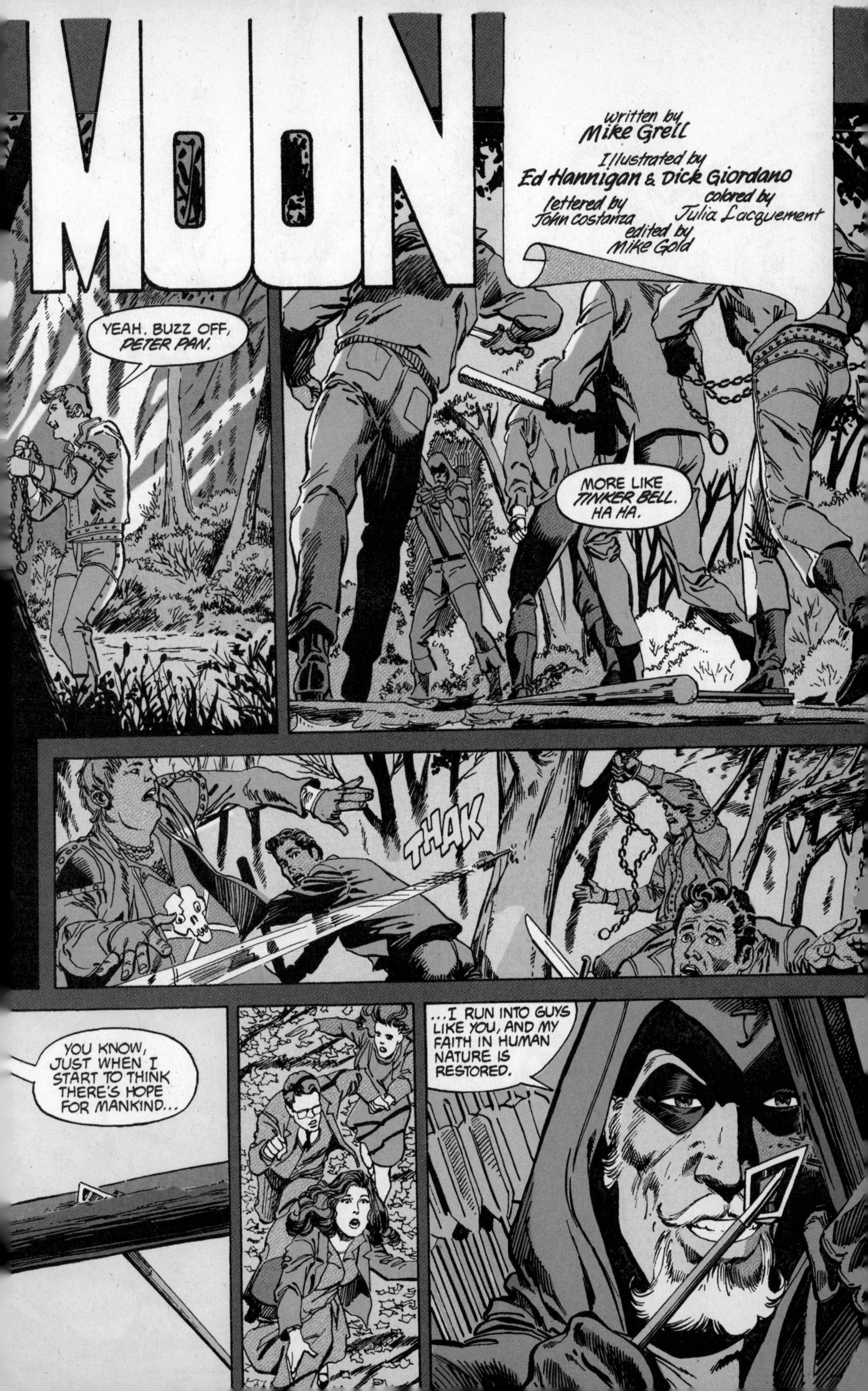
MOON
written by
Mike Grell
Illustrated by
Ed Hannigan & Dick Giordano
lettered by
John costanza
colored by
Julia Lacquement
edited by
Mike Gold
YEAH. BUZZ OFF, PETER PAN.
MORE LIKE TINKER BELL. HA HA.
THAK
YOU KNOW, JUST WHEN I START TO THINK THERE'S HOPE FOR MANKIND...
...I RUN INTO GUYS LIKE YOU, AND MY FAITH IN HUMAN NATURE IS RESTORED.

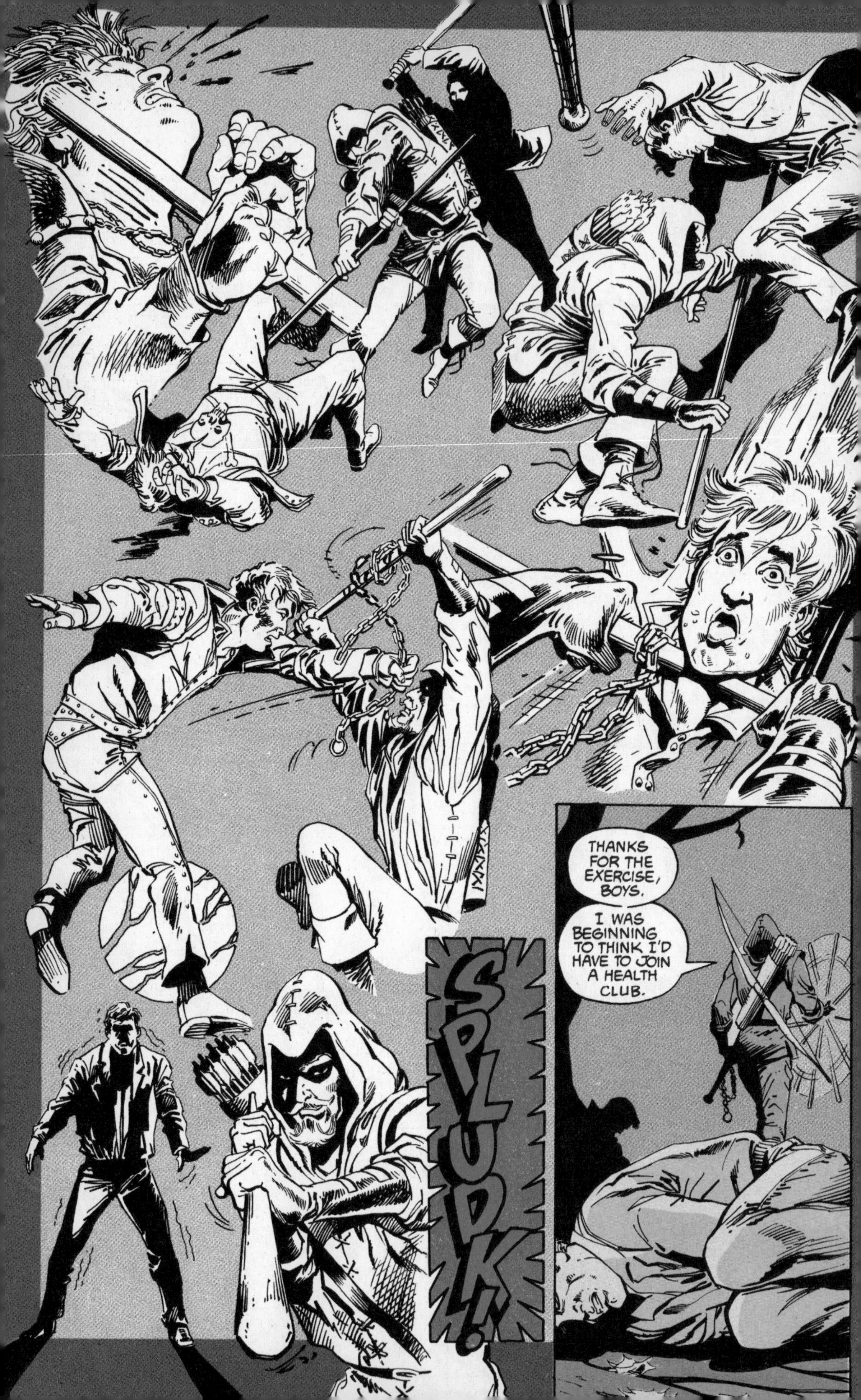
SPLUDK!
THANKS FOR THE EXERCISE, BOYS.
I WAS BEGINNING TO THINK I'D HAVE TO JOIN A HEALTH CLUB.

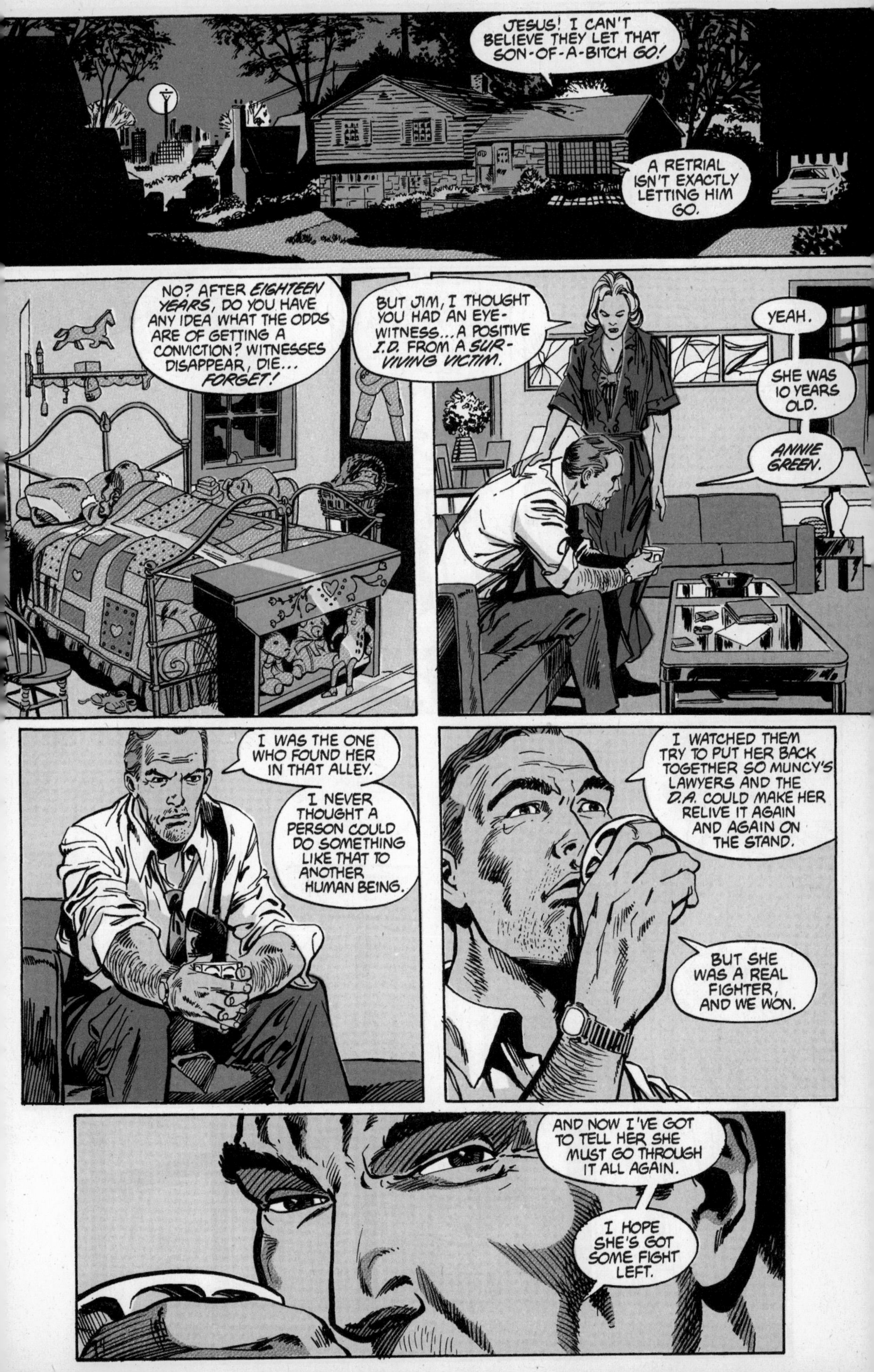
JESUS! I CAN'T BELIEVE THEY LET THAT SON-OF-A-BITCH GO!
A RETRIAL ISN'T EXACTLY LETTING HIM GO.
NO? AFTER EIGHTEEN YEARS, DO YOU HAVE ANY IDEA WHAT THE ODDS ARE OF GETTING A CONVICTION? WITNESSES DISAPPEAR, DIE... FORGET!
BUT JIM, I THOUGHT YOU HAD AN EYE-WITNESS... A POSITIVE I.D. FROM A SURVIVING VICTIM.
YEAH.
SHE WAS 10 YEARS OLD.
ANNIE GREEN.
I WAS THE ONE WHO FOUND HER IN THAT ALLEY.
I NEVER THOUGHT A PERSON COULD DO SOMETHING LIKE THAT TO ANOTHER HUMAN BEING.
I WATCHED THEM TRY TO PUT HER BACK TOGETHER SO MUNCY'S LAWYERS AND THE D.A. COULD MAKE HER RELIVE IT AGAIN AND AGAIN ON THE STAND.
BUT SHE WAS A REAL FIGHTER, AND WE WON.
AND NOW I'VE GOT TO TELL HER SHE MUST GO THROUGH IT ALL AGAIN.
I HOPE SHE'S GOT SOME FIGHT LEFT.

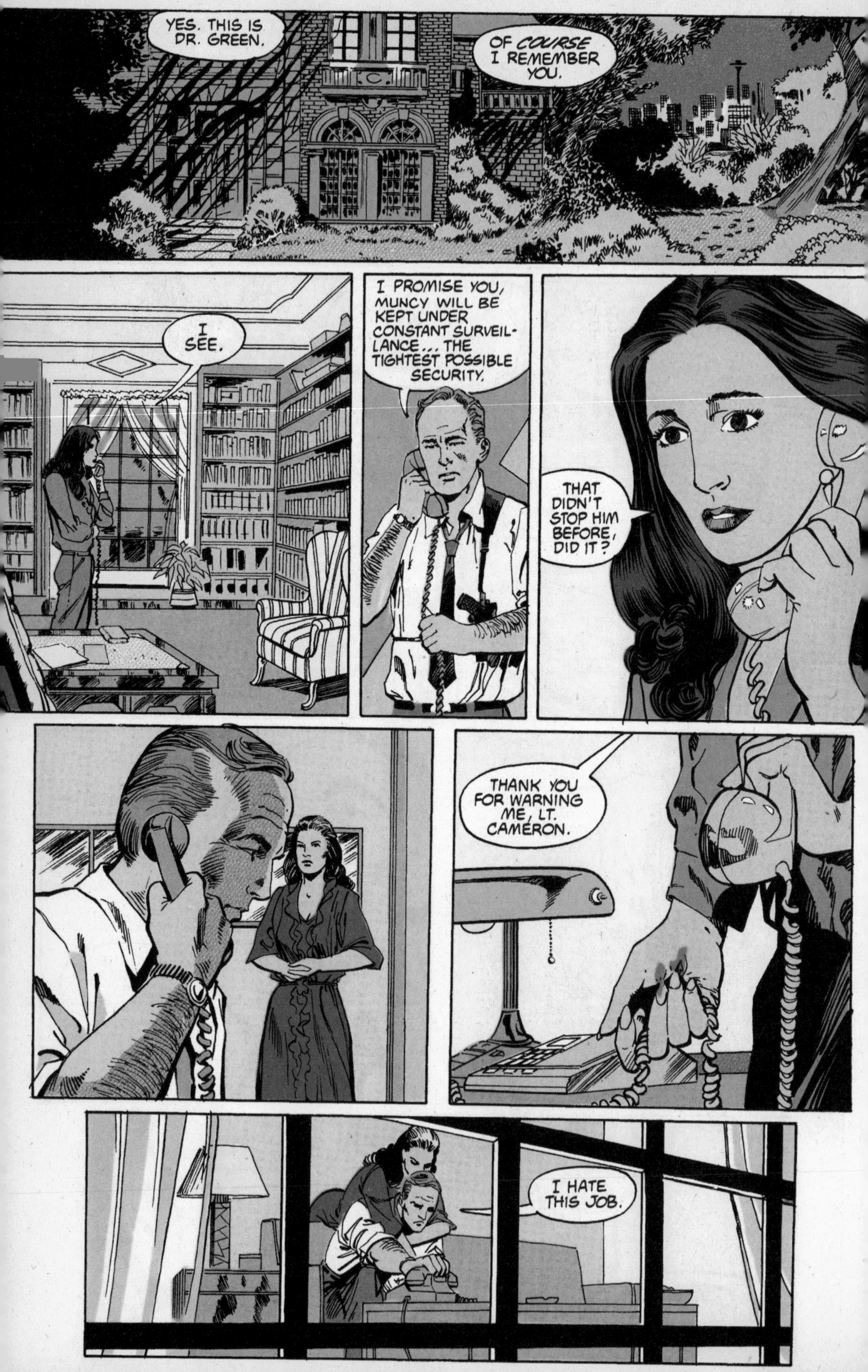
YES. THIS IS DR. GREEN.
OF COURSE I REMEMBER YOU.
I SEE.
I PROMISE YOU, MUNCY WILL BE KEPT UNDER CONSTANT SURVEIL-LANCE... THE TIGHTEST POSSIBLE SECURITY.
THAT DIDN'T STOP HIM BEFORE, DID IT?
THANK YOU FOR WARNING ME, LT. CAMERON.
I HATE THIS JOB.

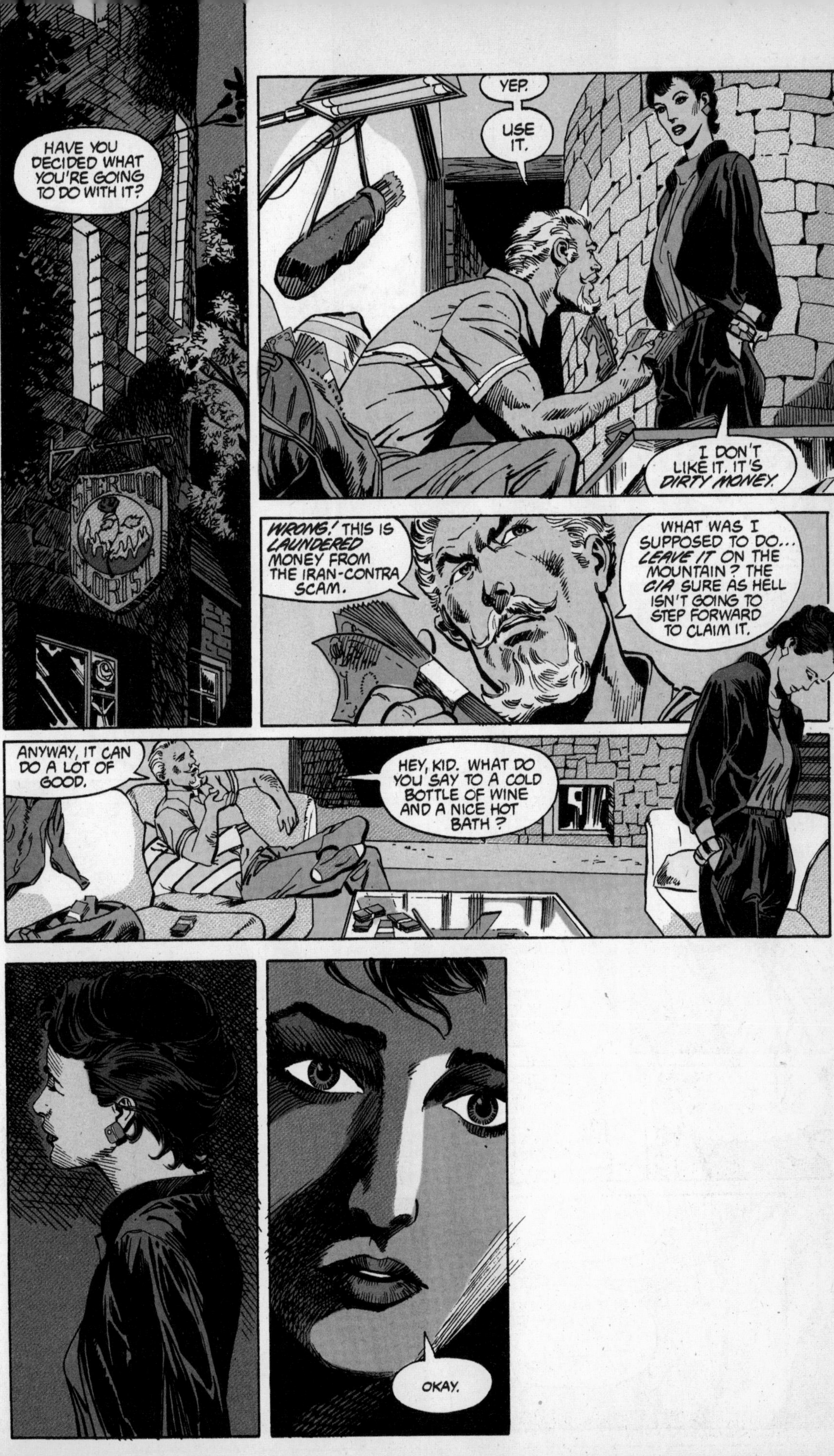
HAVE YOU DECIDED WHAT YOU'RE GOING TO DO WITH IT?
YEP.
USE IT.
I DON'T LIKE IT. IT'S DIRTY MONEY.
WRONG! THIS IS LAUNDERED MONEY FROM THE IRAN-CONTRA SCAM.
WHAT WAS I SUPPOSED TO DO... LEAVE IT ON THE MOUNTAIN? THE CIA SURE AS HELL ISN'T GOING TO STEP FORWARD TO CLAIM IT.
ANYWAY, IT CAN DO A LOT OF GOOD.
HEY, KID. WHAT DO YOU SAY TO A COLD BOTTLE OF WINE AND A NICE HOT BATH?
OKAY.

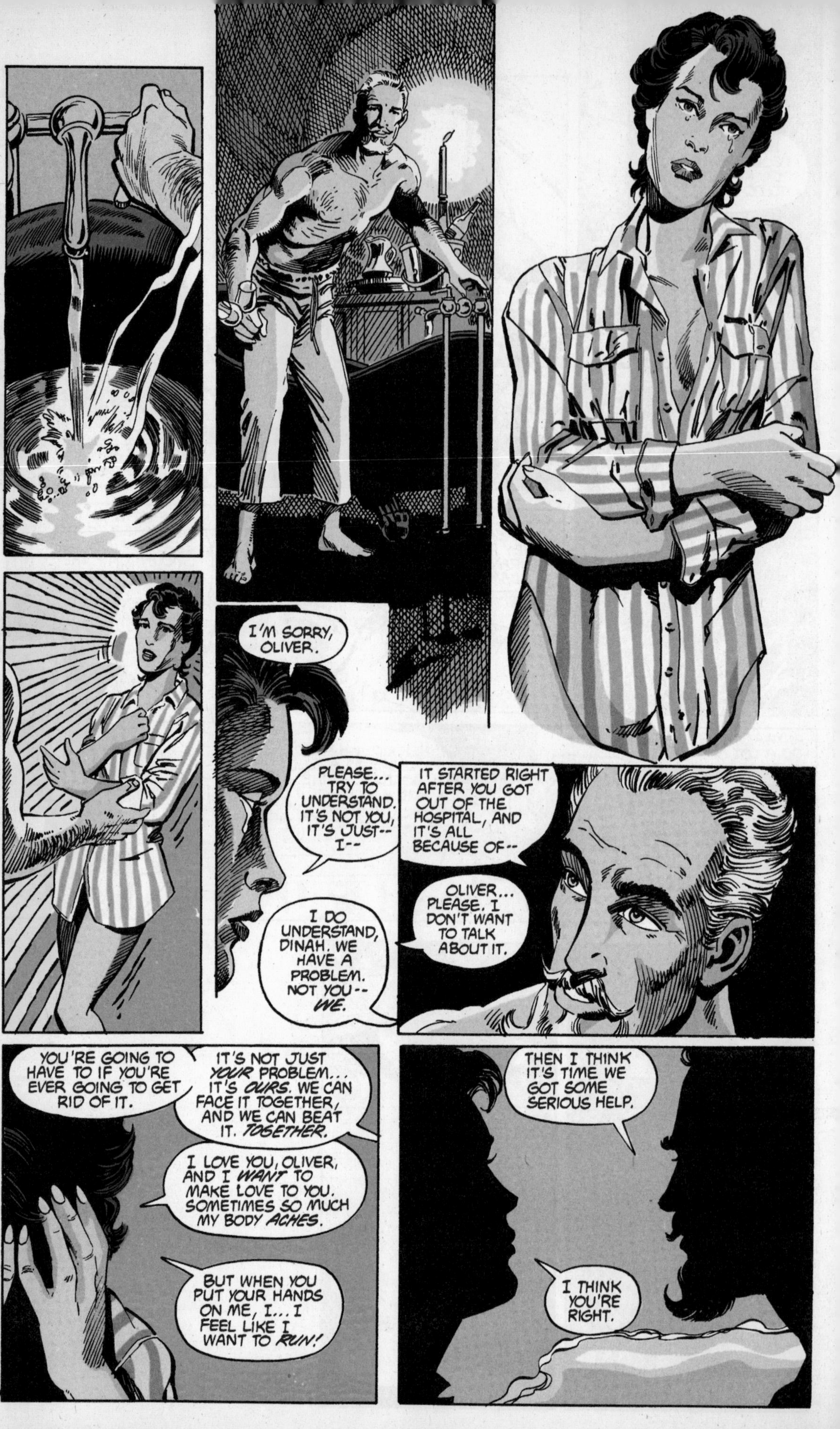
I'M SORRY, OLIVER.
PLEASE... TRY TO UNDERSTAND. IT'S NOT YOU, IT'S JUST-- I--
I DO UNDERSTAND, DINAH. WE HAVE A PROBLEM. NOT YOU-- WE.
IT STARTED RIGHT AFTER YOU GOT OUT OF THE HOSPITAL, AND IT'S ALL BECAUSE OF--
OLIVER... PLEASE. I DON'T WANT TO TALK ABOUT IT.
YOU'RE GOING TO HAVE TO IF YOU'RE EVER GOING TO GET RID OF IT.
IT'S NOT JUST YOUR PROBLEM... IT'S OURS. WE CAN FACE IT TOGETHER, AND WE CAN BEAT IT. TOGETHER.
I LOVE YOU, OLIVER, AND I WANT TO MAKE LOVE TO YOU. SOMETIMES SO MUCH MY BODY ACHES.
BUT WHEN YOU PUT YOUR HANDS ON ME, I... I FEEL LIKE I WANT TO RUN!
THEN I THINK IT'S TIME WE GOT SOME SERIOUS HELP.
I THINK YOU'RE RIGHT.

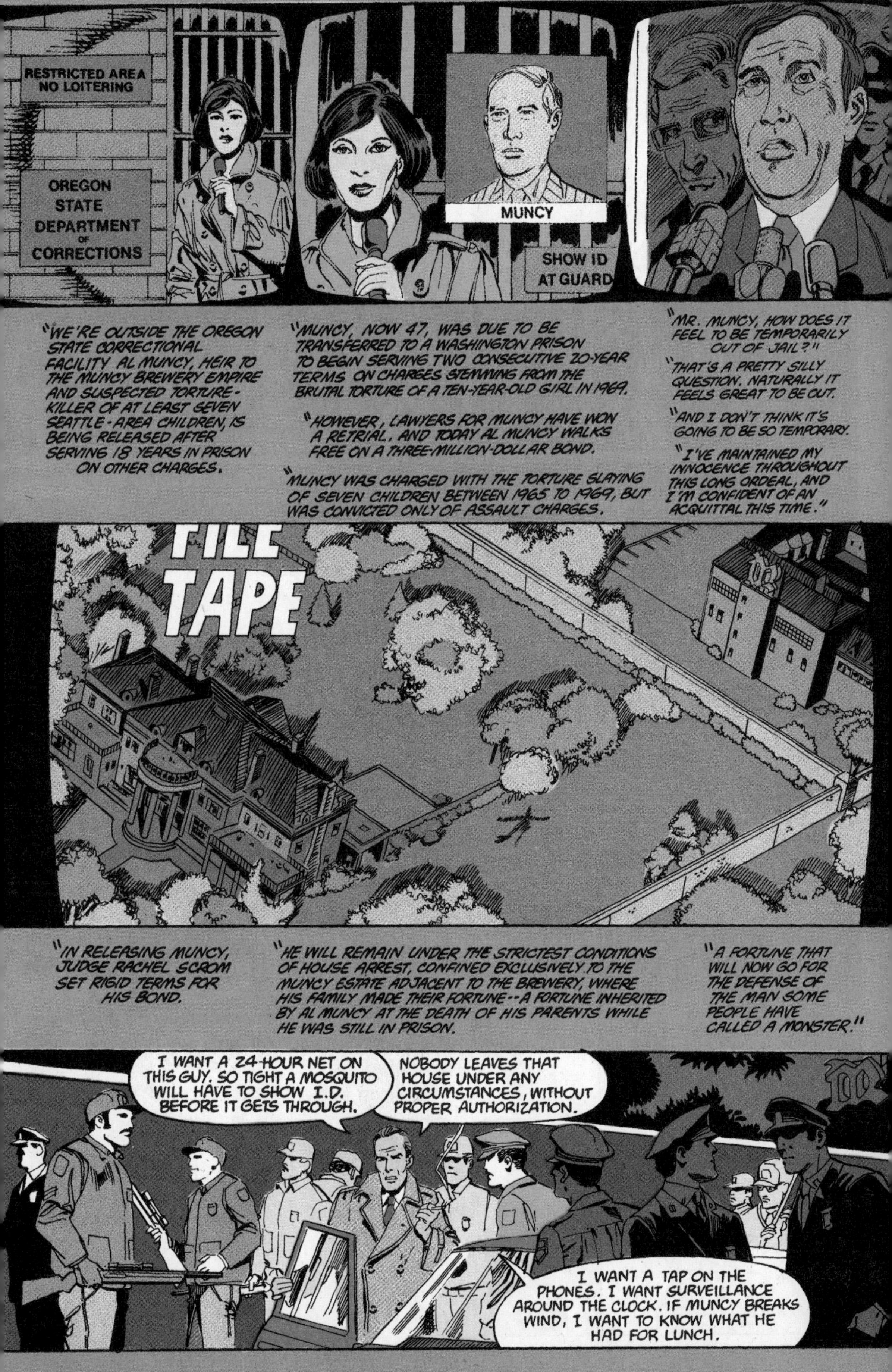
RESTRICTED AREA NO LOITERING
OREGON STATE DEPARTMENT OF CORRECTIONS
MUNCY
SHOW ID AT GUARD
"WE'RE OUTSIDE THE OREGON STATE CORRECTIONAL FACILITY. AL MUNCY, HEIR TO THE MUNCY BREWERY EMPIRE AND SUSPECTED TORTURE-KILLER OF AT LEAST SEVEN SEATTLE-AREA CHILDREN, IS BEING RELEASED AFTER SERVING 18 YEARS IN PRISON ON OTHER CHARGES.
"MUNCY, NOW 47, WAS DUE TO BE TRANSFERRED TO A WASHINGTON PRISON TO BEGIN SERVING TWO CONSECUTIVE 20-YEAR TERMS ON CHARGES STEMMING FROM THE BRUTAL TORTURE OF A TEN-YEAR-OLD GIRL IN 1969.
"HOWEVER, LAWYERS FOR MUNCY HAVE WON A RETRIAL. AND TODAY AL MUNCY WALKS FREE ON A THREE-MILLION-DOLLAR BOND.
"MUNCY WAS CHARGED WITH THE TORTURE SLAYING OF SEVEN CHILDREN BETWEEN 1965 TO 1969, BUT WAS CONVICTED ONLY OF ASSAULT CHARGES.
"MR. MUNCY, HOW DOES IT FEEL TO BE TEMPORARILY OUT OF JAIL?"
"THAT'S A PRETTY SILLY QUESTION. NATURALLY IT FEELS GREAT TO BE OUT.
"AND I DON'T THINK IT'S GOING TO BE SO TEMPORARY.
"I'VE MAINTAINED MY INNOCENCE THROUGHOUT THIS LONG ORDEAL, AND I'M CONFIDENT OF AN ACQUITTAL THIS TIME."
FILE TAPE
"IN RELEASING MUNCY, JUDGE RACHEL SCROM SET RIGID TERMS FOR HIS BOND.
"HE WILL REMAIN UNDER THE STRICTEST CONDITIONS OF HOUSE ARREST, CONFINED EXCLUSIVELY TO THE MUNCY ESTATE ADJACENT TO THE BREWERY, WHERE HIS FAMILY MADE THEIR FORTUNE--A FORTUNE INHERITED BY AL MUNCY AT THE DEATH OF HIS PARENTS WHILE HE WAS STILL IN PRISON.
"A FORTUNE THAT WILL NOW GO FOR THE DEFENSE OF THE MAN SOME PEOPLE HAVE CALLED A MONSTER."
I WANT A 24-HOUR NET ON THIS GUY. SO TIGHT A MOSQUITO WILL HAVE TO SHOW I.D. BEFORE IT GETS THROUGH.
NOBODY LEAVES THAT HOUSE UNDER ANY CIRCUMSTANCES, WITHOUT PROPER AUTHORIZATION.
I WANT A TAP ON THE PHONES. I WANT SURVEILLANCE AROUND THE CLOCK. IF MUNCY BREAKS WIND, I WANT TO KNOW WHAT HE HAD FOR LUNCH.

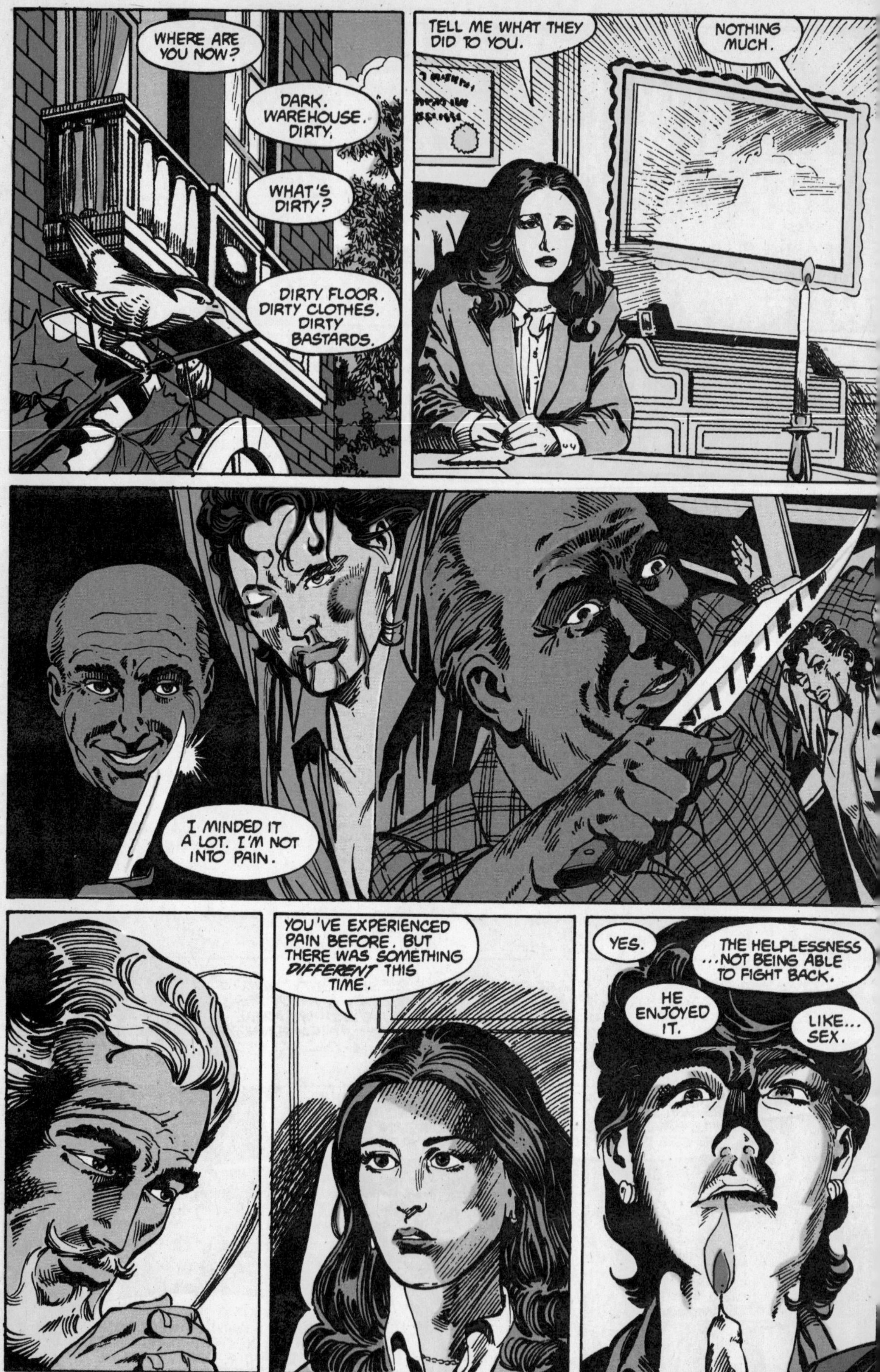
WHERE ARE YOU NOW?
DARK. WAREHOUSE. DIRTY.
WHAT'S DIRTY?
DIRTY FLOOR. DIRTY CLOTHES. DIRTY BASTARDS.
TELL ME WHAT THEY DID TO YOU.
NOTHING MUCH.
I MINDED IT A LOT. I'M NOT INTO PAIN.
YOU'VE EXPERIENCED PAIN BEFORE. BUT THERE WAS SOMETHING *DIFFERENT* THIS TIME.
YES.
THE HELPLESSNESS ...NOT BEING ABLE TO FIGHT BACK.
HE ENJOYED IT.
LIKE... SEX.

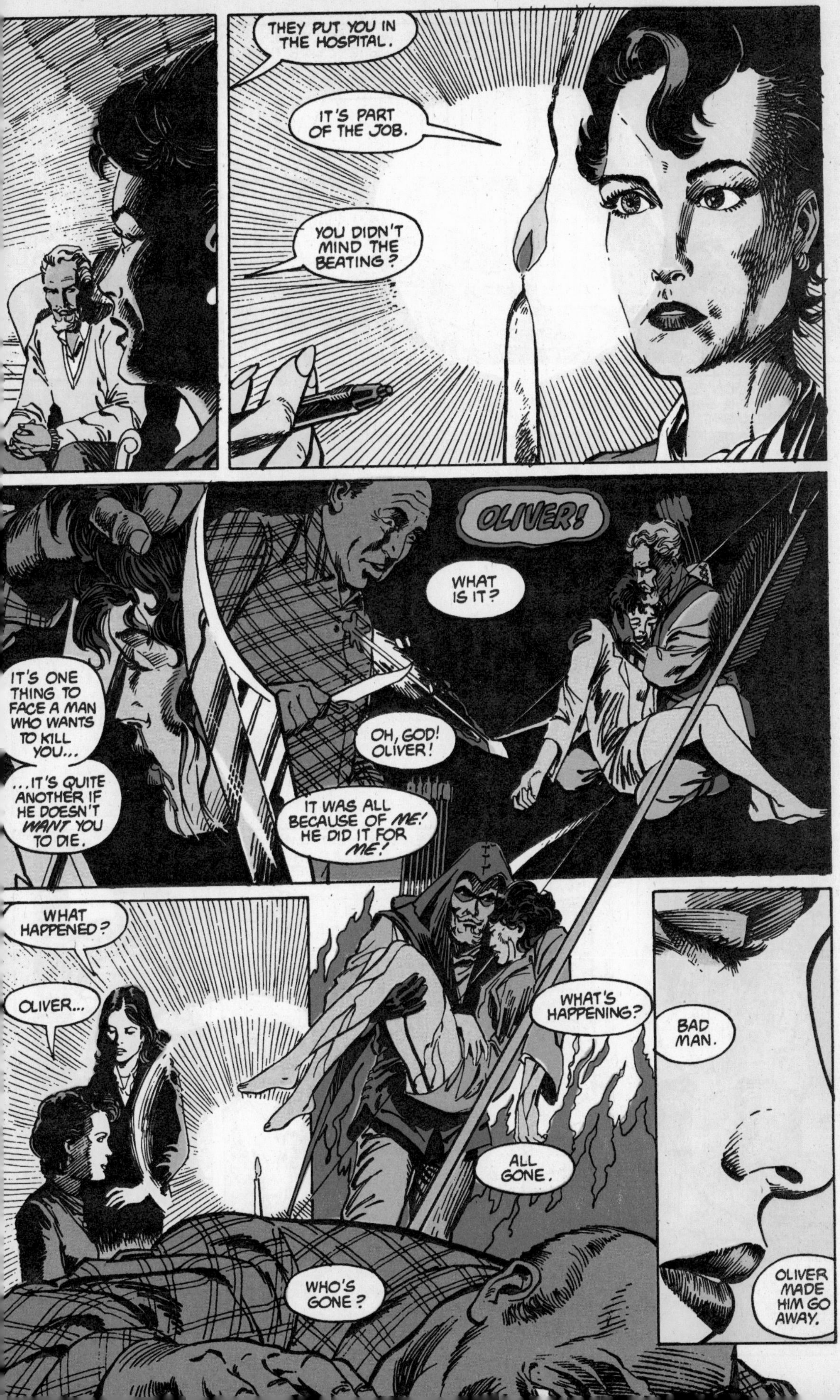
THEY PUT YOU IN THE HOSPITAL.
IT'S PART OF THE JOB.
YOU DIDN'T MIND THE BEATING?
IT'S ONE THING TO FACE A MAN WHO WANTS TO KILL YOU...
...IT'S QUITE ANOTHER IF HE DOESN'T *WANT* YOU TO DIE.
OLIVER!
WHAT IS IT?
OH, GOD! OLIVER!
IT WAS ALL BECAUSE OF *ME!* HE DID IT FOR *ME!*
WHAT HAPPENED?
OLIVER...
WHAT'S HAPPENING?
BAD MAN.
ALL GONE.
WHO'S GONE?
OLIVER MADE HIM GO AWAY.

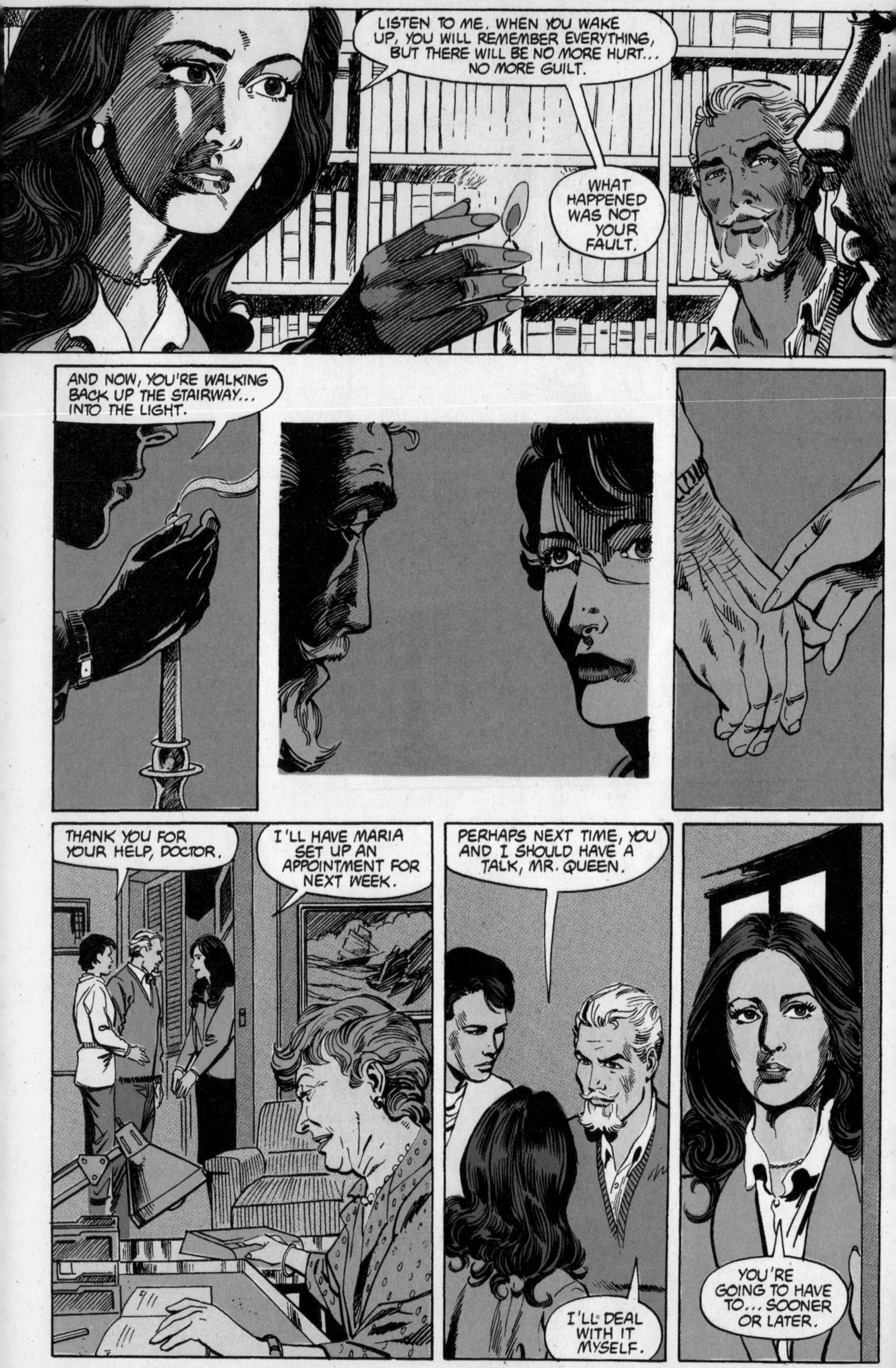
LISTEN TO ME. WHEN YOU WAKE UP, YOU WILL REMEMBER EVERYTHING, BUT THERE WILL BE NO MORE HURT... NO MORE GUILT.
WHAT HAPPENED WAS NOT YOUR FAULT.
AND NOW, YOU'RE WALKING BACK UP THE STAIRWAY... INTO THE LIGHT.
THANK YOU FOR YOUR HELP, DOCTOR.
I'LL HAVE MARIA SET UP AN APPOINTMENT FOR NEXT WEEK.
PERHAPS NEXT TIME, YOU AND I SHOULD HAVE A TALK, MR. QUEEN.
I'LL DEAL WITH IT MYSELF.
YOU'RE GOING TO HAVE TO... SOONER OR LATER.

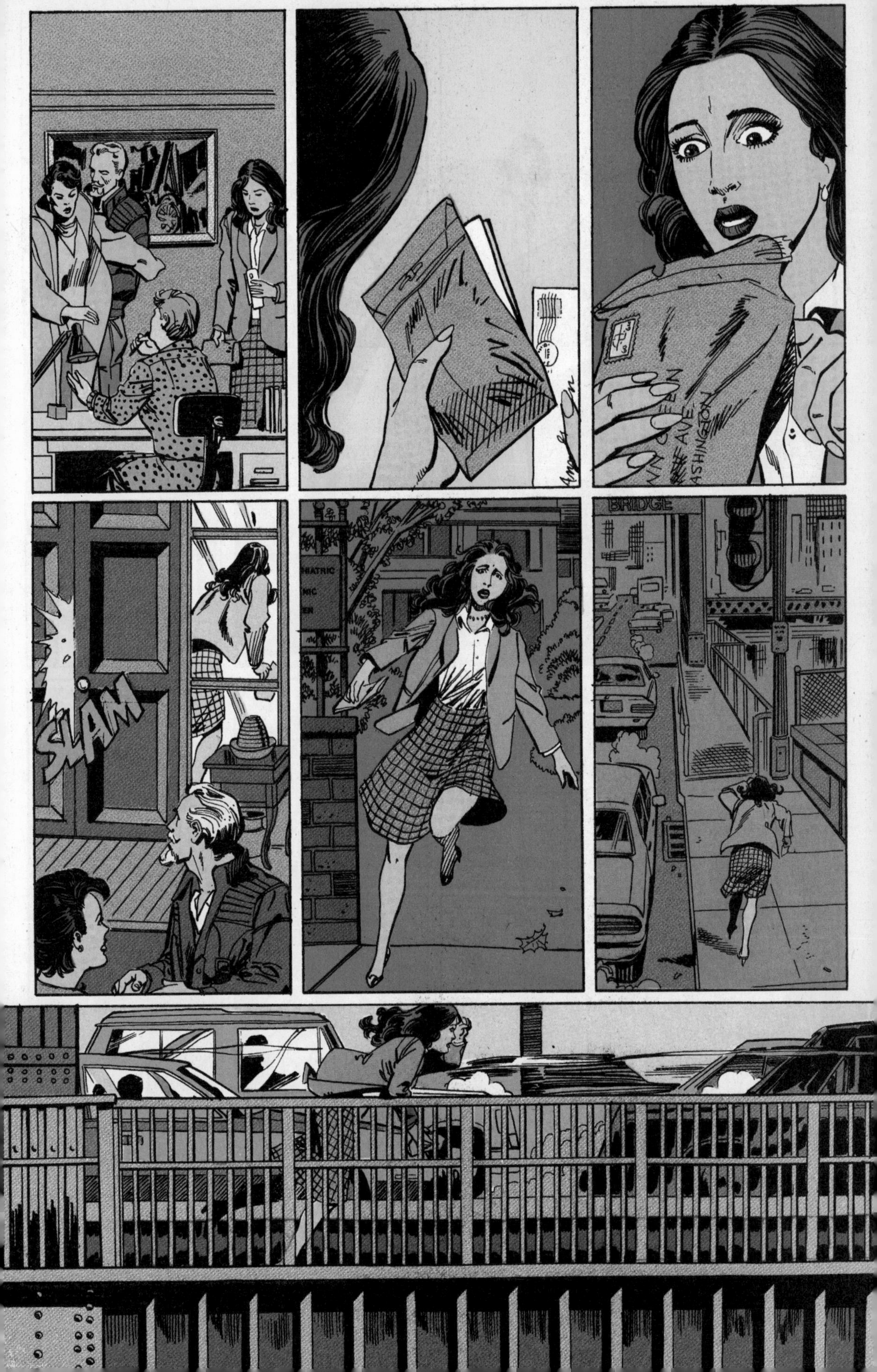
SLAM
BRIDGE

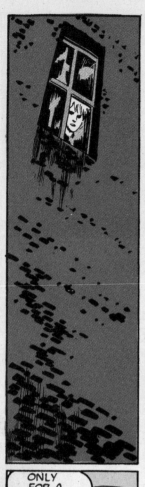

LOSE SOME-THING?

ONLY FOR A MOMENT.

ARE YOU ALL RIGHT?

I REALLY DON'T KNOW, MR. QUEEN.

YOU HELPED US... MAYBE I CAN HELP YOU.

GIVE ME A CHANCE. IT'S WHAT I DO.

I'M NOT SO SURE ANYONE CAN.

HONEST. I'M IN THE BOOK UNDER "GOOD GUYS."

ARE YOU STILL?

A GOOD GUY?

I DON'T KNOW.

MAYBE WE'LL FIND OUT.

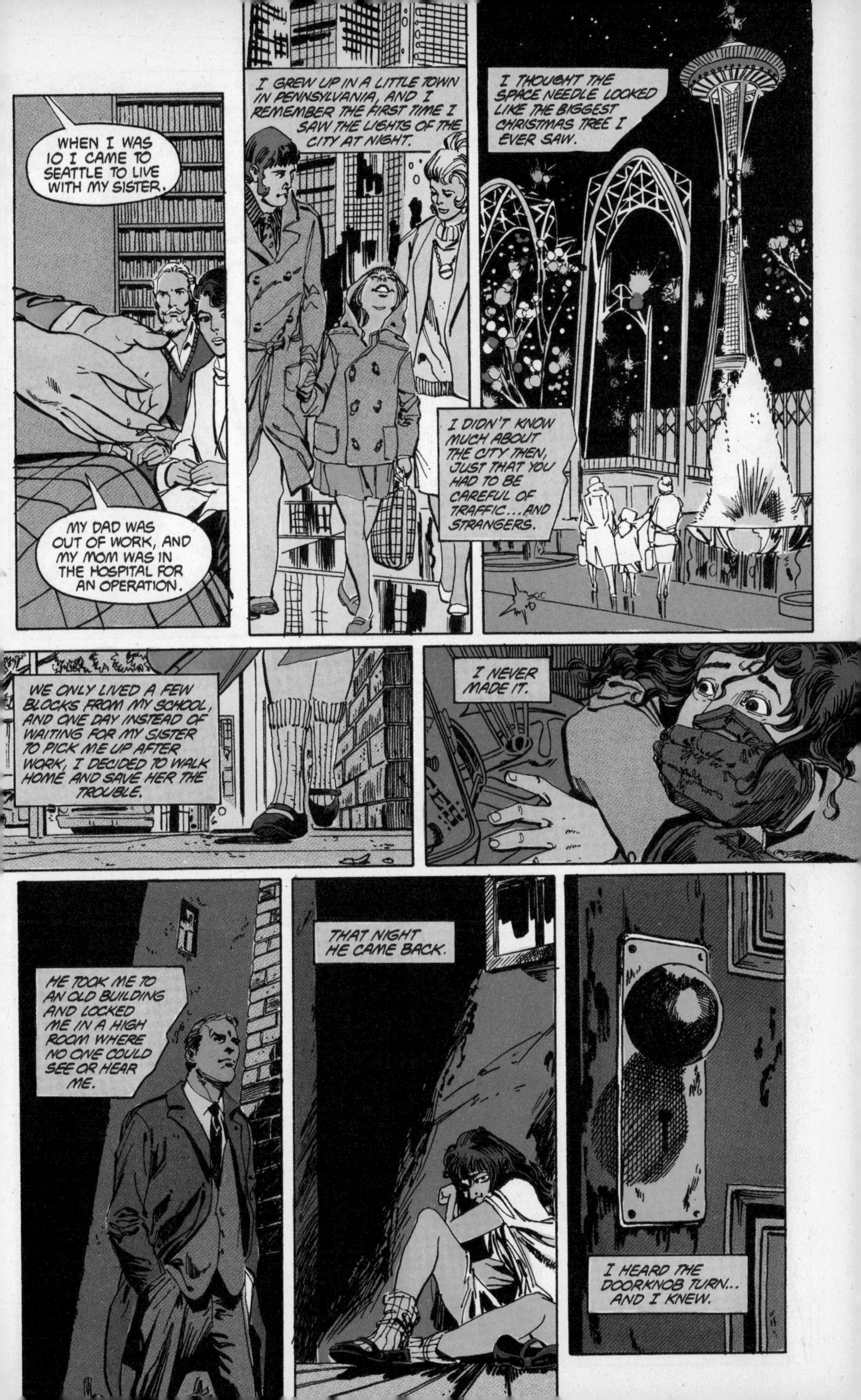
WHEN I WAS 10 I CAME TO SEATTLE TO LIVE WITH MY SISTER.
MY DAD WAS OUT OF WORK, AND MY MOM WAS IN THE HOSPITAL FOR AN OPERATION.
I GREW UP IN A LITTLE TOWN IN PENNSYLVANIA, AND I REMEMBER THE FIRST TIME I SAW THE LIGHTS OF THE CITY AT NIGHT.
I THOUGHT THE SPACE NEEDLE LOOKED LIKE THE BIGGEST CHRISTMAS TREE I EVER SAW.
I DIDN'T KNOW MUCH ABOUT THE CITY THEN, JUST THAT YOU HAD TO BE CAREFUL OF TRAFFIC... AND STRANGERS.
WE ONLY LIVED A FEW BLOCKS FROM MY SCHOOL, AND ONE DAY INSTEAD OF WAITING FOR MY SISTER TO PICK ME UP AFTER WORK, I DECIDED TO WALK HOME AND SAVE HER THE TROUBLE.
I NEVER MADE IT.
HE TOOK ME TO AN OLD BUILDING AND LOCKED ME IN A HIGH ROOM WHERE NO ONE COULD SEE OR HEAR ME.
THAT NIGHT HE CAME BACK.
I HEARD THE DOORKNOB TURN... AND I KNEW.

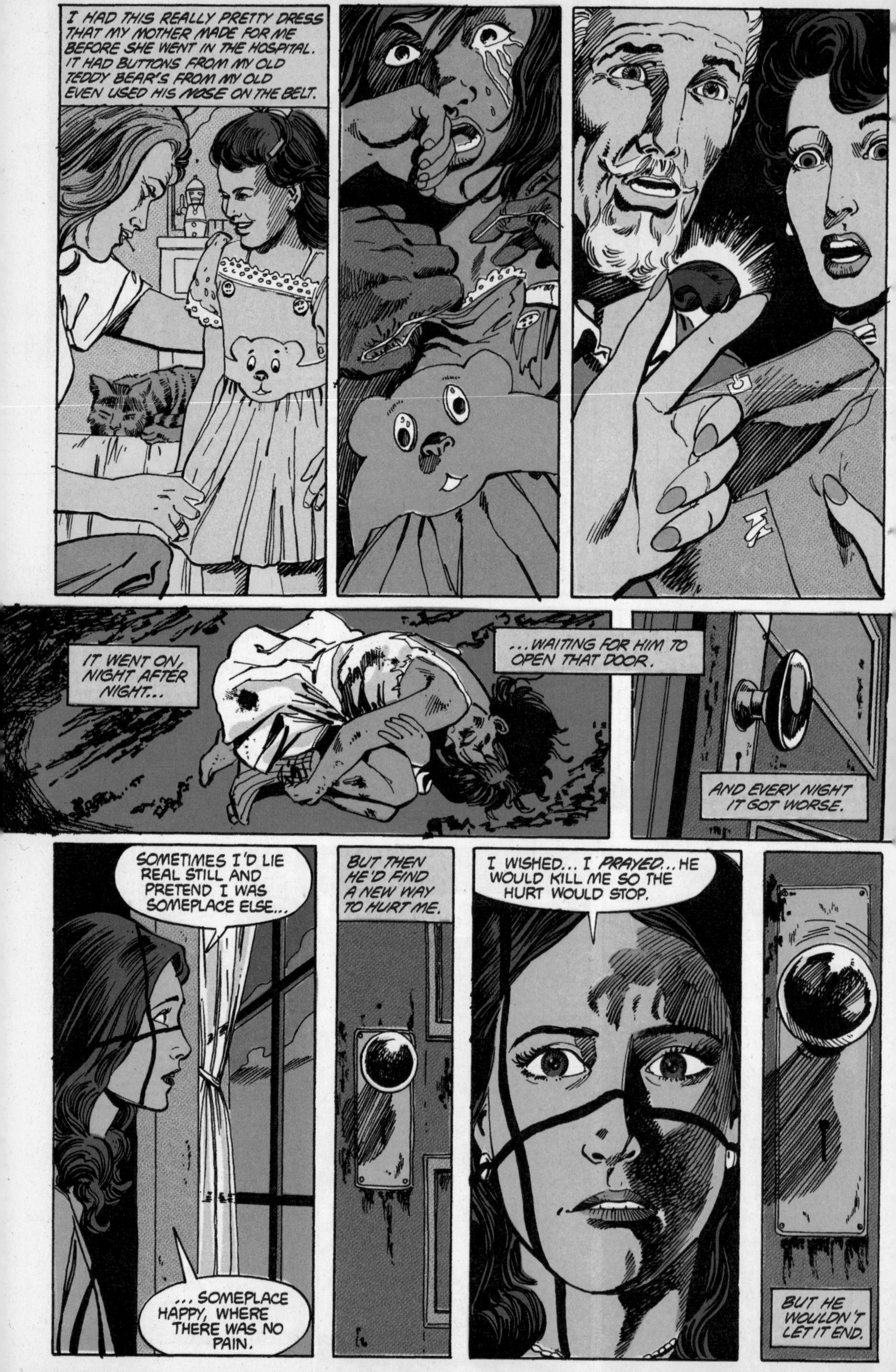
I HAD THIS REALLY PRETTY DRESS THAT MY MOTHER MADE FOR ME BEFORE SHE WENT IN THE HOSPITAL. IT HAD BUTTONS FROM MY OLD TEDDY BEAR'S FROM MY OLD EVEN USED HIS NOSE ON THE BELT.
IT WENT ON, NIGHT AFTER NIGHT...
...WAITING FOR HIM TO OPEN THAT DOOR.
AND EVERY NIGHT IT GOT WORSE.
SOMETIMES I'D LIE REAL STILL AND PRETEND I WAS SOMEPLACE ELSE...
...SOMEPLACE HAPPY, WHERE THERE WAS NO PAIN.
BUT THEN HE'D FIND A NEW WAY TO HURT ME.
I WISHED... I PRAYED... HE WOULD KILL ME SO THE HURT WOULD STOP.
BUT HE WOULDN'T LET IT END.

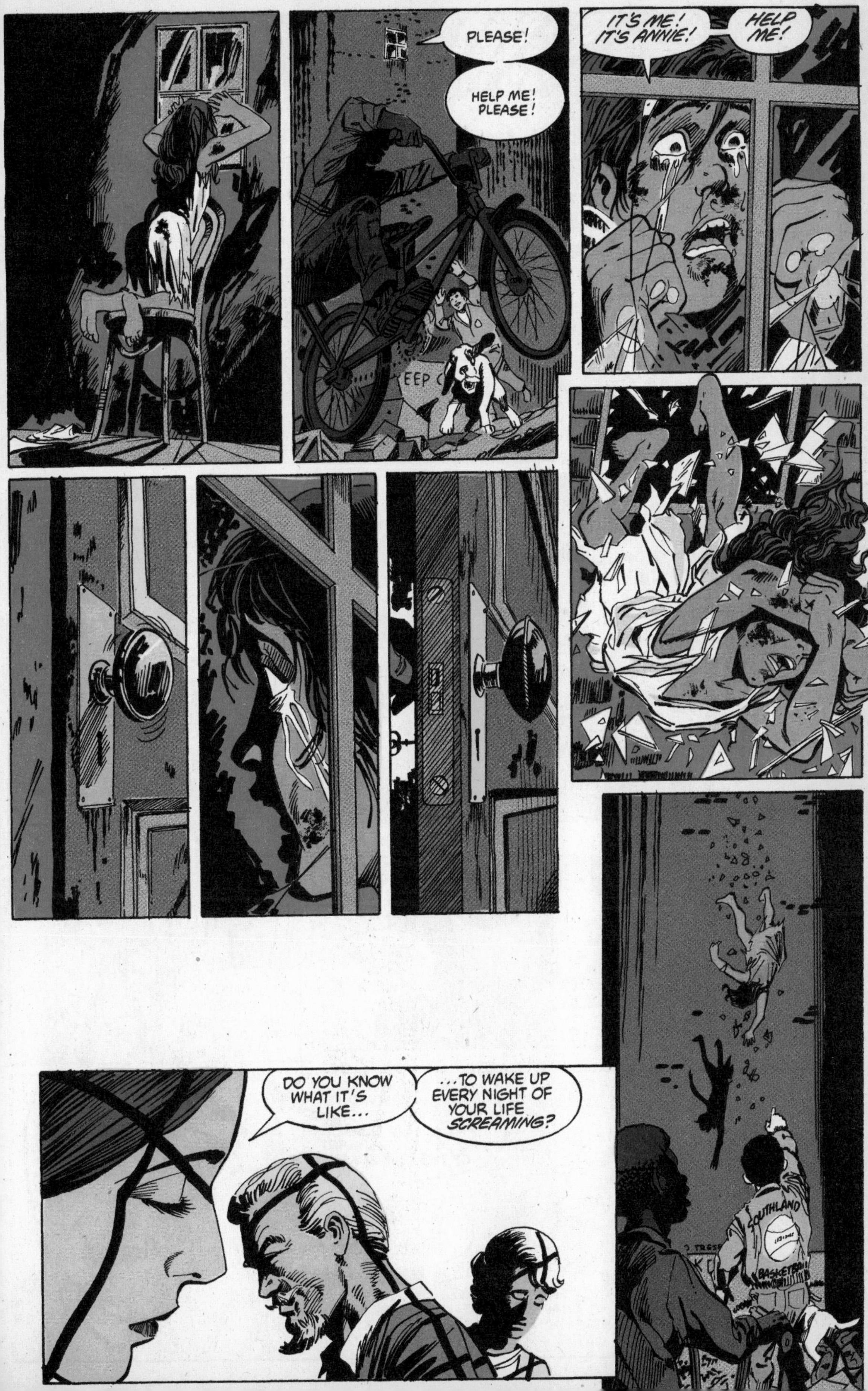
PLEASE!
HELP ME! PLEASE!
IT'S ME! IT'S ANNIE!
HELP ME!
DO YOU KNOW WHAT IT'S LIKE...
...TO WAKE UP EVERY NIGHT OF YOUR LIFE SCREAMING?
SOUTHLAND

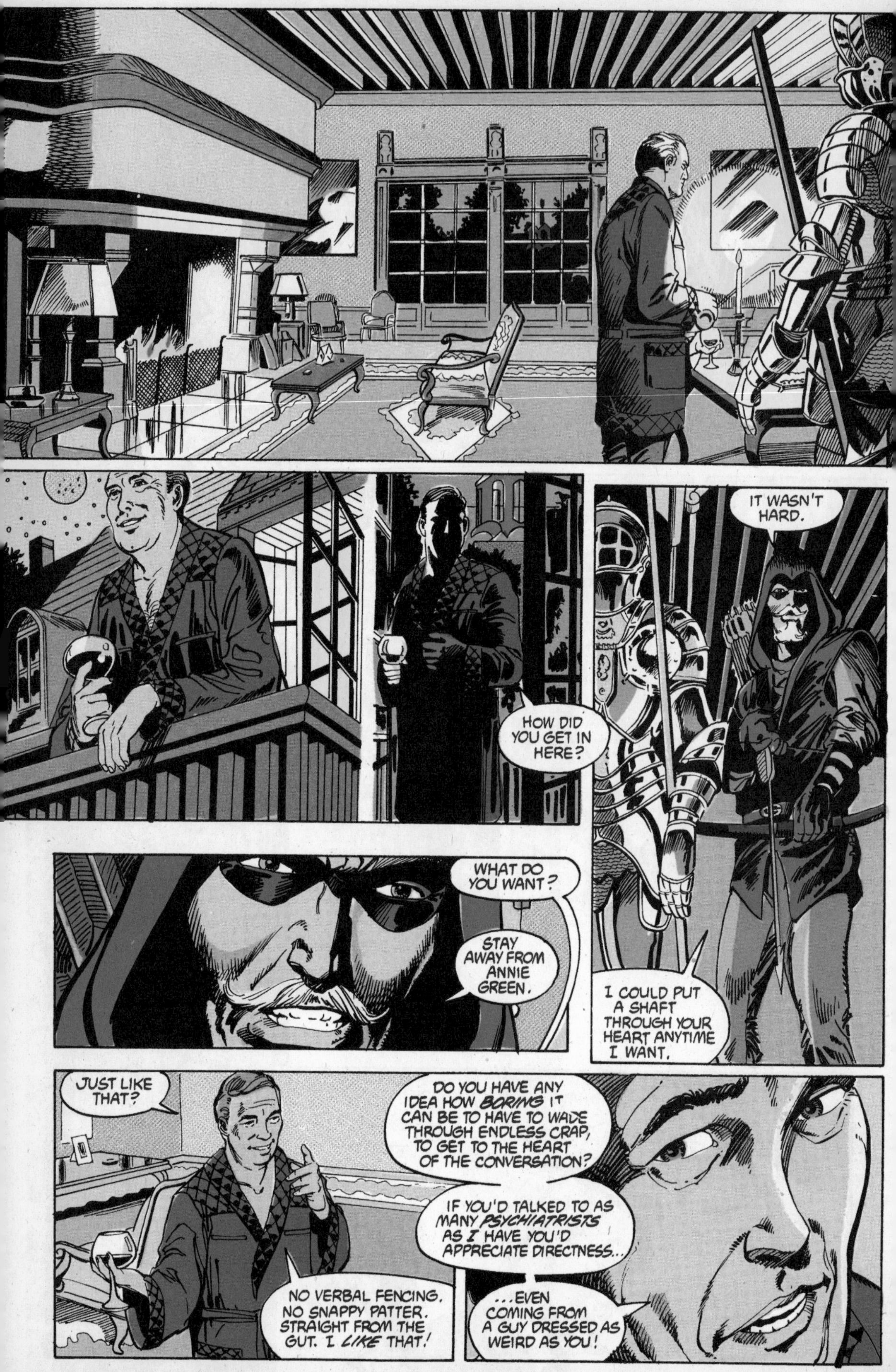
IT WASN'T HARD.
HOW DID YOU GET IN HERE?
WHAT DO YOU WANT?
STAY AWAY FROM ANNIE GREEN.
I COULD PUT A SHAFT THROUGH YOUR HEART ANYTIME I WANT.
JUST LIKE THAT?
DO YOU HAVE ANY IDEA HOW BORING IT CAN BE TO HAVE TO WADE THROUGH ENDLESS CRAP, TO GET TO THE HEART OF THE CONVERSATION?
IF YOU'D TALKED TO AS MANY PSYCHIATRISTS AS I HAVE YOU'D APPRECIATE DIRECTNESS...
NO VERBAL FENCING. NO SNAPPY PATTER. STRAIGHT FROM THE GUT. I LIKE THAT!
...EVEN COMING FROM A GUY DRESSED AS WEIRD AS YOU!

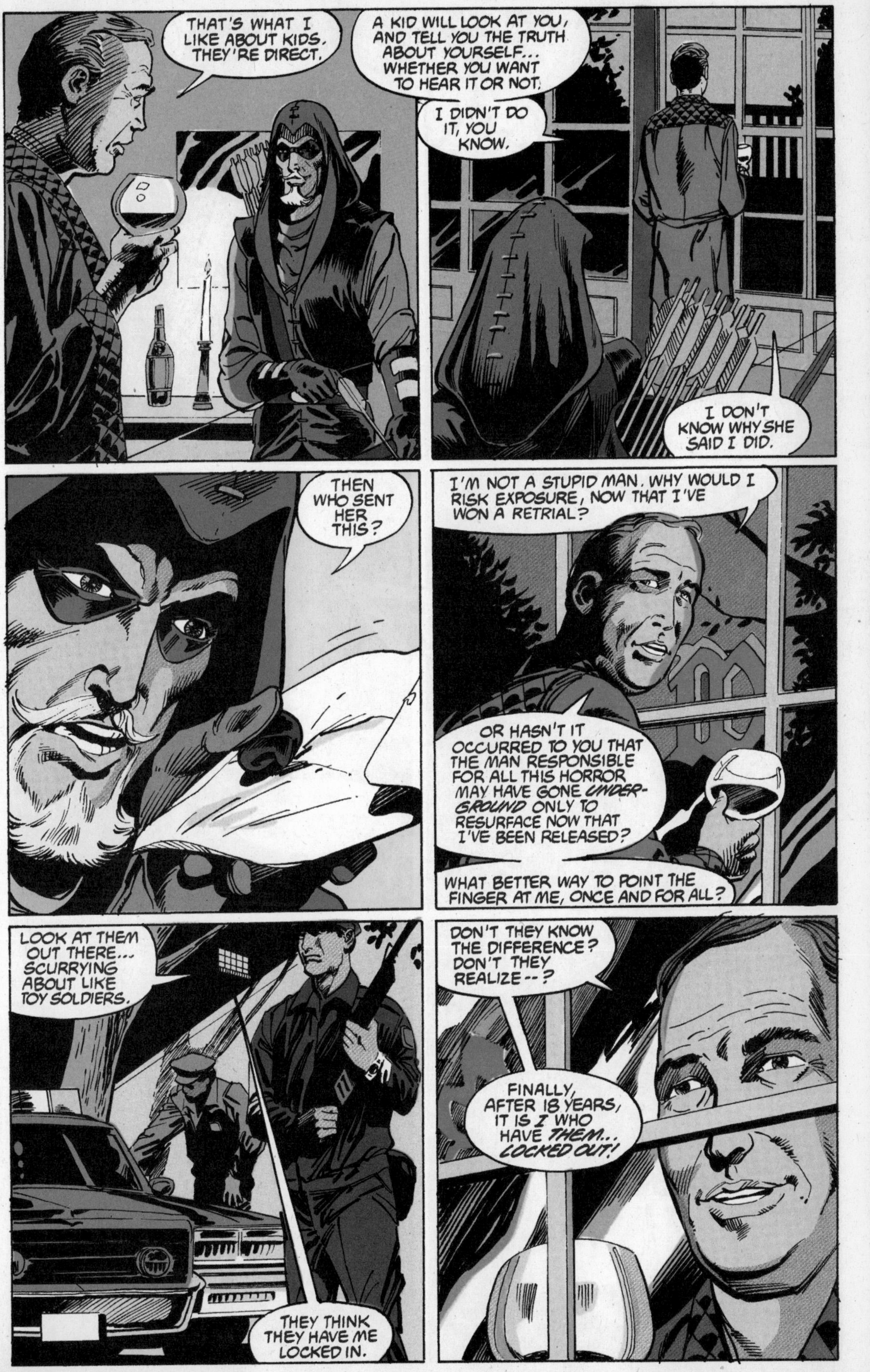
THAT'S WHAT I LIKE ABOUT KIDS. THEY'RE DIRECT.
A KID WILL LOOK AT YOU, AND TELL YOU THE TRUTH ABOUT YOURSELF... WHETHER YOU WANT TO HEAR IT OR NOT.
I DIDN'T DO IT, YOU KNOW.
I DON'T KNOW WHY SHE SAID I DID.
THEN WHO SENT HER THIS?
I'M NOT A STUPID MAN. WHY WOULD I RISK EXPOSURE, NOW THAT I'VE WON A RETRIAL?
OR HASN'T IT OCCURRED TO YOU THAT THE MAN RESPONSIBLE FOR ALL THIS HORROR MAY HAVE GONE UNDERGROUND ONLY TO RESURFACE NOW THAT I'VE BEEN RELEASED?
WHAT BETTER WAY TO POINT THE FINGER AT ME, ONCE AND FOR ALL?
LOOK AT THEM OUT THERE... SCURRYING ABOUT LIKE TOY SOLDIERS.
THEY THINK THEY HAVE ME LOCKED IN.
DON'T THEY KNOW THE DIFFERENCE? DON'T THEY REALIZE--?
FINALLY, AFTER 18 YEARS, IT IS I WHO HAVE THEM... LOCKED OUT!

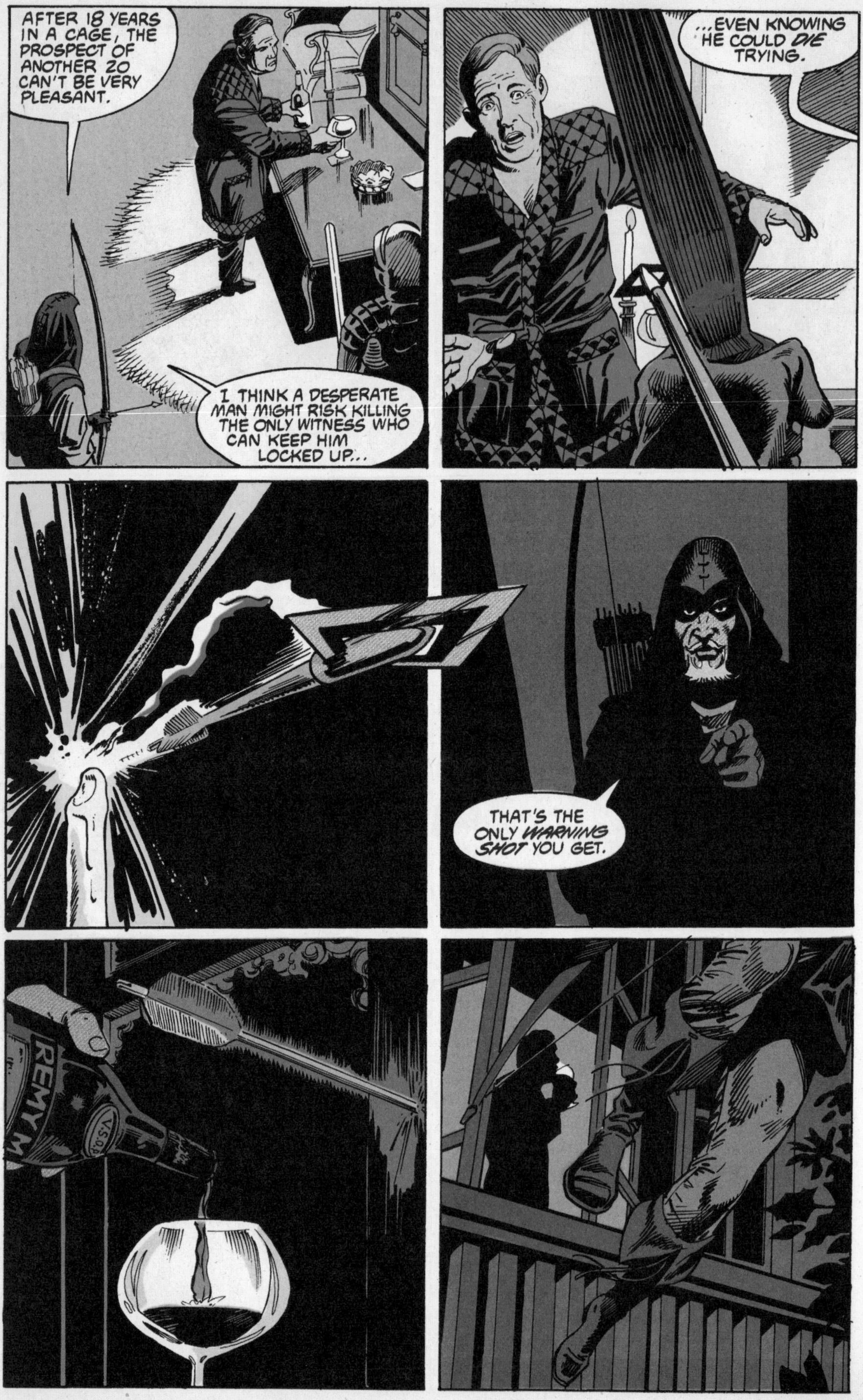
AFTER 18 YEARS IN A CAGE, THE PROSPECT OF ANOTHER 20 CAN'T BE VERY PLEASANT.
I THINK A DESPERATE MAN MIGHT RISK KILLING THE ONLY WITNESS WHO CAN KEEP HIM LOCKED UP...
...EVEN KNOWING HE COULD *DIE* TRYING.
THAT'S THE ONLY *WARNING SHOT* YOU GET.

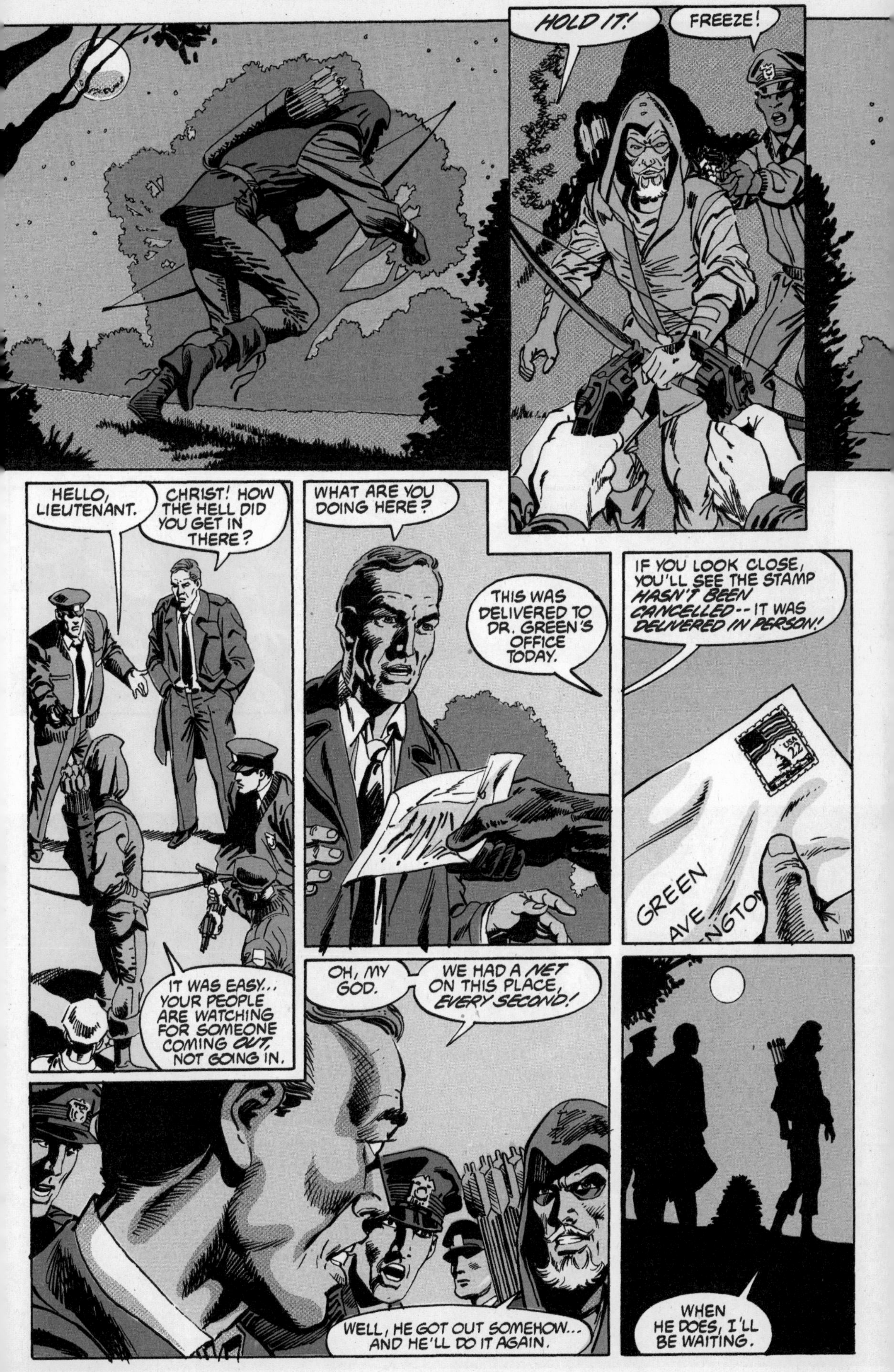
HOLD IT!
FREEZE!
HELLO, LIEUTENANT.
CHRIST! HOW THE HELL DID YOU GET IN THERE?
IT WAS EASY... YOUR PEOPLE ARE WATCHING FOR SOMEONE COMING OUT, NOT GOING IN.
WHAT ARE YOU DOING HERE?
THIS WAS DELIVERED TO DR. GREEN'S OFFICE TODAY.
IF YOU LOOK CLOSE, YOU'LL SEE THE STAMP HASN'T BEEN CANCELLED-- IT WAS DELIVERED IN PERSON!
GREEN
AVE
OH, MY GOD.
WE HAD A NET ON THIS PLACE, EVERY SECOND!
WELL, HE GOT OUT SOMEHOW... AND HE'LL DO IT AGAIN.
WHEN HE DOES, I'LL BE WAITING.

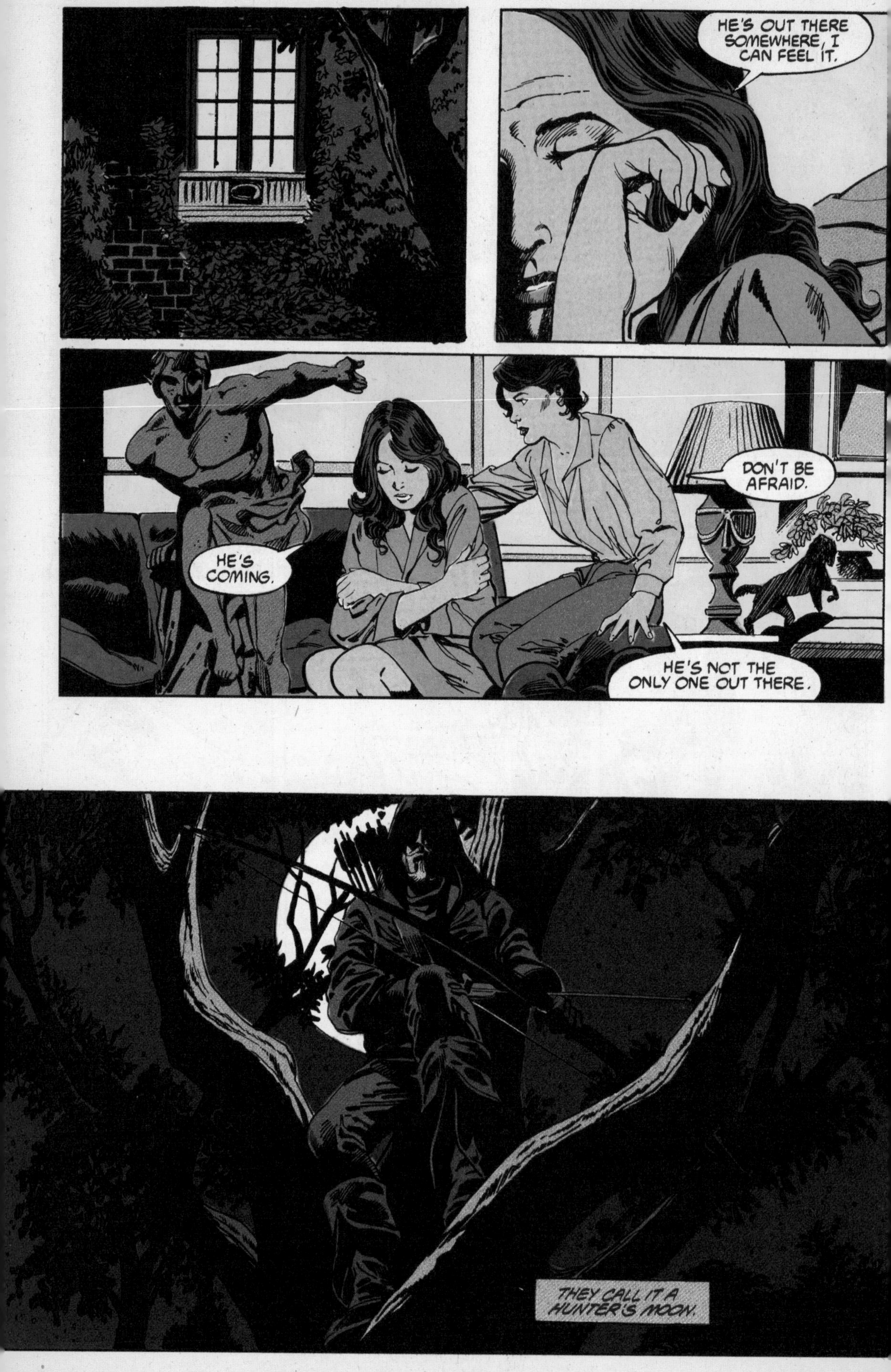
HE'S OUT THERE SOMEWHERE, I CAN FEEL IT.
HE'S COMING.
DON'T BE AFRAID.
HE'S NOT THE ONLY ONE OUT THERE.
THEY CALL IT A HUNTER'S MOON.

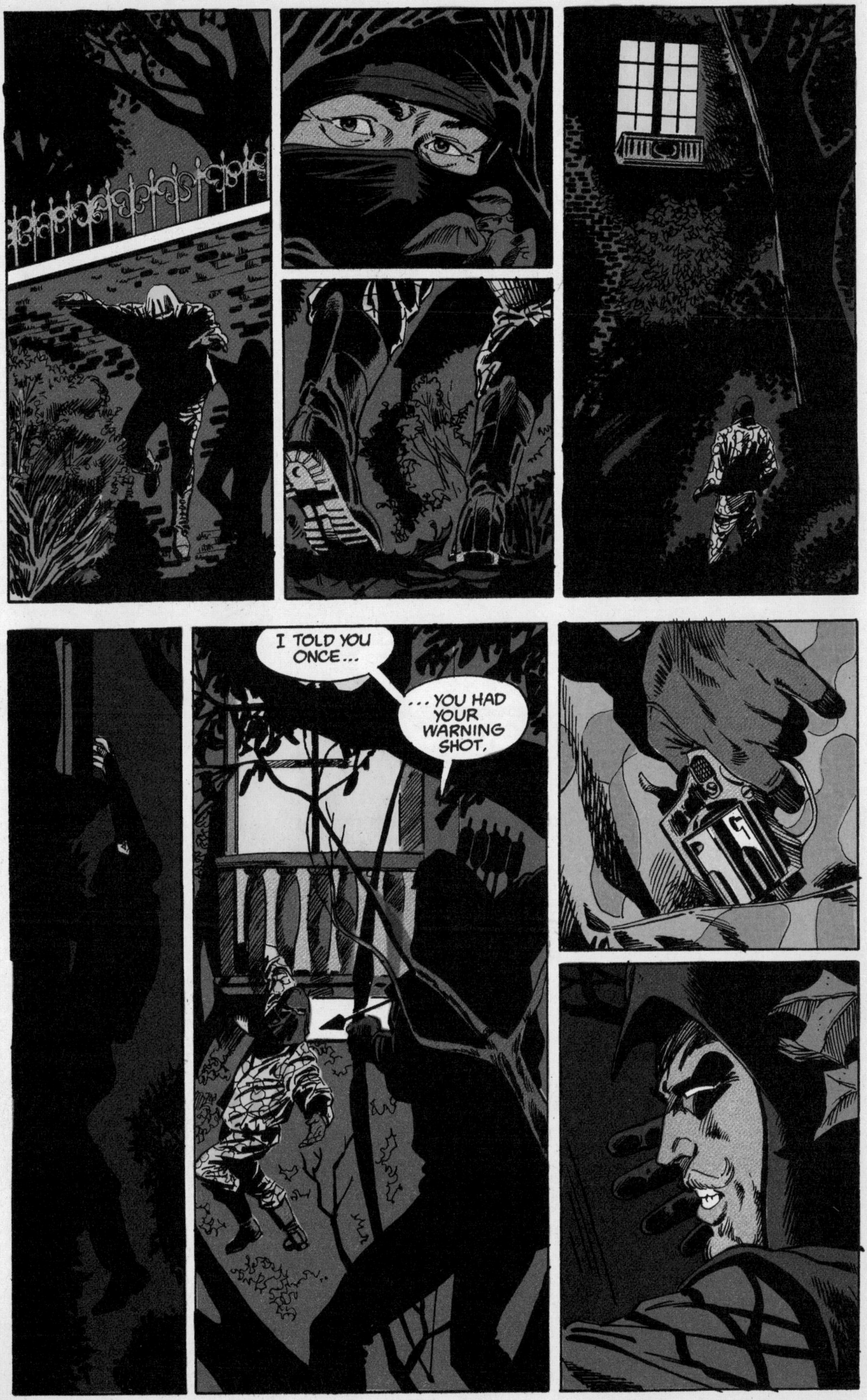
I TOLD YOU ONCE...
...YOU HAD YOUR WARNING SHOT.

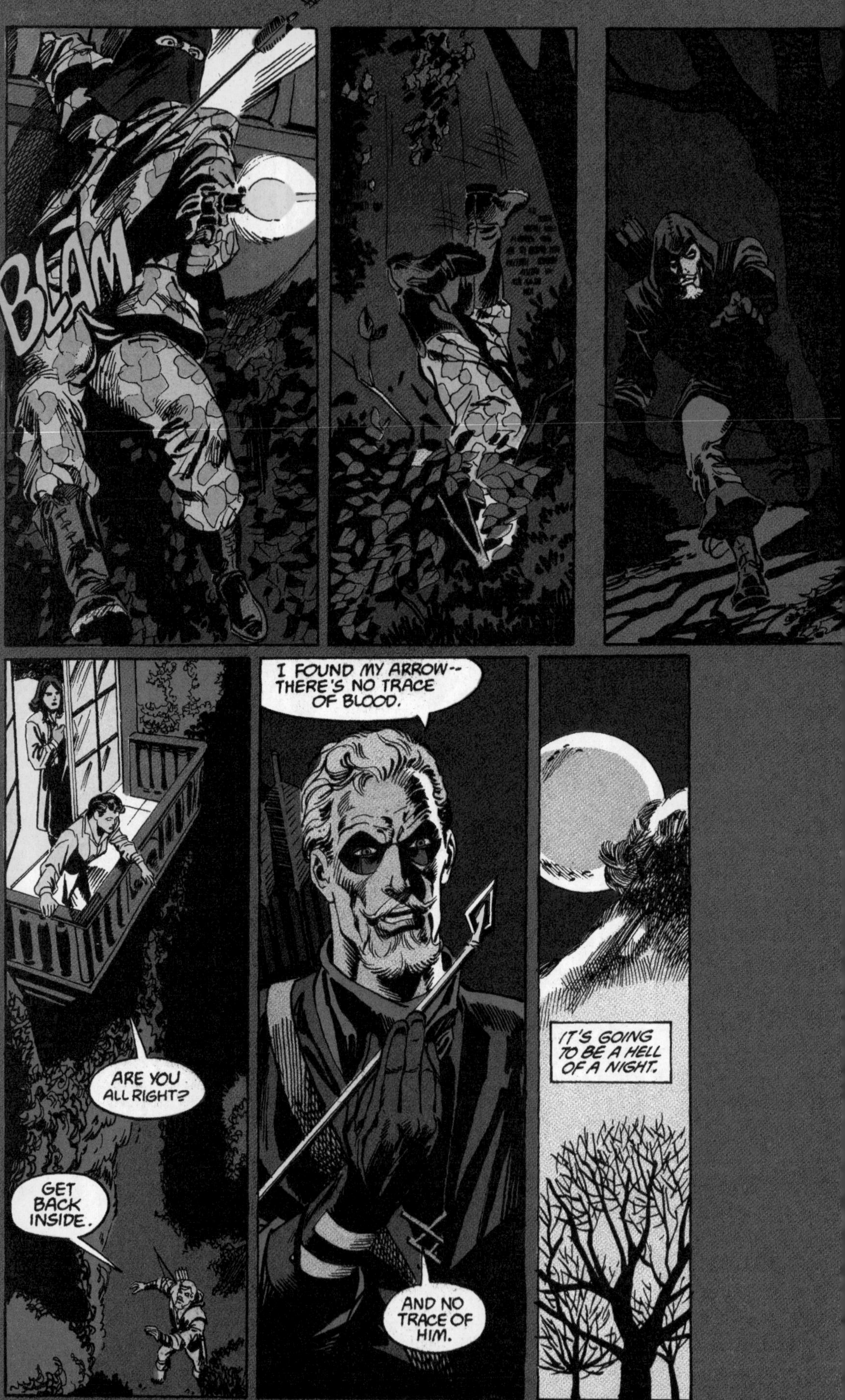
BLAM
ARE YOU ALL RIGHT?
GET BACK INSIDE.
I FOUND MY ARROW-- THERE'S NO TRACE OF BLOOD.
AND NO TRACE OF HIM.
IT'S GOING TO BE A HELL OF A NIGHT.

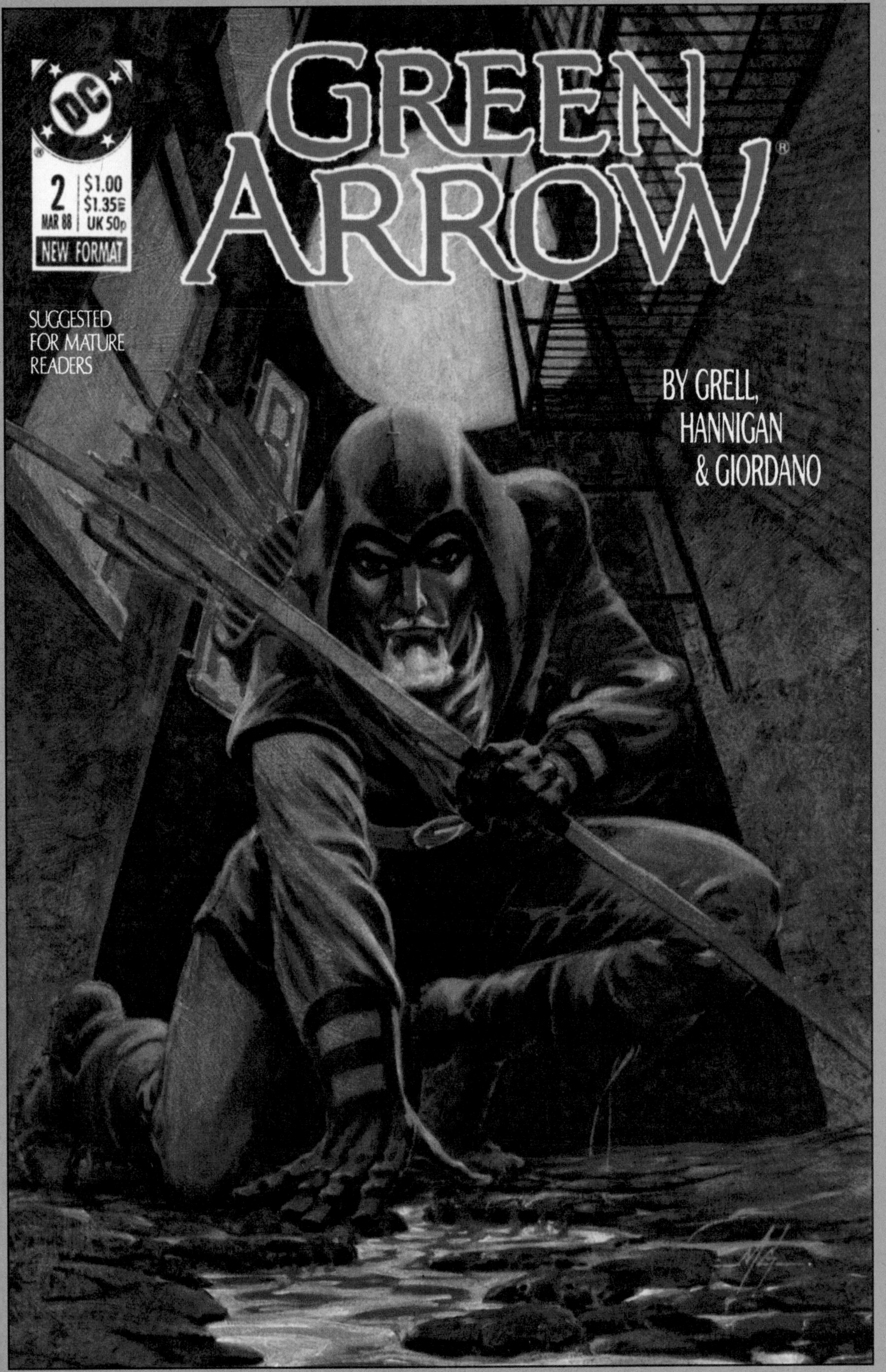
GREEN ARROW
DC
2 $1.00 $1.35 MAR 88 UK 50p
NEW FORMAT
SUGGESTED FOR MATURE READERS
BY GRELL, HANNIGAN & GIORDANO

Cover art by Mike Grell

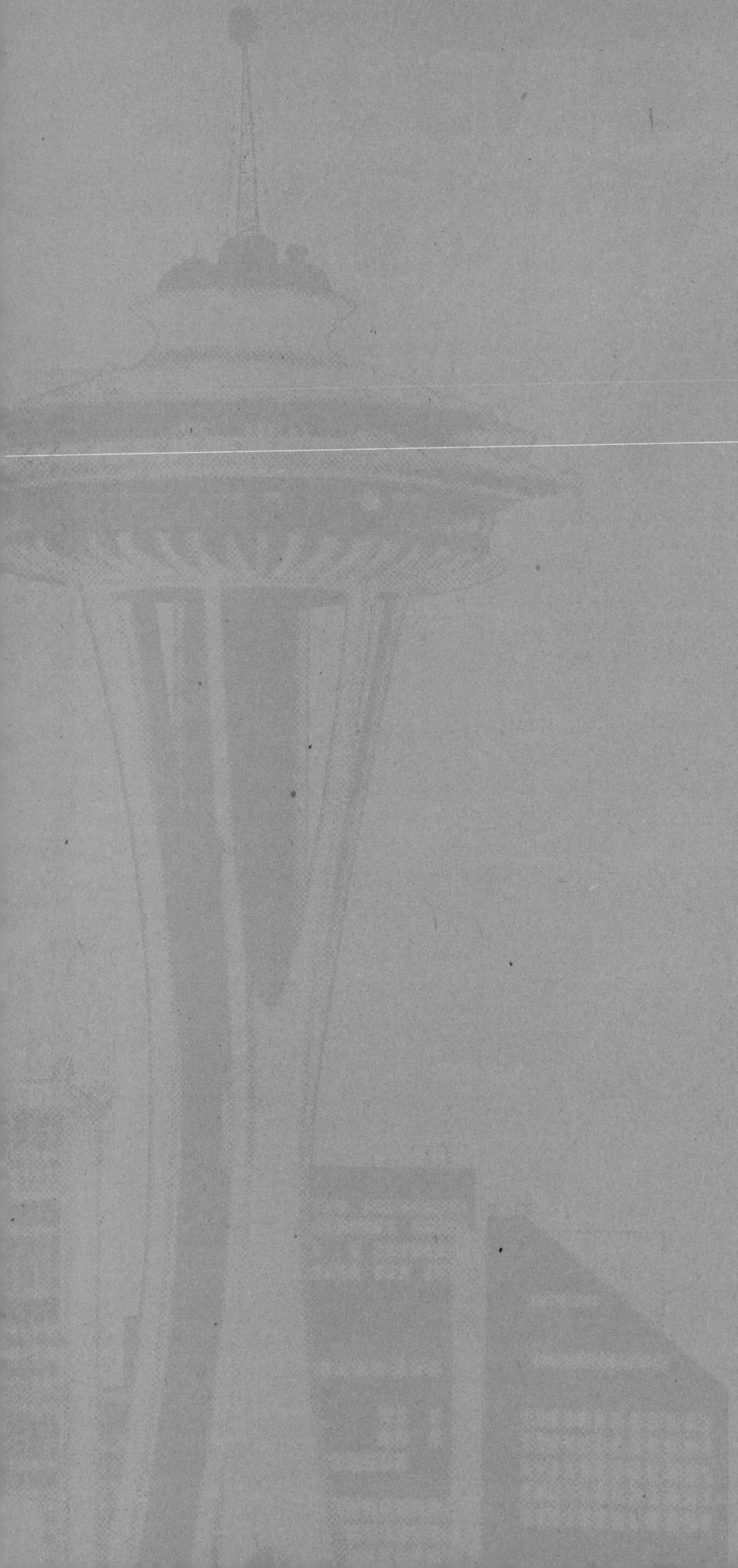

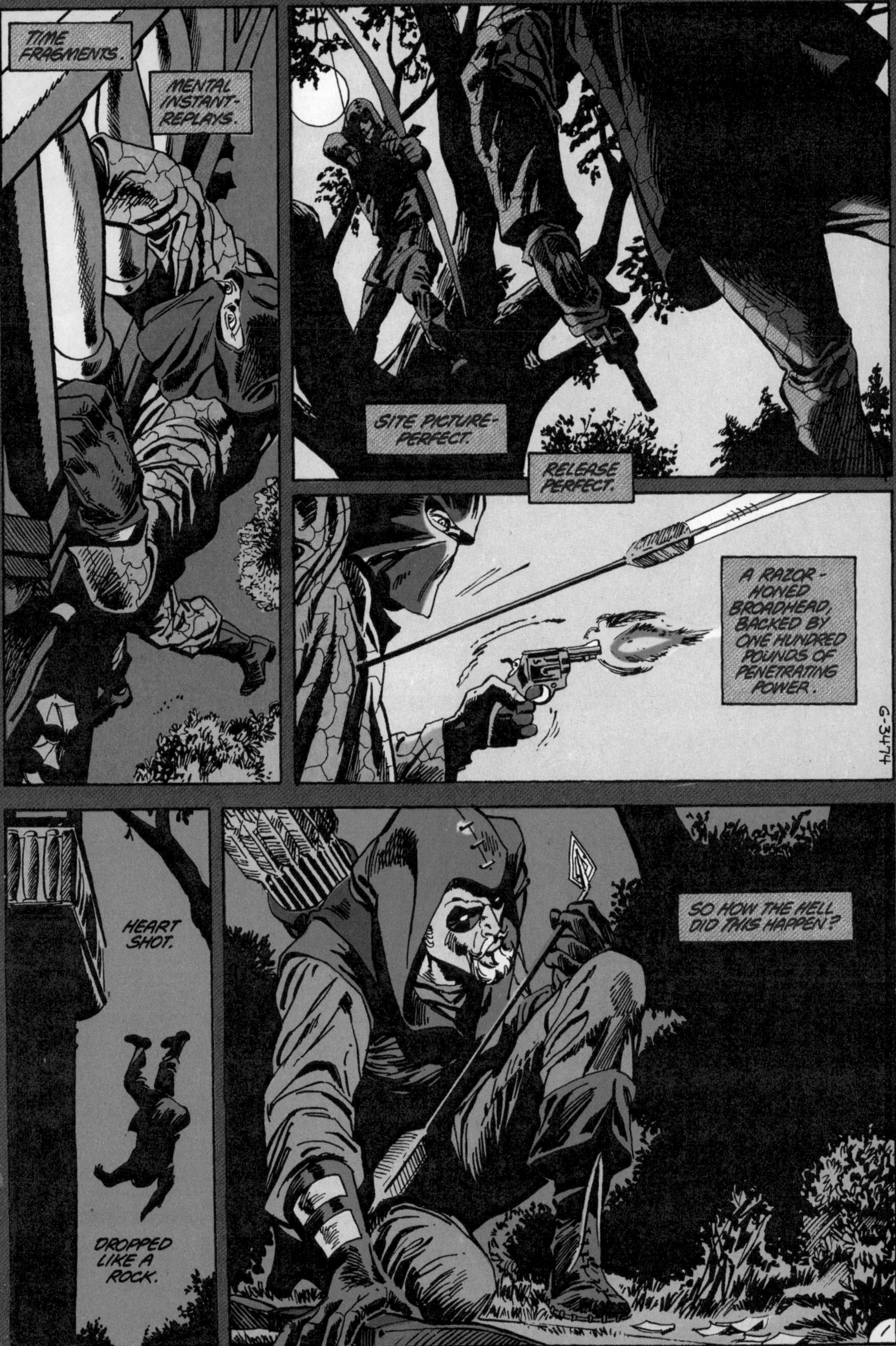

TIME FRAGMENTS.
MENTAL INSTANT-REPLAYS.
SITE PICTURE-PERFECT.
RELEASE PERFECT.
A RAZOR-HONED BROADHEAD, BACKED BY ONE HUNDRED POUNDS OF PENETRATING POWER.
G-3474
HEART SHOT.
DROPPED LIKE A ROCK.
SO HOW THE HELL DID THIS HAPPEN?
1

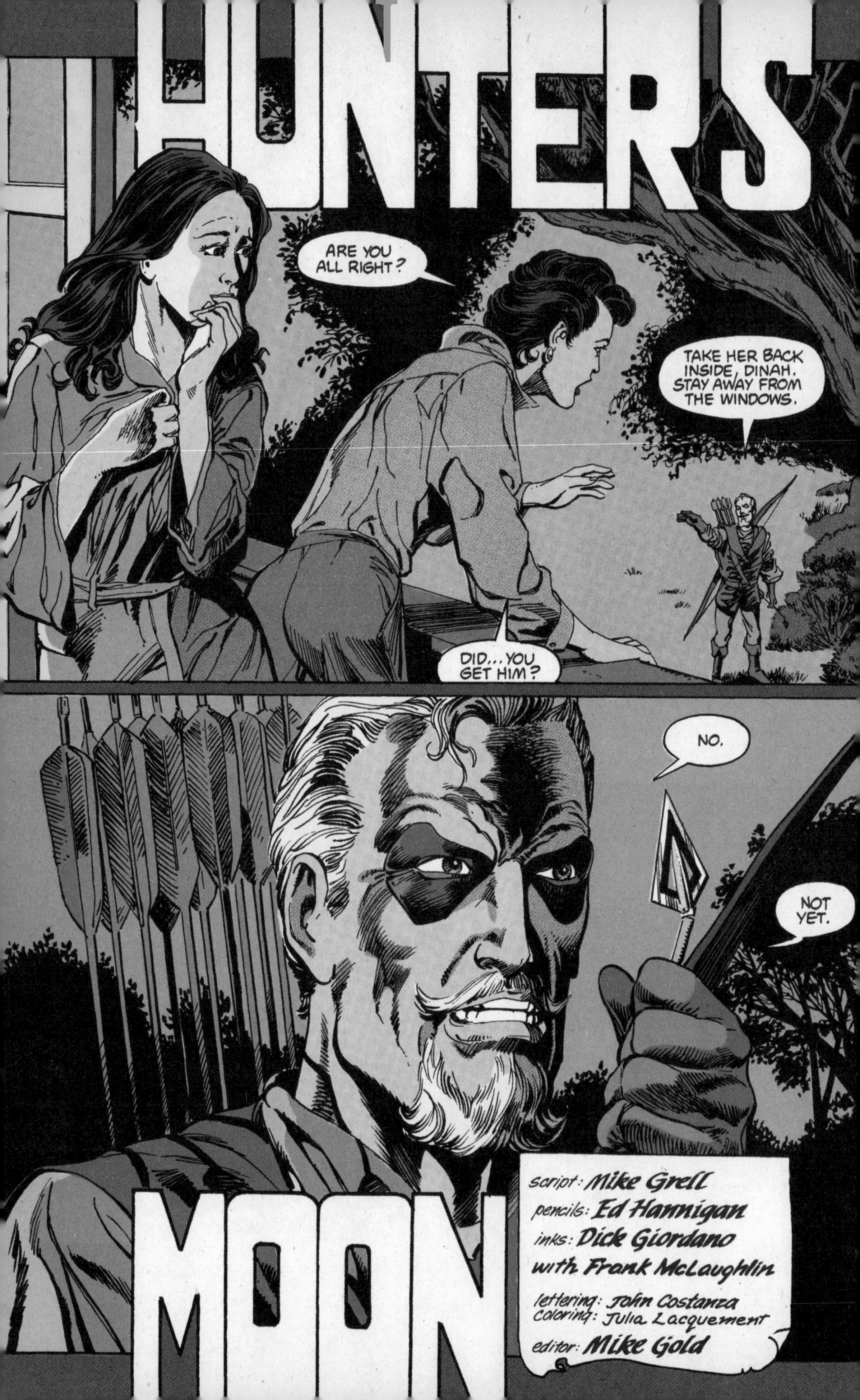
HUNTER'S
ARE YOU ALL RIGHT?
TAKE HER BACK INSIDE, DINAH. STAY AWAY FROM THE WINDOWS.
DID... YOU GET HIM?
NO.
NOT YET.
MOON
script: Mike Grell
pencils: Ed Hannigan
inks: Dick Giordano
with Frank McLaughlin
lettering: John Costanza
Coloring: Julia Lacquement
editor: Mike Gold

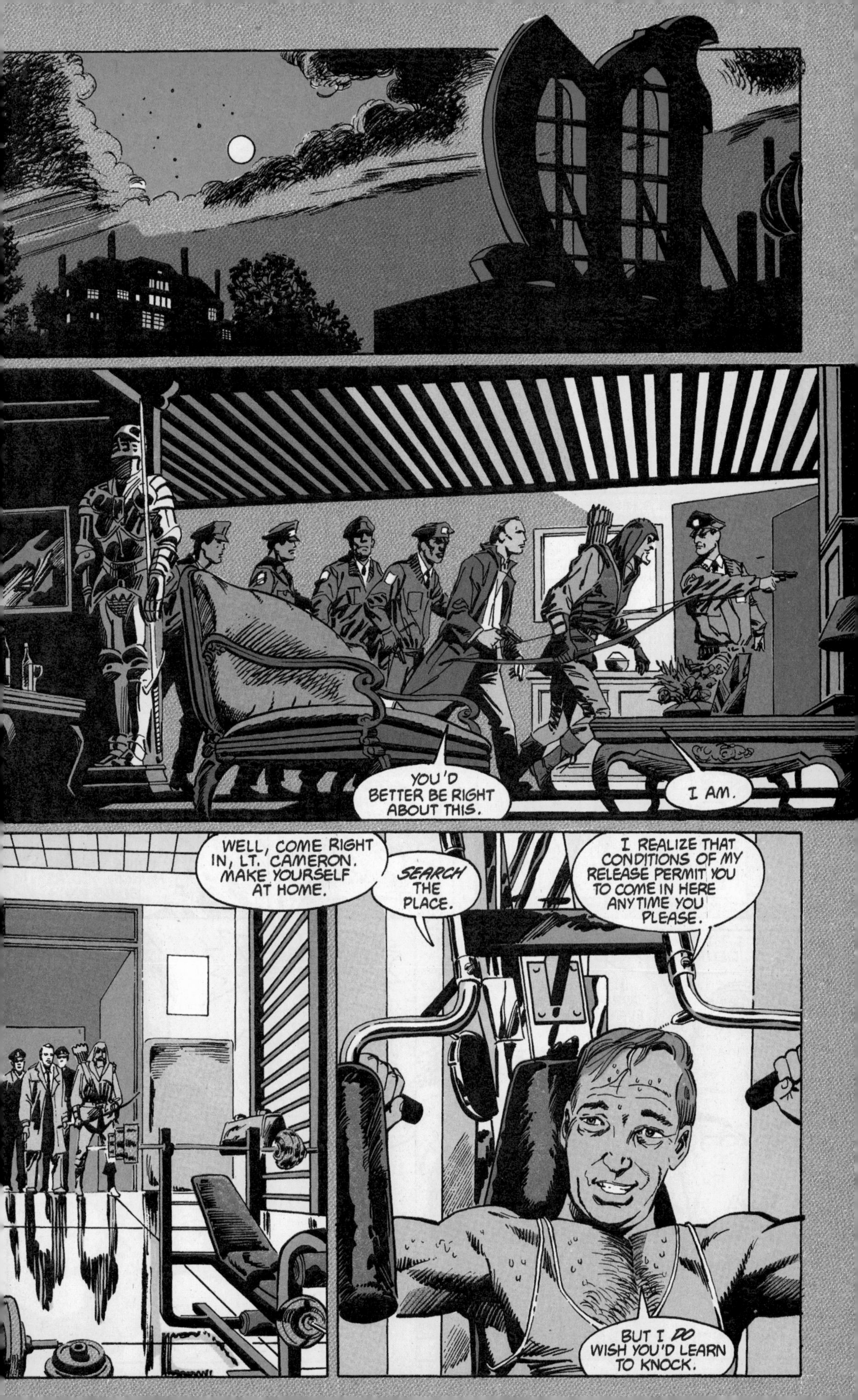
YOU'D BETTER BE RIGHT ABOUT THIS.
I AM.
WELL, COME RIGHT IN, LT. CAMERON. MAKE YOURSELF AT HOME.
SEARCH THE PLACE.
I REALIZE THAT CONDITIONS OF MY RELEASE PERMIT YOU TO COME IN HERE ANYTIME YOU PLEASE.
BUT I DO WISH YOU'D LEARN TO KNOCK.

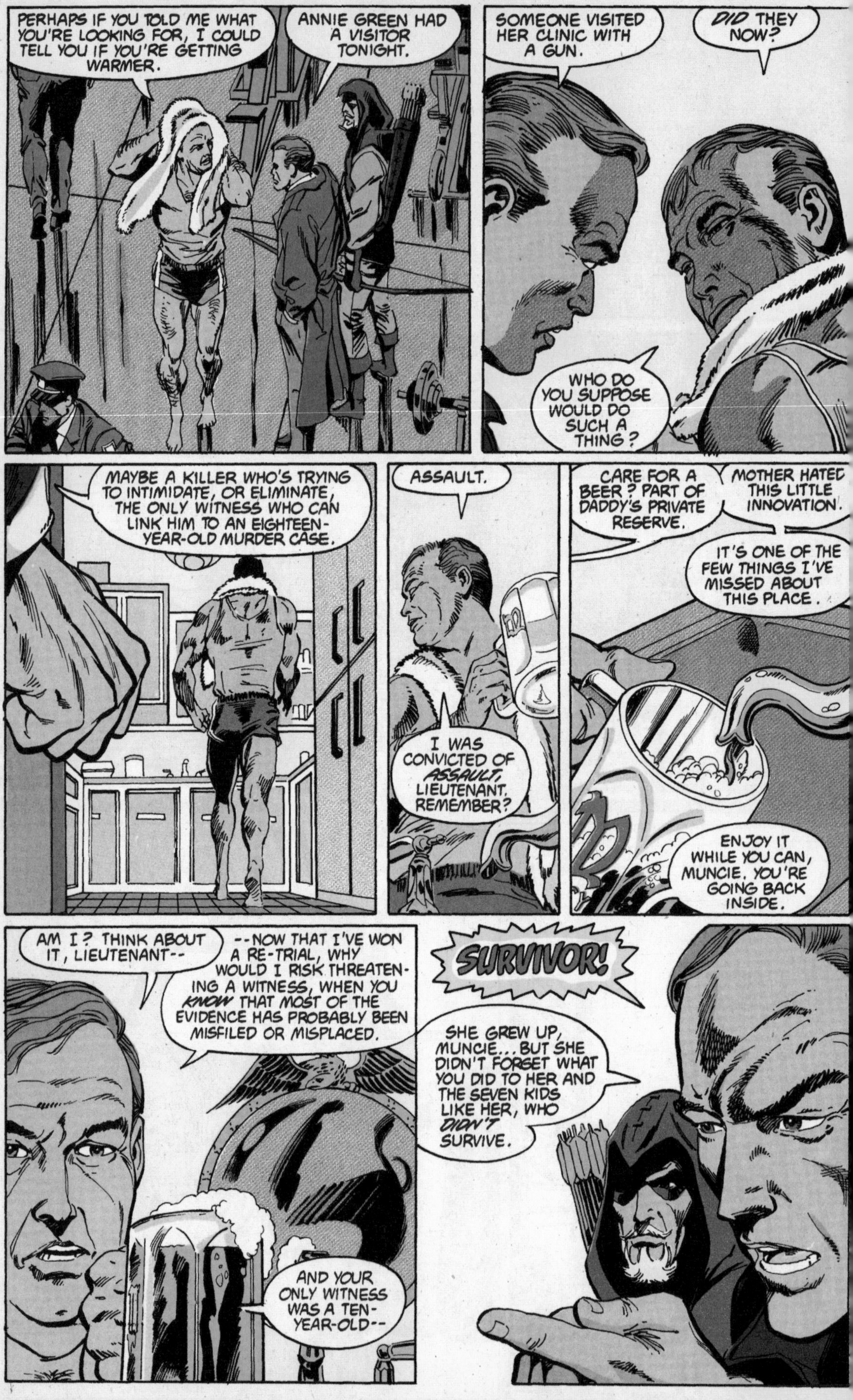
PERHAPS IF YOU TOLD ME WHAT YOU'RE LOOKING FOR, I COULD TELL YOU IF YOU'RE GETTING WARMER.
ANNIE GREEN HAD A VISITOR TONIGHT.
SOMEONE VISITED HER CLINIC WITH A GUN.
DID THEY NOW?
WHO DO YOU SUPPOSE WOULD DO SUCH A THING?
MAYBE A KILLER WHO'S TRYING TO INTIMIDATE, OR ELIMINATE, THE ONLY WITNESS WHO CAN LINK HIM TO AN EIGHTEEN-YEAR-OLD MURDER CASE.
ASSAULT.
I WAS CONVICTED OF ASSAULT, LIEUTENANT. REMEMBER?
CARE FOR A BEER? PART OF DADDY'S PRIVATE RESERVE.
MOTHER HATED THIS LITTLE INNOVATION.
IT'S ONE OF THE FEW THINGS I'VE MISSED ABOUT THIS PLACE.
ENJOY IT WHILE YOU CAN, MUNCIE. YOU'RE GOING BACK INSIDE.
AM I? THINK ABOUT IT, LIEUTENANT--
--NOW THAT I'VE WON A RE-TRIAL, WHY WOULD I RISK THREATENING A WITNESS, WHEN YOU KNOW THAT MOST OF THE EVIDENCE HAS PROBABLY BEEN MISFILED OR MISPLACED.
AND YOUR ONLY WITNESS WAS A TEN-YEAR-OLD--
SURVIVOR!
SHE GREW UP, MUNCIE... BUT SHE DIDN'T FORGET WHAT YOU DID TO HER AND THE SEVEN KIDS LIKE HER, WHO DIDN'T SURVIVE.

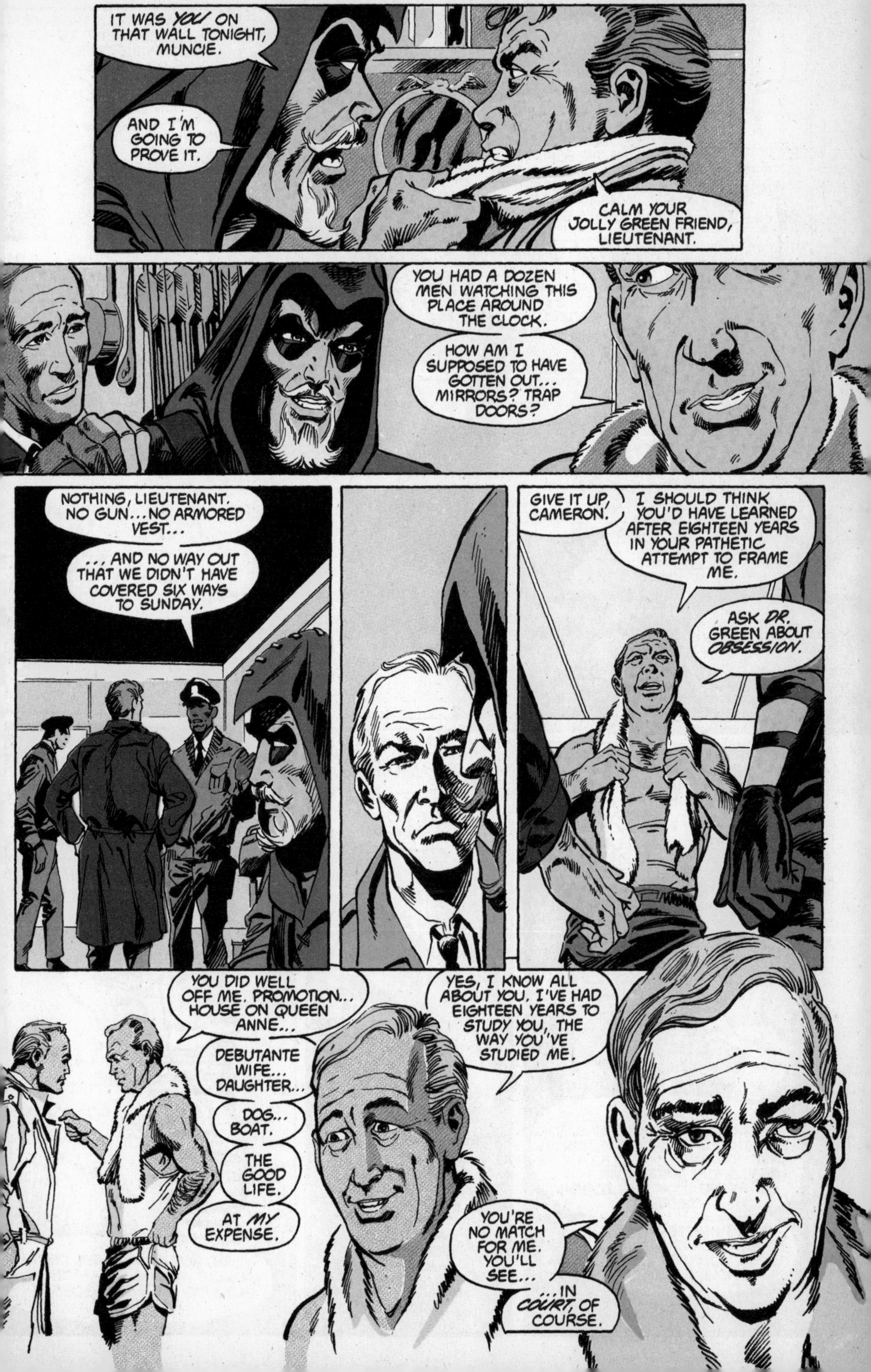
IT WAS YOU ON THAT WALL TONIGHT, MUNCIE.
AND I'M GOING TO PROVE IT.
CALM YOUR JOLLY GREEN FRIEND, LIEUTENANT.
YOU HAD A DOZEN MEN WATCHING THIS PLACE AROUND THE CLOCK.
HOW AM I SUPPOSED TO HAVE GOTTEN OUT... MIRRORS? TRAP DOORS?
NOTHING, LIEUTENANT. NO GUN... NO ARMORED VEST...
..., AND NO WAY OUT THAT WE DIDN'T HAVE COVERED SIX WAYS TO SUNDAY.
GIVE IT UP, CAMERON.
I SHOULD THINK YOU'D HAVE LEARNED AFTER EIGHTEEN YEARS IN YOUR PATHETIC ATTEMPT TO FRAME ME.
ASK DR. GREEN ABOUT OBSESSION.
YOU DID WELL OFF ME. PROMOTION... HOUSE ON QUEEN ANNE...
DEBUTANTE WIFE... DAUGHTER...
DOG... BOAT.
THE GOOD LIFE.
AT MY EXPENSE.
YES, I KNOW ALL ABOUT YOU. I'VE HAD EIGHTEEN YEARS TO STUDY YOU, THE WAY YOU'VE STUDIED ME.
YOU'RE NO MATCH FOR ME. YOU'LL SEE...
...IN COURT, OF COURSE.

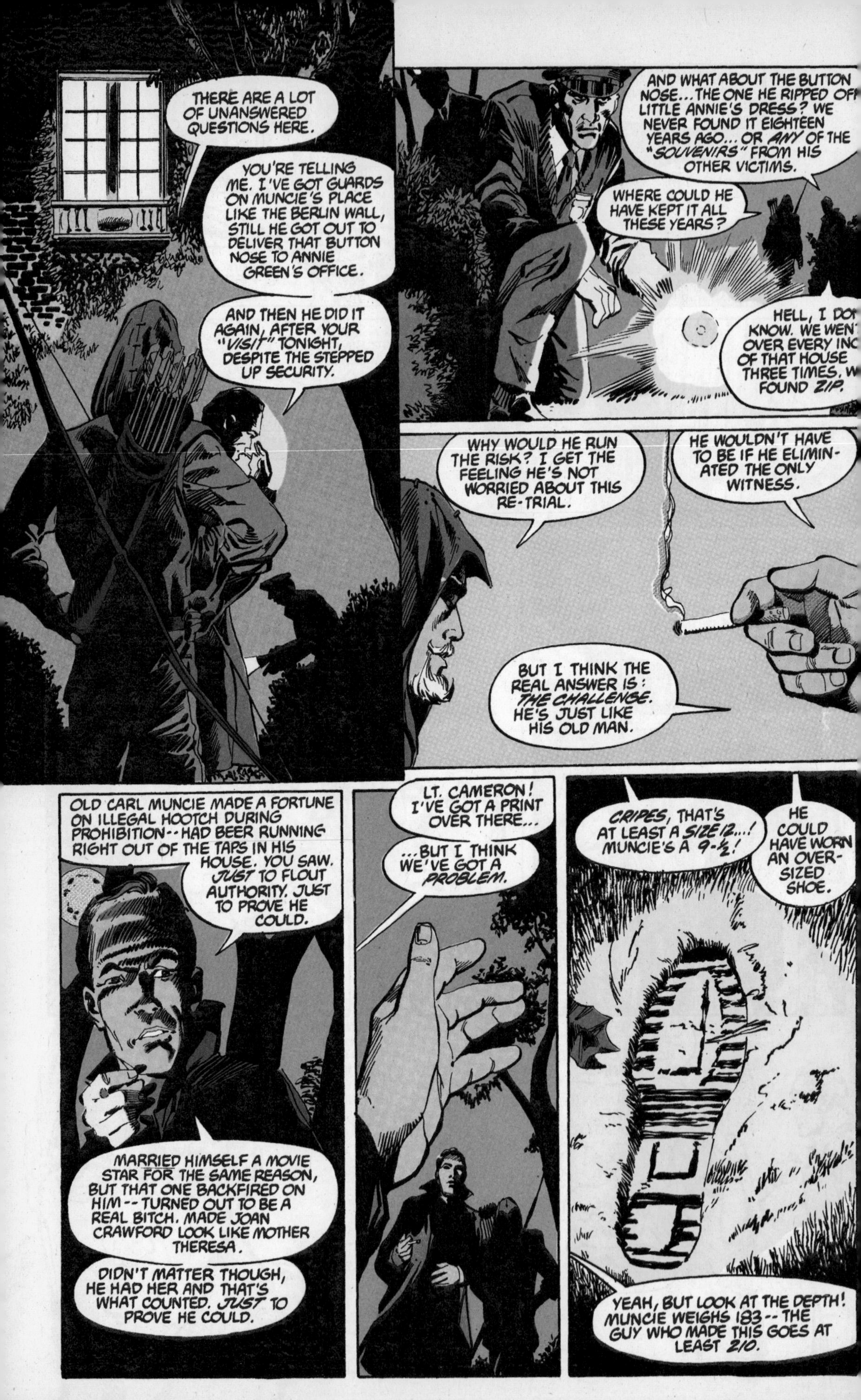
THERE ARE A LOT OF UNANSWERED QUESTIONS HERE.
YOU'RE TELLING ME. I'VE GOT GUARDS ON MUNCIE'S PLACE LIKE THE BERLIN WALL, STILL HE GOT OUT TO DELIVER THAT BUTTON NOSE TO ANNIE GREEN'S OFFICE.
AND THEN HE DID IT AGAIN, AFTER YOUR "VISIT" TONIGHT, DESPITE THE STEPPED UP SECURITY.
AND WHAT ABOUT THE BUTTON NOSE... THE ONE HE RIPPED OFF LITTLE ANNIE'S DRESS? WE NEVER FOUND IT EIGHTEEN YEARS AGO... OR ANY OF THE "SOUVENIRS" FROM HIS OTHER VICTIMS.
WHERE COULD HE HAVE KEPT IT ALL THESE YEARS?
HELL, I DON' KNOW. WE WENT OVER EVERY INC OF THAT HOUSE THREE TIMES. W FOUND ZIP.
WHY WOULD HE RUN THE RISK? I GET THE FEELING HE'S NOT WORRIED ABOUT THIS RE-TRIAL.
HE WOULDN'T HAVE TO BE IF HE ELIMINATED THE ONLY WITNESS.
BUT I THINK THE REAL ANSWER IS: THE CHALLENGE. HE'S JUST LIKE HIS OLD MAN.
OLD CARL MUNCIE MADE A FORTUNE ON ILLEGAL HOOTCH DURING PROHIBITION--HAD BEER RUNNING RIGHT OUT OF THE TAPS IN HIS HOUSE. YOU SAW. JUST TO FLOUT AUTHORITY. JUST TO PROVE HE COULD.
MARRIED HIMSELF A MOVIE STAR FOR THE SAME REASON, BUT THAT ONE BACKFIRED ON HIM--TURNED OUT TO BE A REAL BITCH. MADE JOAN CRAWFORD LOOK LIKE MOTHER THERESA.
DIDN'T MATTER THOUGH, HE HAD HER AND THAT'S WHAT COUNTED. JUST TO PROVE HE COULD.
LT. CAMERON! I'VE GOT A PRINT OVER THERE...
...BUT I THINK WE'VE GOT A PROBLEM.
CRIPES, THAT'S AT LEAST A SIZE 12...! MUNCIE'S A 9-1/2!
HE COULD HAVE WORN AN OVER-SIZED SHOE.
YEAH, BUT LOOK AT THE DEPTH! MUNCIE WEIGHS 183--THE GUY WHO MADE THIS GOES AT LEAST 210.

I DON'T KNOW WHY PEOPLE SAY THINGS LIKE "AT LEAST YOU WEREN'T RAPED."

AS IF THAT WERE THE WORST THING THAT ANYONE COULD DO TO YOU.

YOU KNOW FROM YOUR OWN EXPERIENCE THAT SEX HAS *NOTHING* TO DO WITH THIS TYPE OF INDIVIDUAL.

IT'S THE PAIN.

AND THE FEAR.

IT'S NOT SOMETHING YOU CAN JUST FORGET ABOUT, AND MAKE IT GO AWAY. YOU HAVE TO LEARN TO LIVE WITH THE MEMORY...

...NOT TRY TO FORCE IT INTO A DARK CORNER OF YOUR MIND, WHERE IT CAN HAUNT YOU THE REST OF YOUR LIFE.

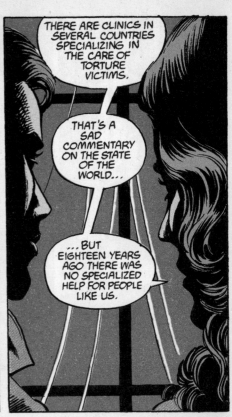

THERE ARE CLINICS IN SEVERAL COUNTRIES SPECIALIZING IN THE CARE OF TORTURE VICTIMS.

THAT'S A SAD COMMENTARY ON THE STATE OF THE WORLD...

...BUT EIGHTEEN YEARS AGO THERE WAS NO SPECIALIZED HELP FOR PEOPLE LIKE US.

"AT LEAST SHE WASN'T RAPED," THEY SAID.

WHEN I WAS SIXTEEN I SPENT TWO MONTHS IN A MENTAL WARD BECAUSE A BOY I REALLY LIKED PUT HIS HANDS ON ME.

I FELT SORRY FOR HIM.

HE DIDN'T KNOW THAT TOUCHING IS ONE OF THE HARDEST THINGS TO ACCEPT.

I'VE NEVER BEEN ABLE TO BEAR THE TOUCH OF A MAN...

...I STILL HAVE TO STEEL MYSELF TO SHAKE HANDS.

IT'S A MATTER OF *TRUST.*

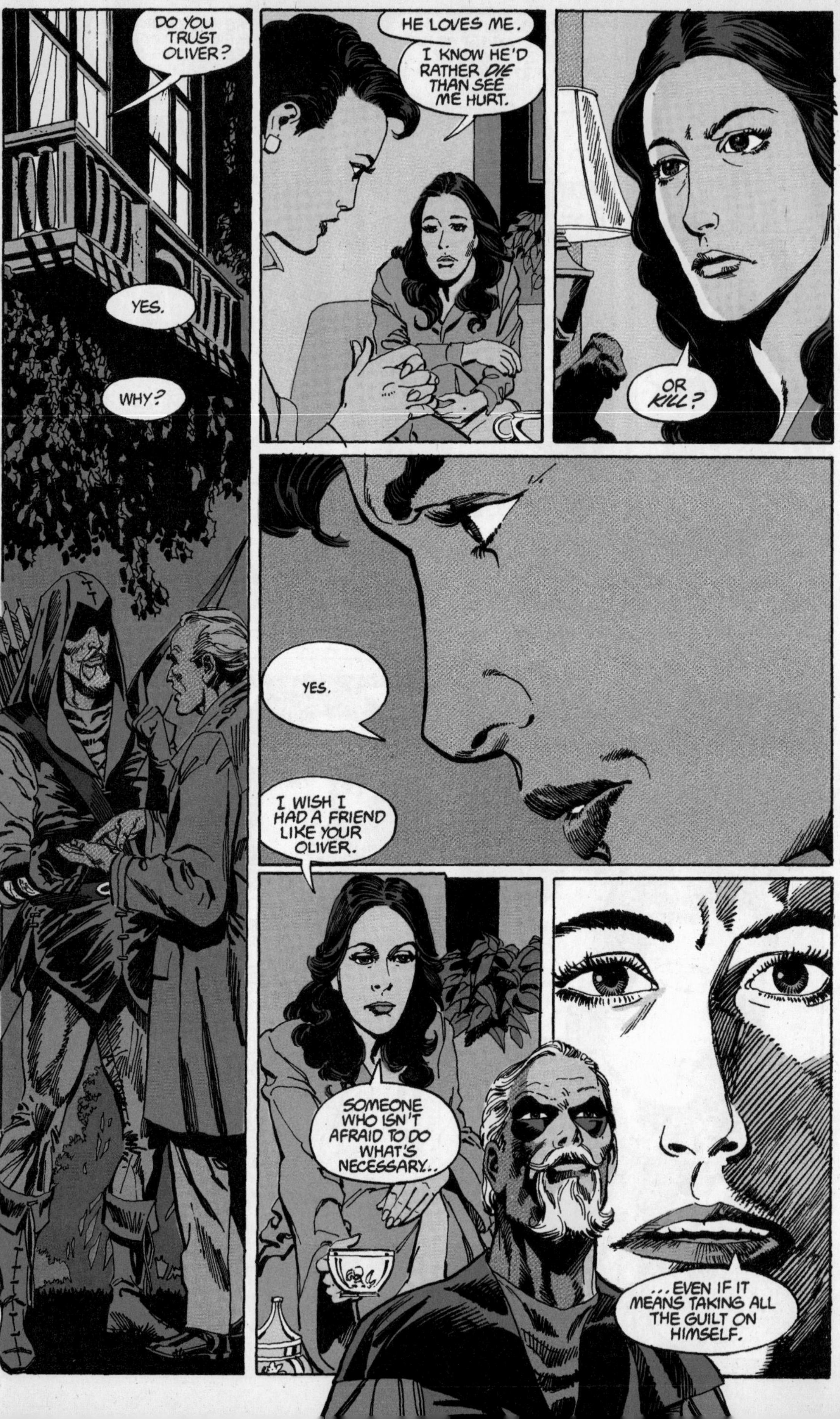
DO YOU TRUST OLIVER?
YES.
WHY?
HE LOVES ME.
I KNOW HE'D RATHER *DIE* THAN SEE ME HURT.
OR *KILL*?
YES.
I WISH I HAD A FRIEND LIKE YOUR OLIVER.
SOMEONE WHO ISN'T AFRAID TO DO WHAT'S NECESSARY...
...EVEN IF IT MEANS TAKING ALL THE GUILT ON HIMSELF.

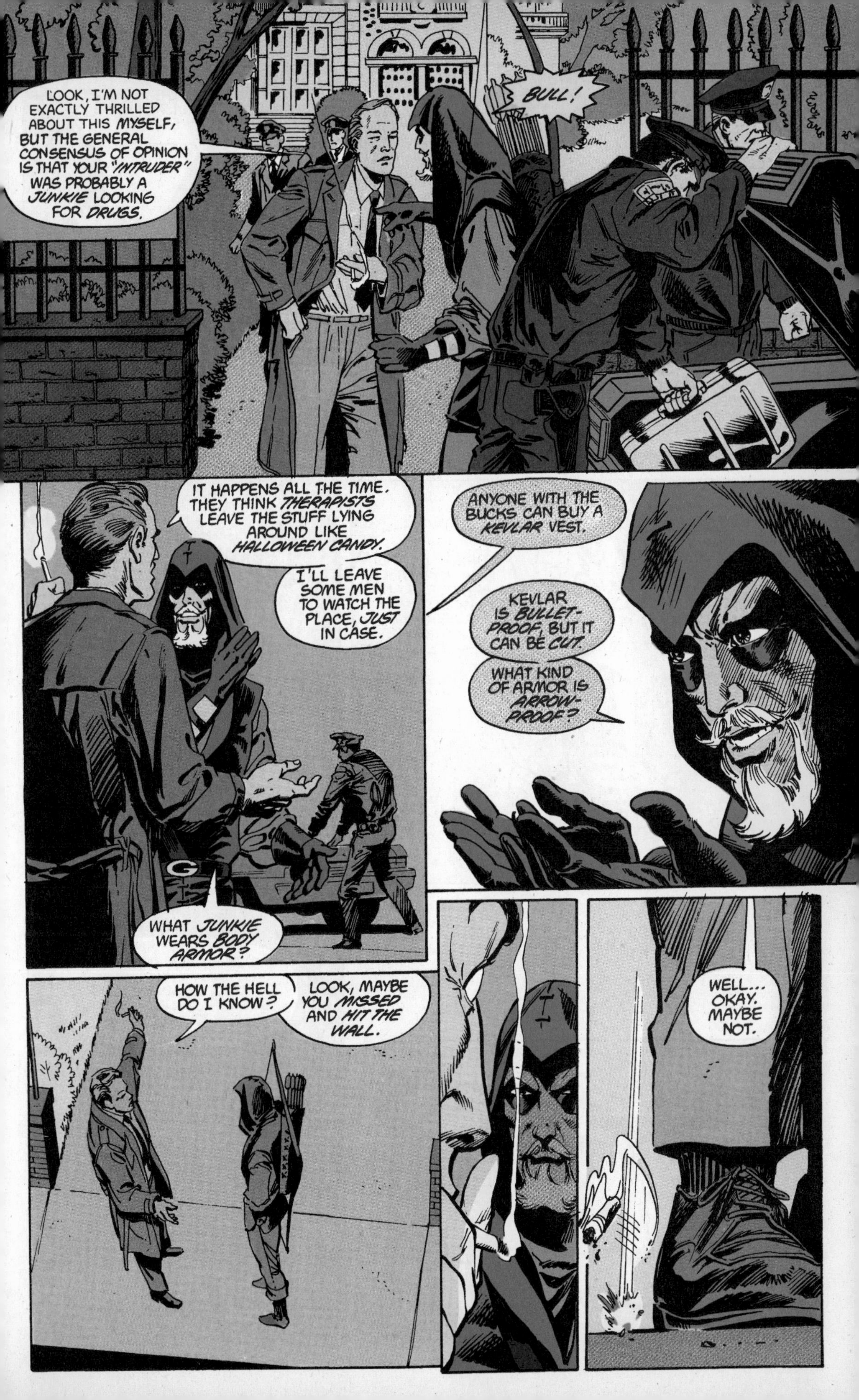

LOOK, I'M NOT EXACTLY THRILLED ABOUT THIS MYSELF, BUT THE GENERAL CONSENSUS OF OPINION IS THAT YOUR "INTRUDER" WAS PROBABLY A JUNKIE LOOKING FOR DRUGS.
BULL!
IT HAPPENS ALL THE TIME. THEY THINK THERAPISTS LEAVE THE STUFF LYING AROUND LIKE HALLOWEEN CANDY.
I'LL LEAVE SOME MEN TO WATCH THE PLACE, JUST IN CASE.
WHAT JUNKIE WEARS BODY ARMOR?
ANYONE WITH THE BUCKS CAN BUY A KEVLAR VEST.
KEVLAR IS BULLET-PROOF, BUT IT CAN BE CUT.
WHAT KIND OF ARMOR IS ARROW-PROOF?
HOW THE HELL DO I KNOW?
LOOK, MAYBE YOU MISSED AND HIT THE WALL.
WELL... OKAY. MAYBE NOT.

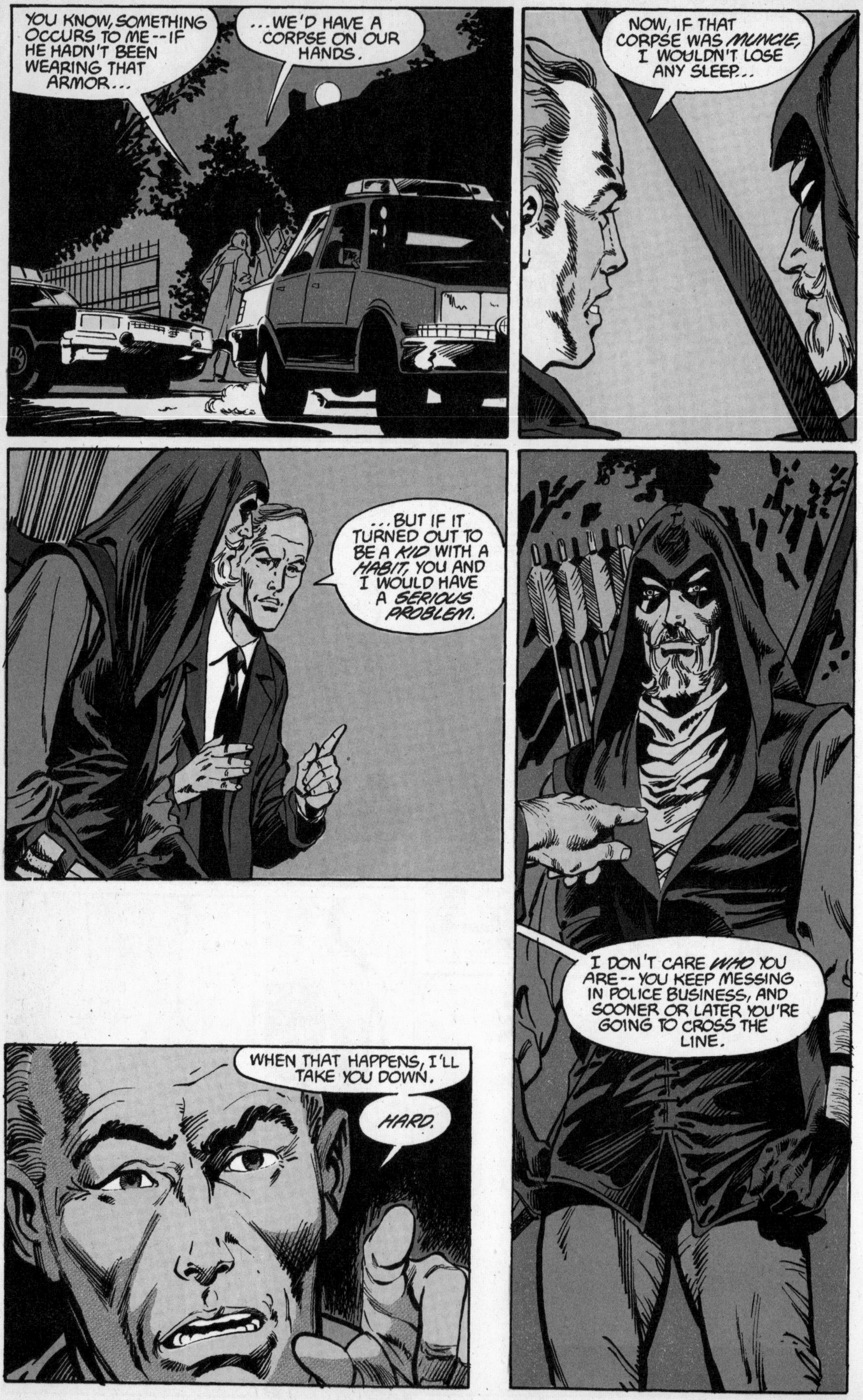
YOU KNOW, SOMETHING OCCURS TO ME--IF HE HADN'T BEEN WEARING THAT ARMOR...
...WE'D HAVE A CORPSE ON OUR HANDS.
NOW, IF THAT CORPSE WAS *MUNCIE*, I WOULDN'T LOSE ANY SLEEP...
...BUT IF IT TURNED OUT TO BE A *KID* WITH A *HABIT*, YOU AND I WOULD HAVE A *SERIOUS PROBLEM*.
I DON'T CARE *WHO* YOU ARE--YOU KEEP MESSING IN POLICE BUSINESS, AND SOONER OR LATER YOU'RE GOING TO CROSS THE LINE.
WHEN THAT HAPPENS, I'LL TAKE YOU DOWN.
HARD.

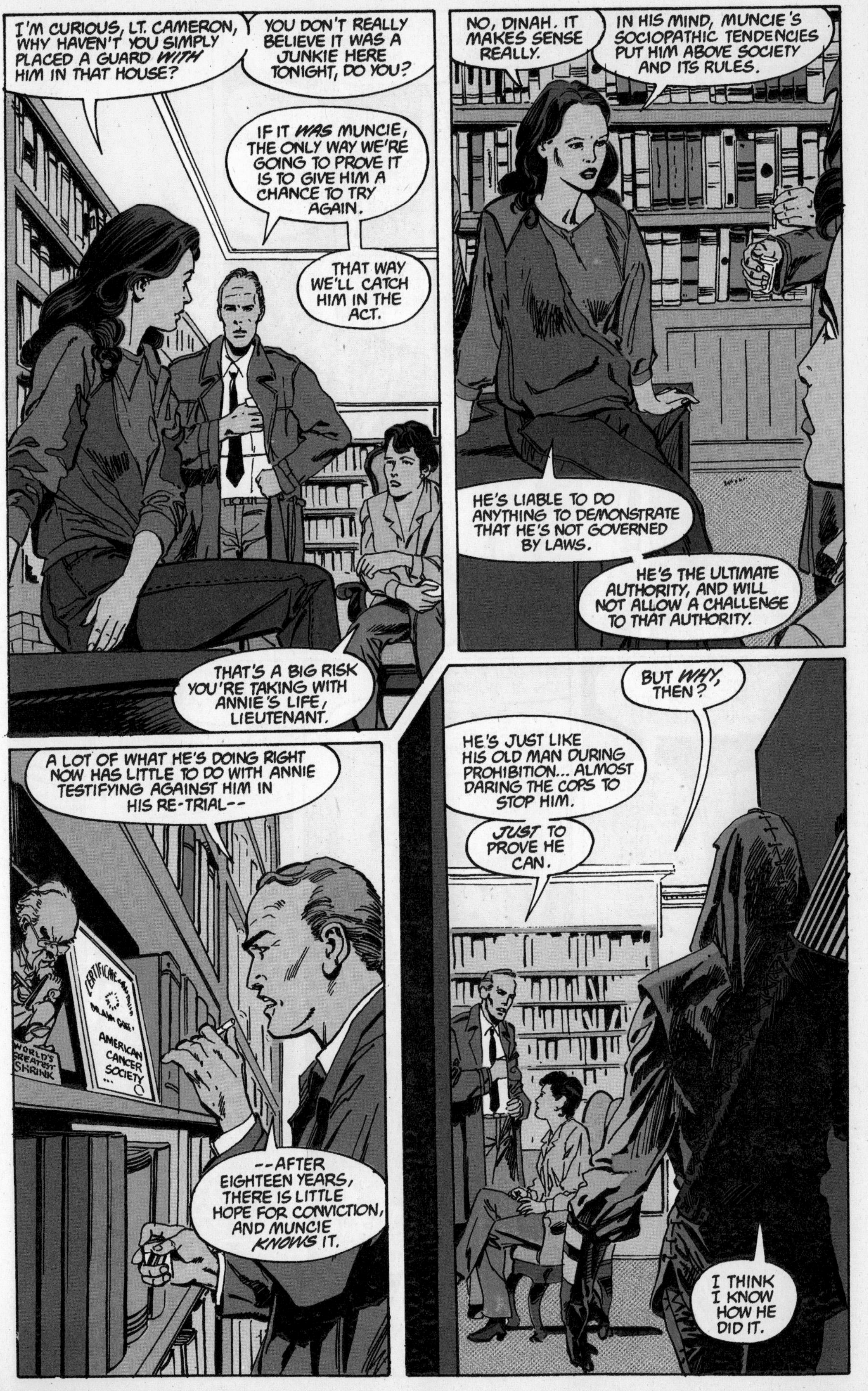
I'M CURIOUS, LT. CAMERON, WHY HAVEN'T YOU SIMPLY PLACED A GUARD WITH HIM IN THAT HOUSE?
YOU DON'T REALLY BELIEVE IT WAS A JUNKIE HERE TONIGHT, DO YOU?
IF IT WAS MUNCIE, THE ONLY WAY WE'RE GOING TO PROVE IT IS TO GIVE HIM A CHANCE TO TRY AGAIN.
THAT WAY WE'LL CATCH HIM IN THE ACT.
THAT'S A BIG RISK YOU'RE TAKING WITH ANNIE'S LIFE, LIEUTENANT.
NO, DINAH. IT MAKES SENSE REALLY.
IN HIS MIND, MUNCIE'S SOCIOPATHIC TENDENCIES PUT HIM ABOVE SOCIETY AND ITS RULES.
HE'S LIABLE TO DO ANYTHING TO DEMONSTRATE THAT HE'S NOT GOVERNED BY LAWS.
HE'S THE ULTIMATE AUTHORITY, AND WILL NOT ALLOW A CHALLENGE TO THAT AUTHORITY.
A LOT OF WHAT HE'S DOING RIGHT NOW HAS LITTLE TO DO WITH ANNIE TESTIFYING AGAINST HIM IN HIS RE-TRIAL--
WORLD'S GREATEST SHRINK
AMERICAN CANCER SOCIETY
--AFTER EIGHTEEN YEARS, THERE IS LITTLE HOPE FOR CONVICTION, AND MUNCIE KNOWS IT.
BUT WHY, THEN?
HE'S JUST LIKE HIS OLD MAN DURING PROHIBITION... ALMOST DARING THE COPS TO STOP HIM.
JUST TO PROVE HE CAN.
I THINK I KNOW HOW HE DID IT.

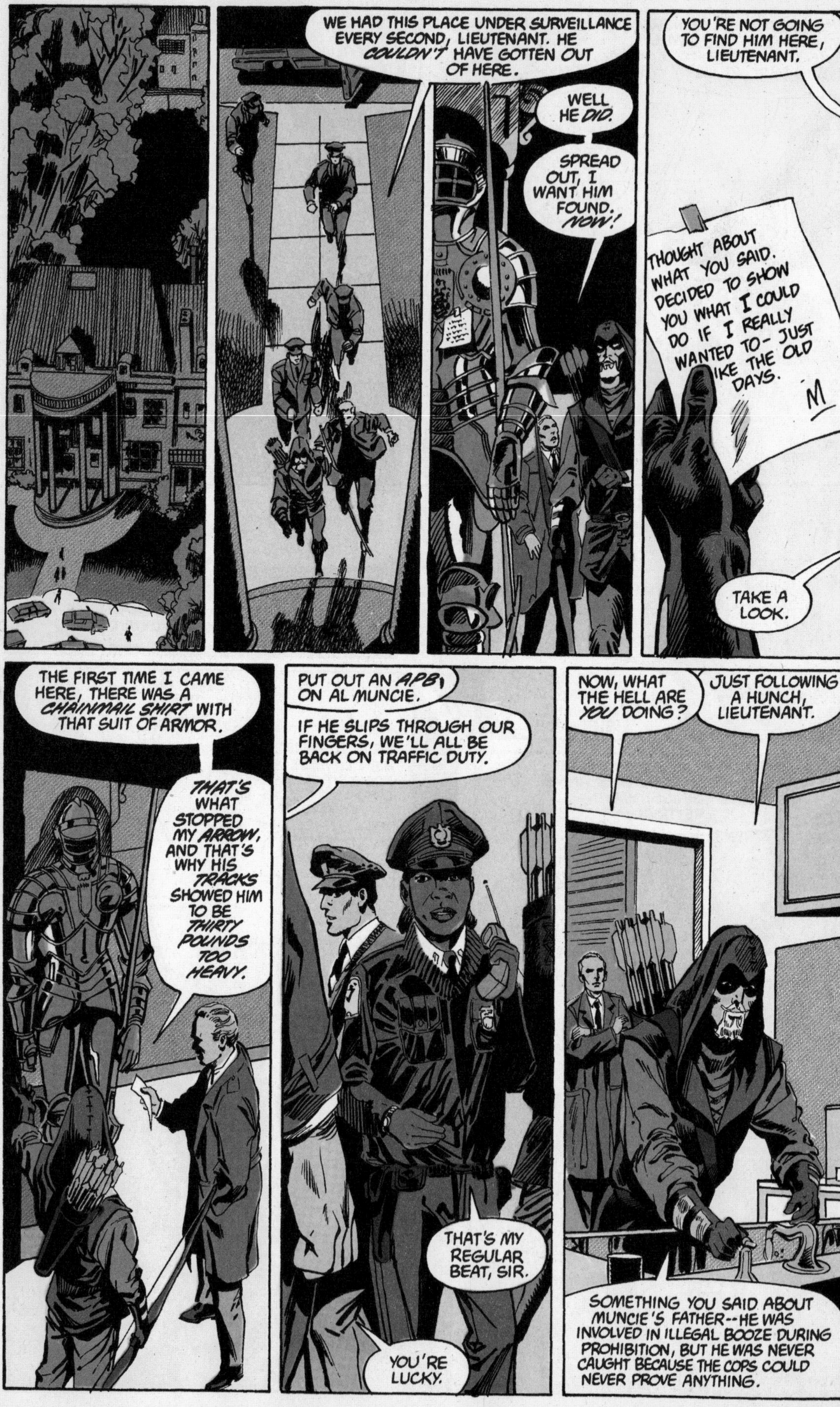

WE HAD THIS PLACE UNDER SURVEILLANCE EVERY SECOND, LIEUTENANT. HE COULDN'T HAVE GOTTEN OUT OF HERE.
WELL HE DID.
SPREAD OUT, I WANT HIM FOUND. NOW!
YOU'RE NOT GOING TO FIND HIM HERE, LIEUTENANT.
THOUGHT ABOUT WHAT YOU SAID. DECIDED TO SHOW YOU WHAT I COULD DO IF I REALLY WANTED TO- JUST LIKE THE OLD DAYS. M
TAKE A LOOK.
THE FIRST TIME I CAME HERE, THERE WAS A CHAINMAIL SHIRT WITH THAT SUIT OF ARMOR.
THAT'S WHAT STOPPED MY ARROW, AND THAT'S WHY HIS TRACKS SHOWED HIM TO BE THIRTY POUNDS TOO HEAVY.
PUT OUT AN APB, ON AL MUNCIE.
IF HE SLIPS THROUGH OUR FINGERS, WE'LL ALL BE BACK ON TRAFFIC DUTY.
THAT'S MY REGULAR BEAT, SIR.
YOU'RE LUCKY.
NOW, WHAT THE HELL ARE YOU DOING?
JUST FOLLOWING A HUNCH, LIEUTENANT.
SOMETHING YOU SAID ABOUT MUNCIE'S FATHER--HE WAS INVOLVED IN ILLEGAL BOOZE DURING PROHIBITION, BUT HE WAS NEVER CAUGHT BECAUSE THE COPS COULD NEVER PROVE ANYTHING.

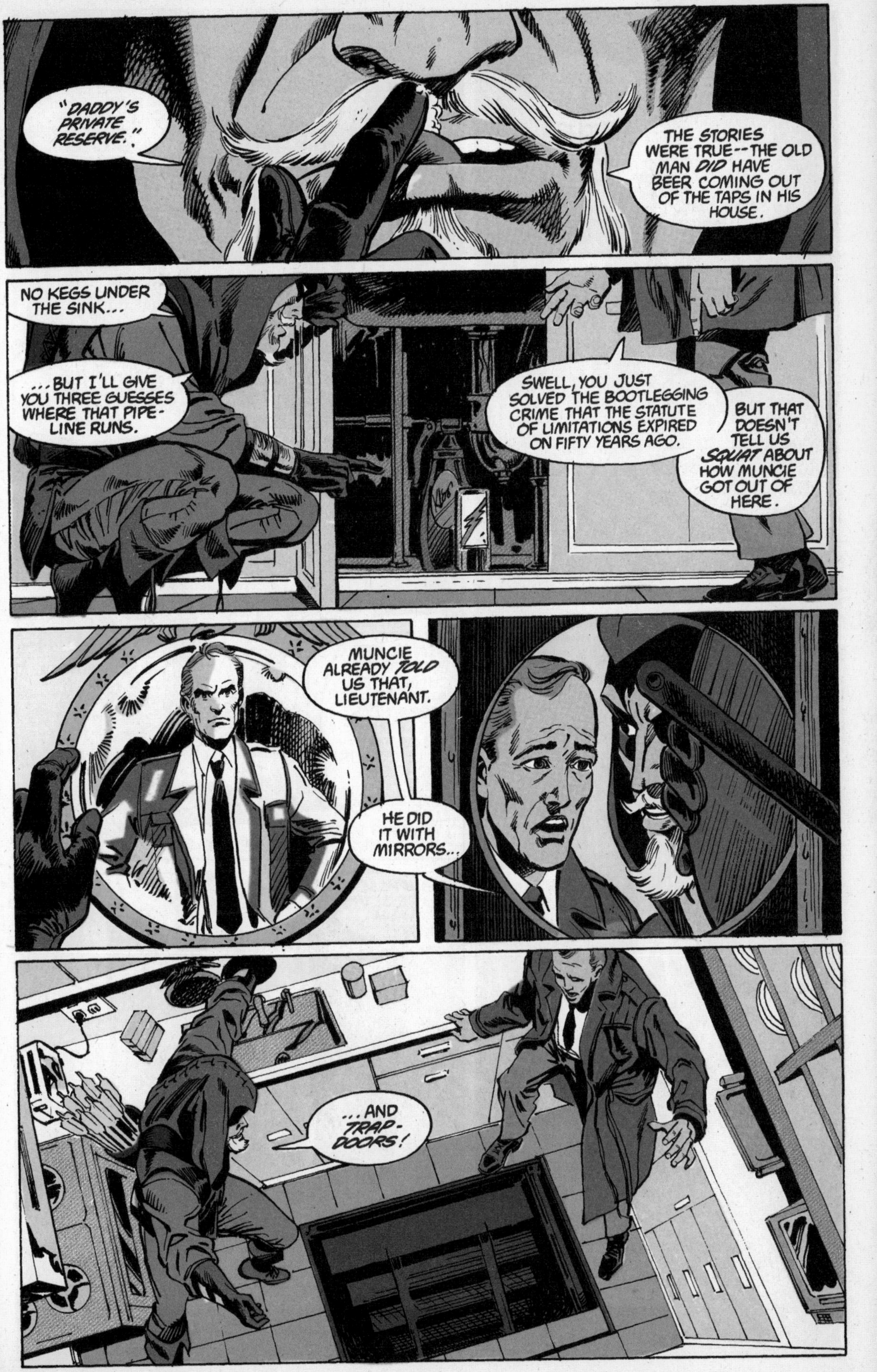
"DADDY'S PRIVATE RESERVE."
THE STORIES WERE TRUE--THE OLD MAN DID HAVE BEER COMING OUT OF THE TAPS IN HIS HOUSE.
NO KEGS UNDER THE SINK...
...BUT I'LL GIVE YOU THREE GUESSES WHERE THAT PIPE-LINE RUNS.
SWELL, YOU JUST SOLVED THE BOOTLEGGING CRIME THAT THE STATUTE OF LIMITATIONS EXPIRED ON FIFTY YEARS AGO.
BUT THAT DOESN'T TELL US SQUAT ABOUT HOW MUNCIE GOT OUT OF HERE.
MUNCIE ALREADY TOLD US THAT, LIEUTENANT.
HE DID IT WITH MIRRORS...
...AND TRAP-DOORS!

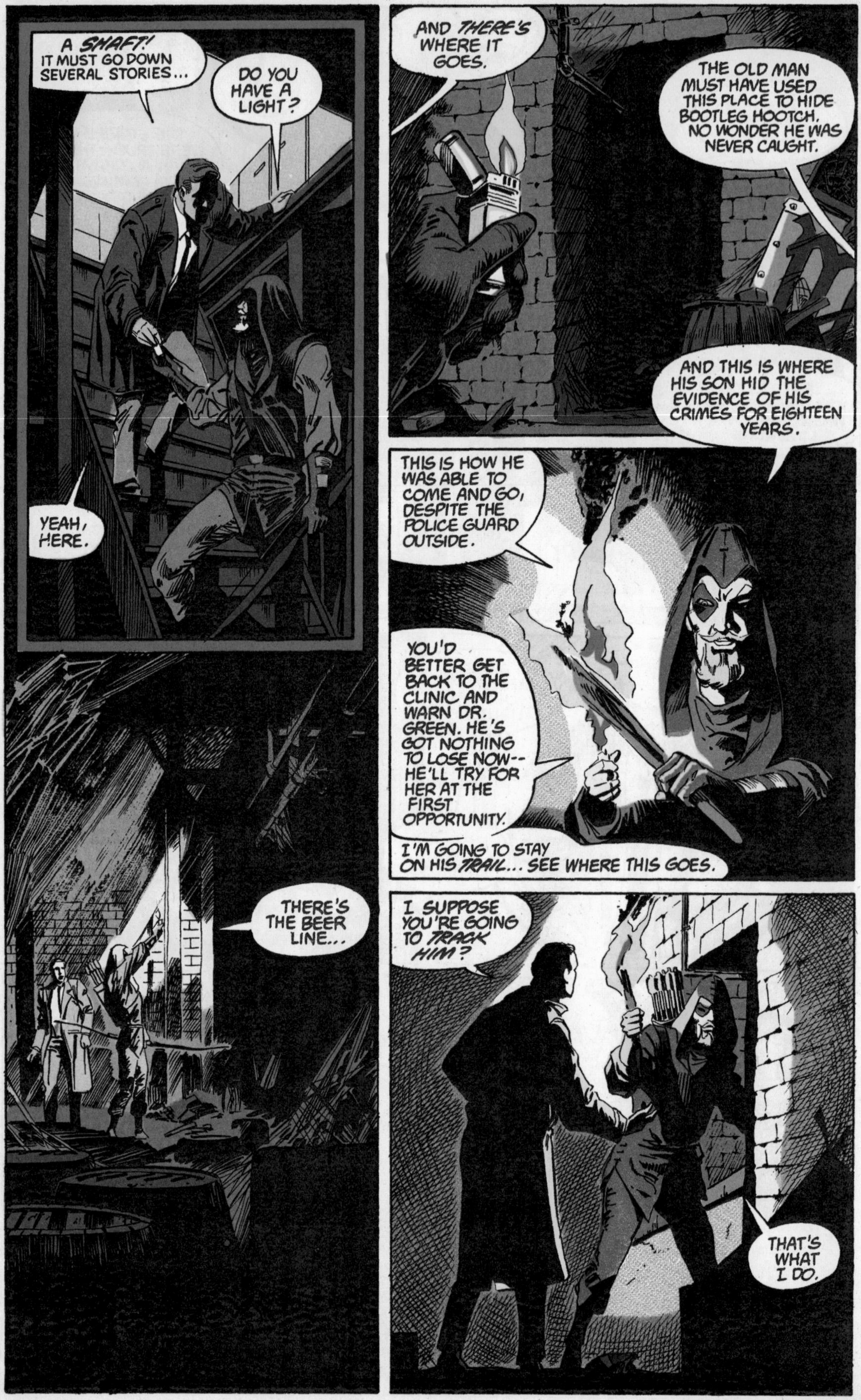
A SHAFT! IT MUST GO DOWN SEVERAL STORIES...
DO YOU HAVE A LIGHT?
YEAH, HERE.
AND THERE'S WHERE IT GOES.
THE OLD MAN MUST HAVE USED THIS PLACE TO HIDE BOOTLEG HOOTCH. NO WONDER HE WAS NEVER CAUGHT.
AND THIS IS WHERE HIS SON HID THE EVIDENCE OF HIS CRIMES FOR EIGHTEEN YEARS.
THERE'S THE BEER LINE...
THIS IS HOW HE WAS ABLE TO COME AND GO, DESPITE THE POLICE GUARD OUTSIDE.
YOU'D BETTER GET BACK TO THE CLINIC AND WARN DR. GREEN. HE'S GOT NOTHING TO LOSE NOW--HE'LL TRY FOR HER AT THE FIRST OPPORTUNITY.
I'M GOING TO STAY ON HIS TRAIL... SEE WHERE THIS GOES.
I SUPPOSE YOU'RE GOING TO TRACK HIM?
THAT'S WHAT I DO.

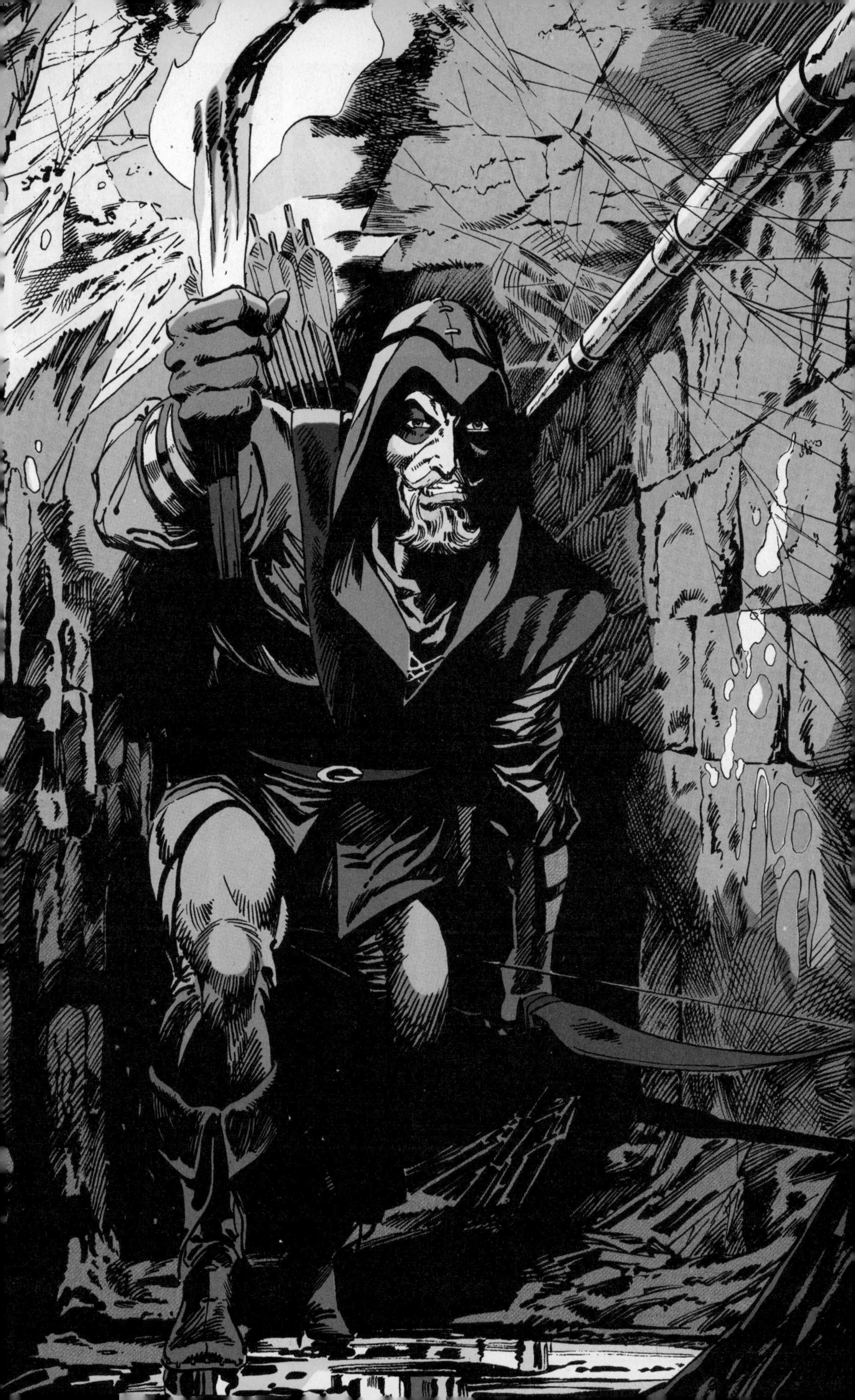

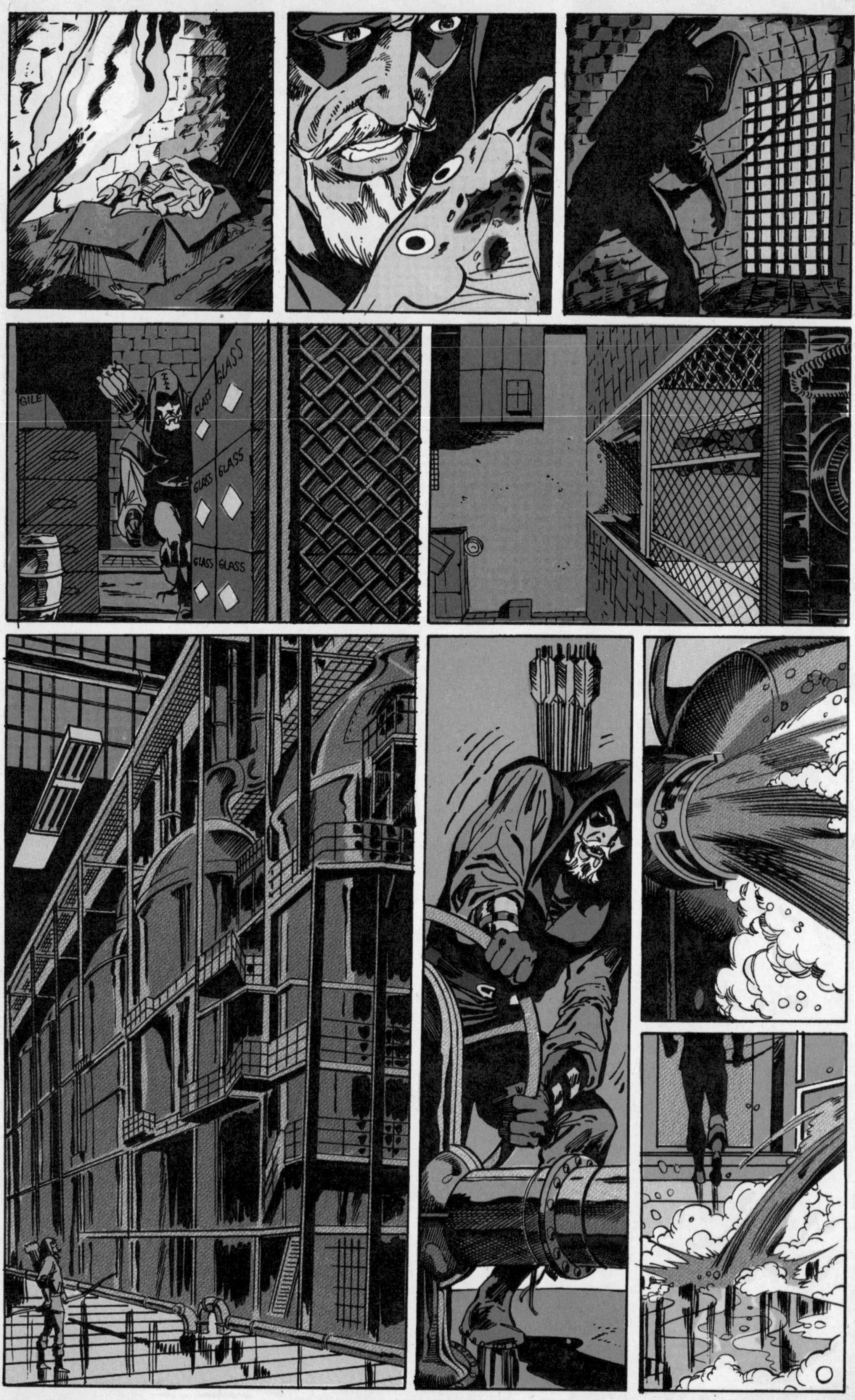
GLASS GLASS
GLASS GLASS
GLASS GLASS

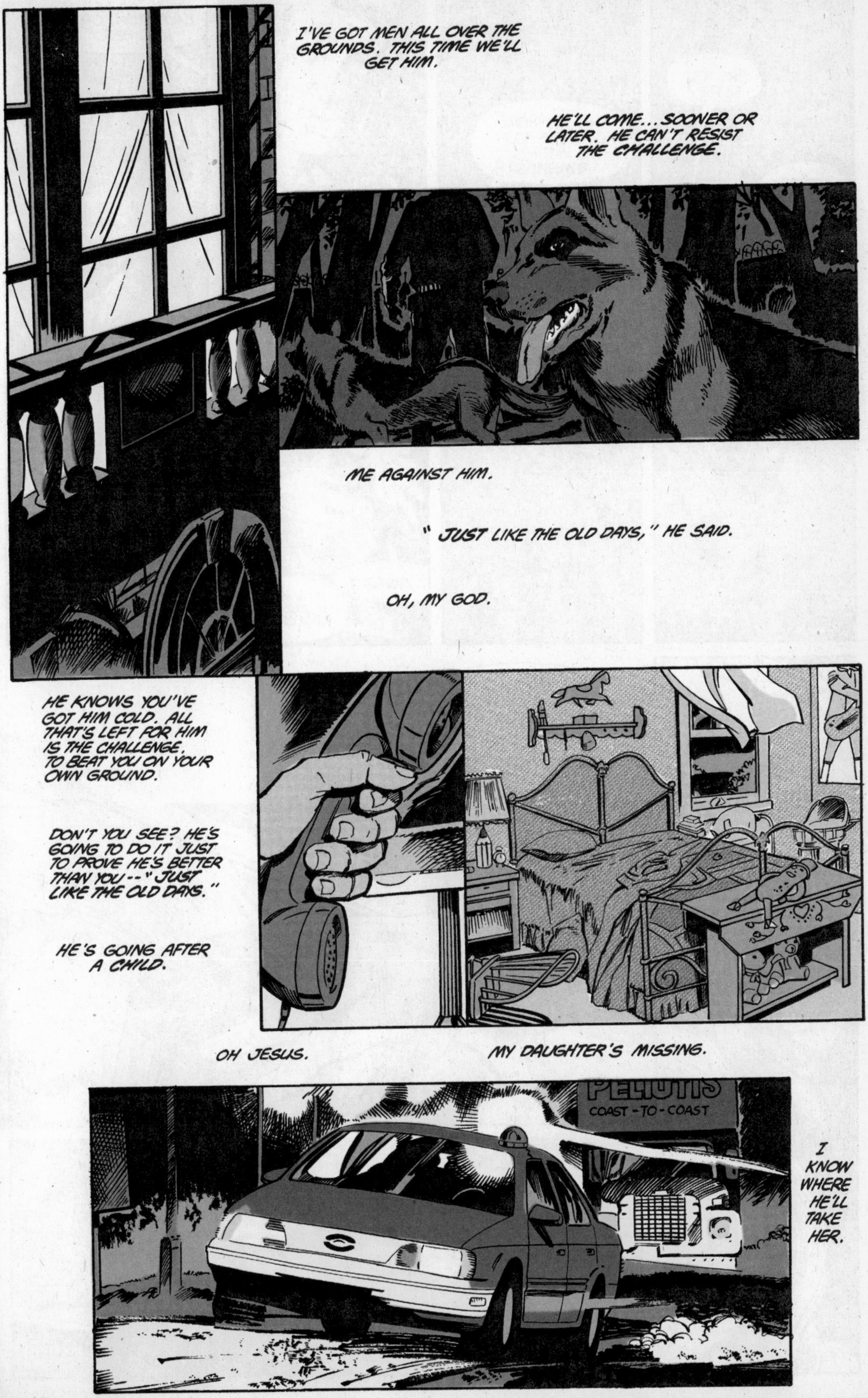
I'VE GOT MEN ALL OVER THE GROUNDS. THIS TIME WE'LL GET HIM.
HE'LL COME... SOONER OR LATER. HE CAN'T RESIST THE CHALLENGE.
ME AGAINST HIM.
" JUST LIKE THE OLD DAYS," HE SAID.
OH, MY GOD.
HE KNOWS YOU'VE GOT HIM COLD. ALL THAT'S LEFT FOR HIM IS THE CHALLENGE. TO BEAT YOU ON YOUR OWN GROUND.
DON'T YOU SEE? HE'S GOING TO DO IT JUST TO PROVE HE'S BETTER THAN YOU -- "JUST LIKE THE OLD DAYS."
HE'S GOING AFTER A CHILD.
OH JESUS.
MY DAUGHTER'S MISSING.
COAST-TO-COAST
I KNOW WHERE HE'LL TAKE HER.

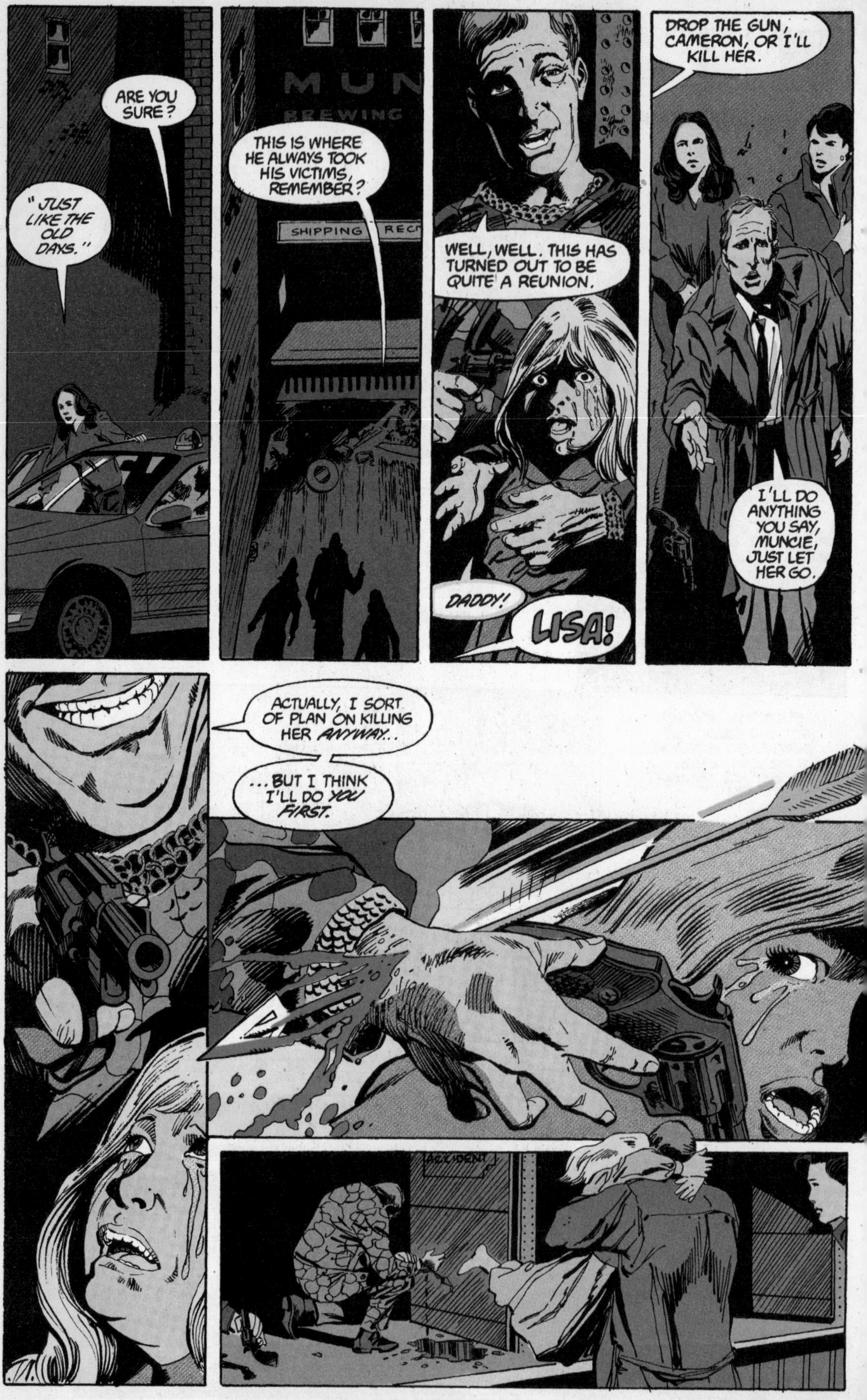
"JUST LIKE THE OLD DAYS."
ARE YOU SURE?
MUN
BREWING
SHIPPING
THIS IS WHERE HE ALWAYS TOOK HIS VICTIMS, REMEMBER?
WELL, WELL. THIS HAS TURNED OUT TO BE QUITE A REUNION.
DADDY!
LISA!
DROP THE GUN, CAMERON, OR I'LL KILL HER.
I'LL DO ANYTHING YOU SAY, MUNCIE, JUST LET HER GO.
ACTUALLY, I SORT OF PLAN ON KILLING HER ANYWAY...
...BUT I THINK I'LL DO YOU FIRST.
ACCIDENT

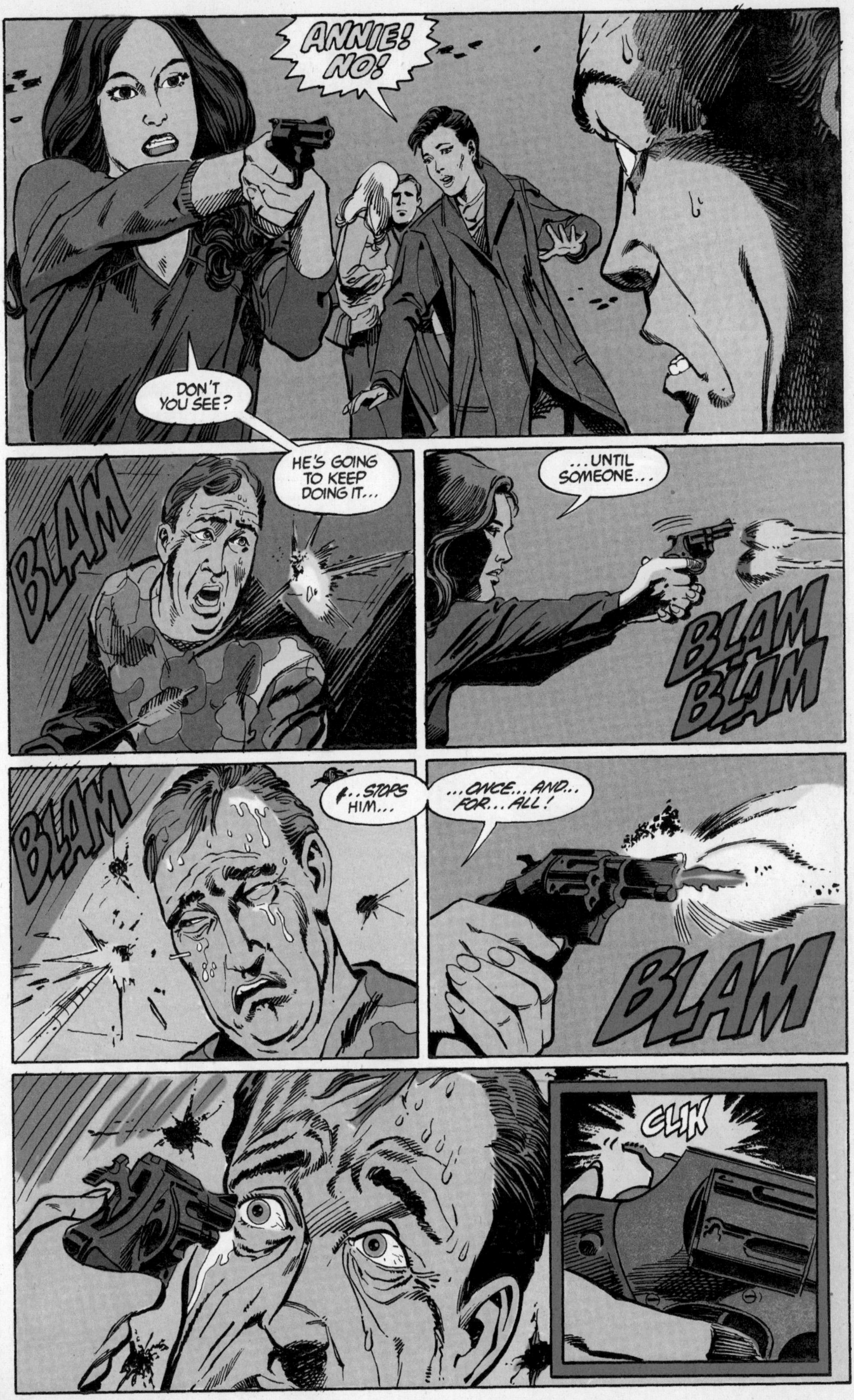
ANNIE! NO!
DON'T YOU SEE?
HE'S GOING TO KEEP DOING IT...
BLAM
...UNTIL SOMEONE...
BLAM BLAM
BLAM
...STOPS HIM...
...ONCE... AND... FOR... ALL!
BLAM
CLIK

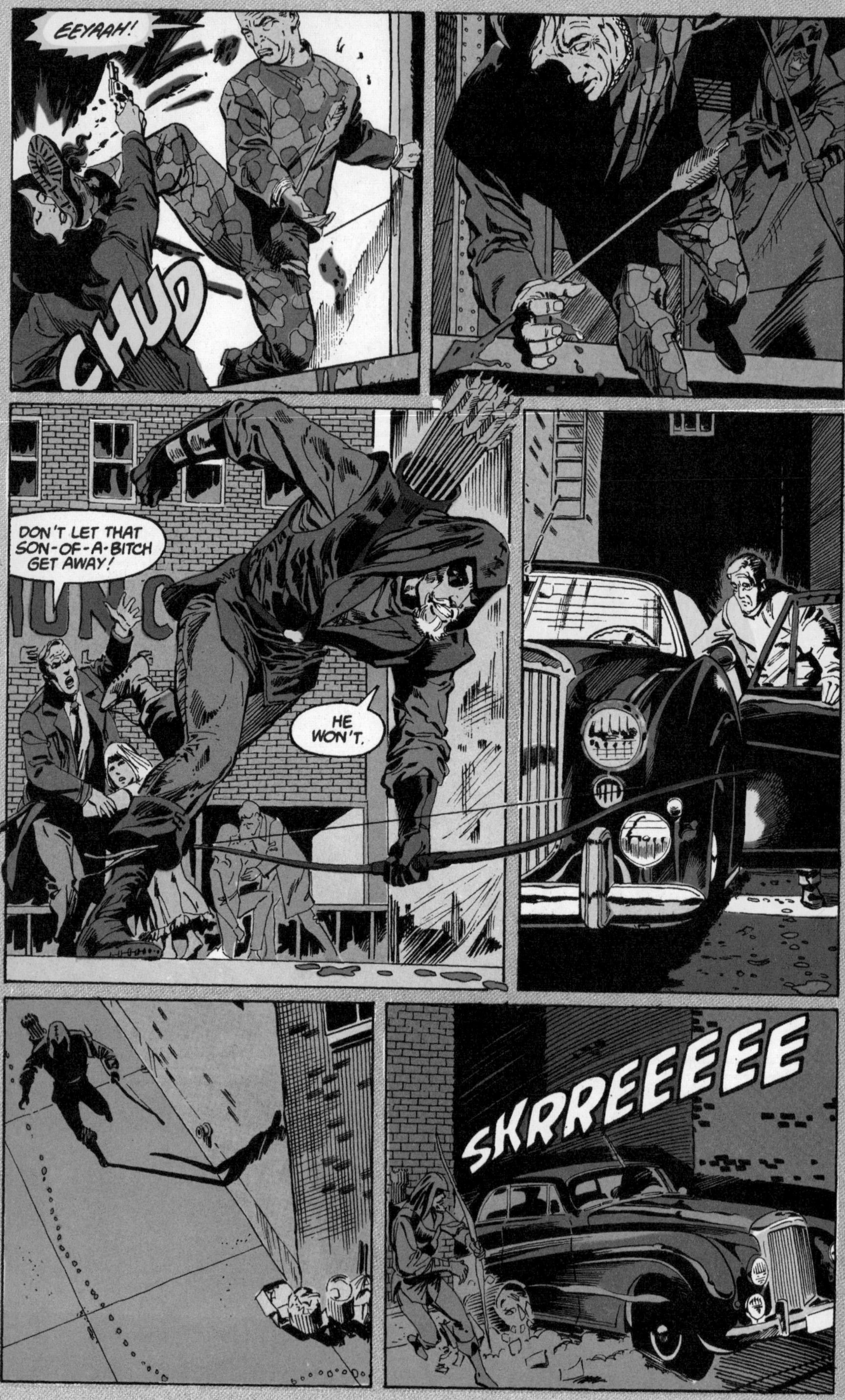
EEYAAH!
CHUD
DON'T LET THAT SON-OF-A-BITCH GET AWAY!
HE WON'T.
SKRREEEEEE

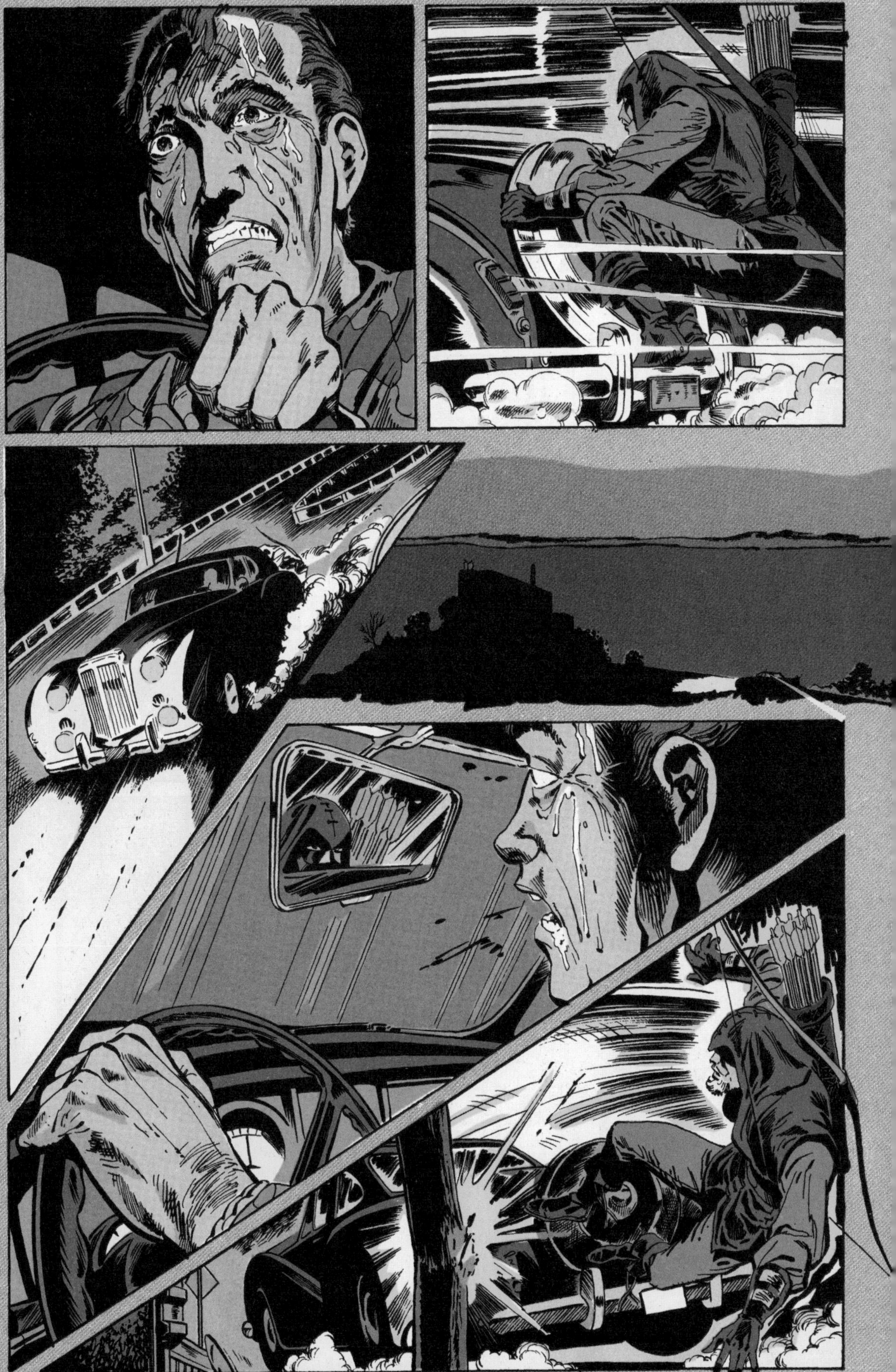

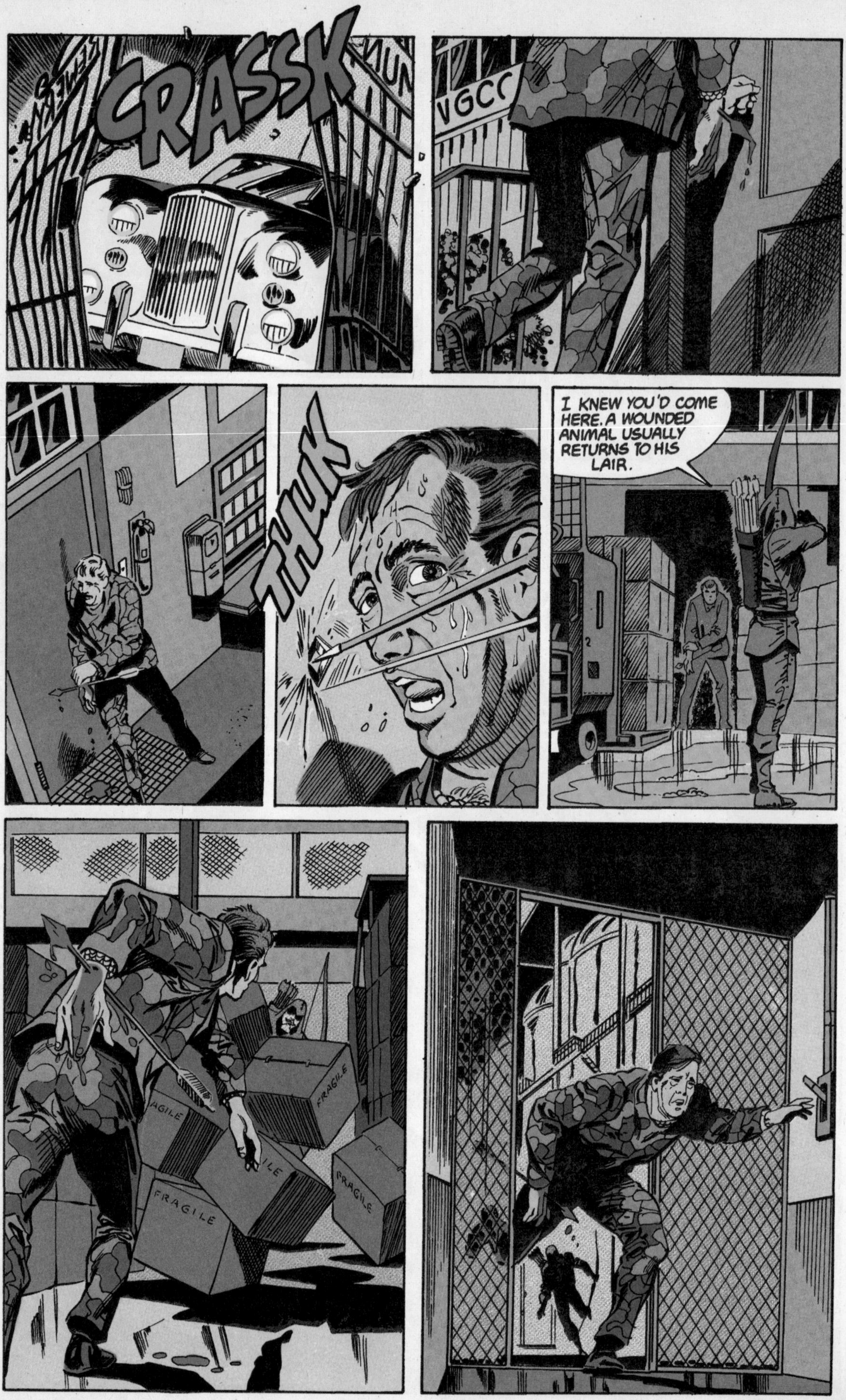
CRASSK
VGCC
THUK
I KNEW YOU'D COME HERE. A WOUNDED ANIMAL USUALLY RETURNS TO HIS LAIR.
FRAGILE
FRAGILE
FRAGILE
FRAGILE

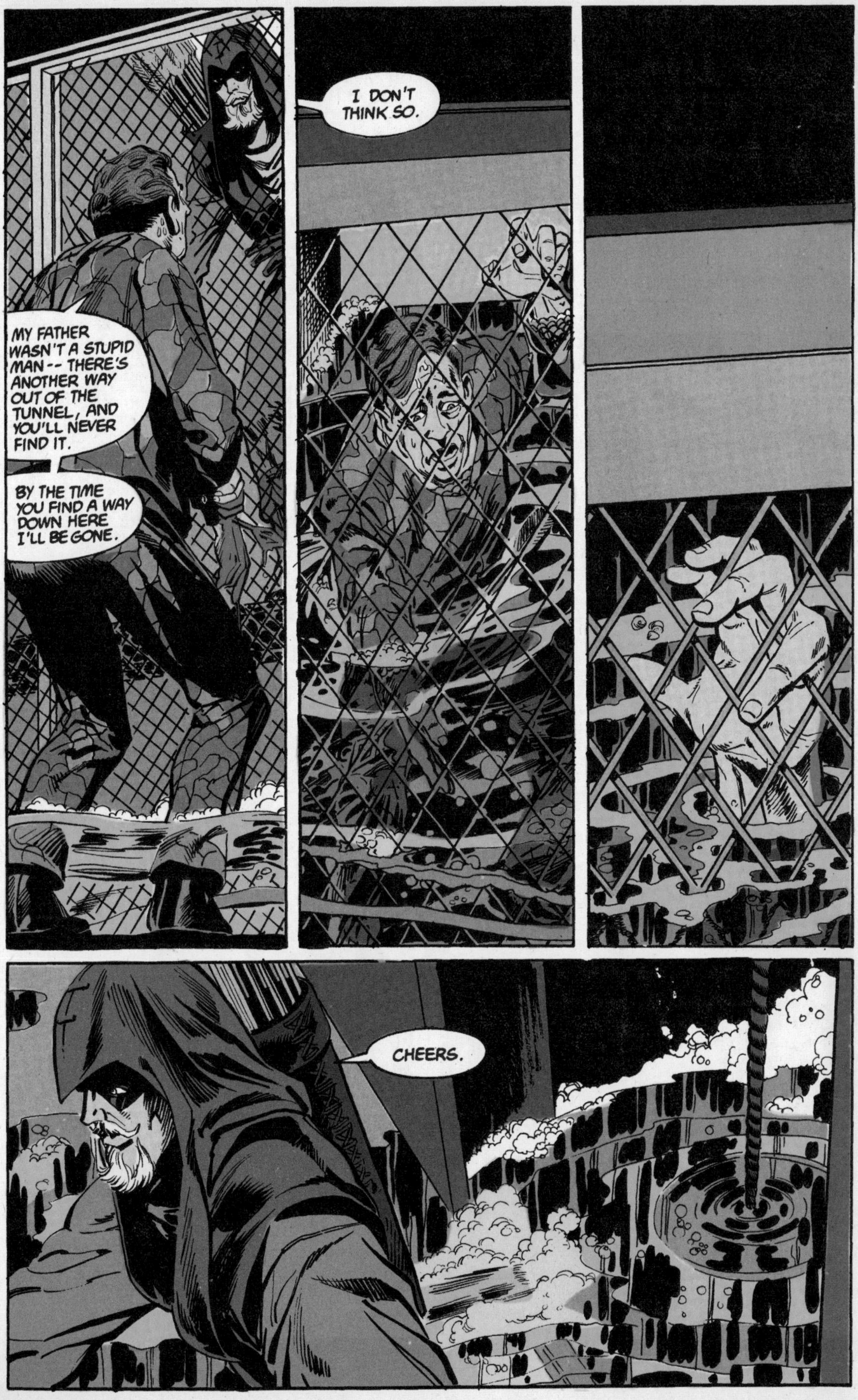
MY FATHER WASN'T A STUPID MAN-- THERE'S ANOTHER WAY OUT OF THE TUNNEL, AND YOU'LL NEVER FIND IT.
BY THE TIME YOU FIND A WAY DOWN HERE I'LL BE GONE.
I DON'T THINK SO.
CHEERS.

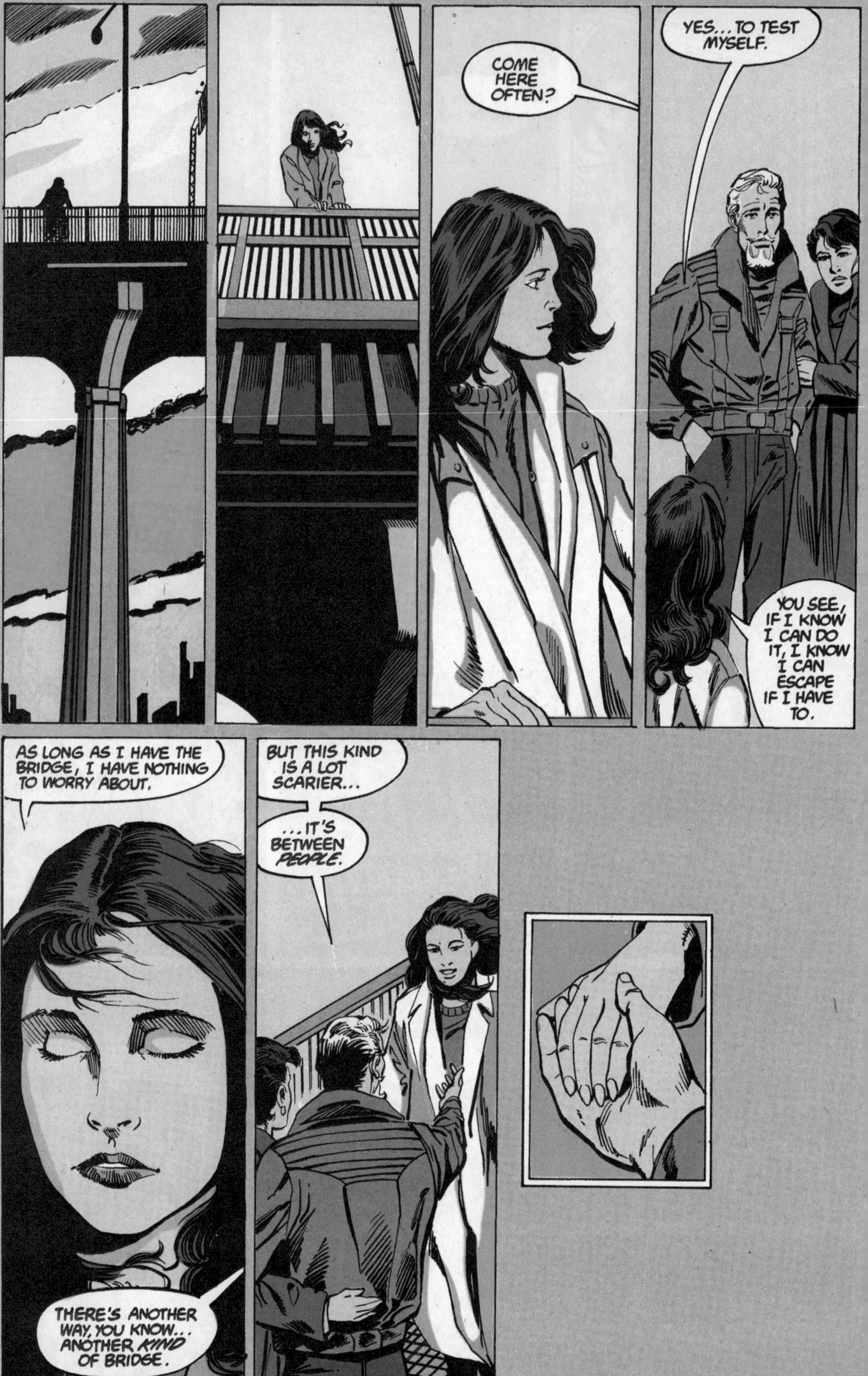
COME HERE OFTEN?
YES... TO TEST MYSELF.
YOU SEE, IF I KNOW I CAN DO IT, I KNOW I CAN ESCAPE IF I HAVE TO.
AS LONG AS I HAVE THE BRIDGE, I HAVE NOTHING TO WORRY ABOUT.
THERE'S ANOTHER WAY, YOU KNOW... ANOTHER KIND OF BRIDGE.
BUT THIS KIND IS A LOT SCARIER...
...IT'S BETWEEN PEOPLE.

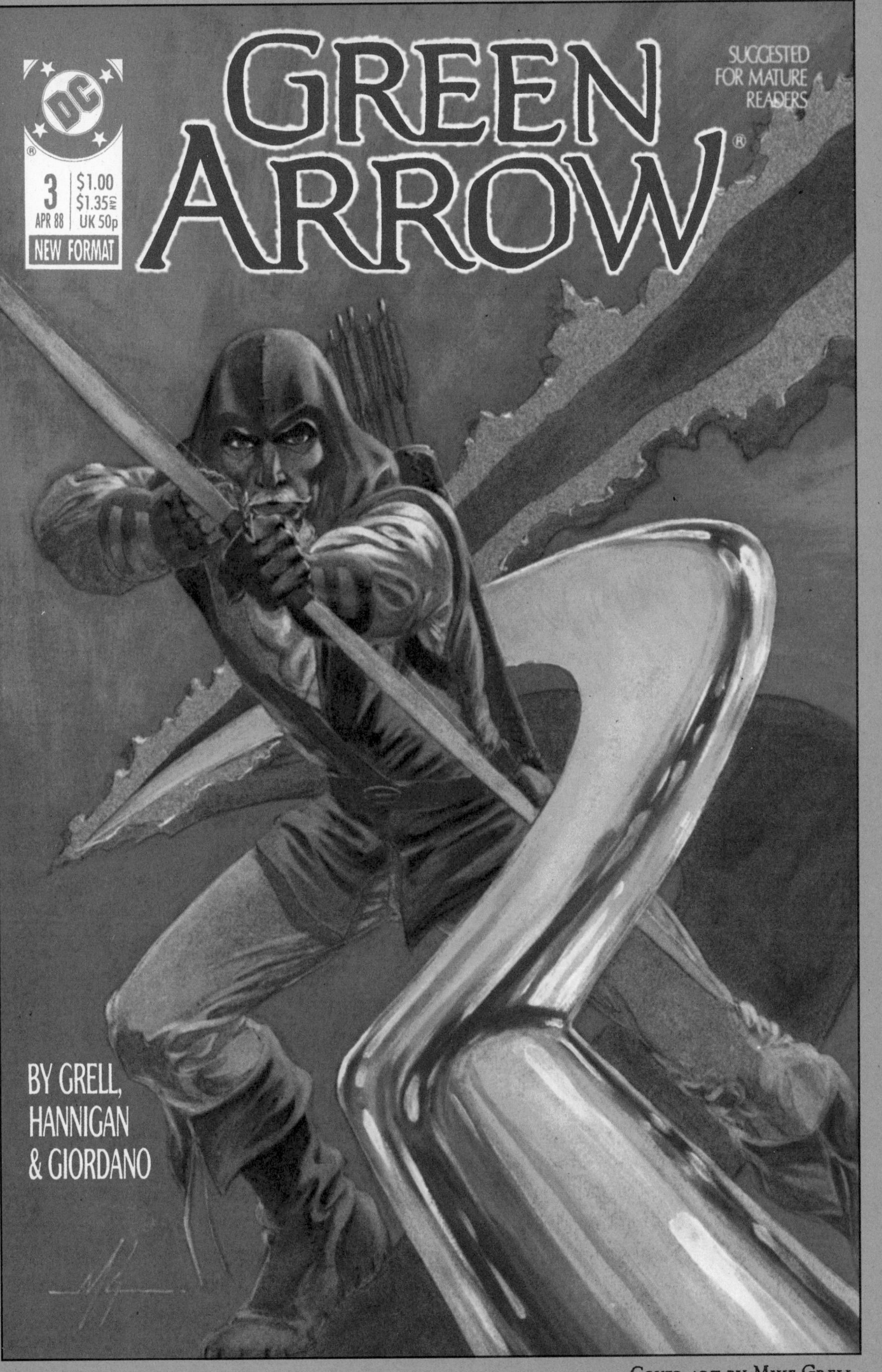

DC
3
APR 88
$1.00
$1.35 CAN
UK 50p
NEW FORMAT
GREEN ARROW
SUGGESTED FOR MATURE READERS
BY GRELL, HANNIGAN & GIORDANO

Cover art by Mike Grell

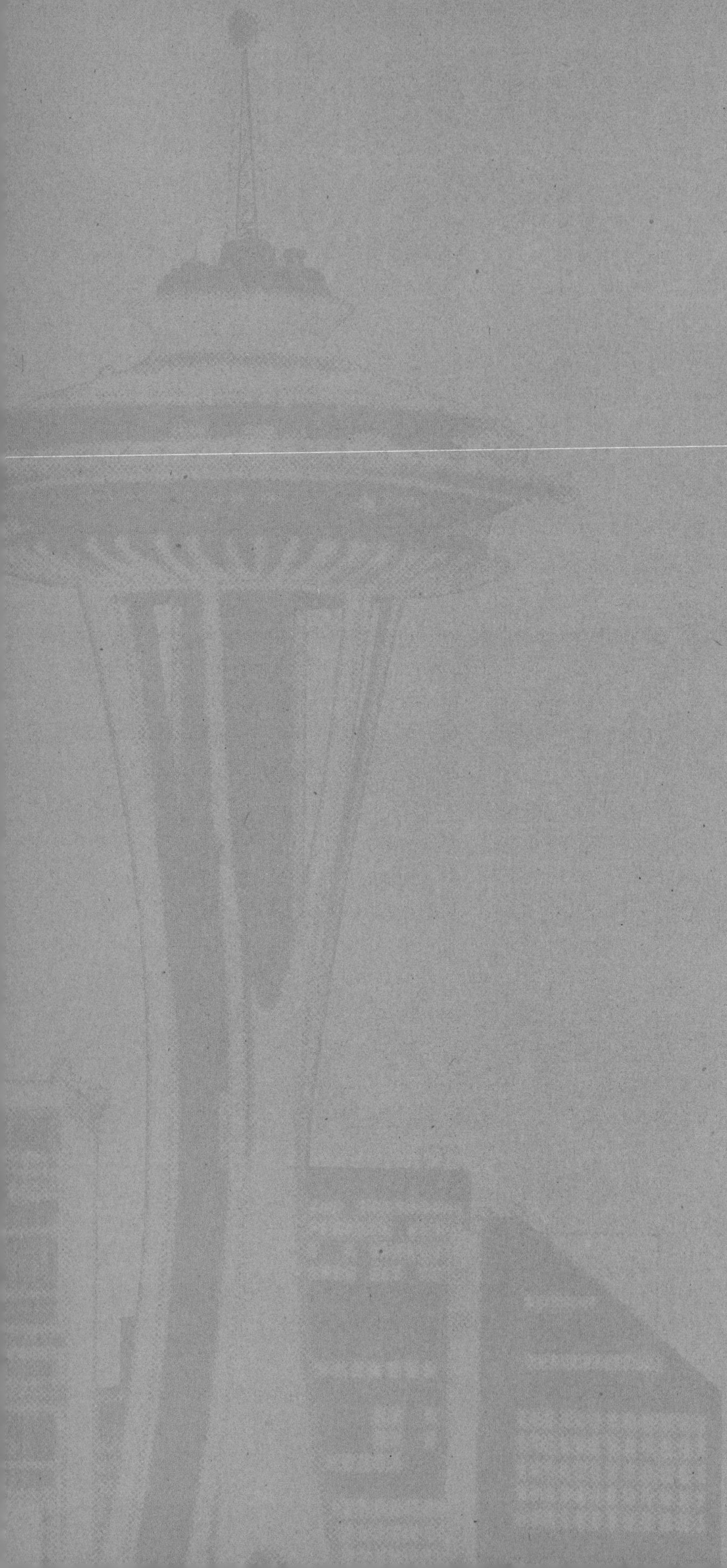

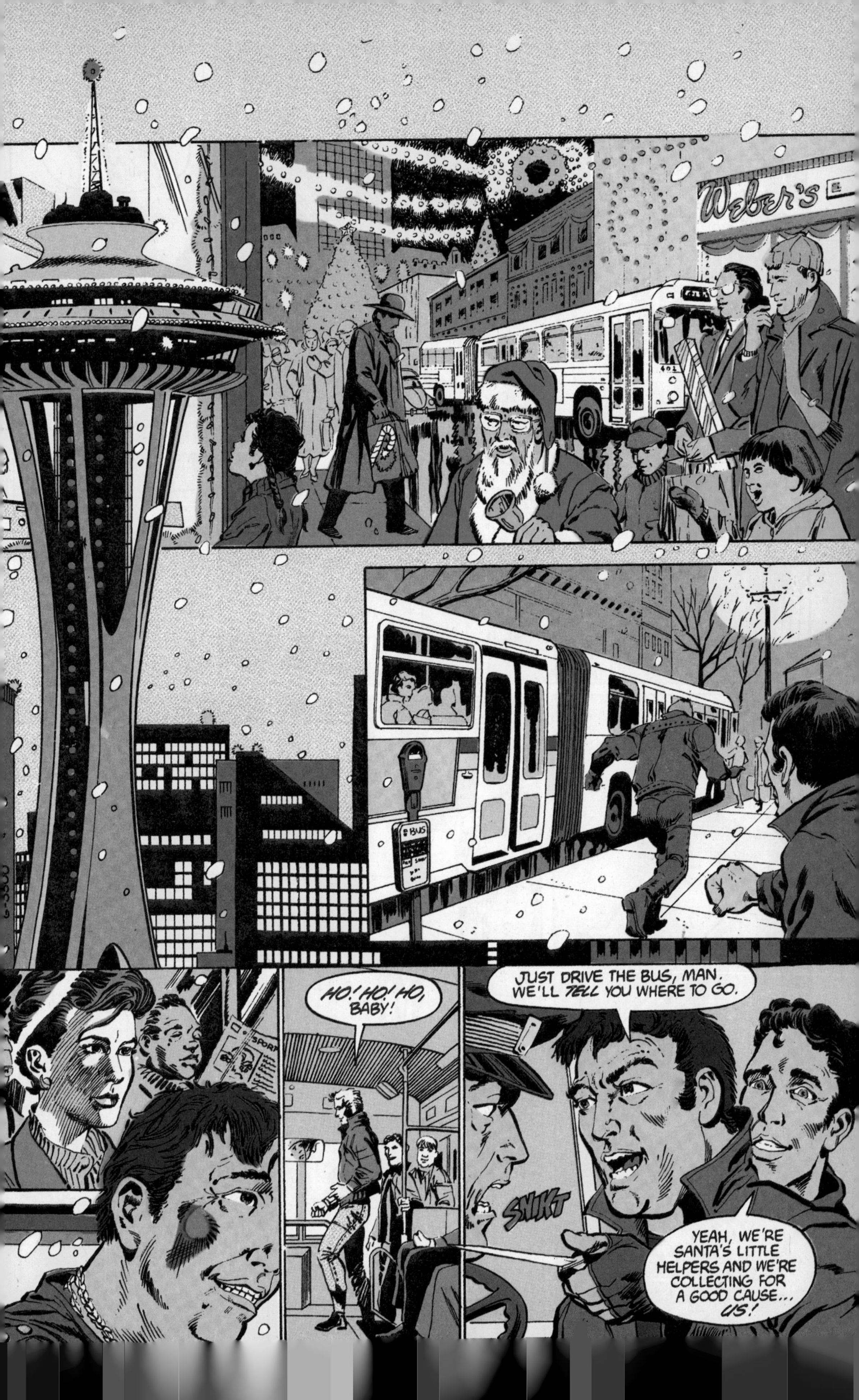
Weber's
BUS
HO! HO! HO, BABY!
JUST DRIVE THE BUS, MAN. WE'LL TELL YOU WHERE TO GO.
SNIKT
YEAH, WE'RE SANTA'S LITTLE HELPERS AND WE'RE COLLECTING FOR A GOOD CAUSE... US!

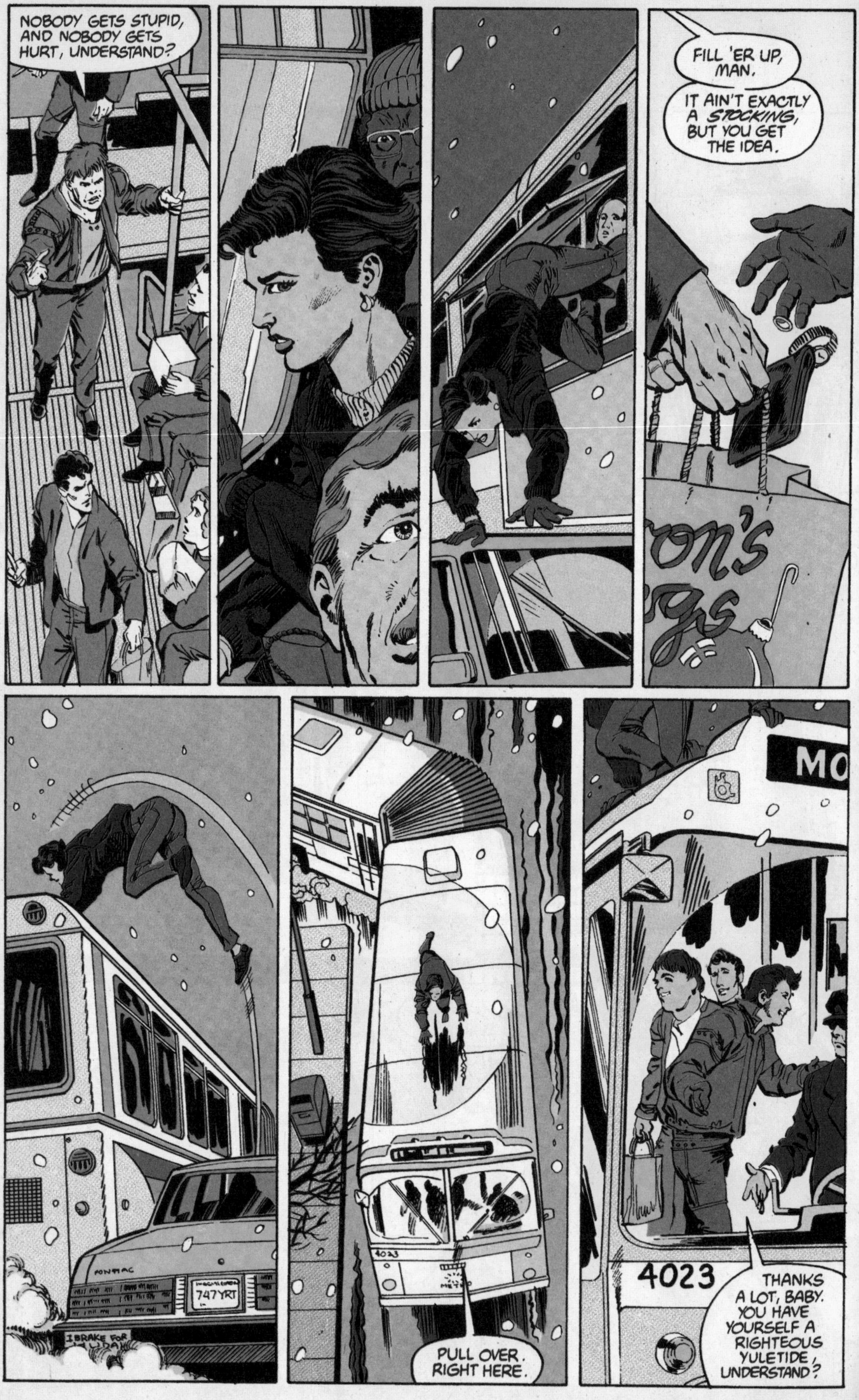
NOBODY GETS STUPID, AND NOBODY GETS HURT, UNDERSTAND?
FILL 'ER UP, MAN.
IT AIN'T EXACTLY A STOCKING, BUT YOU GET THE IDEA.
747 YRT
I BRAKE FOR
PULL OVER. RIGHT HERE.
4023
THANKS A LOT, BABY. YOU HAVE YOURSELF A RIGHTEOUS YULETIDE, UNDERSTAND?

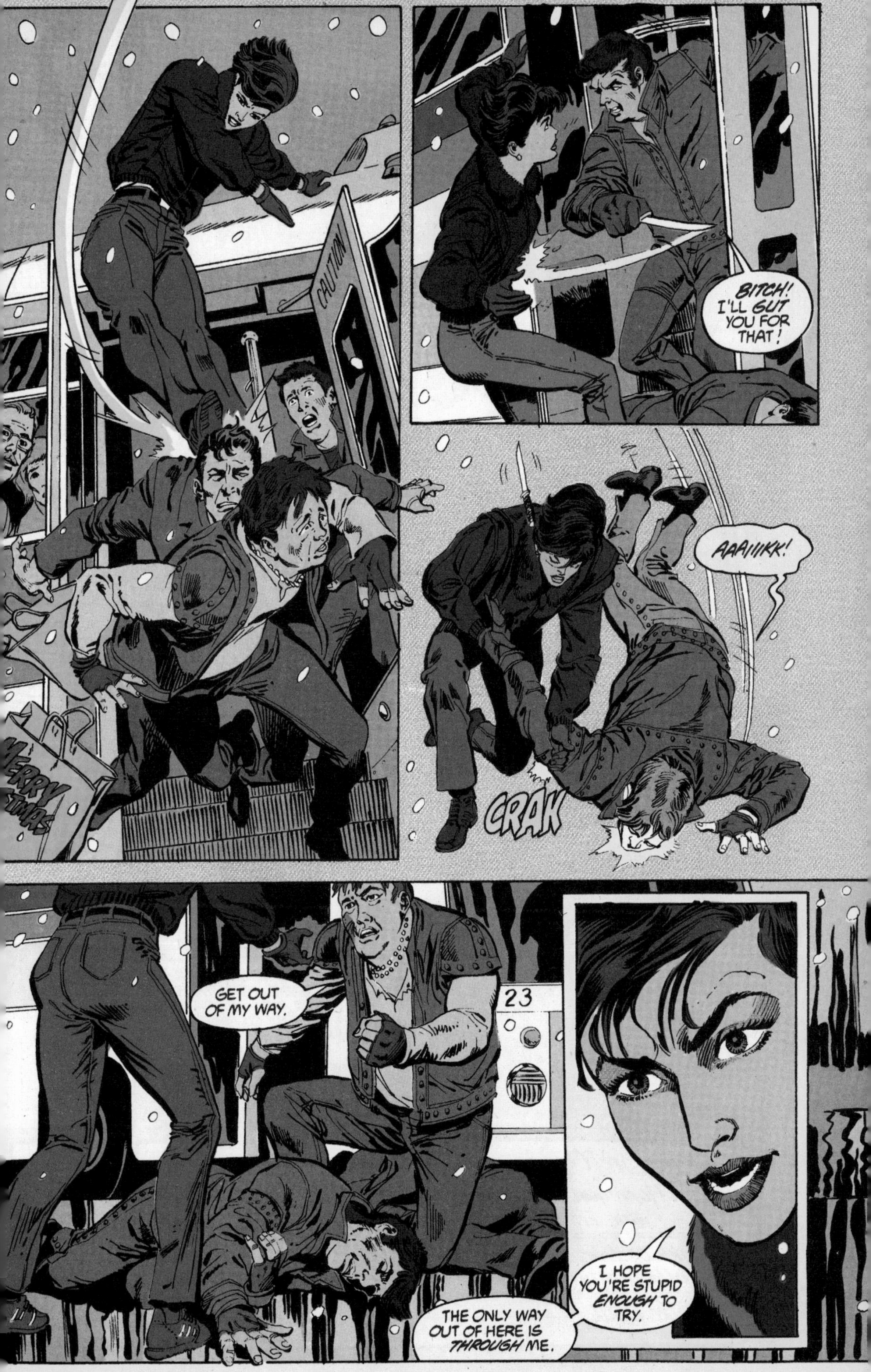
CAUTION
BITCH! I'LL GUT YOU FOR THAT!
MERRY XMAS
AAAIIIKK!
CRAK
GET OUT OF MY WAY.
23
THE ONLY WAY OUT OF HERE IS THROUGH ME.
I HOPE YOU'RE STUPID ENOUGH TO TRY.

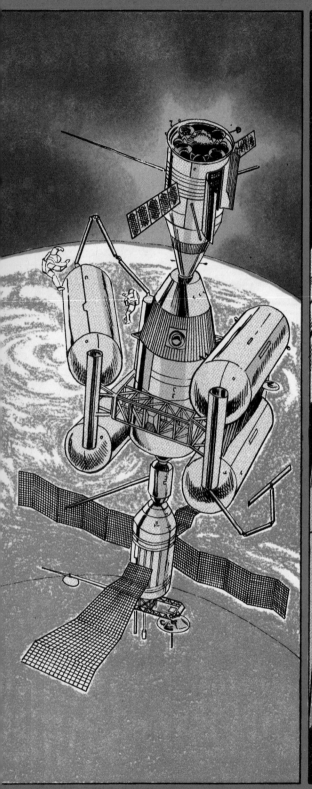

THEY SAY THAT IN SPACE THERE IS NO POLITICS... ONLY THE BROTHERHOOD OF MAN.

THE SUMMIT OF MAN'S KNOWLEDGE LIES AMONG THE STARS, THERE FOR ALL MEN TO REACH OUT AND TOUCH, LED BY THE FEW COURAGEOUS ENOUGH TO CHALLENGE THE VAST SEA OF NIGHT.

Mike Grell —————————— writer

Ed Hannigan & Dick Giordano — artists
with Frank McLaughlin

John Costanza —————————— letterer
Julia Lacquement —————————— colorist

Mike Gold —————————— editor

THE

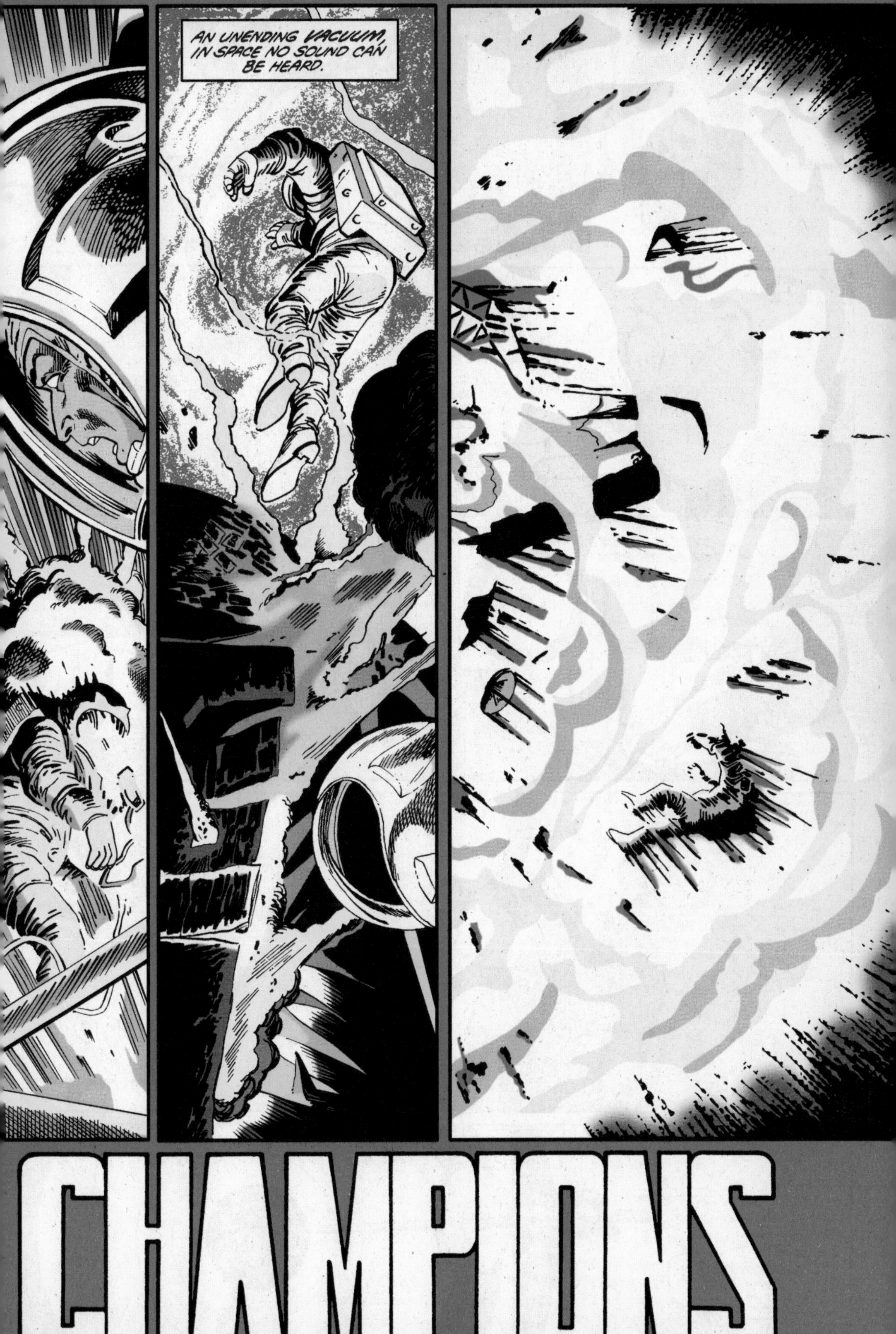
AN UNENDING VACUUM, IN SPACE NO SOUND CAN BE HEARD.

CHAMPIONS

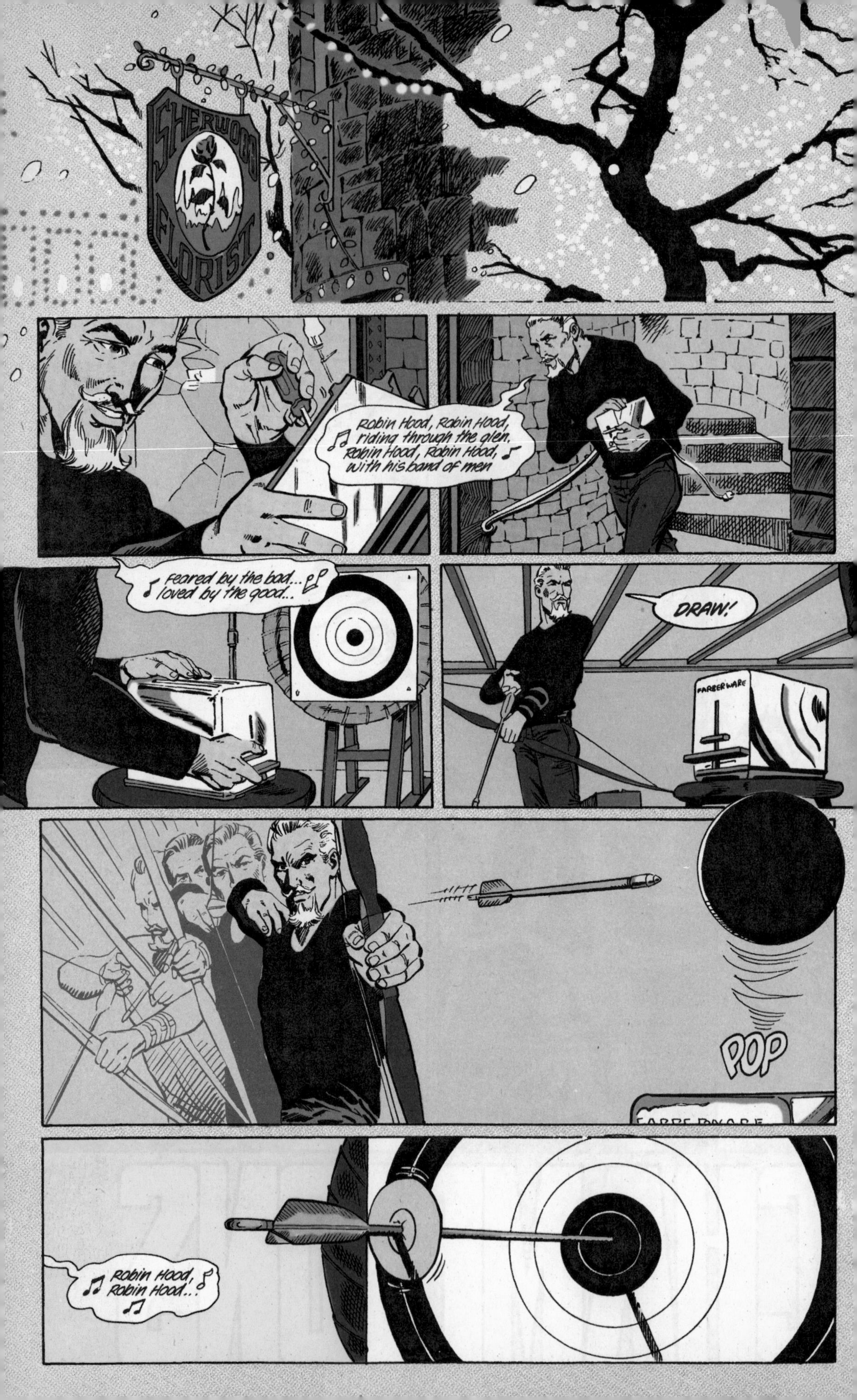
SHERWOOD FLORIST
Robin Hood, Robin Hood, riding through the glen. Robin Hood, Robin Hood, with his band of men
Feared by the bad... loved by the good...
DRAW!
FARBERWARE
POP
Robin Hood, Robin Hood...

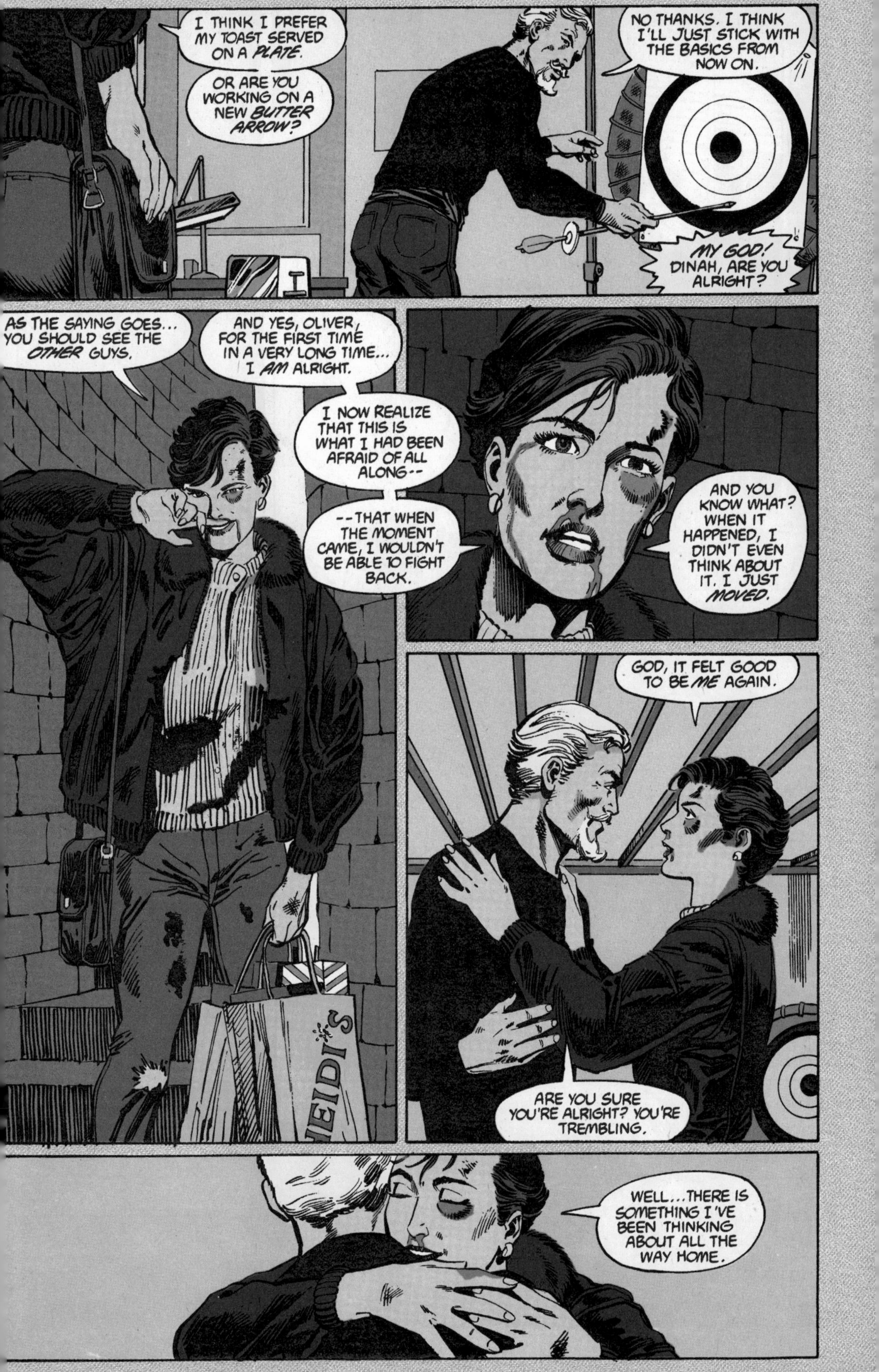

I THINK I PREFER MY TOAST SERVED ON A PLATE.
OR ARE YOU WORKING ON A NEW BUTTER ARROW?
NO THANKS. I THINK I'LL JUST STICK WITH THE BASICS FROM NOW ON.
MY GOD! DINAH, ARE YOU ALRIGHT?
AS THE SAYING GOES... YOU SHOULD SEE THE OTHER GUYS.
AND YES, OLIVER, FOR THE FIRST TIME IN A VERY LONG TIME... I AM ALRIGHT.
I NOW REALIZE THAT THIS IS WHAT I HAD BEEN AFRAID OF ALL ALONG--
--THAT WHEN THE MOMENT CAME, I WOULDN'T BE ABLE TO FIGHT BACK.
AND YOU KNOW WHAT? WHEN IT HAPPENED, I DIDN'T EVEN THINK ABOUT IT. I JUST MOVED.
HEIDI'S
GOD, IT FELT GOOD TO BE ME AGAIN.
ARE YOU SURE YOU'RE ALRIGHT? YOU'RE TREMBLING.
WELL... THERE IS SOMETHING I'VE BEEN THINKING ABOUT ALL THE WAY HOME.

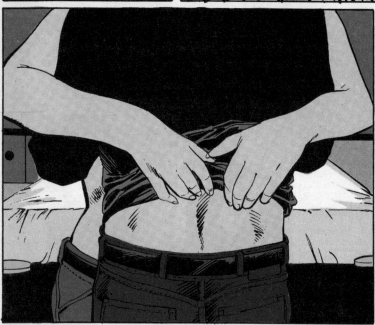

ARE YOU SURE?

I LOVE YOU, OLIVER.

I'M SURE.

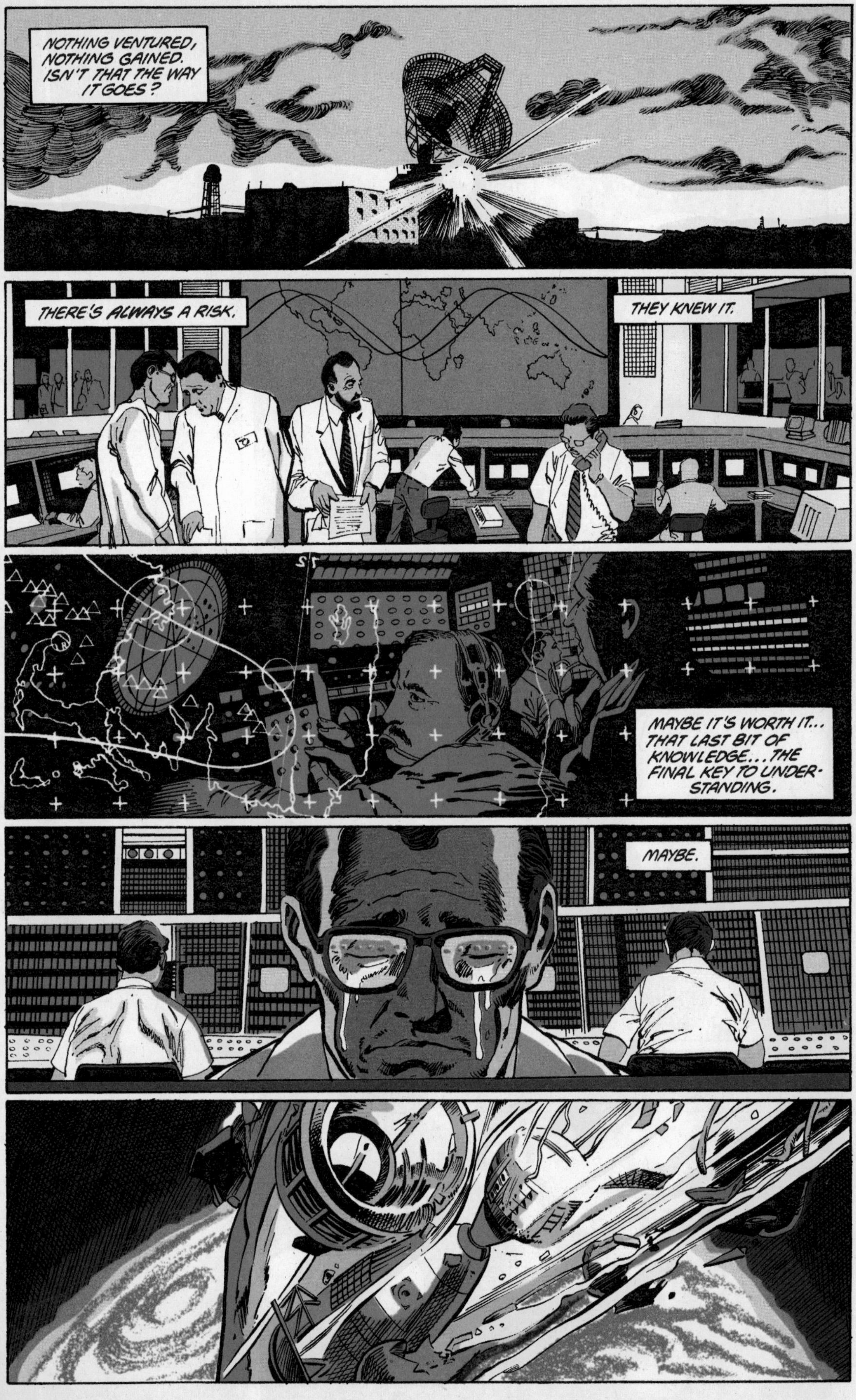
NOTHING VENTURED, NOTHING GAINED. ISN'T THAT THE WAY IT GOES?
THERE'S ALWAYS A RISK.
THEY KNEW IT.
MAYBE IT'S WORTH IT... THAT LAST BIT OF KNOWLEDGE... THE FINAL KEY TO UNDER-STANDING.
MAYBE.

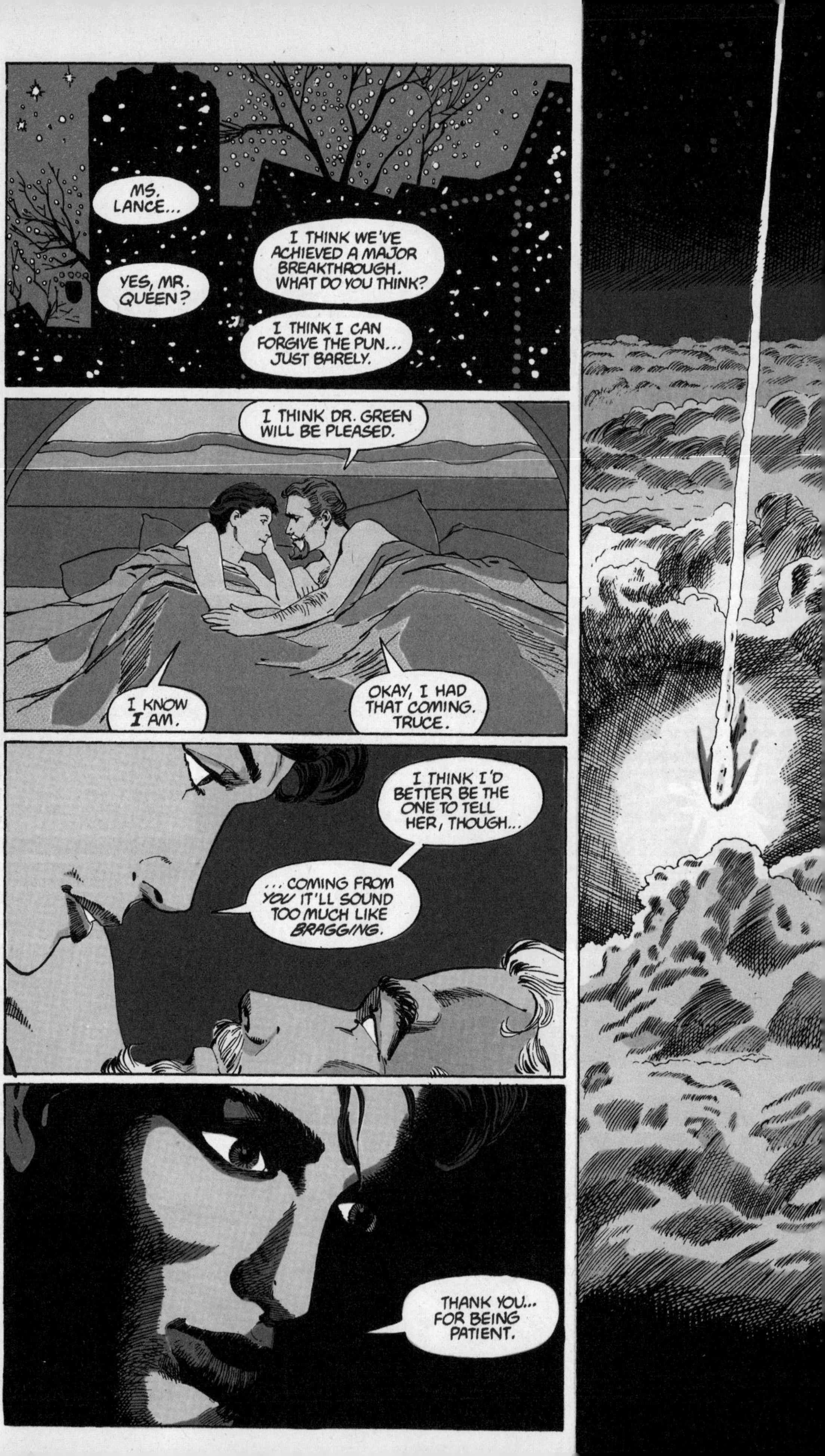
MS. LANCE...
YES, MR. QUEEN?
I THINK WE'VE ACHIEVED A MAJOR BREAKTHROUGH. WHAT DO YOU THINK?
I THINK I CAN FORGIVE THE PUN... JUST BARELY.
I THINK DR. GREEN WILL BE PLEASED.
I KNOW I AM.
OKAY, I HAD THAT COMING. TRUCE.
I THINK I'D BETTER BE THE ONE TO TELL HER, THOUGH...
...COMING FROM YOU IT'LL SOUND TOO MUCH LIKE BRAGGING.
THANK YOU... FOR BEING PATIENT.

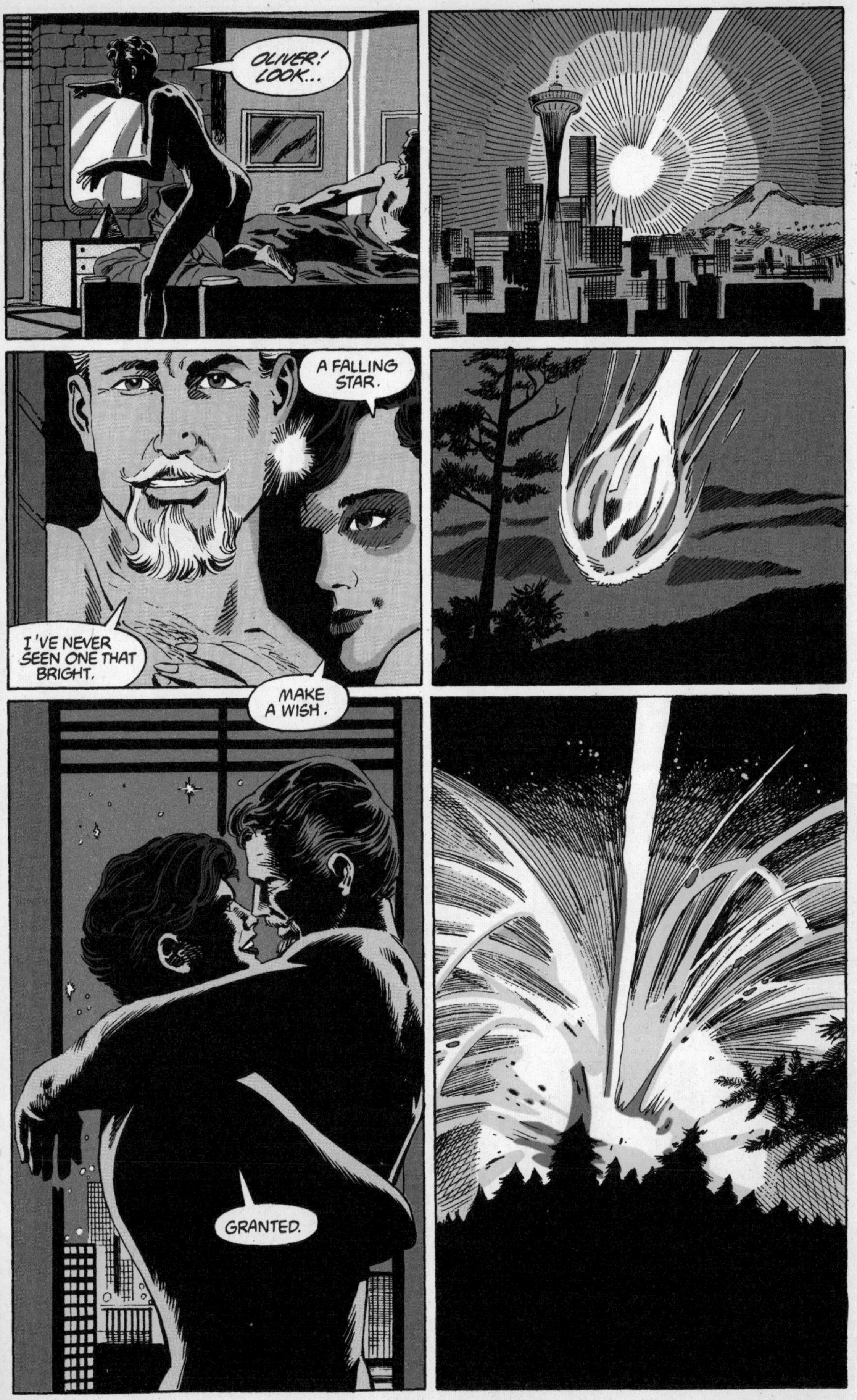
OLIVER! LOOK...
A FALLING STAR.
I'VE NEVER SEEN ONE THAT BRIGHT.
MAKE A WISH.
GRANTED.

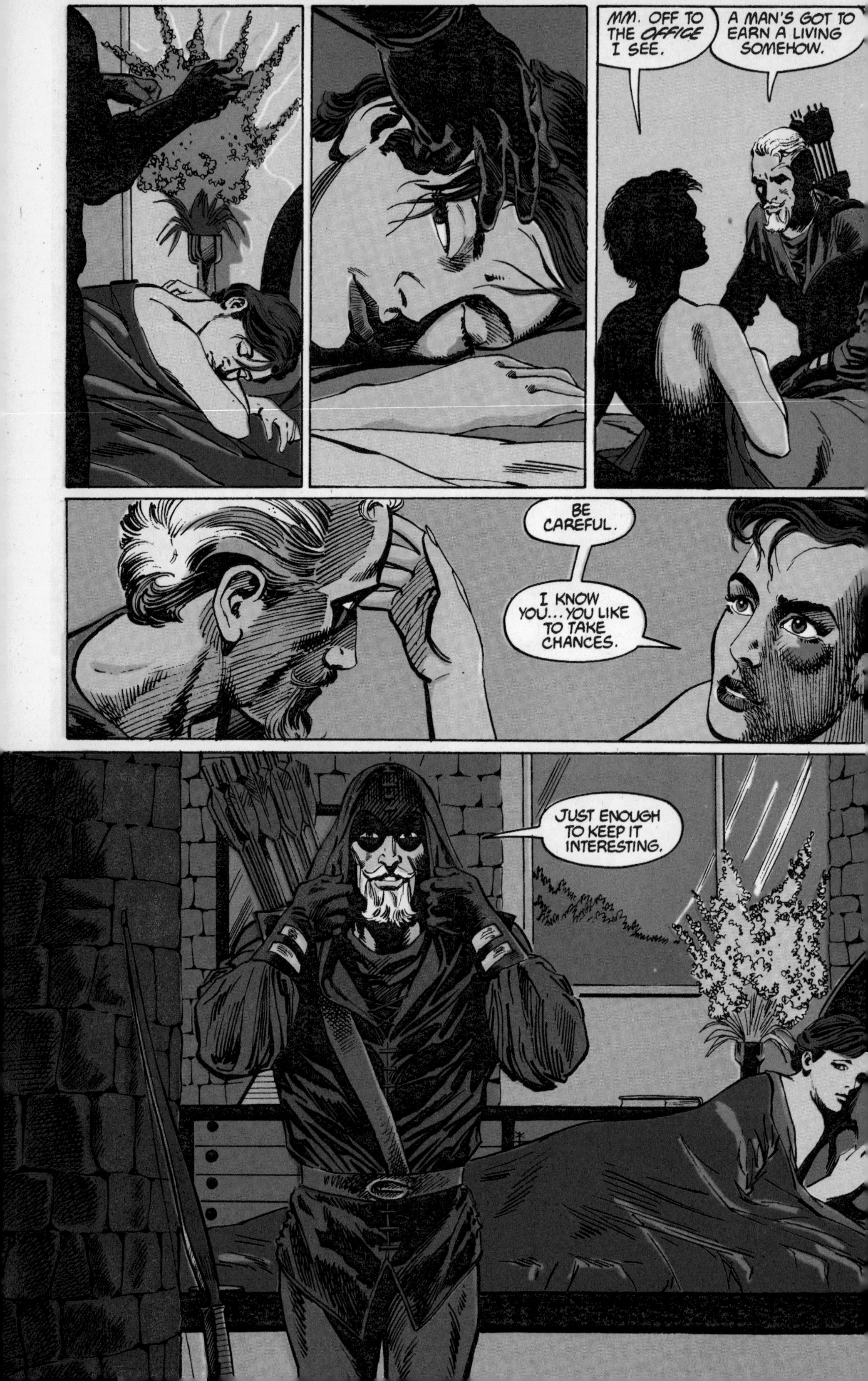
MM. OFF TO THE OFFICE I SEE.
A MAN'S GOT TO EARN A LIVING SOMEHOW.
BE CAREFUL.
I KNOW YOU... YOU LIKE TO TAKE CHANCES.
JUST ENOUGH TO KEEP IT INTERESTING.

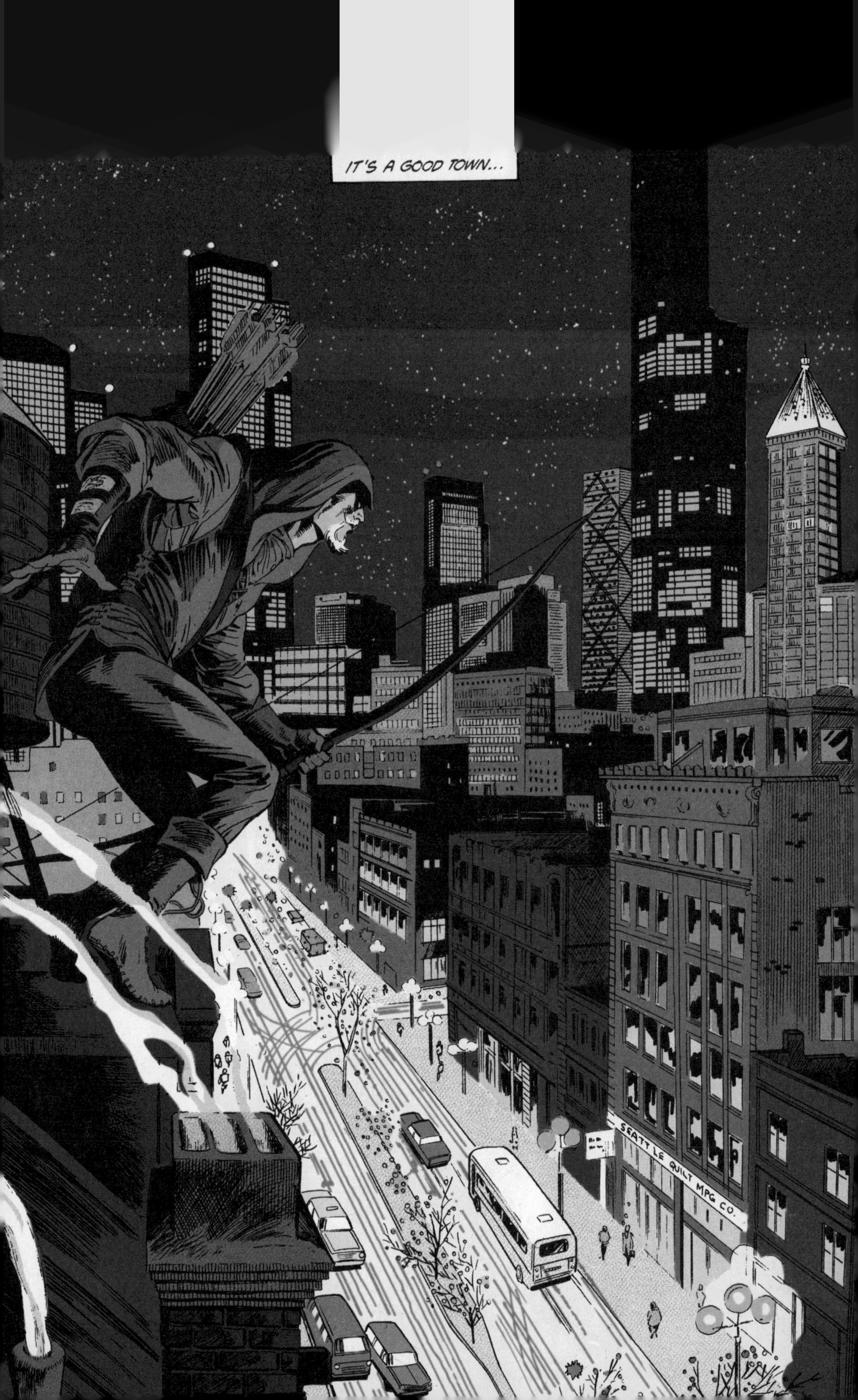
IT'S A GOOD TOWN...
SEATTLE QUILT MFG CO.

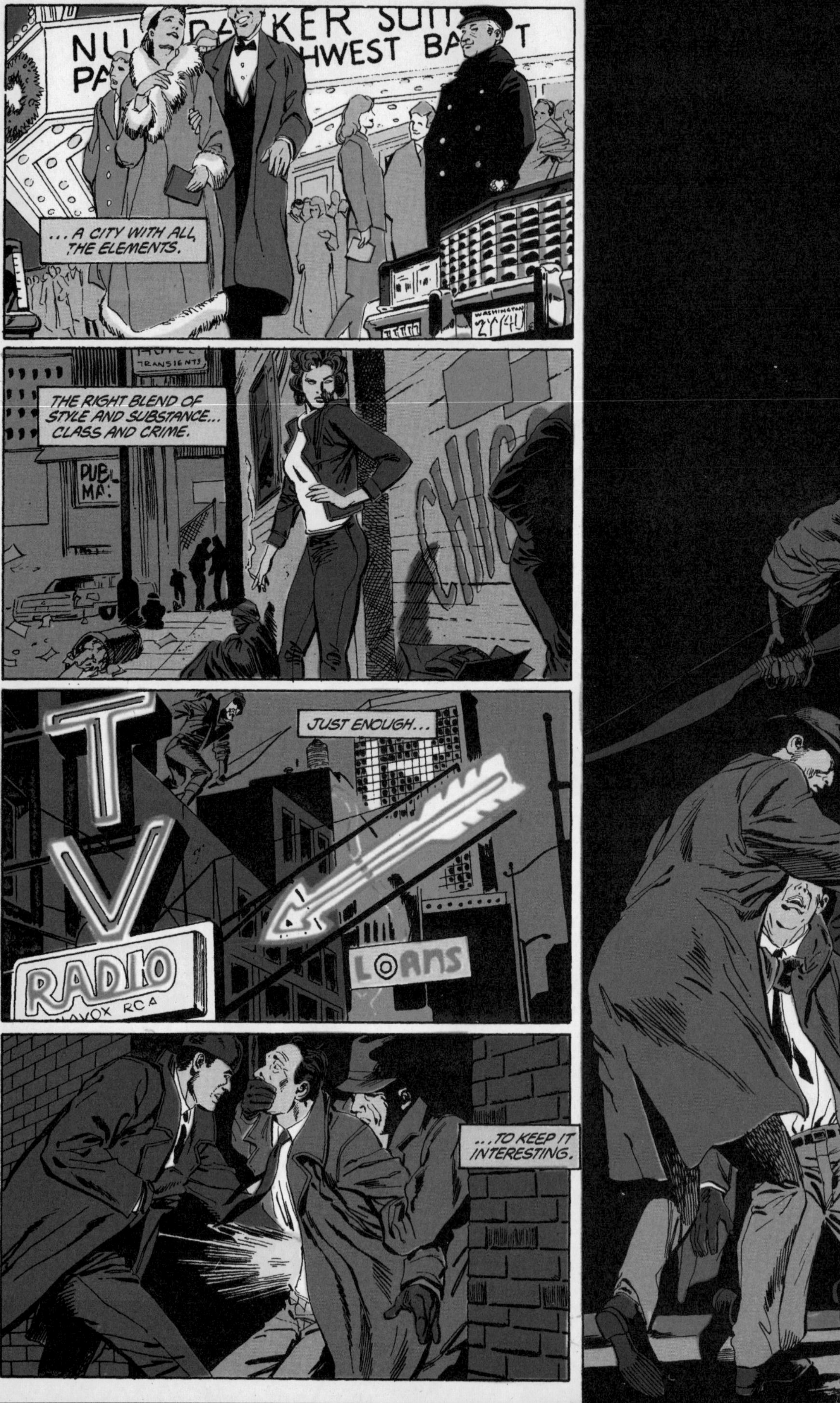
...A CITY WITH ALL THE ELEMENTS.
THE RIGHT BLEND OF STYLE AND SUBSTANCE... CLASS AND CRIME.
TRANSIENTS
JUST ENOUGH...
TV
RADIO
LOANS
...TO KEEP IT INTERESTING.

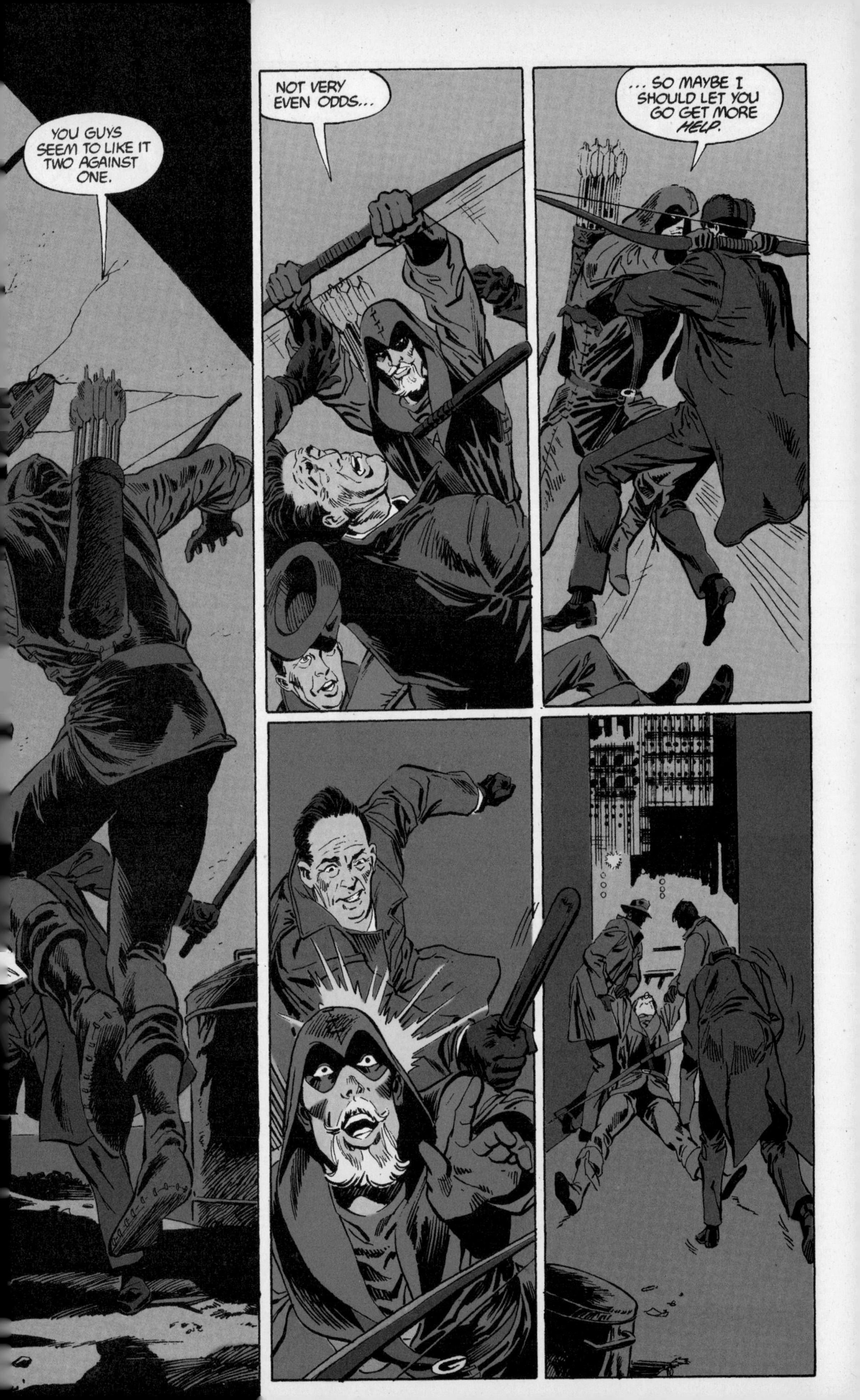
YOU GUYS SEEM TO LIKE IT TWO AGAINST ONE.
NOT VERY EVEN ODDS...
... SO MAYBE I SHOULD LET YOU GO GET MORE *HELP*.

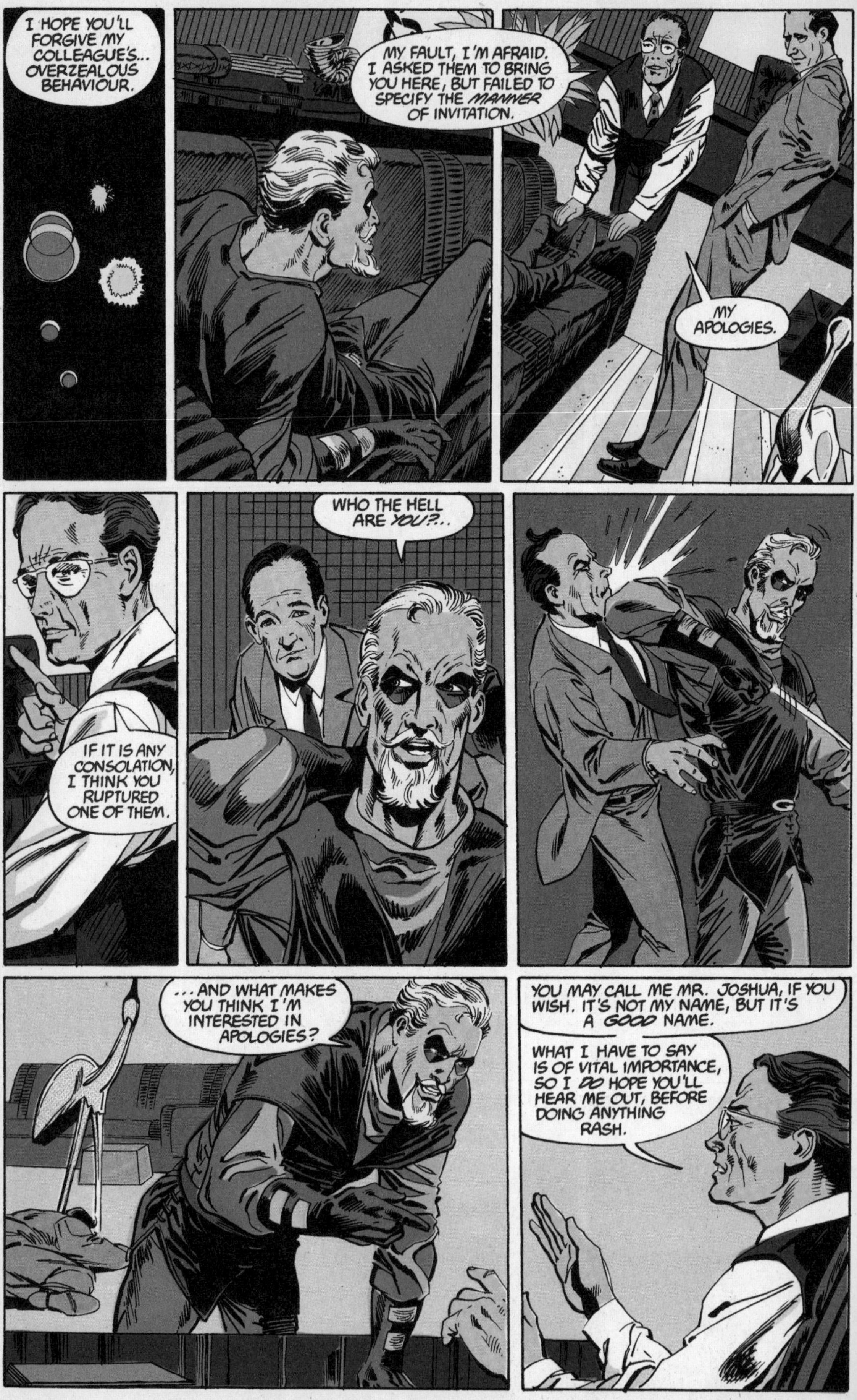
I HOPE YOU'LL FORGIVE MY COLLEAGUE'S... OVERZEALOUS BEHAVIOUR.
MY FAULT, I'M AFRAID. I ASKED THEM TO BRING YOU HERE, BUT FAILED TO SPECIFY THE MANNER OF INVITATION.
MY APOLOGIES.
IF IT IS ANY CONSOLATION, I THINK YOU RUPTURED ONE OF THEM.
WHO THE HELL ARE YOU?..
...AND WHAT MAKES YOU THINK I'M INTERESTED IN APOLOGIES?
YOU MAY CALL ME MR. JOSHUA, IF YOU WISH. IT'S NOT MY NAME, BUT IT'S A GOOD NAME.
WHAT I HAVE TO SAY IS OF VITAL IMPORTANCE, SO I DO HOPE YOU'LL HEAR ME OUT, BEFORE DOING ANYTHING RASH.

FOR THE PAST SEVEN WEEKS, WE HAVE BEEN CONDUCTING A JOINT MISSION WITH THE CHINESE ABOARD AN ORBITING SPACE LABORATORY.

IT'S UNLIKELY YOU WOULD HAVE. IT WAS OF A... *STRATEGIC* NATURE.

THE REENTRY VEHICLE'S MAIN FUEL TANK BLEW, SENDING THE SPACE CRAFT SPINNING FROM ORBIT.

IT BURNED AND EXPLODED ON REENTRY.

FRAGMENTS OF THE CRAFT WERE SCATTERED ALL OVER THE NORTHWEST PACIFIC.

I NEVER HEARD ANYTHING ABOUT A NEW SPACE FLIGHT.

AMONG THE TESTS BEING CONDUCTED ON BOARD WAS A BIO-CHEMICAL RESEARCH EXPERIMENT WHICH COULD ONLY BE CONDUCTED IN A ZERO GRAVITY ENVIRONMENT.

IT RESULTED IN THE CREATION OF A BIOLOGICAL WEAPON MORE TERRIBLE THAN YOU COULD IMAGINE.

A FEW HOURS AGO, MEMBERS OF THE CREW WERE WORKING OUTSIDE THE SPACE-CRAFT TO REPAIR A FAULTY DOCKING MODULE THERE WAS AN EXPLOSION.

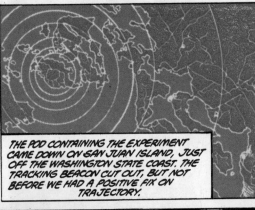

THE POD CONTAINING THE EXPERIMENT CAME DOWN ON SAN JUAN ISLAND, JUST OFF THE WASHINGTON STATE COAST. THE TRACKING BEACON CUT OUT, BUT NOT BEFORE WE HAD A POSITIVE FIX ON TRAJECTORY.

SO? GO PICK IT UP.

I'M AFRAID IT'S NOT AS SIMPLE AS THAT.

YOU SEE, THE CHINESE ARE CLAIMING OWNERSHIP OF THE EXPERIMENT, ALTHOUGH IT WAS, OF COURSE, A JOINT DISCOVERY.

THEY HAVE A LARGE "RECOVERY FORCE" MOVING INTO THE AREA... AS DO *WE*.

WE'RE SCHEDULED TO BEGIN JOINT OFF-SHORE SALVAGE OPERATIONS IN 48 HOURS.

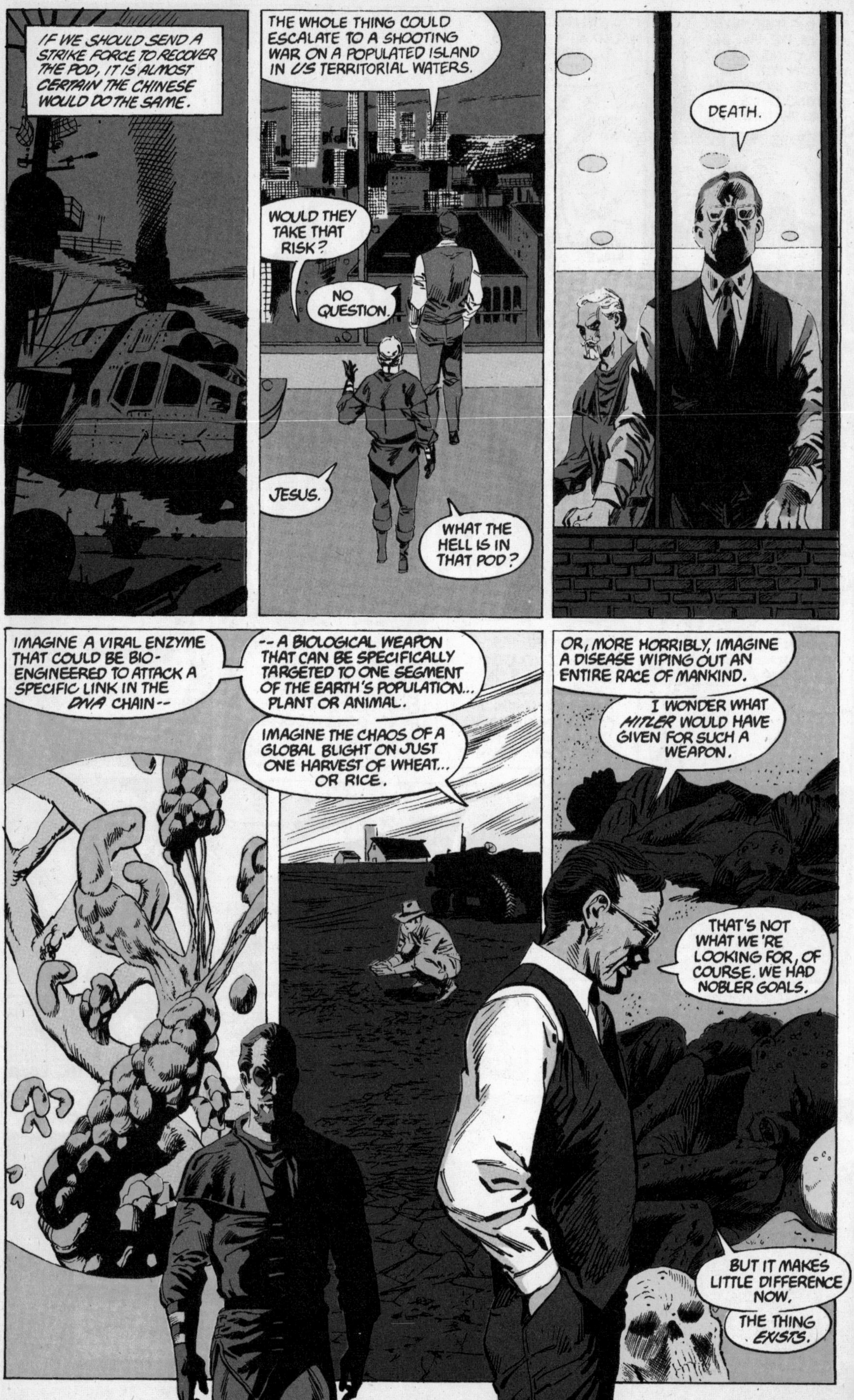
IF WE SHOULD SEND A STRIKE FORCE TO RECOVER THE POD, IT IS ALMOST CERTAIN THE CHINESE WOULD DO THE SAME.
THE WHOLE THING COULD ESCALATE TO A SHOOTING WAR ON A POPULATED ISLAND IN US TERRITORIAL WATERS.
WOULD THEY TAKE THAT RISK?
NO QUESTION.
JESUS.
WHAT THE HELL IS IN THAT POD?
DEATH.
IMAGINE A VIRAL ENZYME THAT COULD BE BIO-ENGINEERED TO ATTACK A SPECIFIC LINK IN THE DNA CHAIN--
-- A BIOLOGICAL WEAPON THAT CAN BE SPECIFICALLY TARGETED TO ONE SEGMENT OF THE EARTH'S POPULATION... PLANT OR ANIMAL.
IMAGINE THE CHAOS OF A GLOBAL BLIGHT ON JUST ONE HARVEST OF WHEAT... OR RICE.
OR, MORE HORRIBLY, IMAGINE A DISEASE WIPING OUT AN ENTIRE RACE OF MANKIND.
I WONDER WHAT HITLER WOULD HAVE GIVEN FOR SUCH A WEAPON.
THAT'S NOT WHAT WE'RE LOOKING FOR, OF COURSE. WE HAD NOBLER GOALS.
BUT IT MAKES LITTLE DIFFERENCE NOW.
THE THING EXISTS.

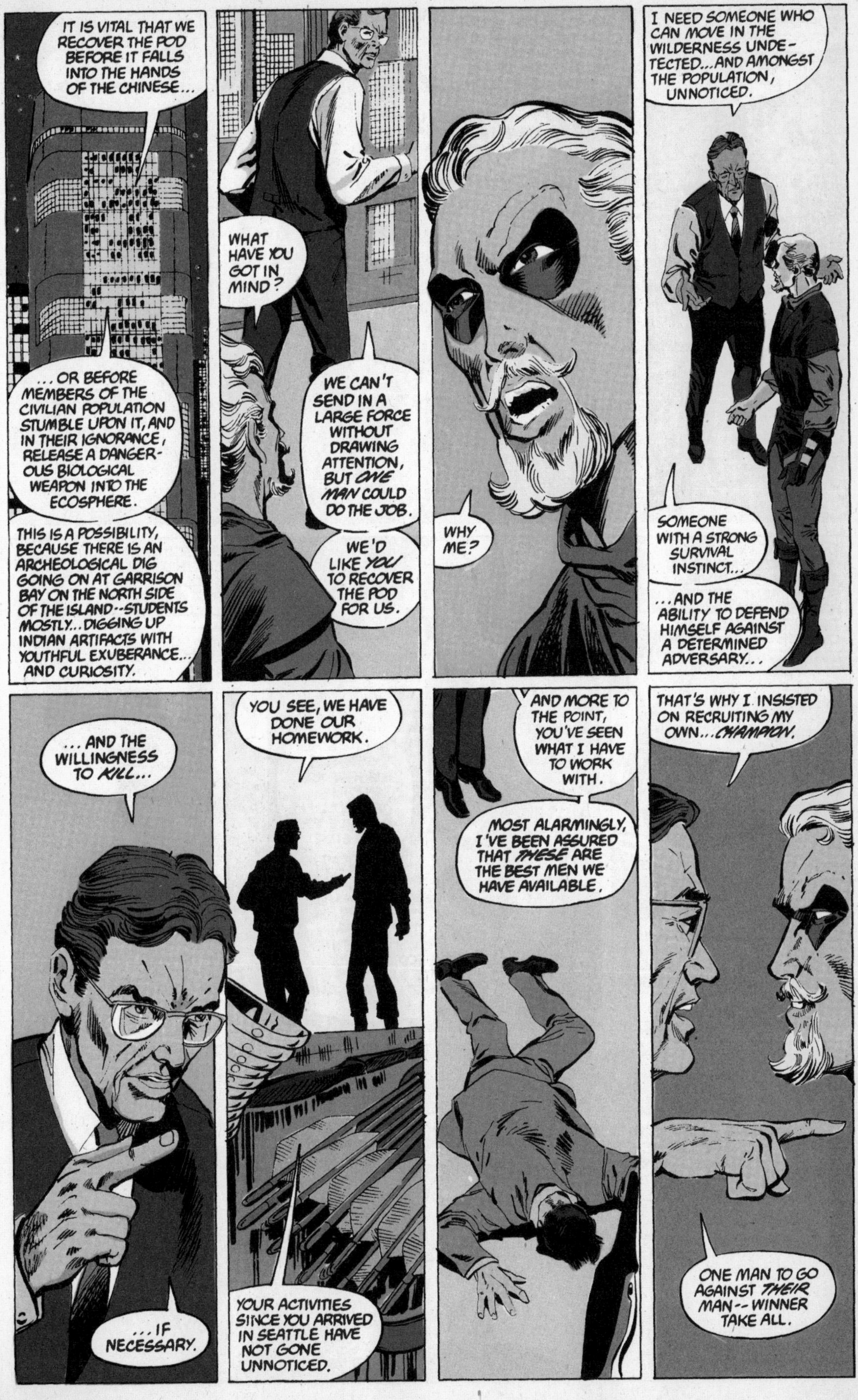
IT IS VITAL THAT WE RECOVER THE POD BEFORE IT FALLS INTO THE HANDS OF THE CHINESE...
...OR BEFORE MEMBERS OF THE CIVILIAN POPULATION STUMBLE UPON IT, AND IN THEIR IGNORANCE, RELEASE A DANGEROUS BIOLOGICAL WEAPON INTO THE ECOSPHERE.
THIS IS A POSSIBILITY, BECAUSE THERE IS AN ARCHEOLOGICAL DIG GOING ON AT GARRISON BAY ON THE NORTH SIDE OF THE ISLAND--STUDENTS MOSTLY...DIGGING UP INDIAN ARTIFACTS WITH YOUTHFUL EXUBERANCE... AND CURIOSITY.
WHAT HAVE YOU GOT IN MIND?
WE CAN'T SEND IN A LARGE FORCE WITHOUT DRAWING ATTENTION, BUT ONE MAN COULD DO THE JOB.
WE'D LIKE YOU TO RECOVER THE POD FOR US.
WHY ME?
I NEED SOMEONE WHO CAN MOVE IN THE WILDERNESS UNDETECTED...AND AMONGST THE POPULATION, UNNOTICED.
SOMEONE WITH A STRONG SURVIVAL INSTINCT...
...AND THE ABILITY TO DEFEND HIMSELF AGAINST A DETERMINED ADVERSARY...
...AND THE WILLINGNESS TO KILL...
...IF NECESSARY.
YOU SEE, WE HAVE DONE OUR HOMEWORK.
YOUR ACTIVITIES SINCE YOU ARRIVED IN SEATTLE HAVE NOT GONE UNNOTICED.
AND MORE TO THE POINT, YOU'VE SEEN WHAT I HAVE TO WORK WITH.
MOST ALARMINGLY, I'VE BEEN ASSURED THAT THESE ARE THE BEST MEN WE HAVE AVAILABLE.
THAT'S WHY I INSISTED ON RECRUITING MY OWN...CHAMPION.
ONE MAN TO GO AGAINST THEIR MAN--WINNER TAKE ALL.

SUPPOSE I TELL YOU TO GO TO HELL.

WHAT YOU'RE SAYING IS THAT THE CHINESE ALSO HAVE MONITORED THE TRAJECTORY OF THE HOMING BEACON...

...AND MOST LIKELY HAVE THEIR *OWN* AGENT MOVING INTO THE AREA.

IN ALL PROBABILITY... YES.

IN FACT--NO OFFENCE--YOU WERE OUR *SECOND* CHOICE.

THE MAN I WOULD HAVE PREFERRED DECLINED ON GROUNDS OF A PRIOR COMMITMENT. I BELIEVE HE HAS BEEN CONTRACTED FOR THIS OPERATION BY THE CHINESE.

TOO BAD, REALLY. HE'S THE BEST I'VE SEEN... TOUGH, SKILLFUL, COLDLY DISPASSIONATE. *TOTALLY* APOLITICAL.

FYERS E.

HERE'S HIS DOSSIER. I SUGGEST YOU STUDY IT CAREFULLY. IT MAY GIVE YOU AN EDGE.

THE MAN IS KNOWN CURRENTLY AS EDDIE FYERS, 5'8", 140 LBS. *DON'T* UNDERESTIMATE HIM.

YOU'RE GOING TO SETTLE THIS LIKE *GENTLEMEN?!?* I DON'T *BELIEVE* YOU GUYS!

WHY THE HELL DON'T YOU JUST CALL OUT THE TROOPS, SURROUND THE ISLAND, AND TRACK DOWN THE DAMN POD YOURSELF.

WE CAN'T VERY WELL DO THAT...

...WITHOUT SOME SERIOUS TROUBLE FROM YOUR GOVERNMENT.

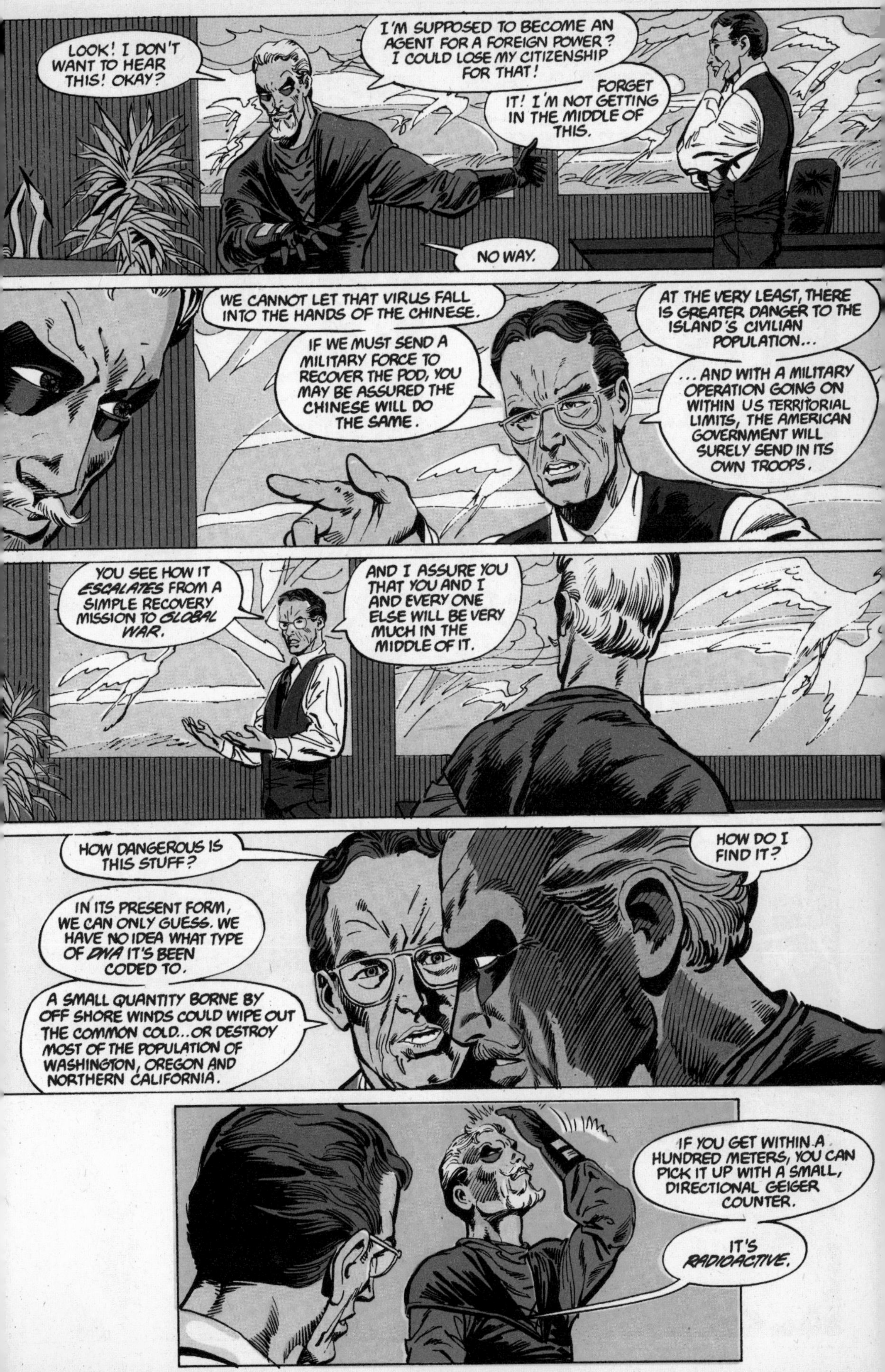
LOOK! I DON'T WANT TO HEAR THIS! OKAY?
I'M SUPPOSED TO BECOME AN AGENT FOR A FOREIGN POWER? I COULD LOSE MY CITIZENSHIP FOR THAT!
FORGET IT! I'M NOT GETTING IN THE MIDDLE OF THIS.
NO WAY.
WE CANNOT LET THAT VIRUS FALL INTO THE HANDS OF THE CHINESE.
IF WE MUST SEND A MILITARY FORCE TO RECOVER THE POD, YOU MAY BE ASSURED THE CHINESE WILL DO THE SAME.
AT THE VERY LEAST, THERE IS GREATER DANGER TO THE ISLAND'S CIVILIAN POPULATION...
...AND WITH A MILITARY OPERATION GOING ON WITHIN US TERRITORIAL LIMITS, THE AMERICAN GOVERNMENT WILL SURELY SEND IN ITS OWN TROOPS.
YOU SEE HOW IT ESCALATES FROM A SIMPLE RECOVERY MISSION TO GLOBAL WAR.
AND I ASSURE YOU THAT YOU AND I AND EVERY ONE ELSE WILL BE VERY MUCH IN THE MIDDLE OF IT.
HOW DANGEROUS IS THIS STUFF?
IN ITS PRESENT FORM, WE CAN ONLY GUESS. WE HAVE NO IDEA WHAT TYPE OF DNA IT'S BEEN CODED TO.
A SMALL QUANTITY BORNE BY OFF SHORE WINDS COULD WIPE OUT THE COMMON COLD...OR DESTROY MOST OF THE POPULATION OF WASHINGTON, OREGON AND NORTHERN CALIFORNIA.
HOW DO I FIND IT?
IF YOU GET WITHIN A HUNDRED METERS, YOU CAN PICK IT UP WITH A SMALL, DIRECTIONAL GEIGER COUNTER.
IT'S RADIOACTIVE.

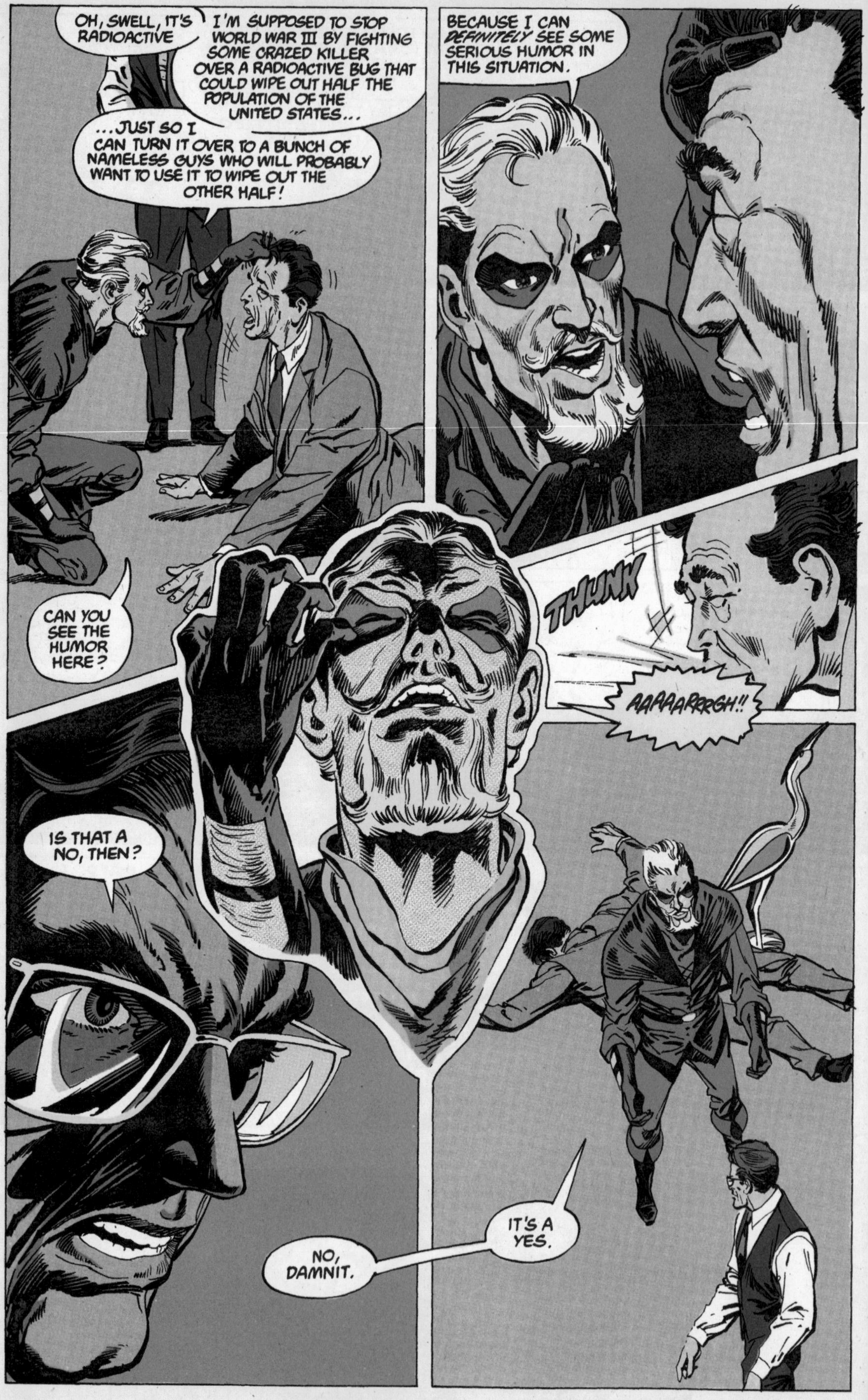

OH, SWELL, IT'S RADIOACTIVE
I'M SUPPOSED TO STOP WORLD WAR III BY FIGHTING SOME CRAZED KILLER OVER A RADIOACTIVE BUG THAT COULD WIPE OUT HALF THE POPULATION OF THE UNITED STATES...
...JUST SO I CAN TURN IT OVER TO A BUNCH OF NAMELESS GUYS WHO WILL PROBABLY WANT TO USE IT TO WIPE OUT THE OTHER HALF!
CAN YOU SEE THE HUMOR HERE?
BECAUSE I CAN DEFINITELY SEE SOME SERIOUS HUMOR IN THIS SITUATION.
THUNK
AAAAARRRGH!!
IS THAT A NO, THEN?
NO, DAMNIT.
IT'S A YES.

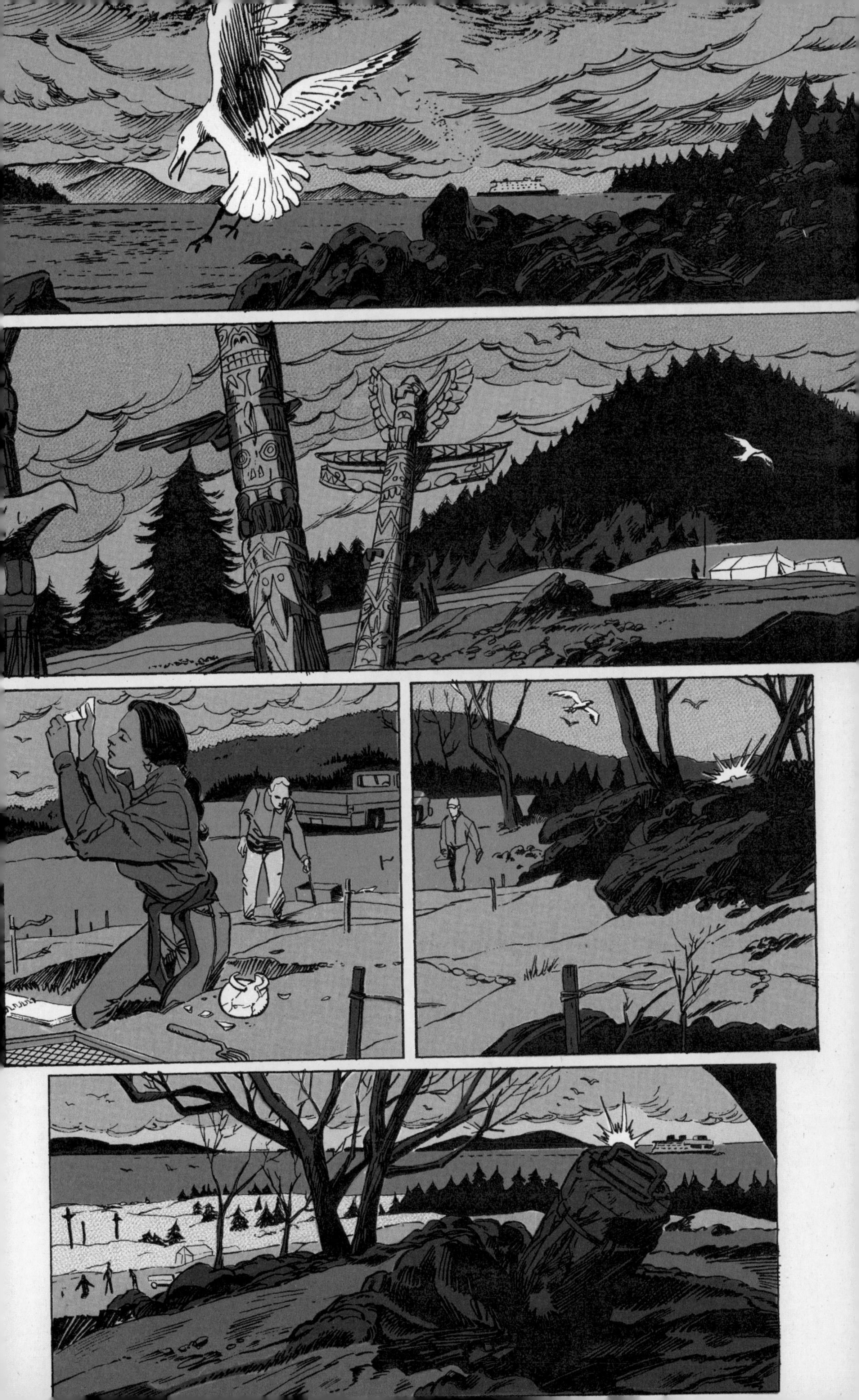

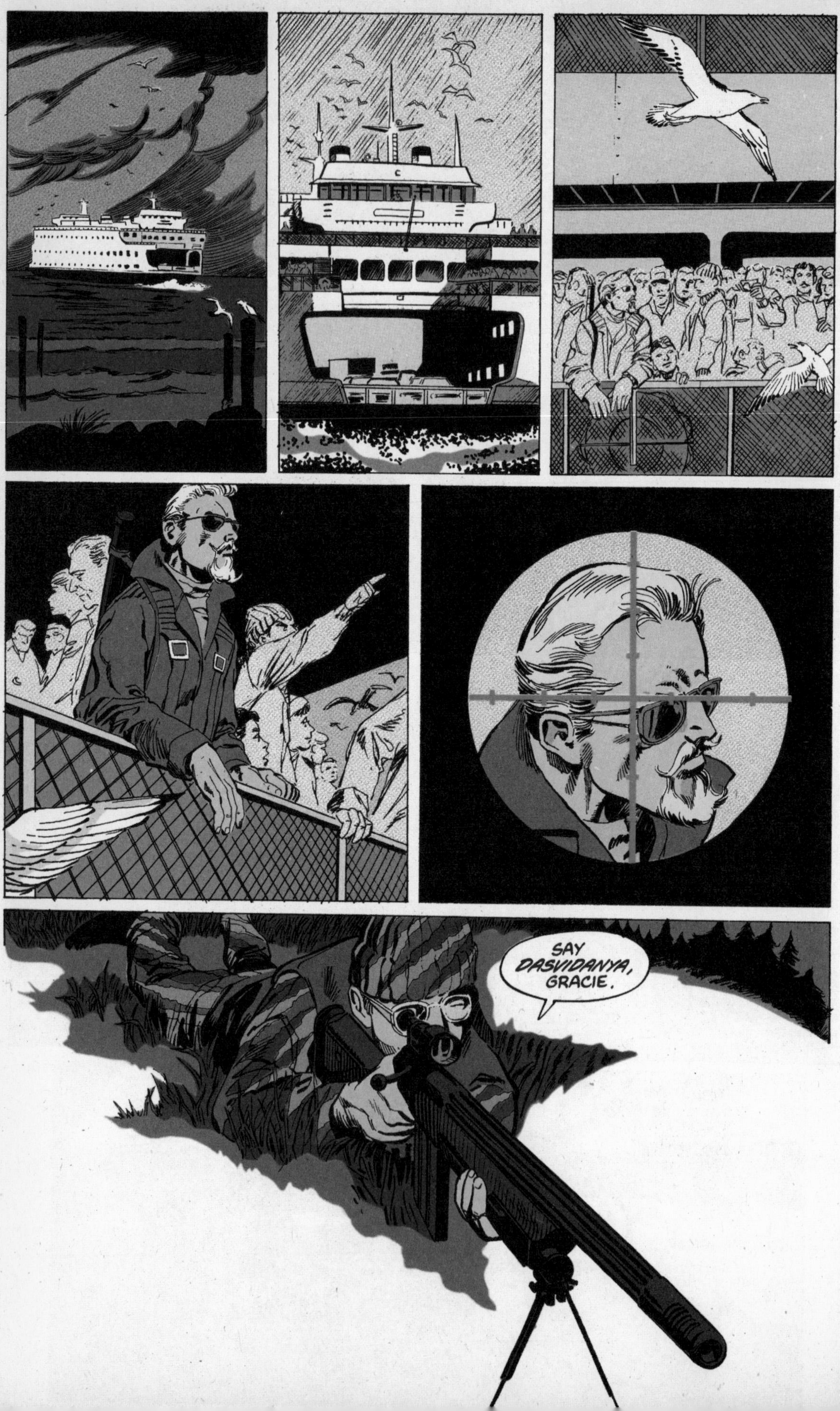
SAY DASVIDANYA, GRACIE.

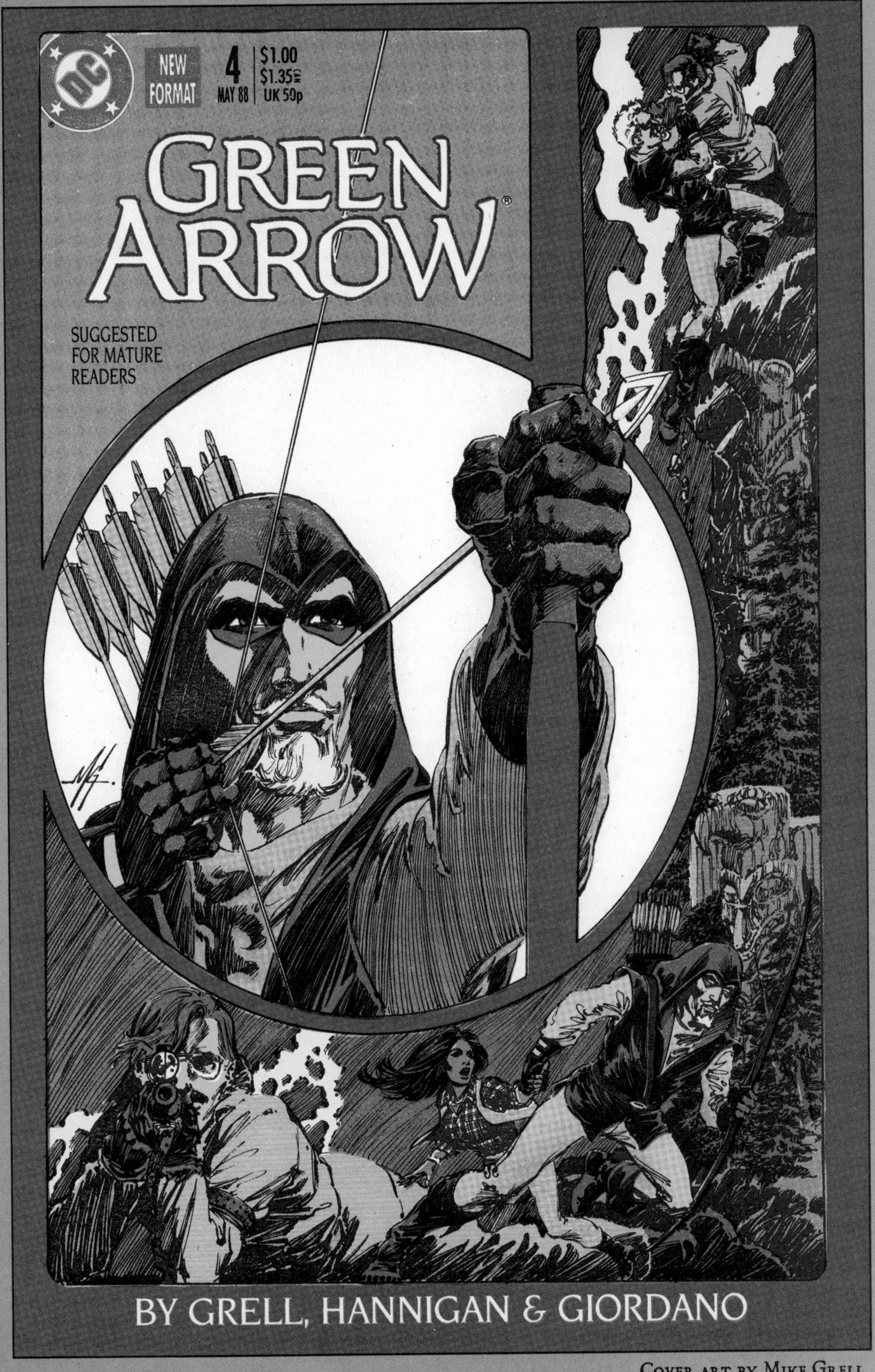
NEW FORMAT
4
MAY 88
$1.00
$1.35
UK 50p
GREEN ARROW
SUGGESTED FOR MATURE READERS
BY GRELL, HANNIGAN & GIORDANO

Cover art by Mike Grell

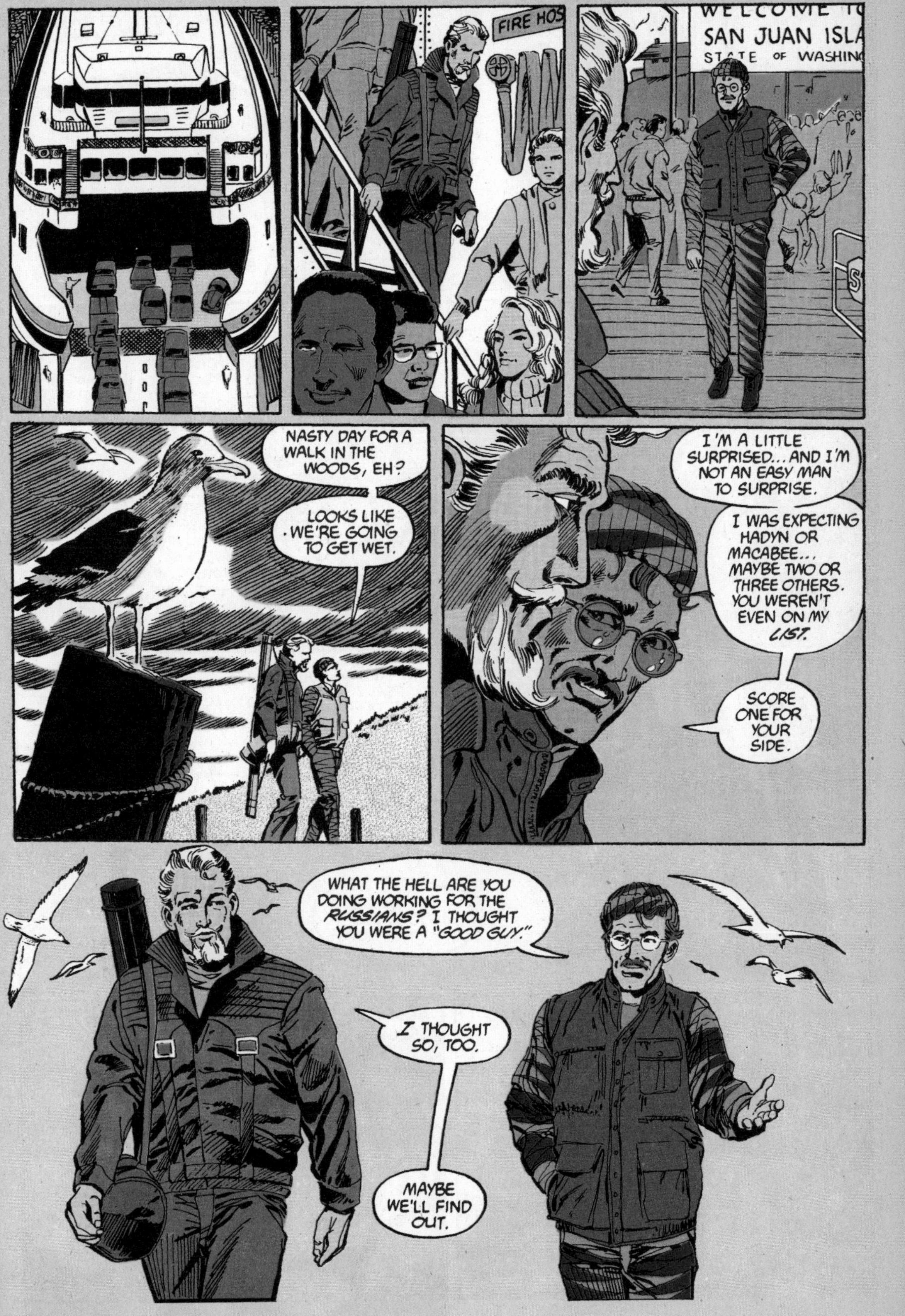
WELCOME TO
SAN JUAN ISLA
STATE OF WASHING
FIRE HOS
NASTY DAY FOR A WALK IN THE WOODS, EH?
LOOKS LIKE WE'RE GOING TO GET WET.
I'M A LITTLE SURPRISED... AND I'M NOT AN EASY MAN TO SURPRISE.
I WAS EXPECTING HADYN OR MACABEE... MAYBE TWO OR THREE OTHERS. YOU WEREN'T EVEN ON MY LIST.
SCORE ONE FOR YOUR SIDE.
WHAT THE HELL ARE YOU DOING WORKING FOR THE RUSSIANS? I THOUGHT YOU WERE A "GOOD GUY."
I THOUGHT SO, TOO.
MAYBE WE'LL FIND OUT.

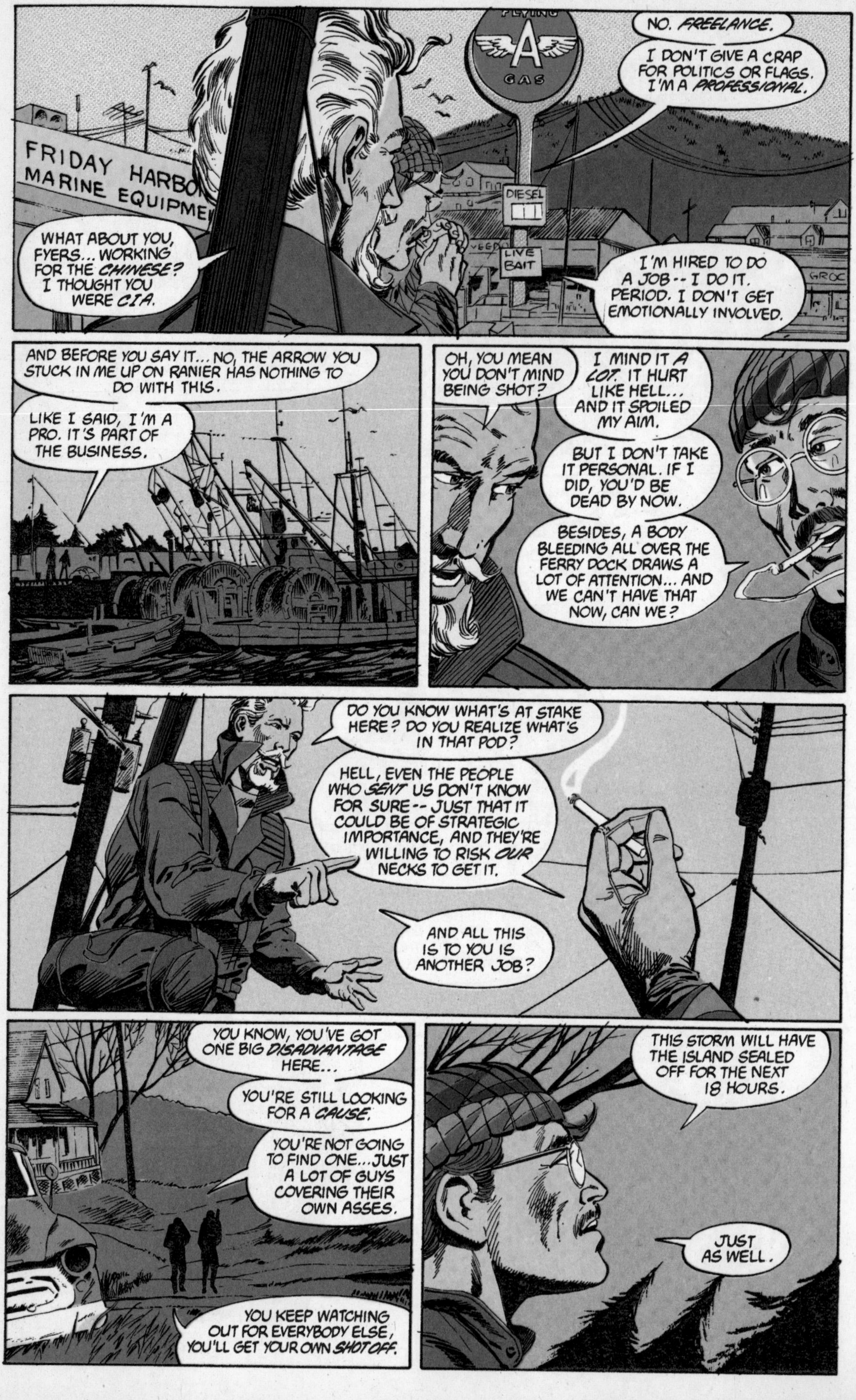
FLYING A GAS
FRIDAY HARBO MARINE EQUIPME
DIESEL
LIVE BAIT
WHAT ABOUT YOU, FYERS... WORKING FOR THE CHINESE? I THOUGHT YOU WERE CIA.
NO. FREELANCE.
I DON'T GIVE A CRAP FOR POLITICS OR FLAGS. I'M A PROFESSIONAL.
I'M HIRED TO DO A JOB -- I DO IT. PERIOD. I DON'T GET EMOTIONALLY INVOLVED.
AND BEFORE YOU SAY IT... NO, THE ARROW YOU STUCK IN ME UP ON RANIER HAS NOTHING TO DO WITH THIS.
LIKE I SAID, I'M A PRO. IT'S PART OF THE BUSINESS.
OH, YOU MEAN YOU DON'T MIND BEING SHOT?
I MIND IT A LOT. IT HURT LIKE HELL... AND IT SPOILED MY AIM.
BUT I DON'T TAKE IT PERSONAL. IF I DID, YOU'D BE DEAD BY NOW.
BESIDES, A BODY BLEEDING ALL OVER THE FERRY DOCK DRAWS A LOT OF ATTENTION... AND WE CAN'T HAVE THAT NOW, CAN WE?
DO YOU KNOW WHAT'S AT STAKE HERE? DO YOU REALIZE WHAT'S IN THAT POD?
HELL, EVEN THE PEOPLE WHO SENT US DON'T KNOW FOR SURE -- JUST THAT IT COULD BE OF STRATEGIC IMPORTANCE, AND THEY'RE WILLING TO RISK OUR NECKS TO GET IT.
AND ALL THIS IS TO YOU IS ANOTHER JOB?
YOU KNOW, YOU'VE GOT ONE BIG DISADVANTAGE HERE...
YOU'RE STILL LOOKING FOR A CAUSE.
YOU'RE NOT GOING TO FIND ONE... JUST A LOT OF GUYS COVERING THEIR OWN ASSES.
YOU KEEP WATCHING OUT FOR EVERYBODY ELSE, YOU'LL GET YOUR OWN SHOT OFF.
THIS STORM WILL HAVE THE ISLAND SEALED OFF FOR THE NEXT 18 HOURS.
JUST AS WELL.

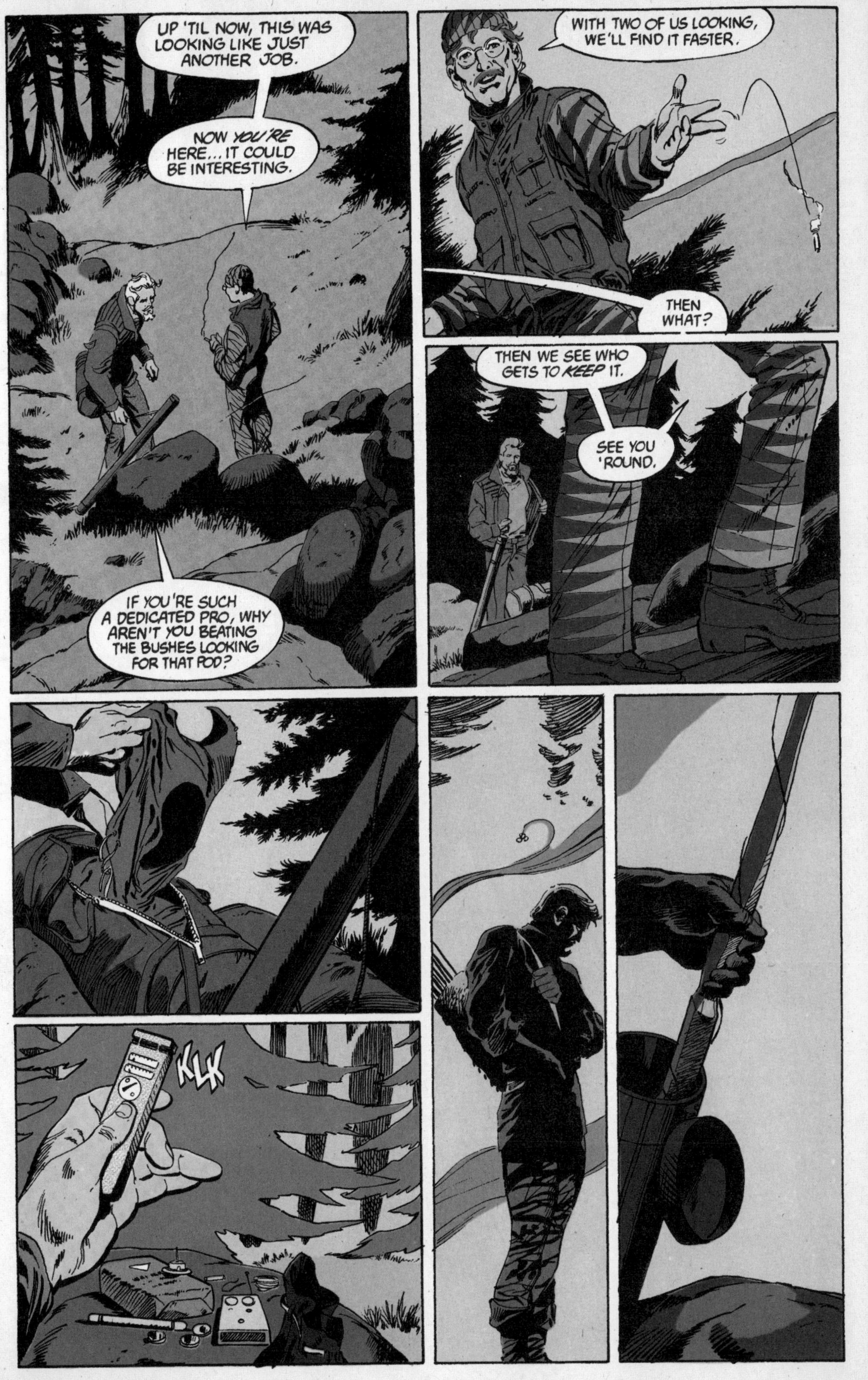
UP 'TIL NOW, THIS WAS LOOKING LIKE JUST ANOTHER JOB.
NOW YOU'RE HERE... IT COULD BE INTERESTING.
IF YOU'RE SUCH A DEDICATED PRO, WHY AREN'T YOU BEATING THE BUSHES LOOKING FOR THAT POD?
WITH TWO OF US LOOKING, WE'LL FIND IT FASTER.
THEN WHAT?
THEN WE SEE WHO GETS TO KEEP IT.
SEE YOU 'ROUND.
KLK

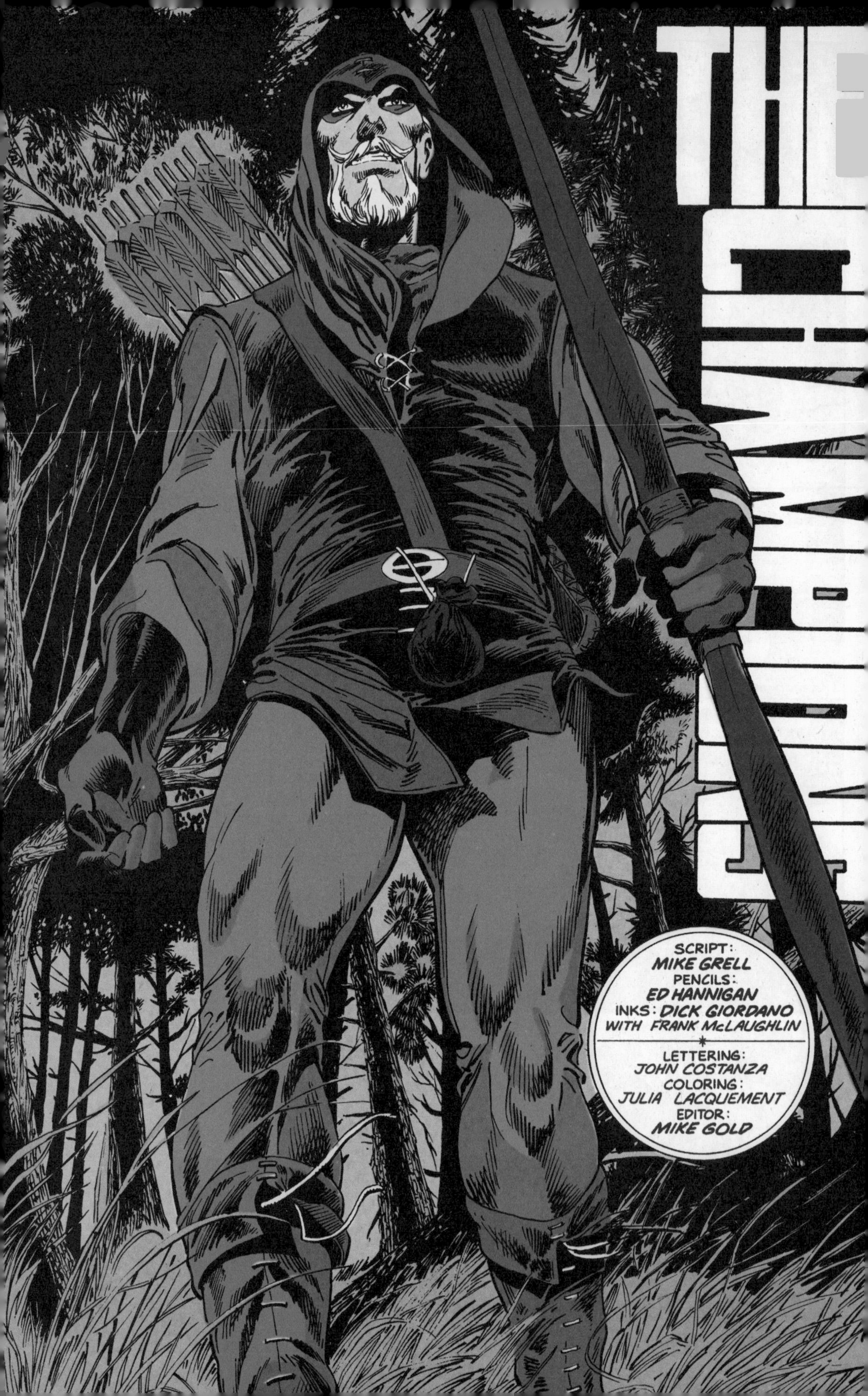

THE
SCRIPT: MIKE GRELL
PENCILS: ED HANNIGAN
INKS: DICK GIORDANO WITH FRANK McLAUGHLIN
LETTERING: JOHN COSTANZA
COLORING: JULIA LACQUEMENT
EDITOR: MIKE GOLD

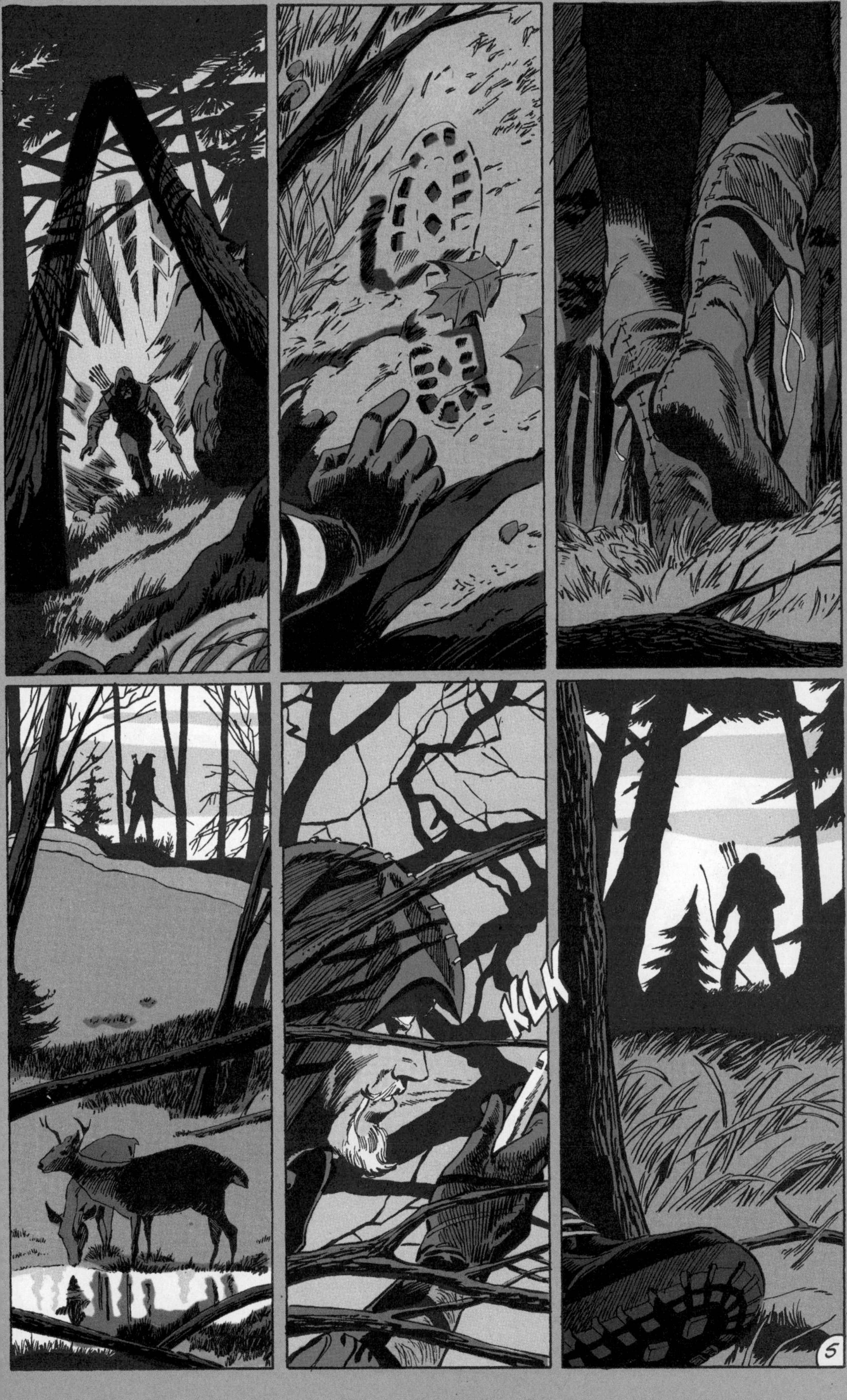
KLK

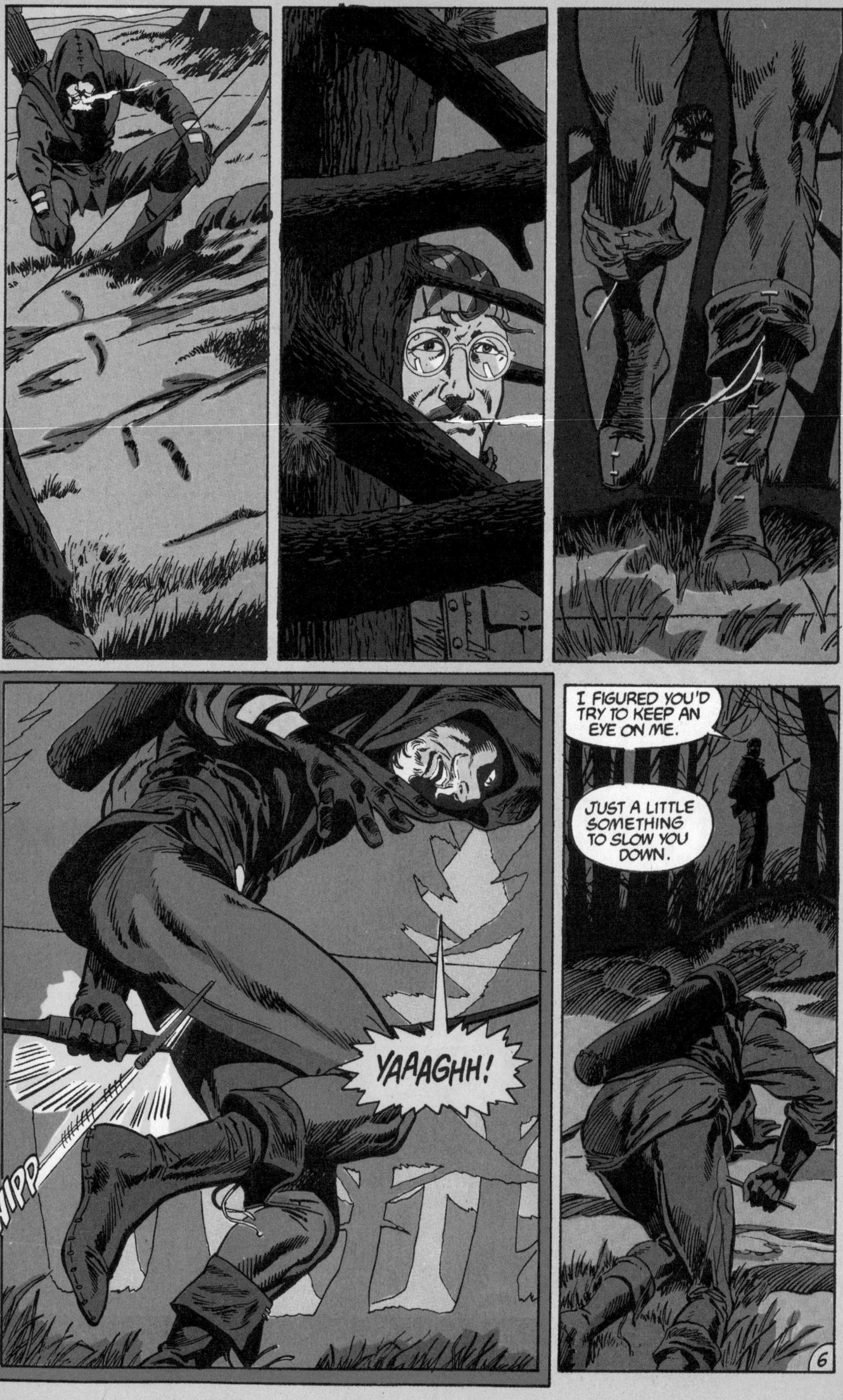
YAAAGHH!
TWIPP
I FIGURED YOU'D TRY TO KEEP AN EYE ON ME.
JUST A LITTLE SOMETHING TO SLOW YOU DOWN.
6

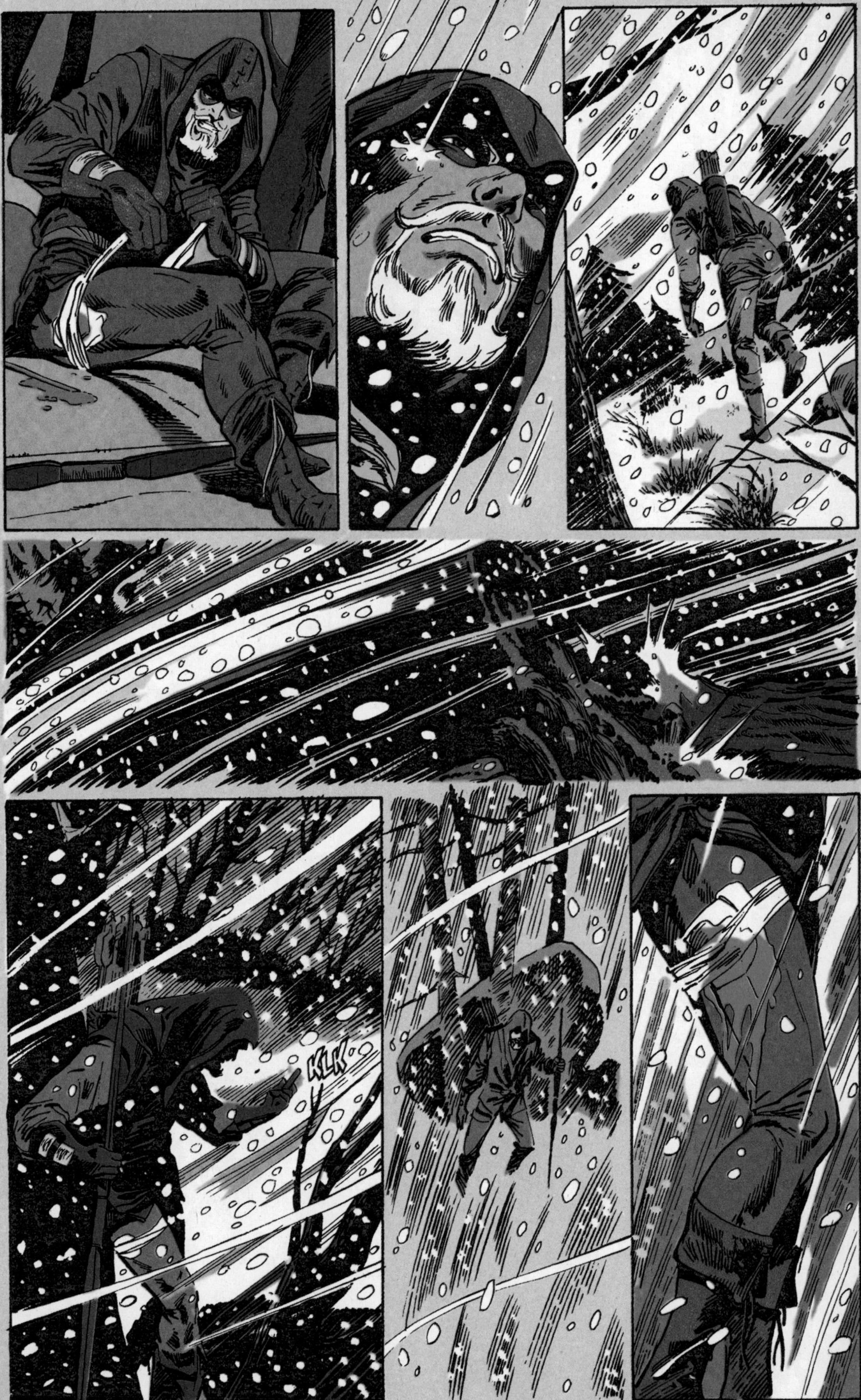
KLK

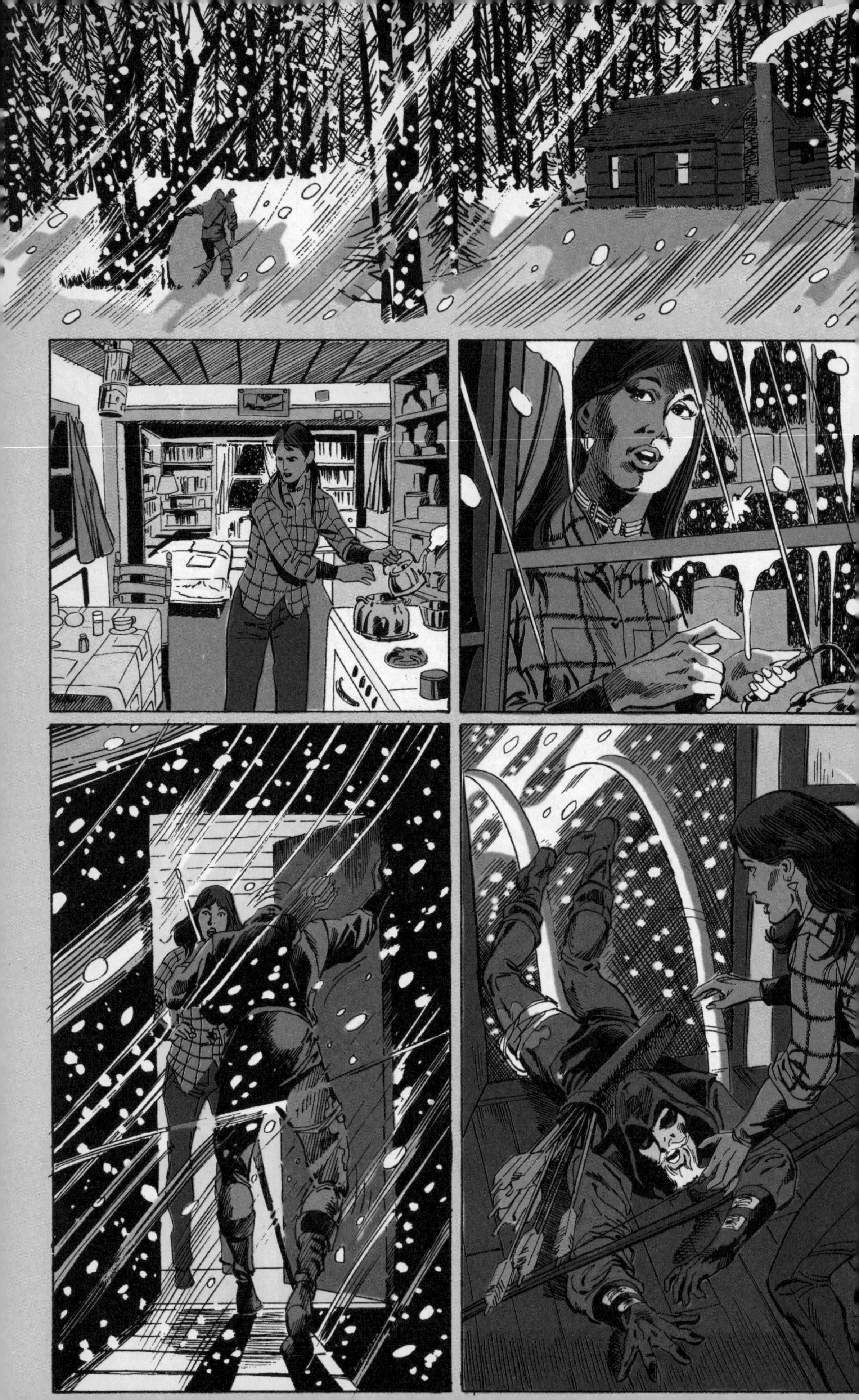

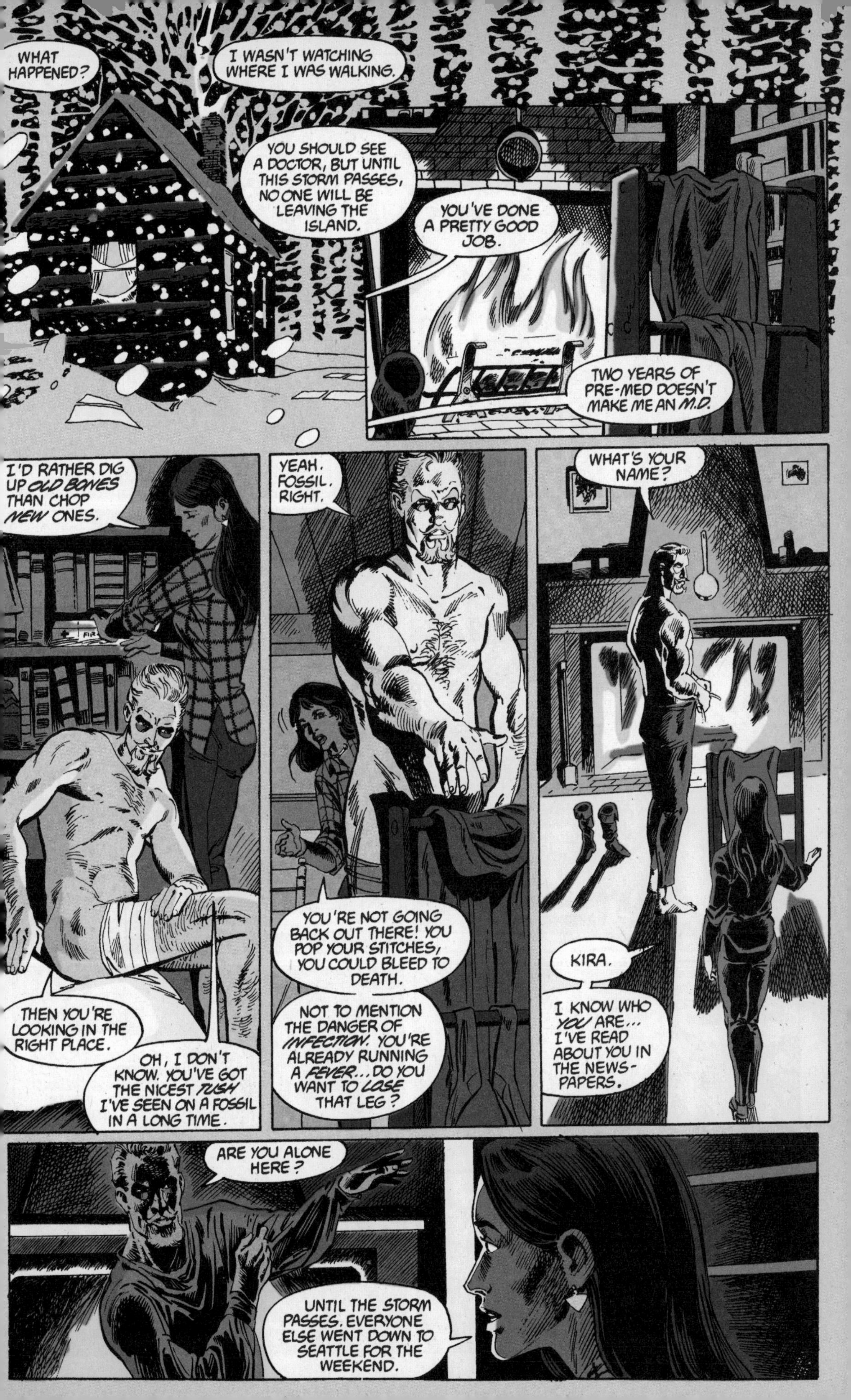
WHAT HAPPENED?
I WASN'T WATCHING WHERE I WAS WALKING.
YOU SHOULD SEE A DOCTOR, BUT UNTIL THIS STORM PASSES, NO ONE WILL BE LEAVING THE ISLAND.
YOU'VE DONE A PRETTY GOOD JOB.
TWO YEARS OF PRE-MED DOESN'T MAKE ME AN M.D.
I'D RATHER DIG UP OLD BONES THAN CHOP NEW ONES.
THEN YOU'RE LOOKING IN THE RIGHT PLACE.
OH, I DON'T KNOW. YOU'VE GOT THE NICEST TUSH I'VE SEEN ON A FOSSIL IN A LONG TIME.
YEAH. FOSSIL. RIGHT.
YOU'RE NOT GOING BACK OUT THERE! YOU POP YOUR STITCHES, YOU COULD BLEED TO DEATH.
NOT TO MENTION THE DANGER OF INFECTION. YOU'RE ALREADY RUNNING A FEVER... DO YOU WANT TO LOSE THAT LEG?
WHAT'S YOUR NAME?
KIRA.
I KNOW WHO YOU ARE... I'VE READ ABOUT YOU IN THE NEWS-PAPERS.
ARE YOU ALONE HERE?
UNTIL THE STORM PASSES. EVERYONE ELSE WENT DOWN TO SEATTLE FOR THE WEEKEND.

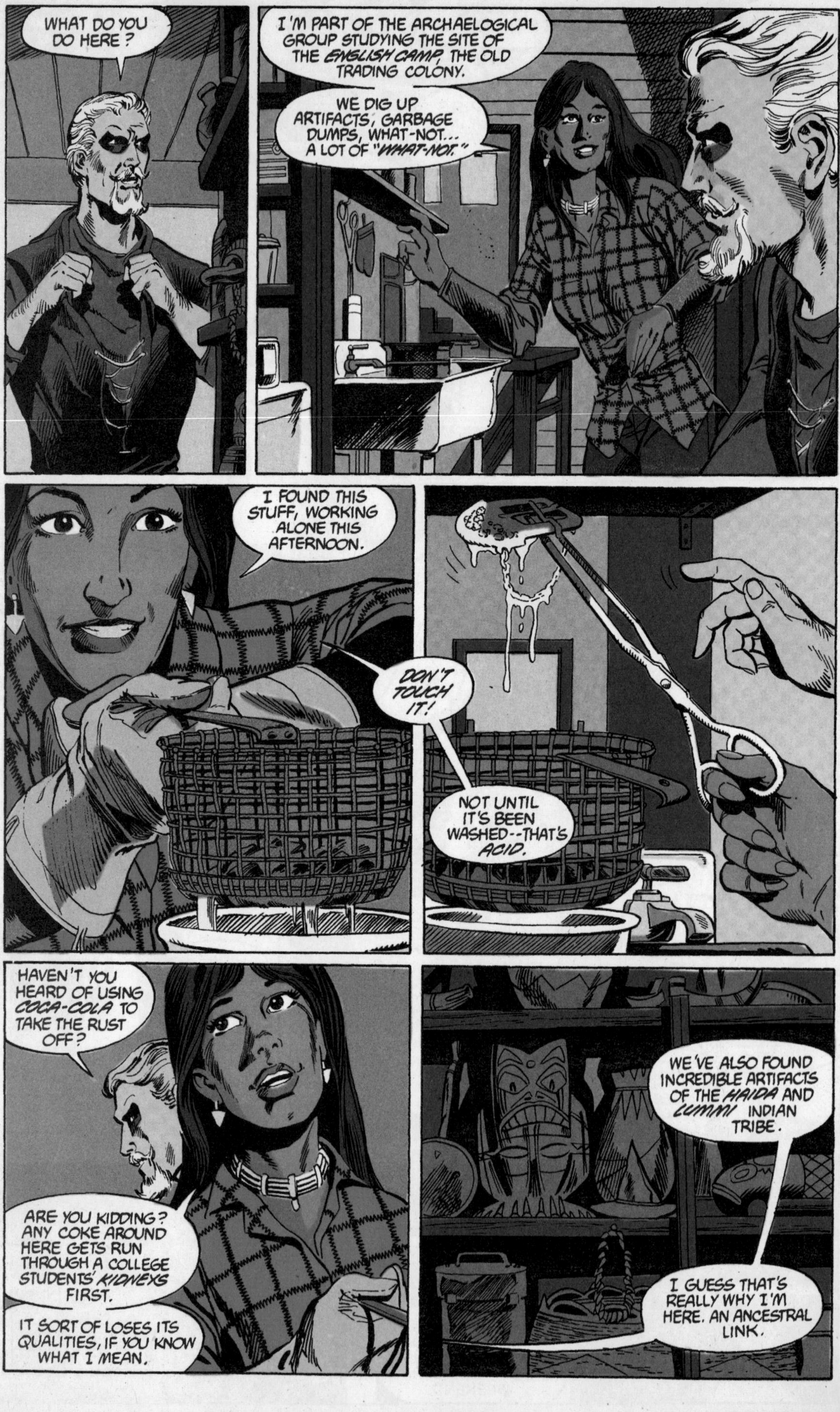
WHAT DO YOU DO HERE?
I'M PART OF THE ARCHAELOGICAL GROUP STUDYING THE SITE OF THE ENGLISH CAMP, THE OLD TRADING COLONY.
WE DIG UP ARTIFACTS, GARBAGE DUMPS, WHAT-NOT... A LOT OF "WHAT-NOT."
I FOUND THIS STUFF, WORKING ALONE THIS AFTERNOON.
DON'T TOUCH IT!
NOT UNTIL IT'S BEEN WASHED--THAT'S ACID.
HAVEN'T YOU HEARD OF USING COCA-COLA TO TAKE THE RUST OFF?
ARE YOU KIDDING? ANY COKE AROUND HERE GETS RUN THROUGH A COLLEGE STUDENTS' KIDNEYS FIRST.
IT SORT OF LOSES ITS QUALITIES, IF YOU KNOW WHAT I MEAN.
WE'VE ALSO FOUND INCREDIBLE ARTIFACTS OF THE HAIDA AND LUMMI INDIAN TRIBE.
I GUESS THAT'S REALLY WHY I'M HERE. AN ANCESTRAL LINK.

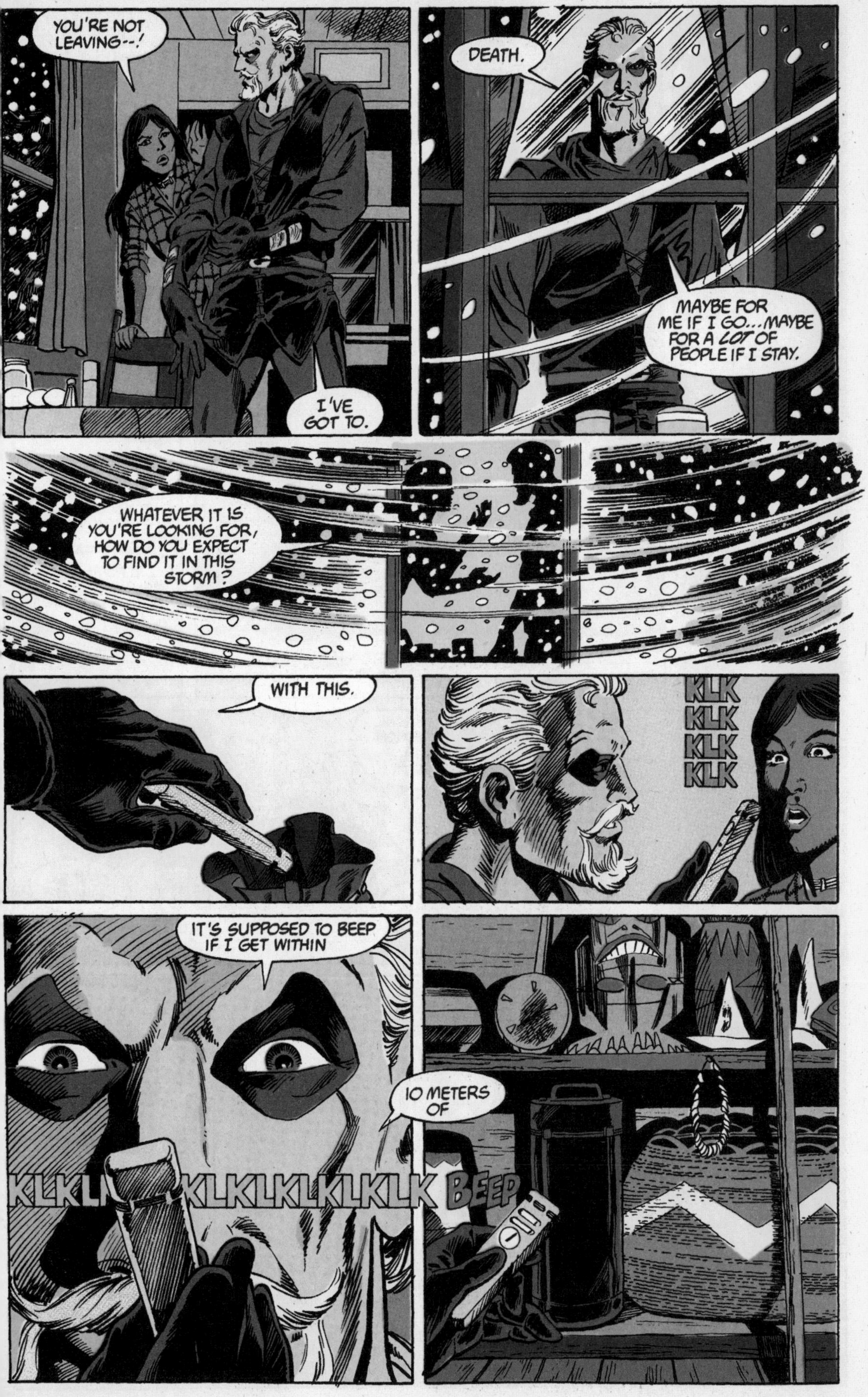
YOU'RE NOT LEAVING--!
I'VE GOT TO.
DEATH.
MAYBE FOR ME IF I GO... MAYBE FOR A *LOT* OF PEOPLE IF I STAY.
WHATEVER IT IS YOU'RE LOOKING FOR, HOW DO YOU EXPECT TO FIND IT IN THIS STORM?
WITH THIS.
KLK KLK KLK KLK
IT'S SUPPOSED TO BEEP IF I GET WITHIN
10 METERS OF
KLKLKLKLKLKLKLK BEEP

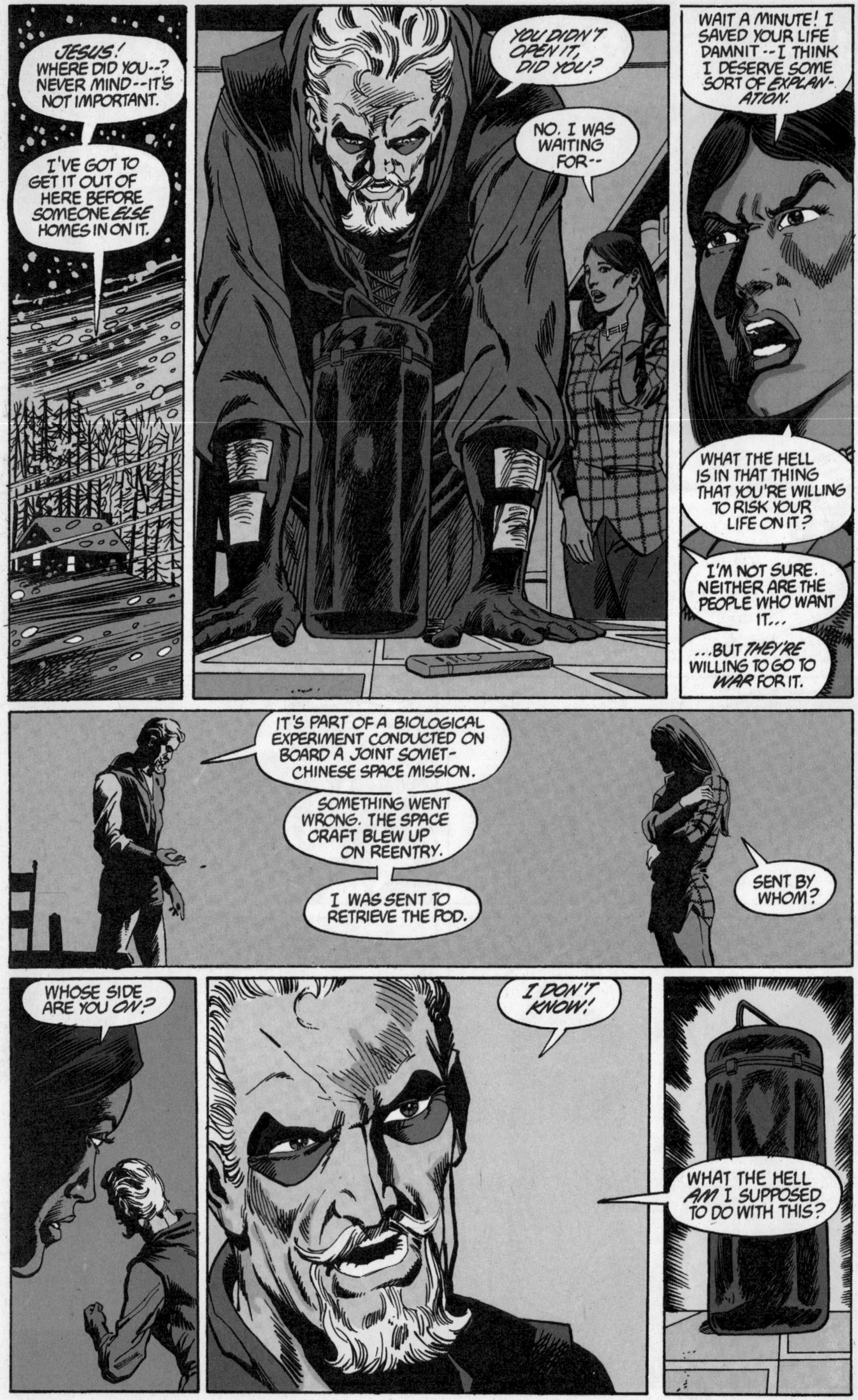
JESUS! WHERE DID YOU--? NEVER MIND--IT'S NOT IMPORTANT.
I'VE GOT TO GET IT OUT OF HERE BEFORE SOMEONE ELSE HOMES IN ON IT.
YOU DIDN'T OPEN IT, DID YOU?
NO. I WAS WAITING FOR--
WAIT A MINUTE! I SAVED YOUR LIFE DAMNIT--I THINK I DESERVE SOME SORT OF EXPLANATION.
WHAT THE HELL IS IN THAT THING THAT YOU'RE WILLING TO RISK YOUR LIFE ON IT?
I'M NOT SURE. NEITHER ARE THE PEOPLE WHO WANT IT...
...BUT THEY'RE WILLING TO GO TO WAR FOR IT.
IT'S PART OF A BIOLOGICAL EXPERIMENT CONDUCTED ON BOARD A JOINT SOVIET-CHINESE SPACE MISSION.
SOMETHING WENT WRONG. THE SPACE CRAFT BLEW UP ON REENTRY.
I WAS SENT TO RETRIEVE THE POD.
SENT BY WHOM?
WHOSE SIDE ARE YOU ON?
I DON'T KNOW!
WHAT THE HELL AM I SUPPOSED TO DO WITH THIS?

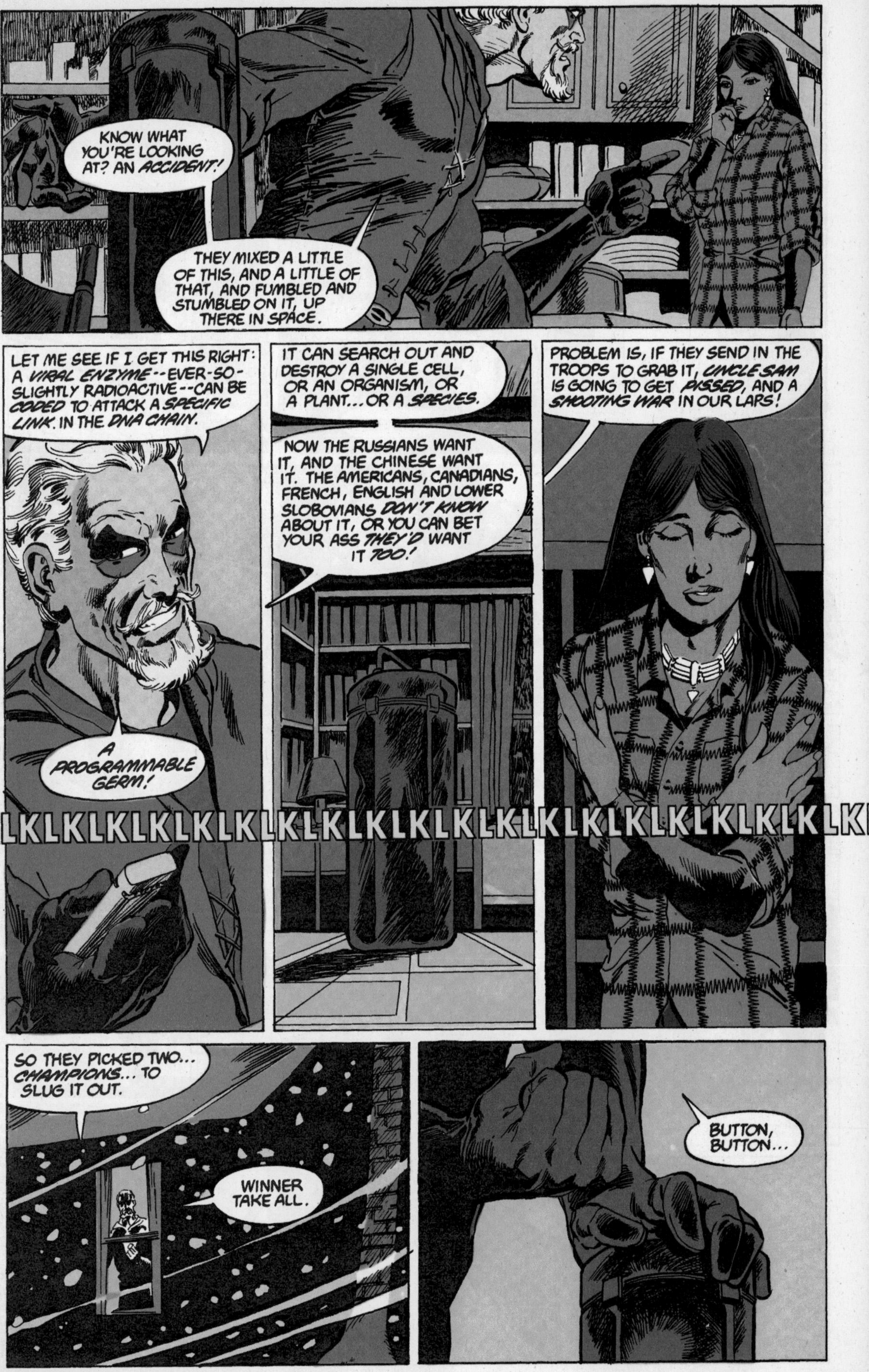
KNOW WHAT YOU'RE LOOKING AT? AN ACCIDENT!
THEY MIXED A LITTLE OF THIS, AND A LITTLE OF THAT, AND FUMBLED AND STUMBLED ON IT, UP THERE IN SPACE.
LET ME SEE IF I GET THIS RIGHT: A VIRAL ENZYME--EVER-SO-SLIGHTLY RADIOACTIVE--CAN BE CODED TO ATTACK A SPECIFIC LINK IN THE DNA CHAIN.
A PROGRAMMABLE GERM!
IT CAN SEARCH OUT AND DESTROY A SINGLE CELL, OR AN ORGANISM, OR A PLANT... OR A SPECIES.
NOW THE RUSSIANS WANT IT, AND THE CHINESE WANT IT. THE AMERICANS, CANADIANS, FRENCH, ENGLISH AND LOWER SLOBOVIANS DON'T KNOW ABOUT IT, OR YOU CAN BET YOUR ASS THEY'D WANT IT TOO!
PROBLEM IS, IF THEY SEND IN THE TROOPS TO GRAB IT, UNCLE SAM IS GOING TO GET PISSED, AND A SHOOTING WAR IN OUR LARS!
KLKLKLKLKLKLKLKLKLKLKLKLKLKLKLKLKLKLKLKLKLK
SO THEY PICKED TWO... CHAMPIONS... TO SLUG IT OUT.
WINNER TAKE ALL.
BUTTON, BUTTON...

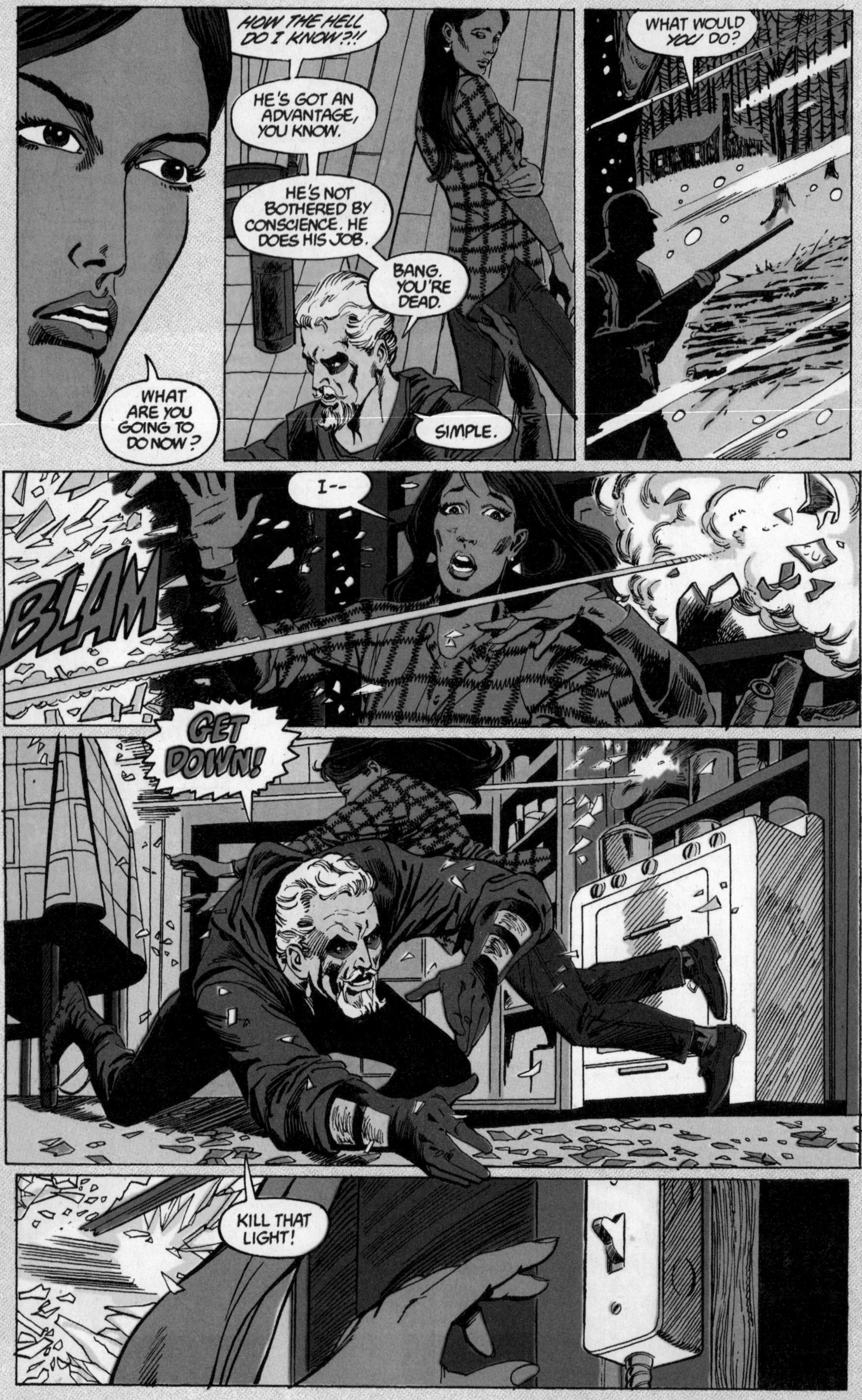
WHAT ARE YOU GOING TO DO NOW?
HOW THE HELL DO I KNOW?!!
HE'S GOT AN ADVANTAGE, YOU KNOW.
HE'S NOT BOTHERED BY CONSCIENCE. HE DOES HIS JOB.
BANG. YOU'RE DEAD.
SIMPLE.
WHAT WOULD YOU DO?
I--
BLAM
GET DOWN!
KILL THAT LIGHT!

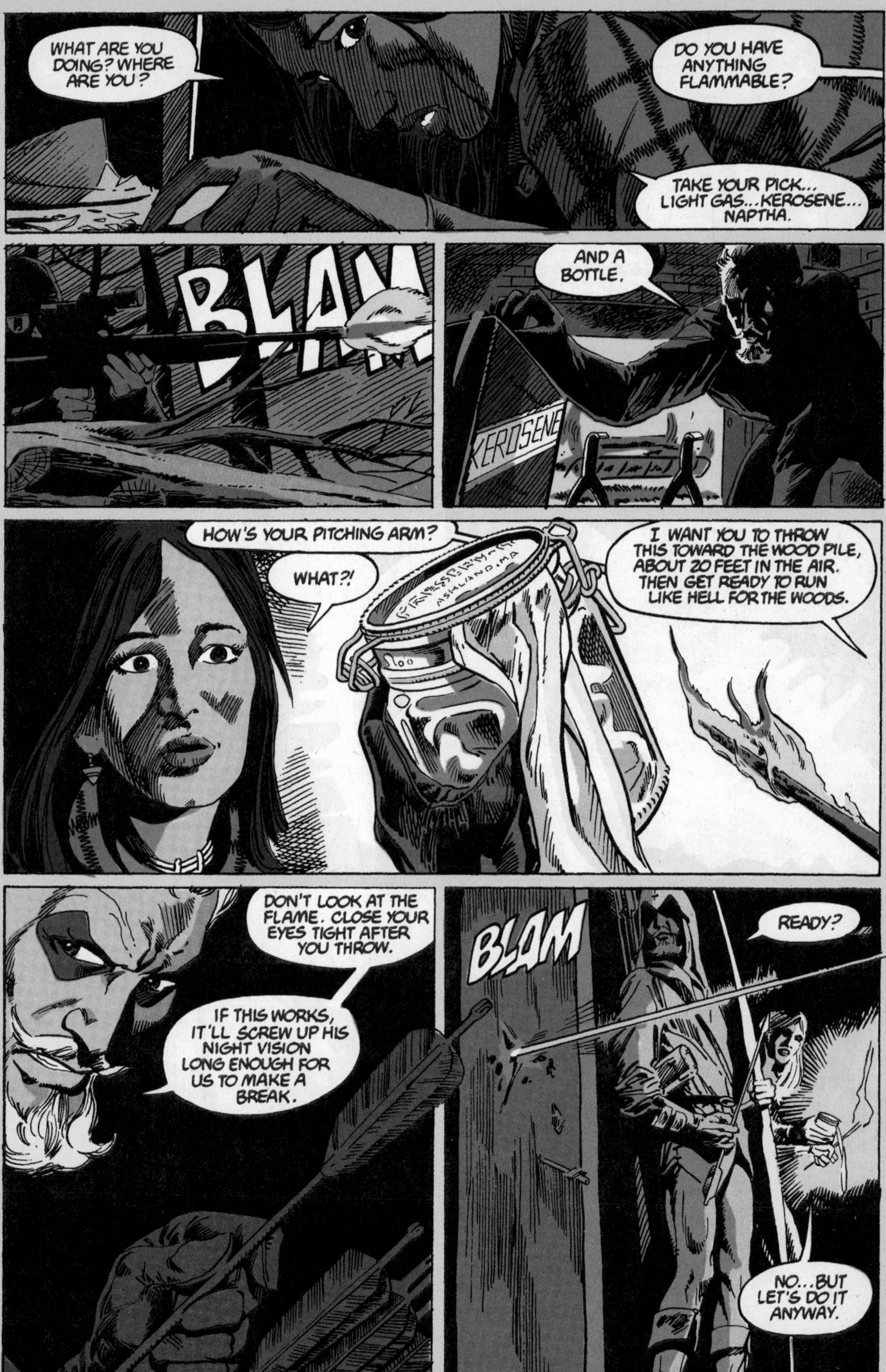
WHAT ARE YOU DOING? WHERE ARE YOU?
DO YOU HAVE ANYTHING FLAMMABLE?
TAKE YOUR PICK... LIGHT GAS...KEROSENE... NAPTHA.
BLAM
AND A BOTTLE.
KEROSENE
HOW'S YOUR PITCHING ARM?
WHAT?!
I WANT YOU TO THROW THIS TOWARD THE WOOD PILE, ABOUT 20 FEET IN THE AIR. THEN GET READY TO RUN LIKE HELL FOR THE WOODS.
DON'T LOOK AT THE FLAME. CLOSE YOUR EYES TIGHT AFTER YOU THROW.
IF THIS WORKS, IT'LL SCREW UP HIS NIGHT VISION LONG ENOUGH FOR US TO MAKE A BREAK.
BLAM
READY?
NO...BUT LET'S DO IT ANYWAY.

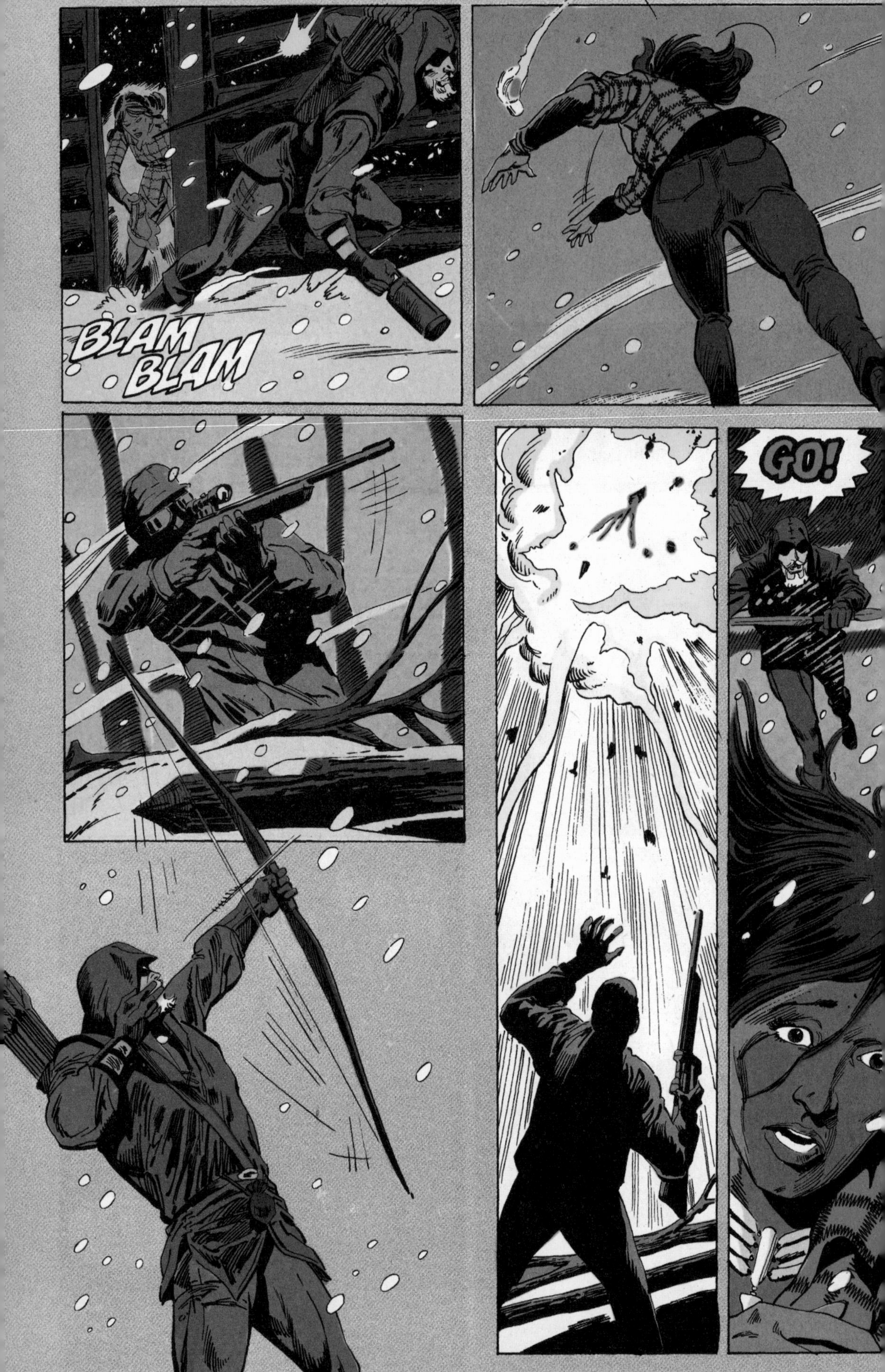
BLAM
BLAM
GO!

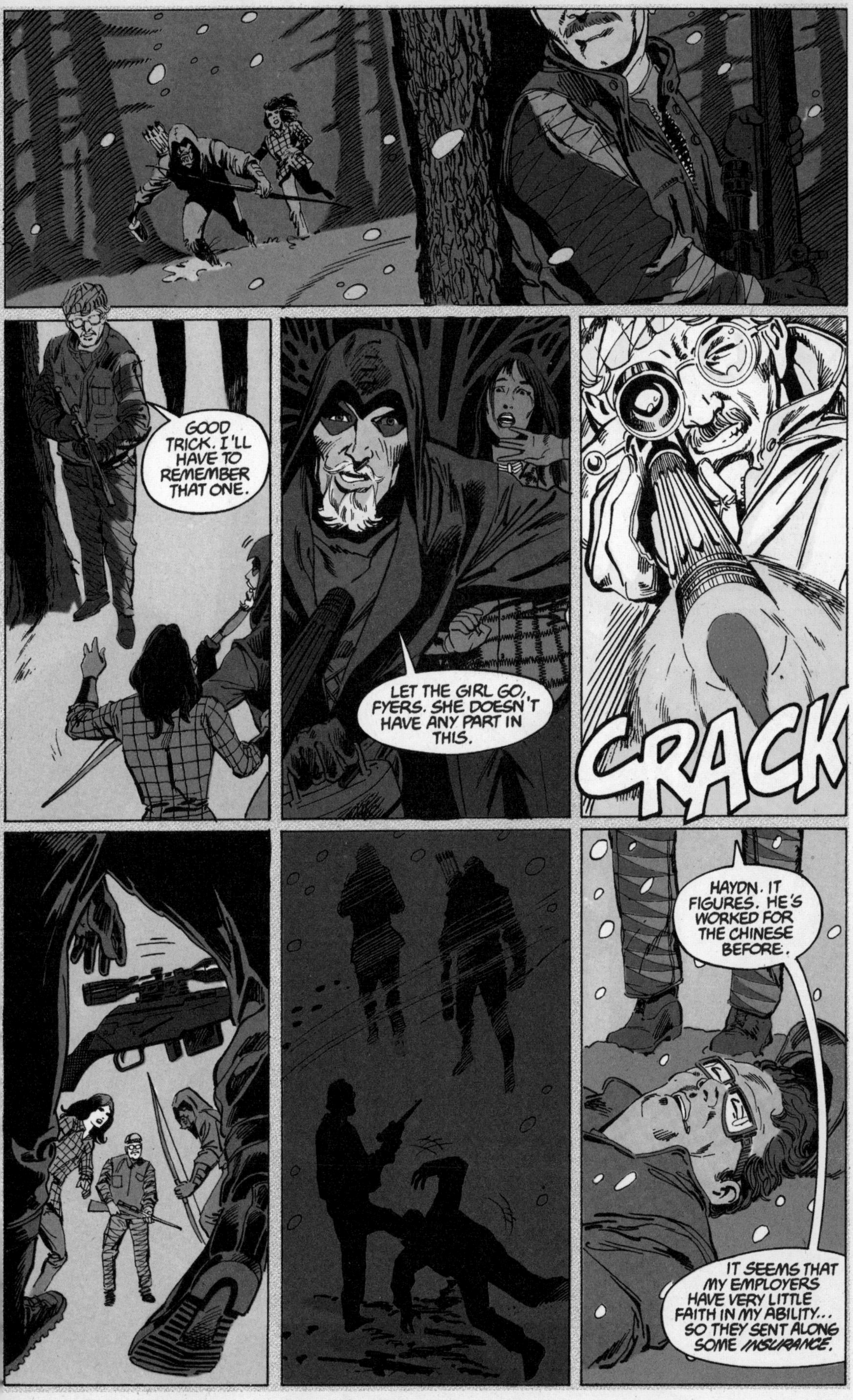
GOOD TRICK. I'LL HAVE TO REMEMBER THAT ONE.
LET THE GIRL GO, FYERS. SHE DOESN'T HAVE ANY PART IN THIS.
CRACK
HAYDN. IT FIGURES. HE'S WORKED FOR THE CHINESE BEFORE.
IT SEEMS THAT MY EMPLOYERS HAVE VERY LITTLE FAITH IN MY ABILITY... SO THEY SENT ALONG SOME *INSURANCE*.

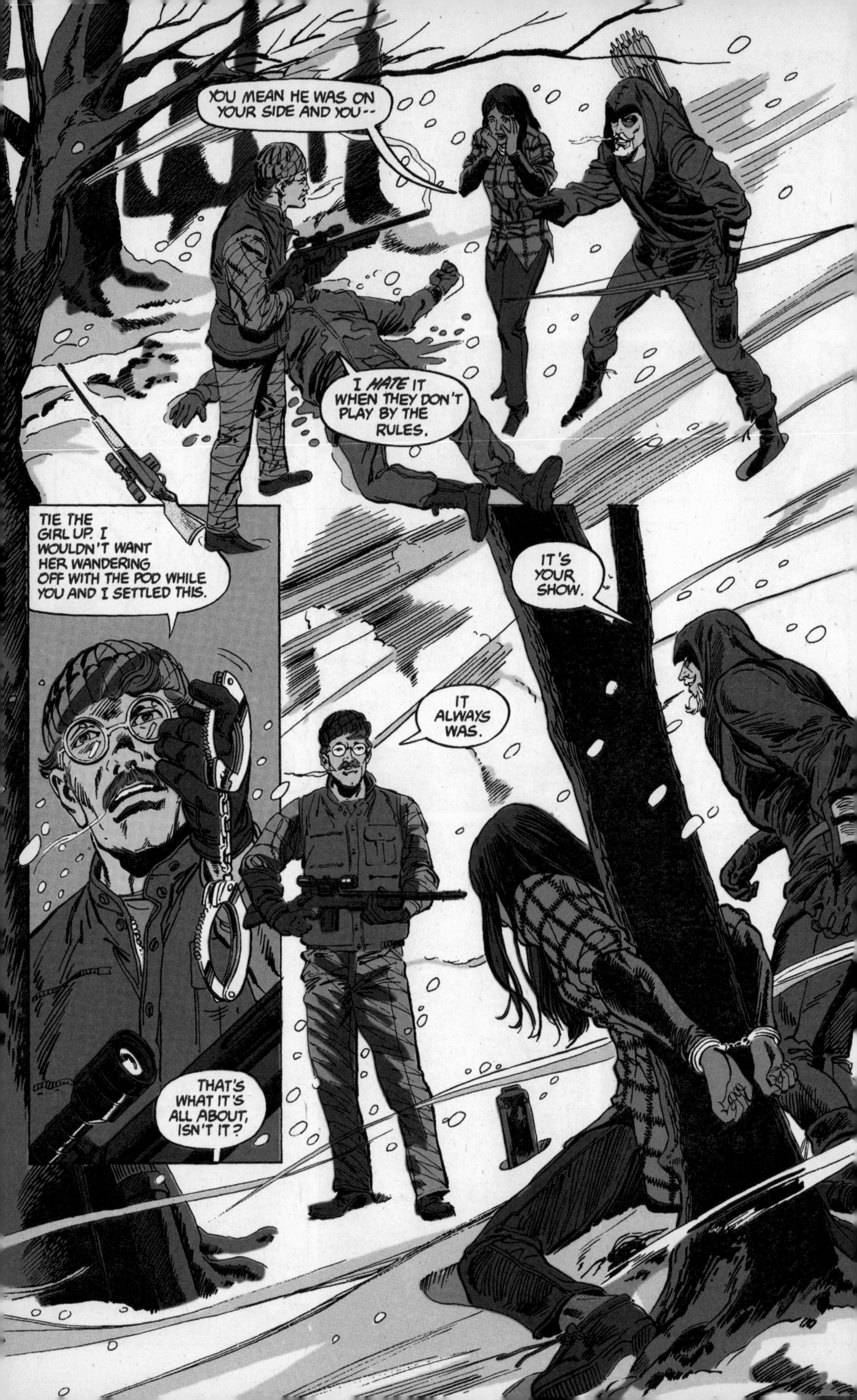
YOU MEAN HE WAS ON YOUR SIDE AND YOU--
I HATE IT WHEN THEY DON'T PLAY BY THE RULES.
TIE THE GIRL UP. I WOULDN'T WANT HER WANDERING OFF WITH THE POD WHILE YOU AND I SETTLED THIS.
IT'S YOUR SHOW.
IT ALWAYS WAS.
THAT'S WHAT IT'S ALL ABOUT, ISN'T IT?

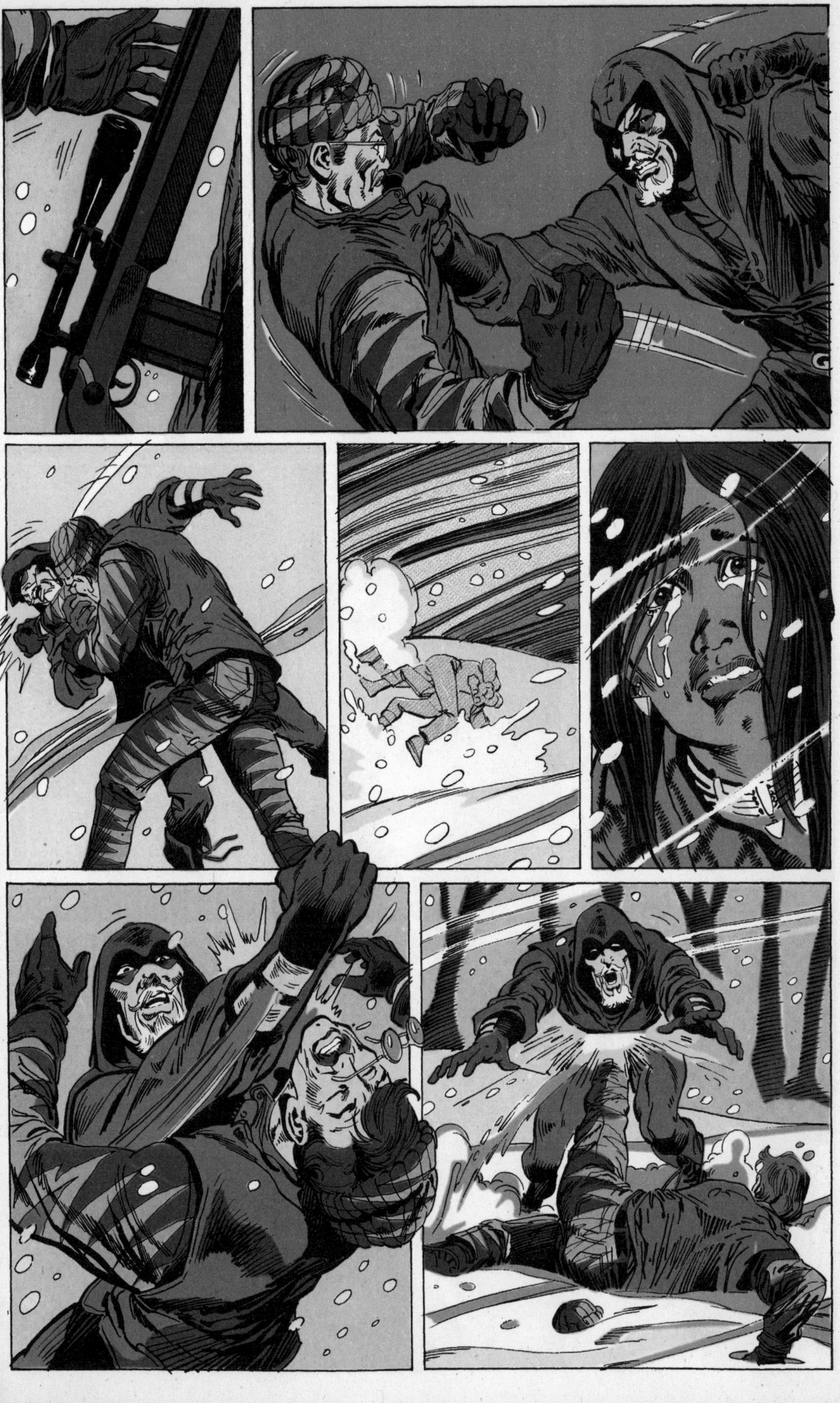

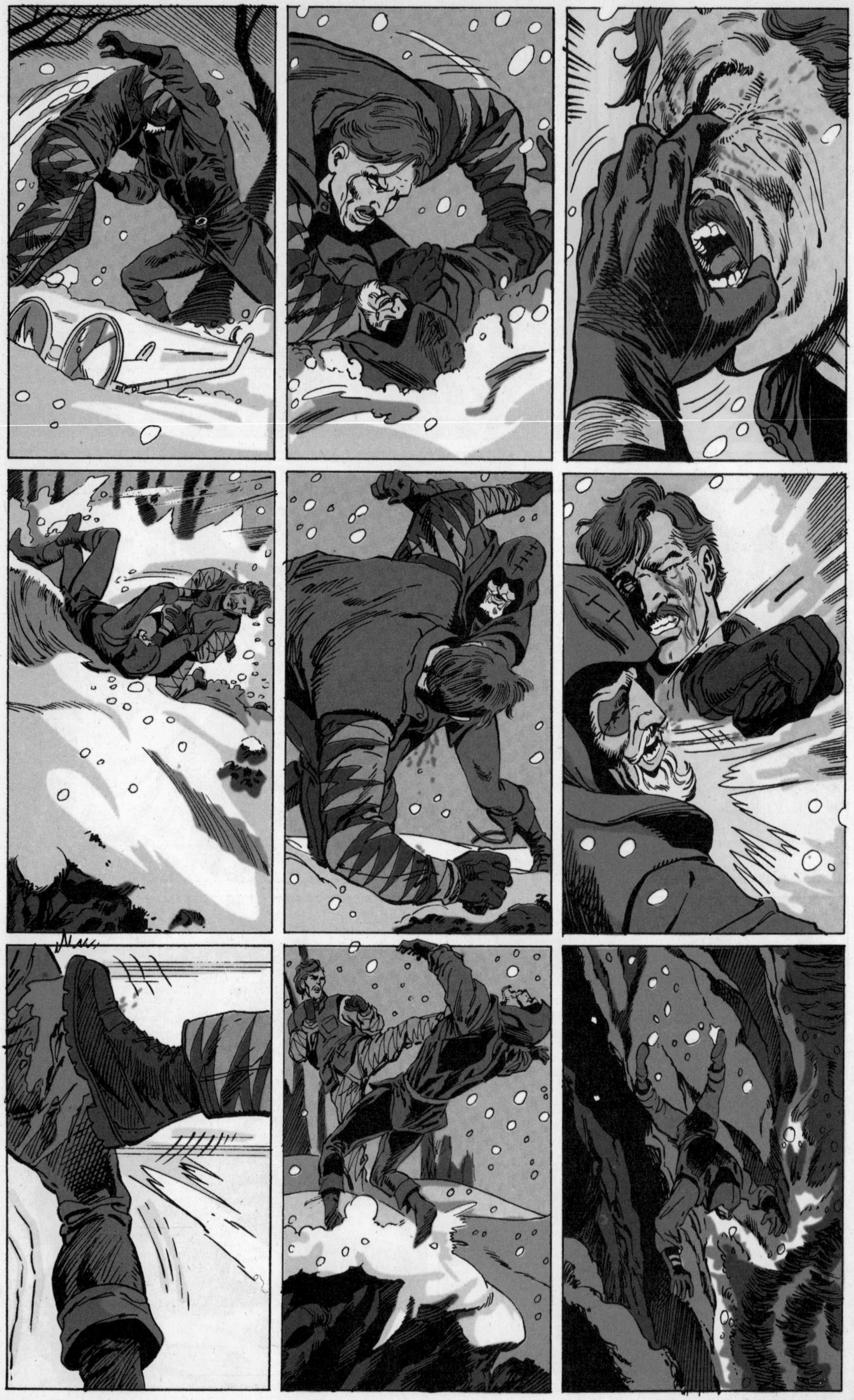

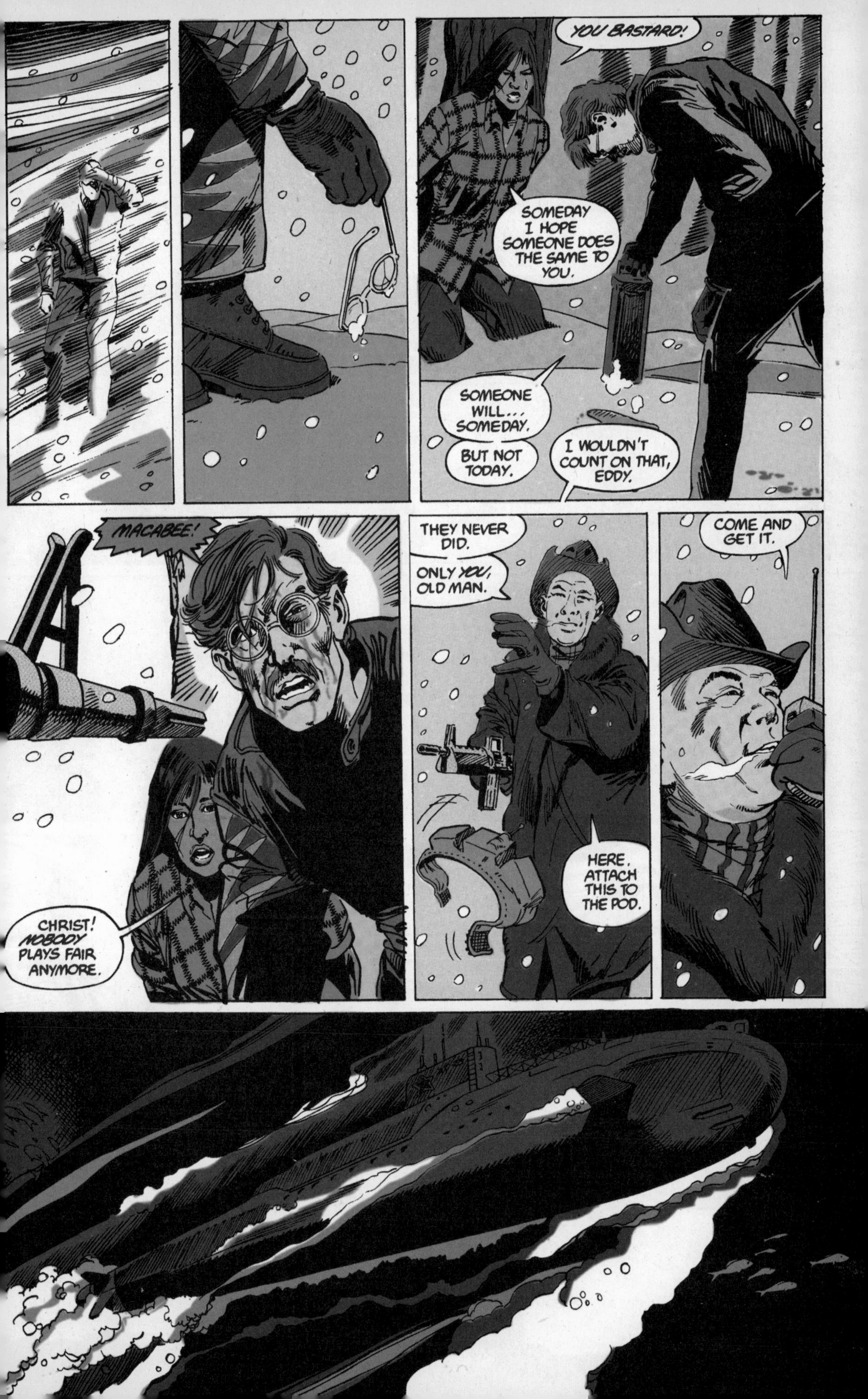
YOU BASTARD!
SOMEDAY I HOPE SOMEONE DOES THE SAME TO YOU.
SOMEONE WILL... SOMEDAY.
BUT NOT TODAY.
I WOULDN'T COUNT ON THAT, EDDY.
MACABEE!
CHRIST! NOBODY PLAYS FAIR ANYMORE.
THEY NEVER DID.
ONLY YOU, OLD MAN.
HERE. ATTACH THIS TO THE POD.
COME AND GET IT.

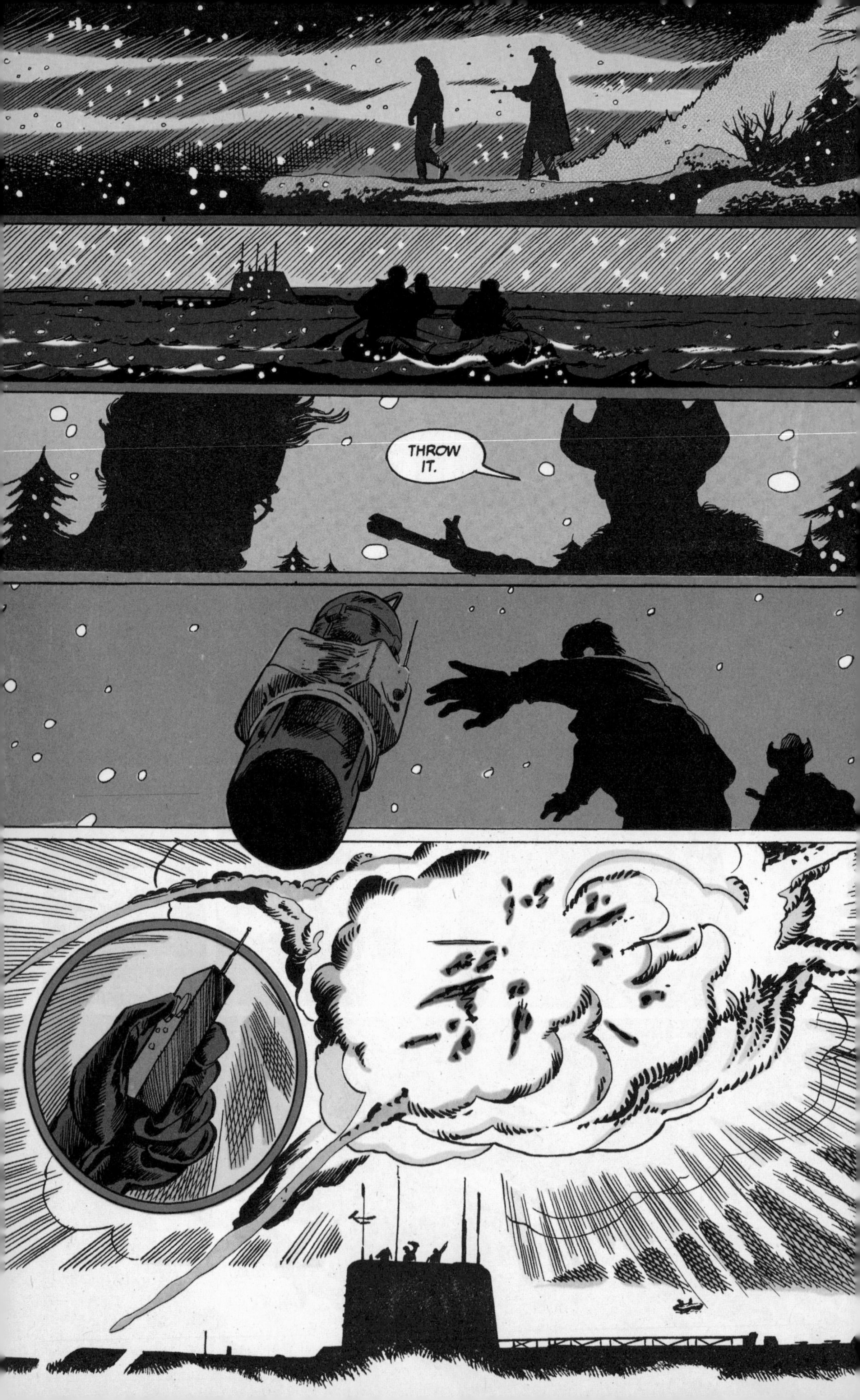
THROW IT.

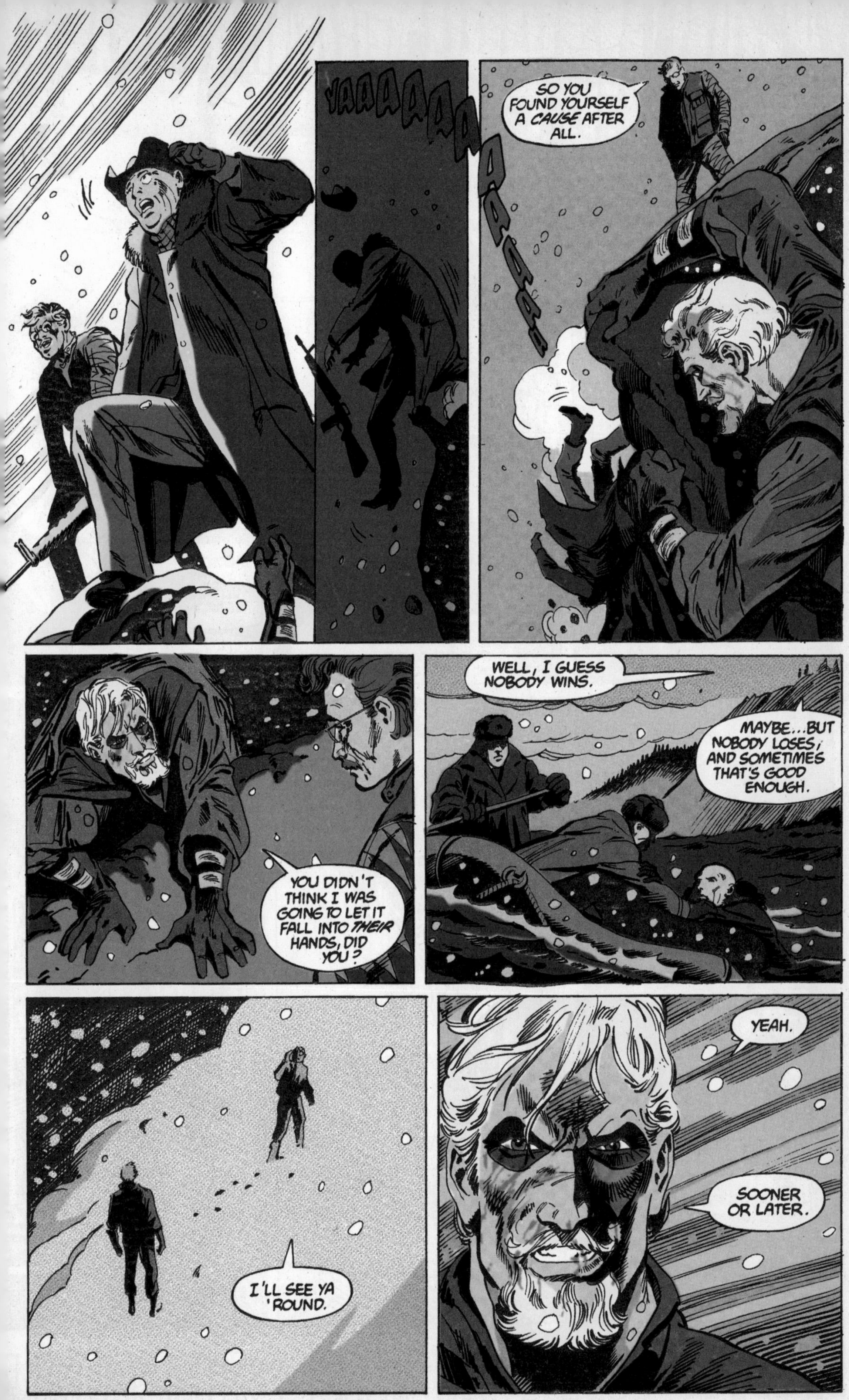
YAAAAAAAAAAAAA
SO YOU FOUND YOURSELF A CAUSE AFTER ALL.
YOU DIDN'T THINK I WAS GOING TO LET IT FALL INTO THEIR HANDS, DID YOU?
WELL, I GUESS NOBODY WINS.
MAYBE...BUT NOBODY LOSES, AND SOMETIMES THAT'S GOOD ENOUGH.
I'LL SEE YA 'ROUND.
YEAH.
SOONER OR LATER.

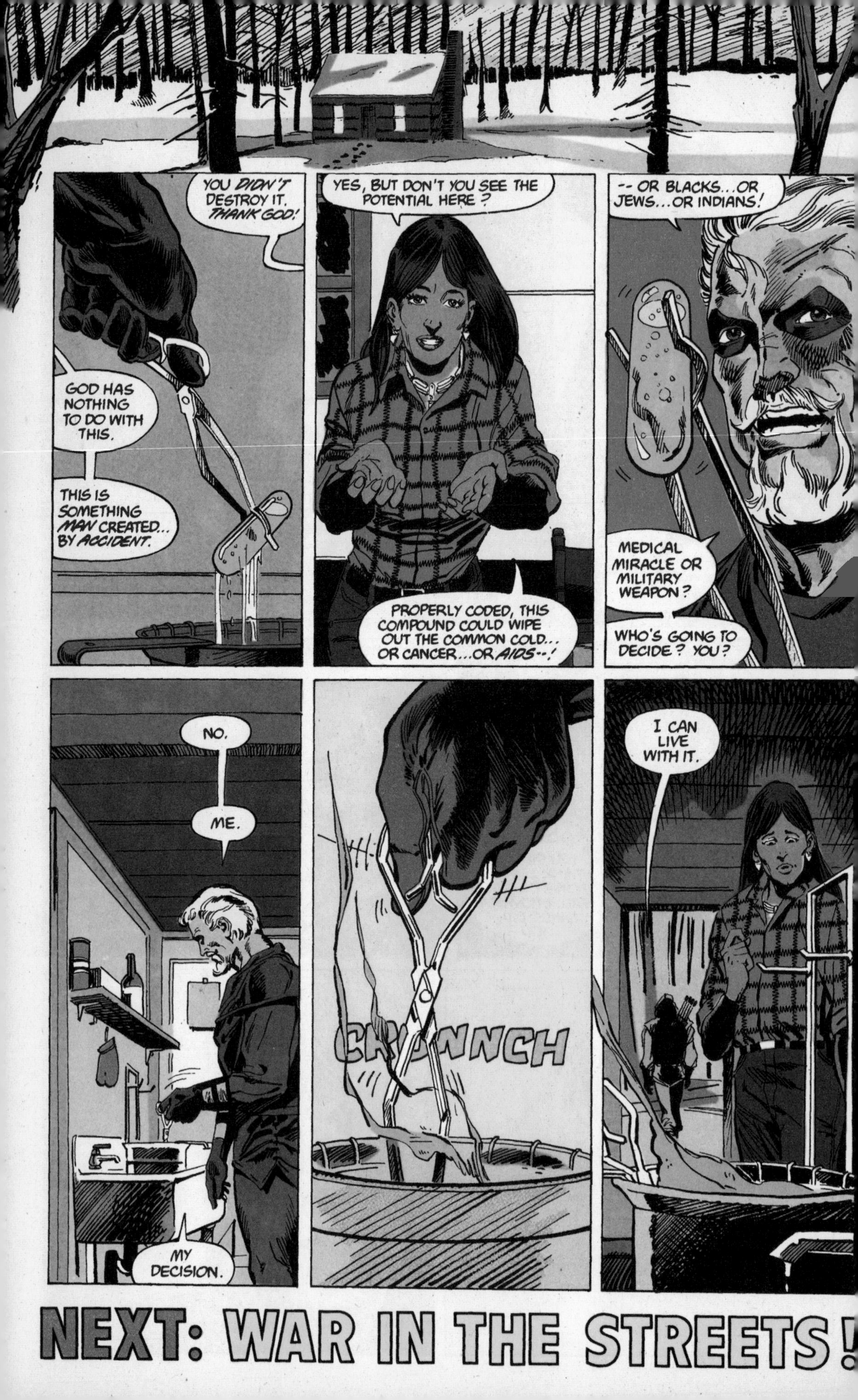
YOU DIDN'T DESTROY IT. THANK GOD!
GOD HAS NOTHING TO DO WITH THIS.
THIS IS SOMETHING MAN CREATED... BY ACCIDENT.
YES, BUT DON'T YOU SEE THE POTENTIAL HERE?
PROPERLY CODED, THIS COMPOUND COULD WIPE OUT THE COMMON COLD... OR CANCER...OR AIDS--!
-- OR BLACKS...OR JEWS...OR INDIANS!
MEDICAL MIRACLE OR MILITARY WEAPON?
WHO'S GOING TO DECIDE? YOU?
NO.
ME.
MY DECISION.
CRUNNCH
I CAN LIVE WITH IT.
NEXT: WAR IN THE STREETS!

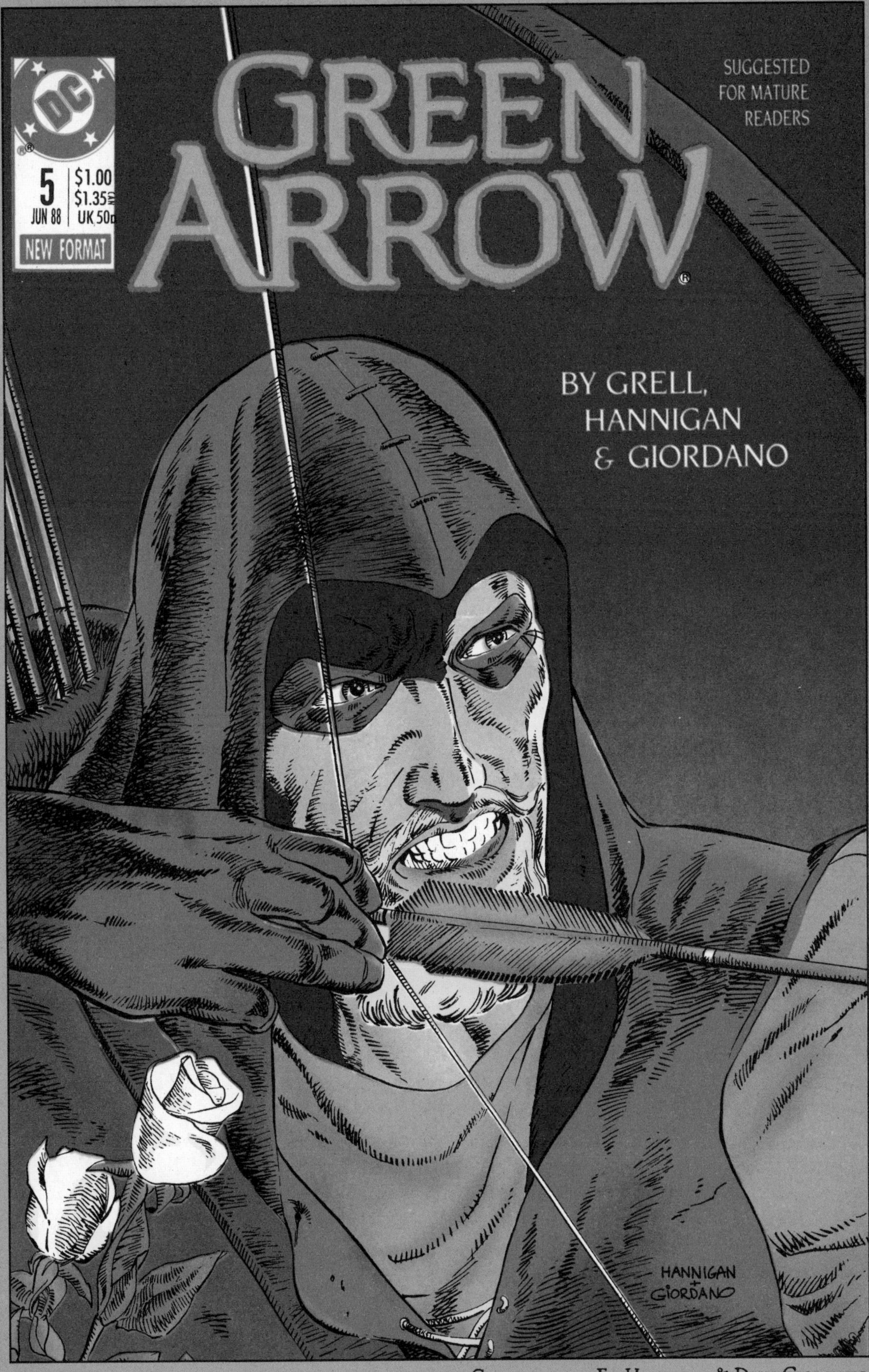

5
JUN 88
$1.00
$1.35
UK 50p
NEW FORMAT
GREEN ARROW
SUGGESTED FOR MATURE READERS
BY GRELL, HANNIGAN & GIORDANO
HANNIGAN + GIORDANO

Cover art by Ed Hannigan & Dick Giordano

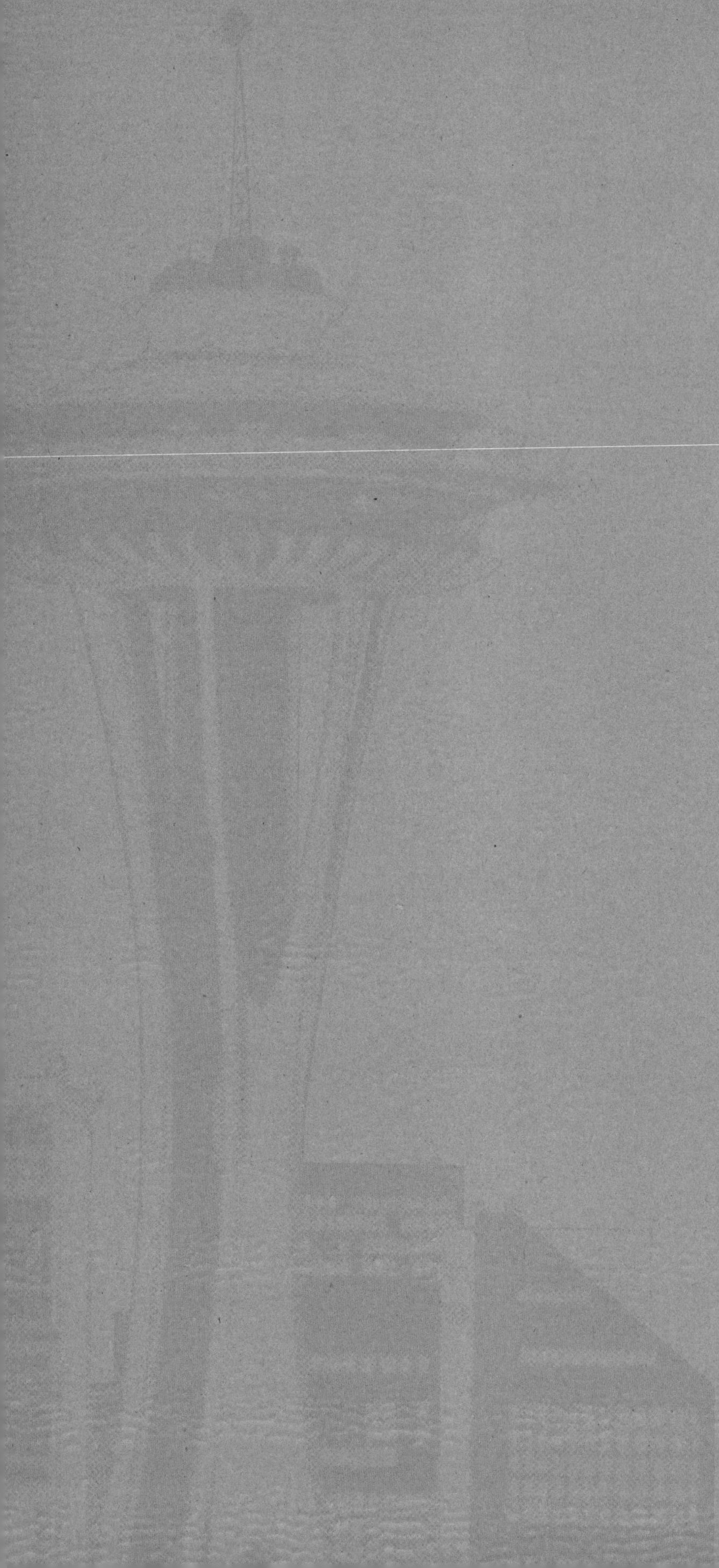

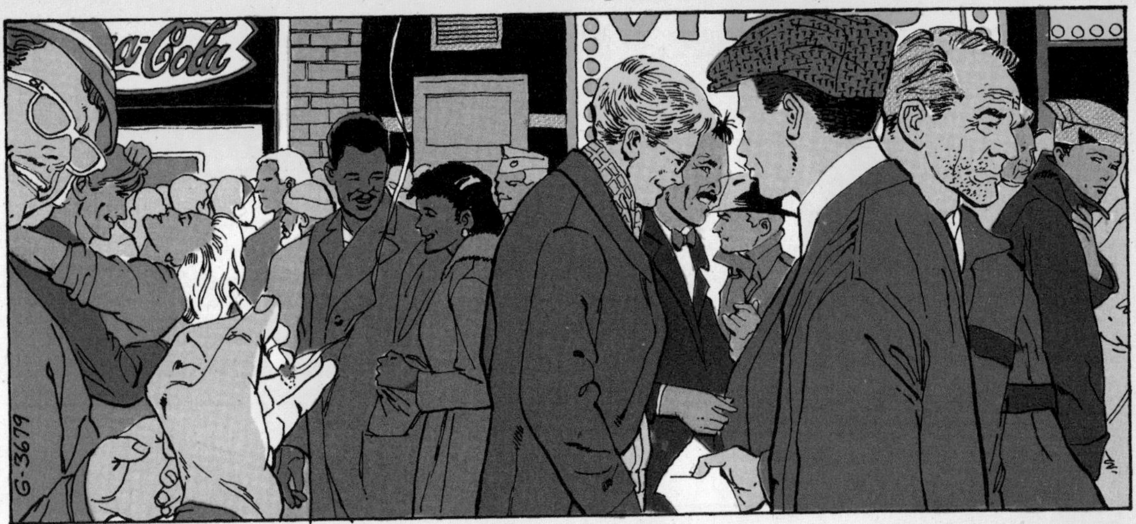
a-Cola
G-3679

IN SEATTLE, LIKE NEW YORK, BROADWAY COMES ALIVE AT NIGHT.

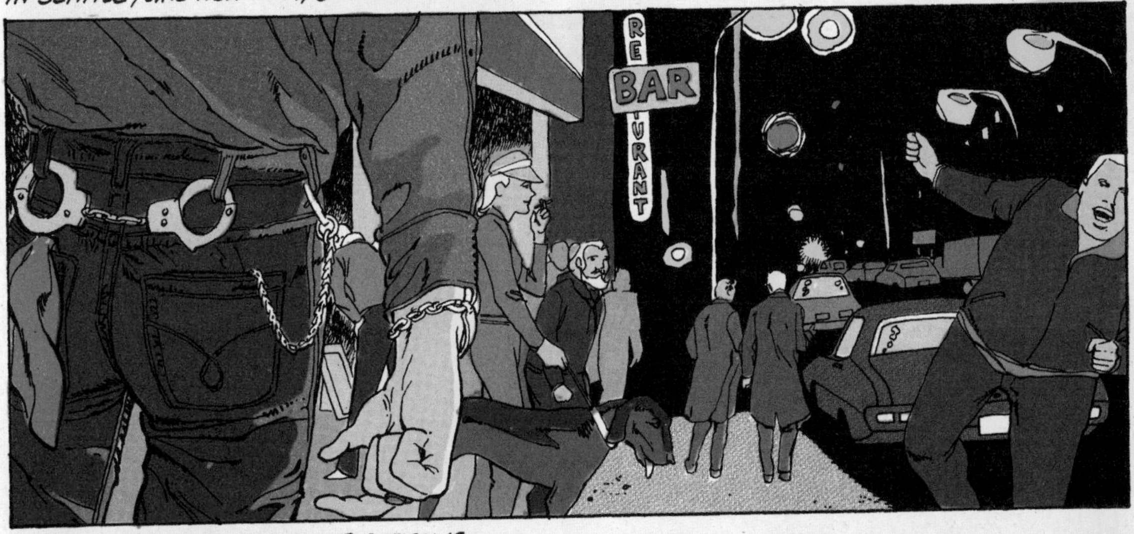
BAR
RESTAURANT

PEOPLE WANT TO BE WHERE THE ACTION IS...

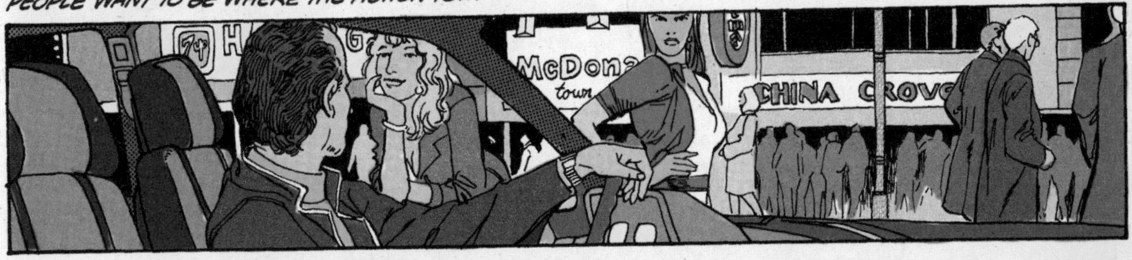
McDona
town
CHINA CROV

...AND THE ACTION IS ON THE STREET.

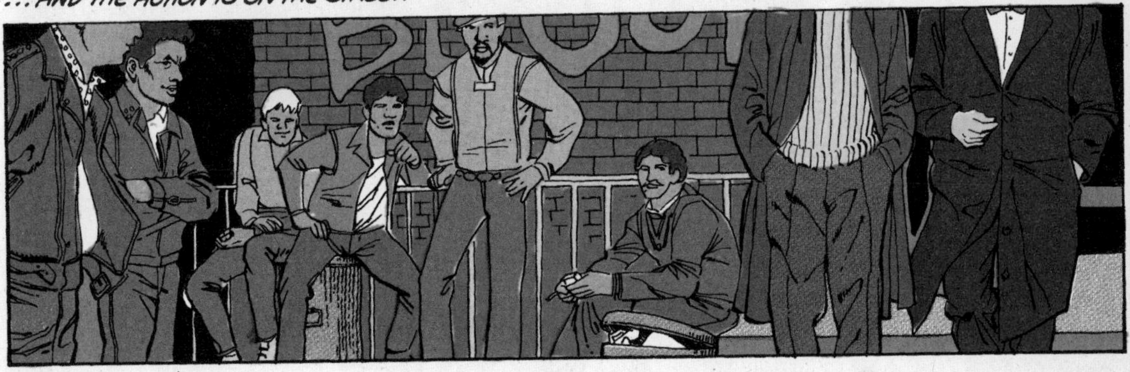

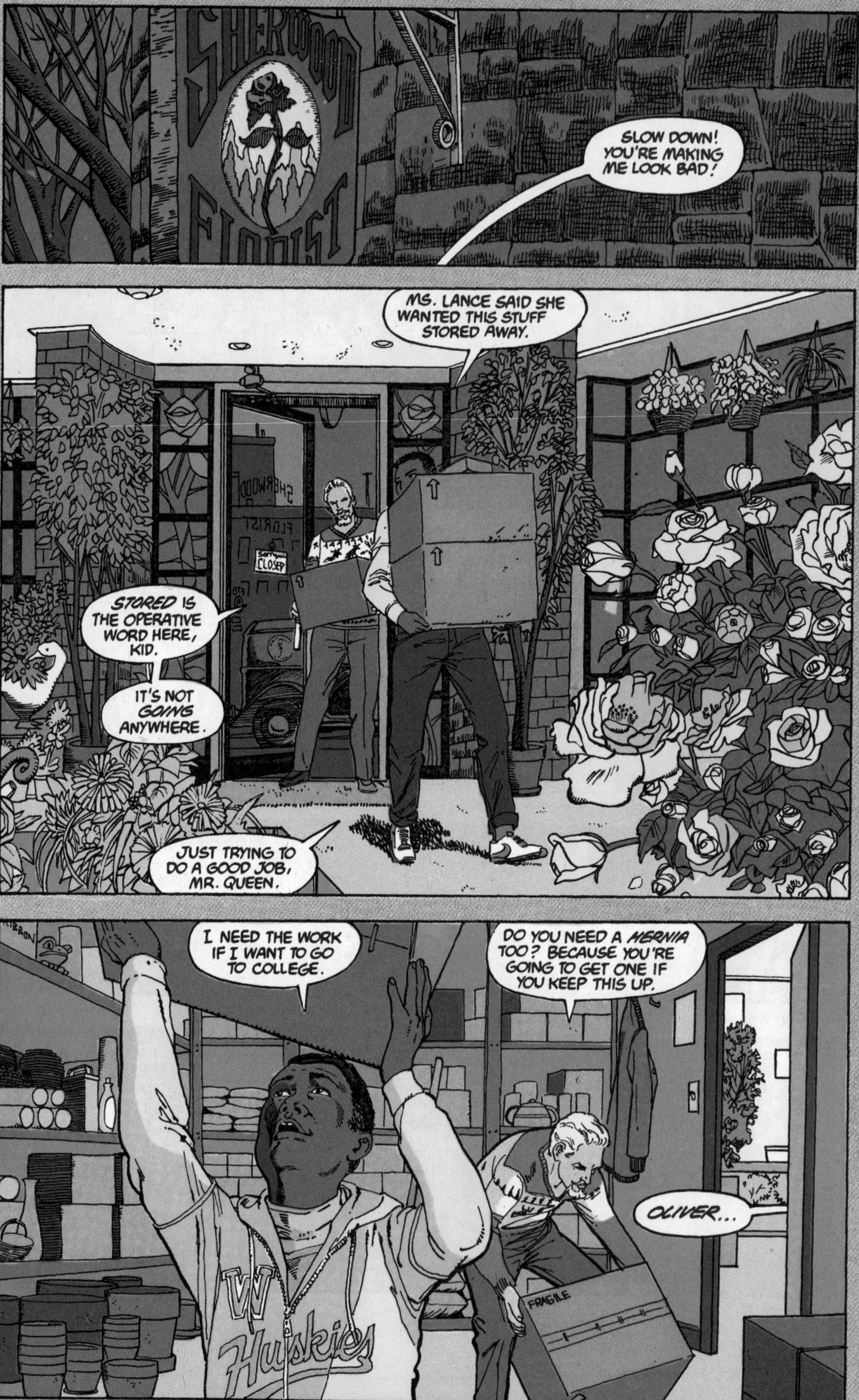
SHERWOOD FLORIST
SLOW DOWN! YOU'RE MAKING ME LOOK BAD!
MS. LANCE SAID SHE WANTED THIS STUFF STORED AWAY.
SHERWOOD FLORIST
SORRY CLOSED
STORED IS THE OPERATIVE WORD HERE, KID.
IT'S NOT GOING ANYWHERE.
JUST TRYING TO DO A GOOD JOB, MR. QUEEN.
I NEED THE WORK IF I WANT TO GO TO COLLEGE.
DO YOU NEED A HERNIA TOO? BECAUSE YOU'RE GOING TO GET ONE IF YOU KEEP THIS UP.
OLIVER...
FRAGILE
W Huskies

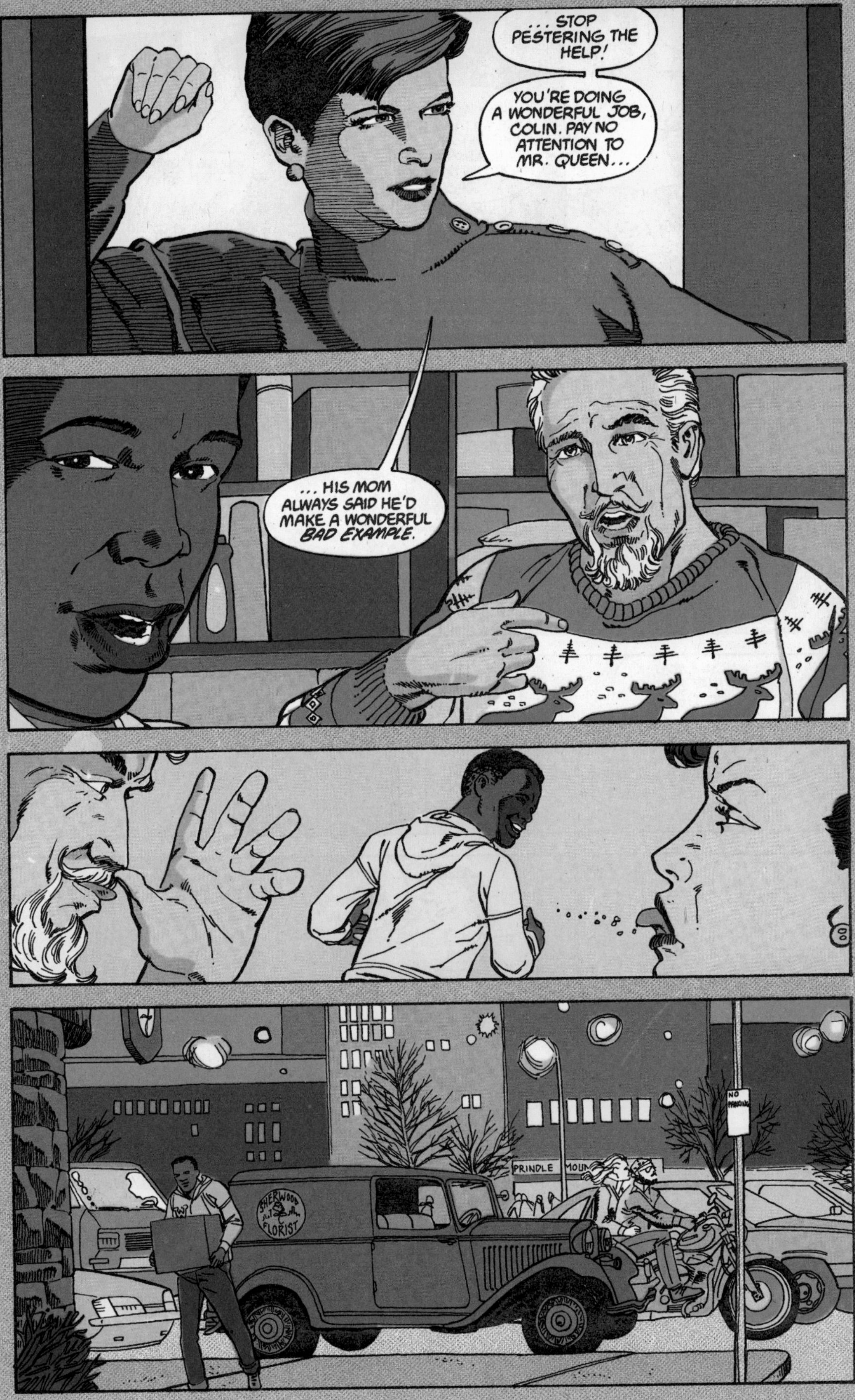
... STOP PESTERING THE HELP!
YOU'RE DOING A WONDERFUL JOB, COLIN. PAY NO ATTENTION TO MR. QUEEN...
... HIS MOM ALWAYS SAID HE'D MAKE A WONDERFUL BAD EXAMPLE.
SHERWOOD FLORIST
PRINDLE MOUN
NO PARKING

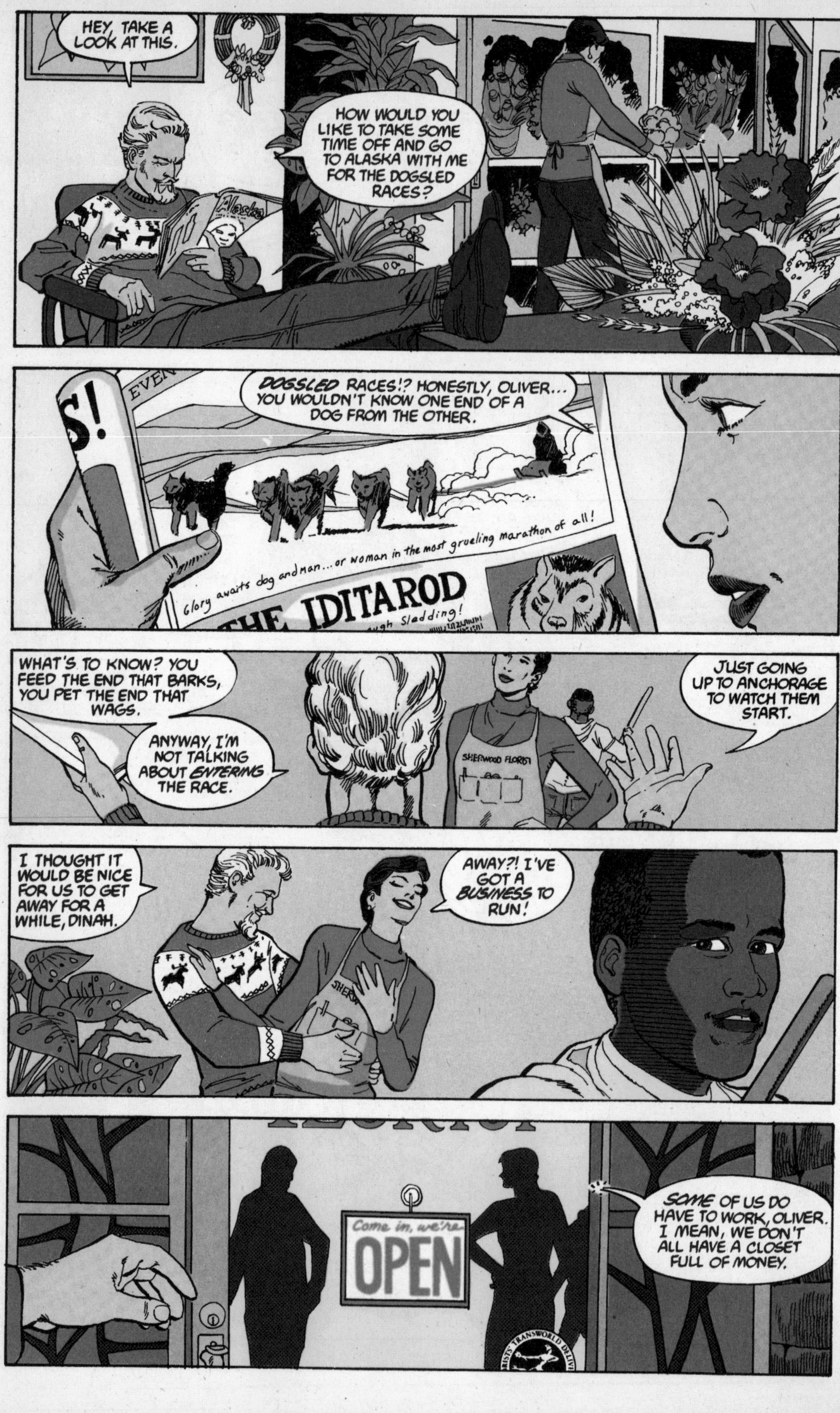

HEY, TAKE A LOOK AT THIS.
HOW WOULD YOU LIKE TO TAKE SOME TIME OFF AND GO TO ALASKA WITH ME FOR THE DOGSLED RACES?
Alaska
DOGSLED RACES!? HONESTLY, OLIVER... YOU WOULDN'T KNOW ONE END OF A DOG FROM THE OTHER.
Glory awaits dog and man... or woman in the most grueling marathon of all!
THE IDITAROD
WHAT'S TO KNOW? YOU FEED THE END THAT BARKS, YOU PET THE END THAT WAGS.
ANYWAY, I'M NOT TALKING ABOUT ENTERING THE RACE.
SHERWOOD FLORIST
JUST GOING UP TO ANCHORAGE TO WATCH THEM START.
I THOUGHT IT WOULD BE NICE FOR US TO GET AWAY FOR A WHILE, DINAH.
AWAY?! I'VE GOT A BUSINESS TO RUN!
Come in, we're OPEN
SOME OF US DO HAVE TO WORK, OLIVER. I MEAN, WE DON'T ALL HAVE A CLOSET FULL OF MONEY.

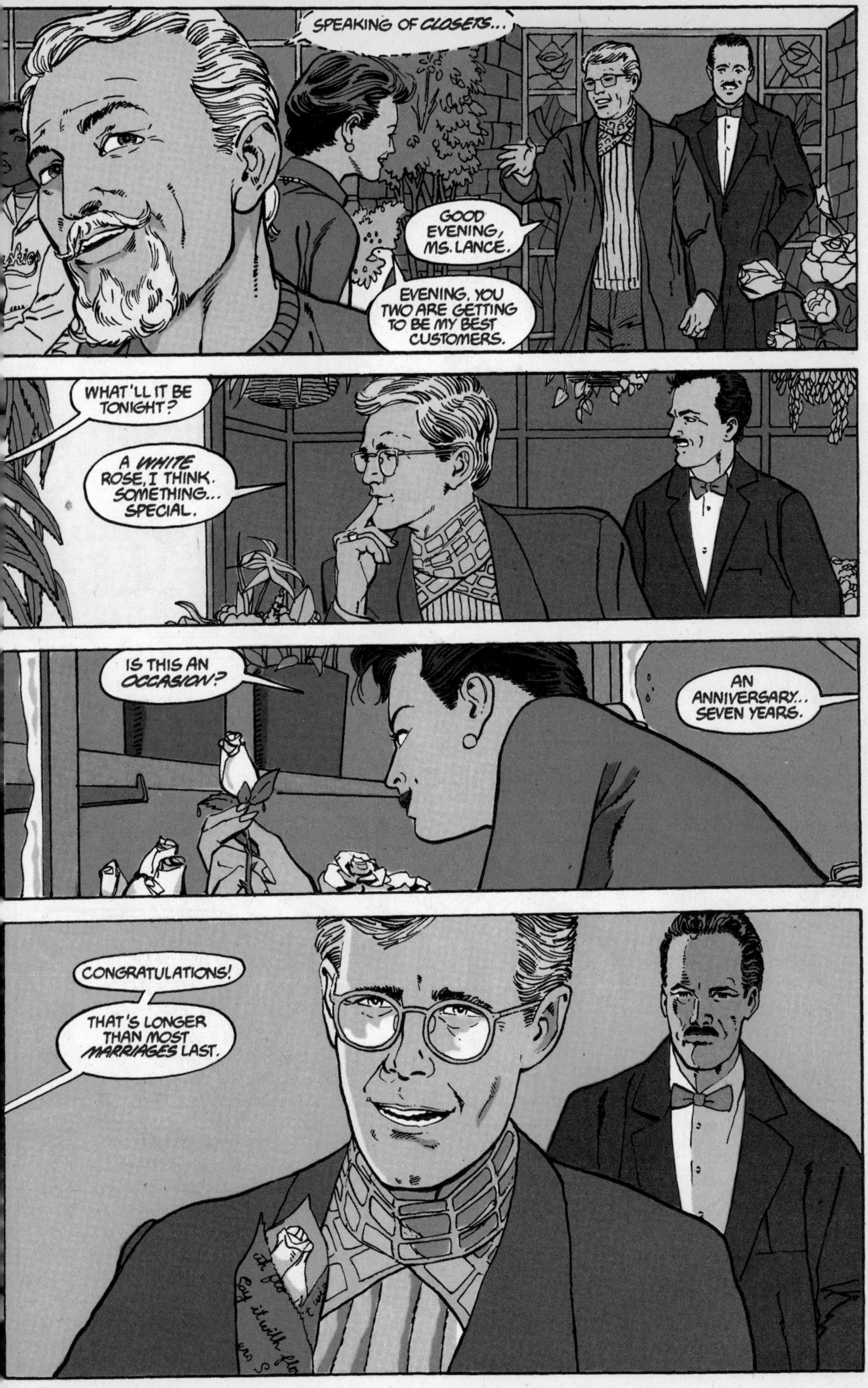
SPEAKING OF CLOSETS...
GOOD EVENING, MS. LANCE.
EVENING. YOU TWO ARE GETTING TO BE MY BEST CUSTOMERS.
WHAT'LL IT BE TONIGHT?
A WHITE ROSE, I THINK. SOMETHING... SPECIAL.
IS THIS AN OCCASION?
AN ANNIVERSARY... SEVEN YEARS.
CONGRATULATIONS!
THAT'S LONGER THAN MOST MARRIAGES LAST.

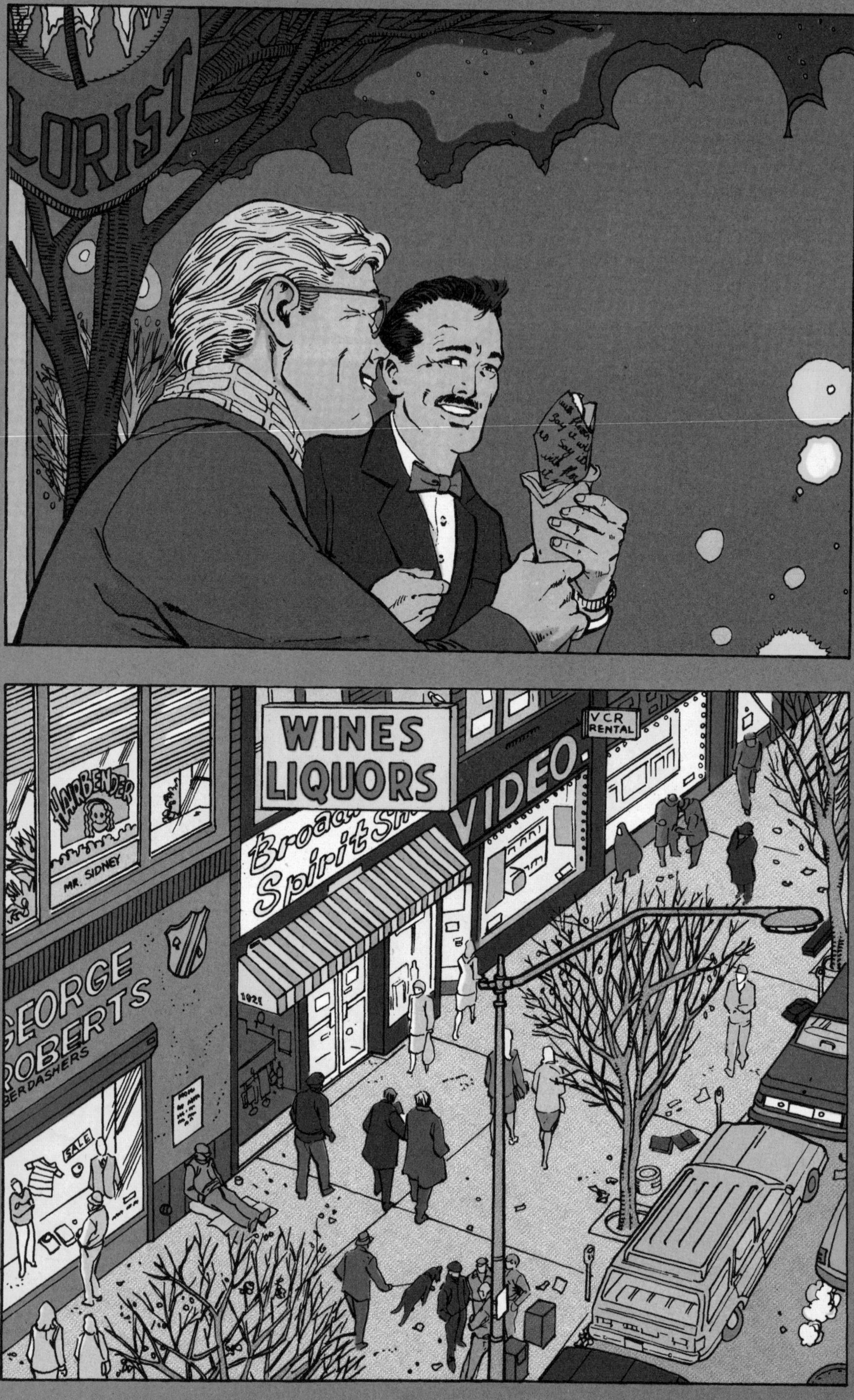
LORIST
WINES
LIQUORS
VCR
RENTAL
VIDEO.
HAIRBENDER
MR. SIDNEY
GEORGE
ROBERTS
BERDASHERS
SALE
1021

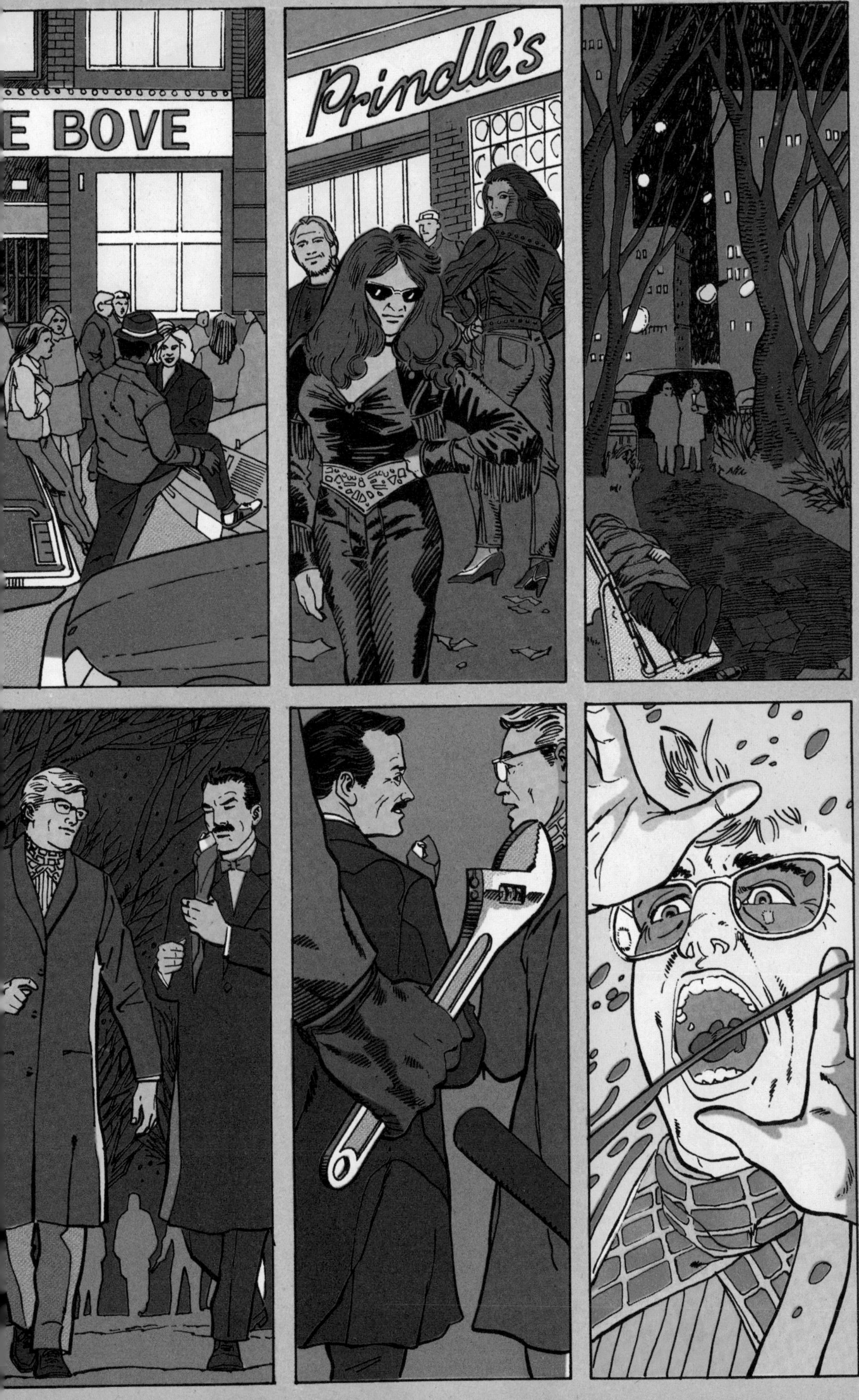
E BOVE
Prindle's

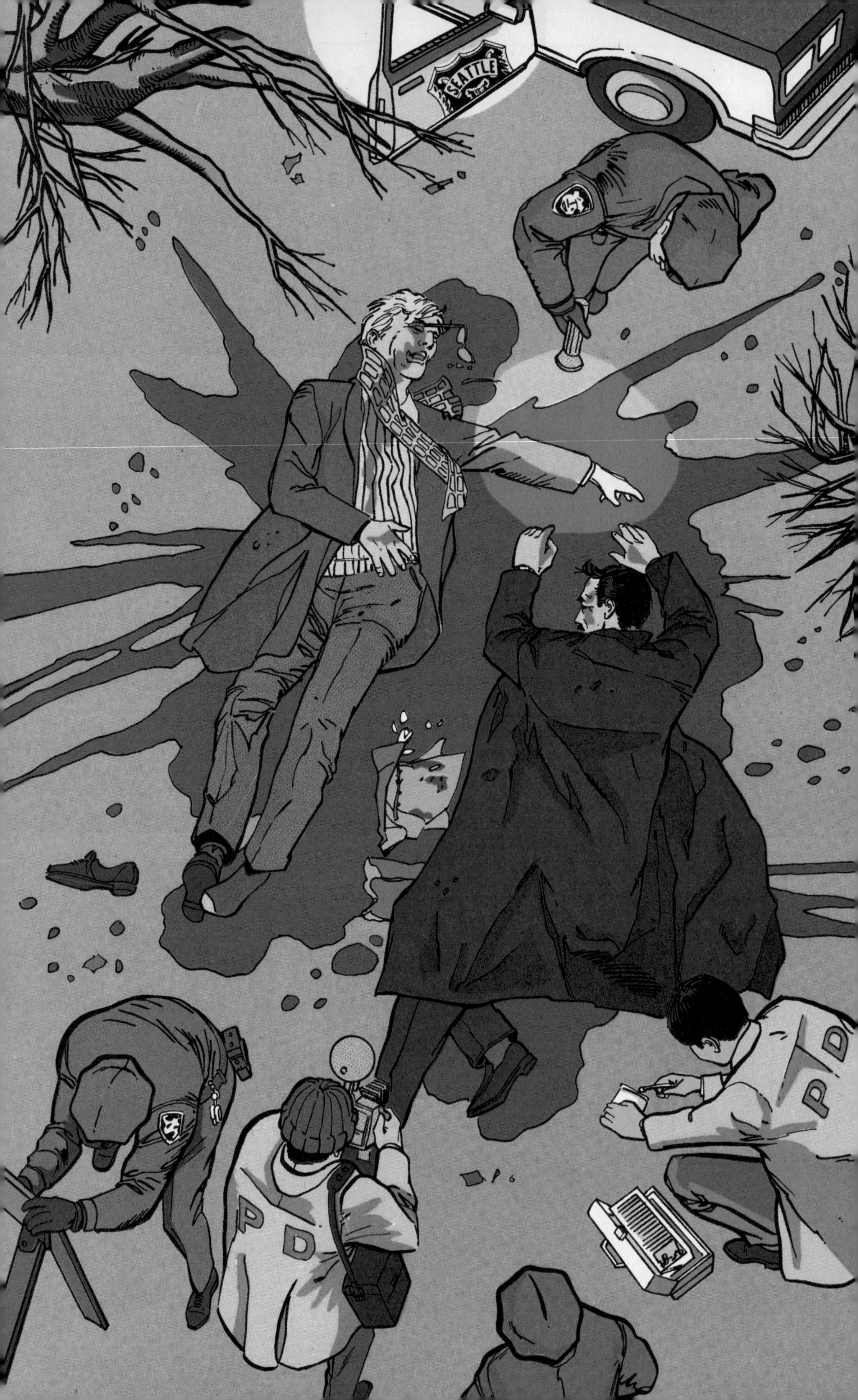
SEATTLE
PD
PD

GAUNTLET

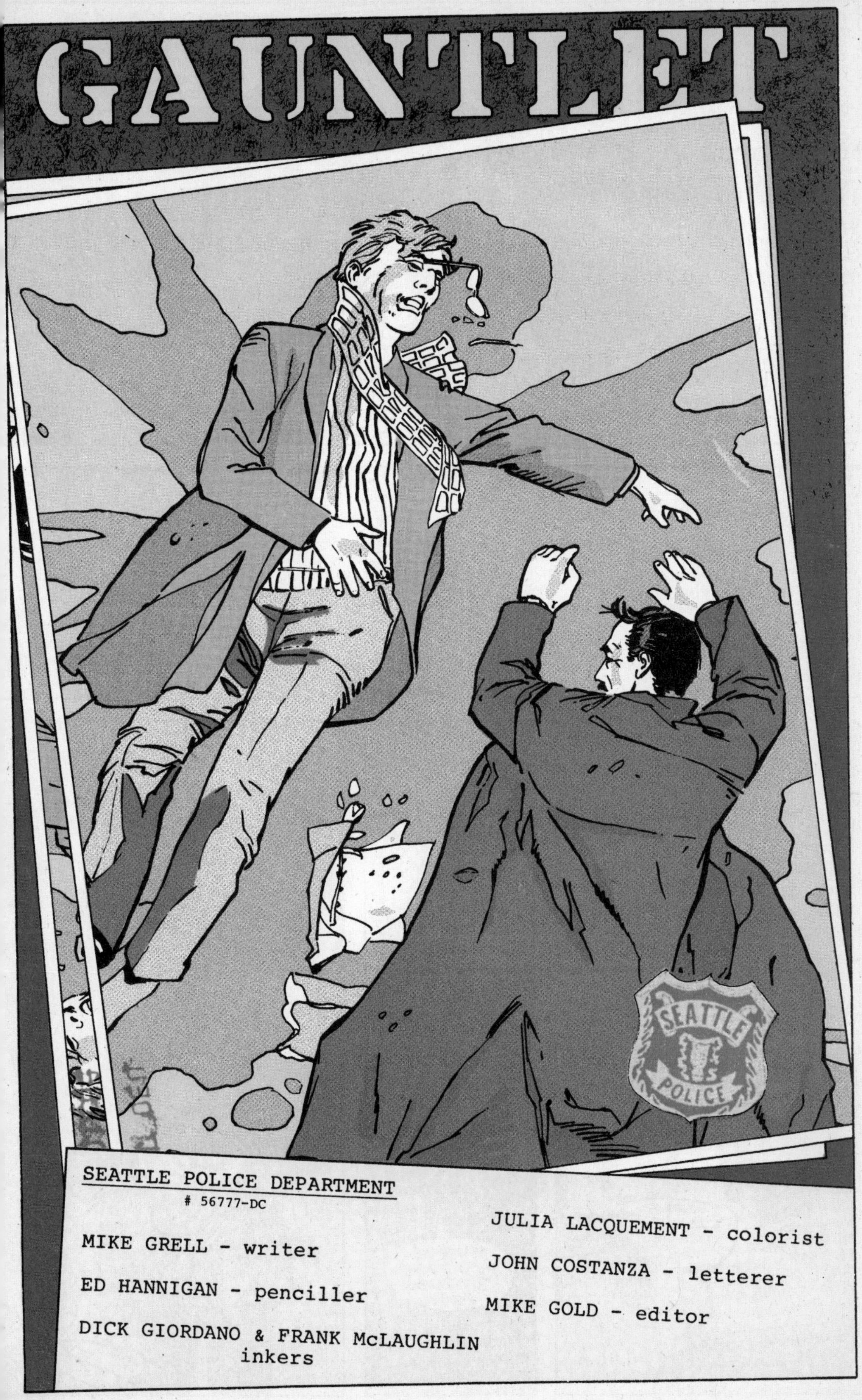

SEATTLE
POLICE

SEATTLE POLICE DEPARTMENT

56777-DC

MIKE GRELL - writer

ED HANNIGAN - penciller

DICK GIORDANO & FRANK McLAUGHLIN
inkers

JULIA LACQUEMENT - colorist

JOHN COSTANZA - letterer

MIKE GOLD - editor

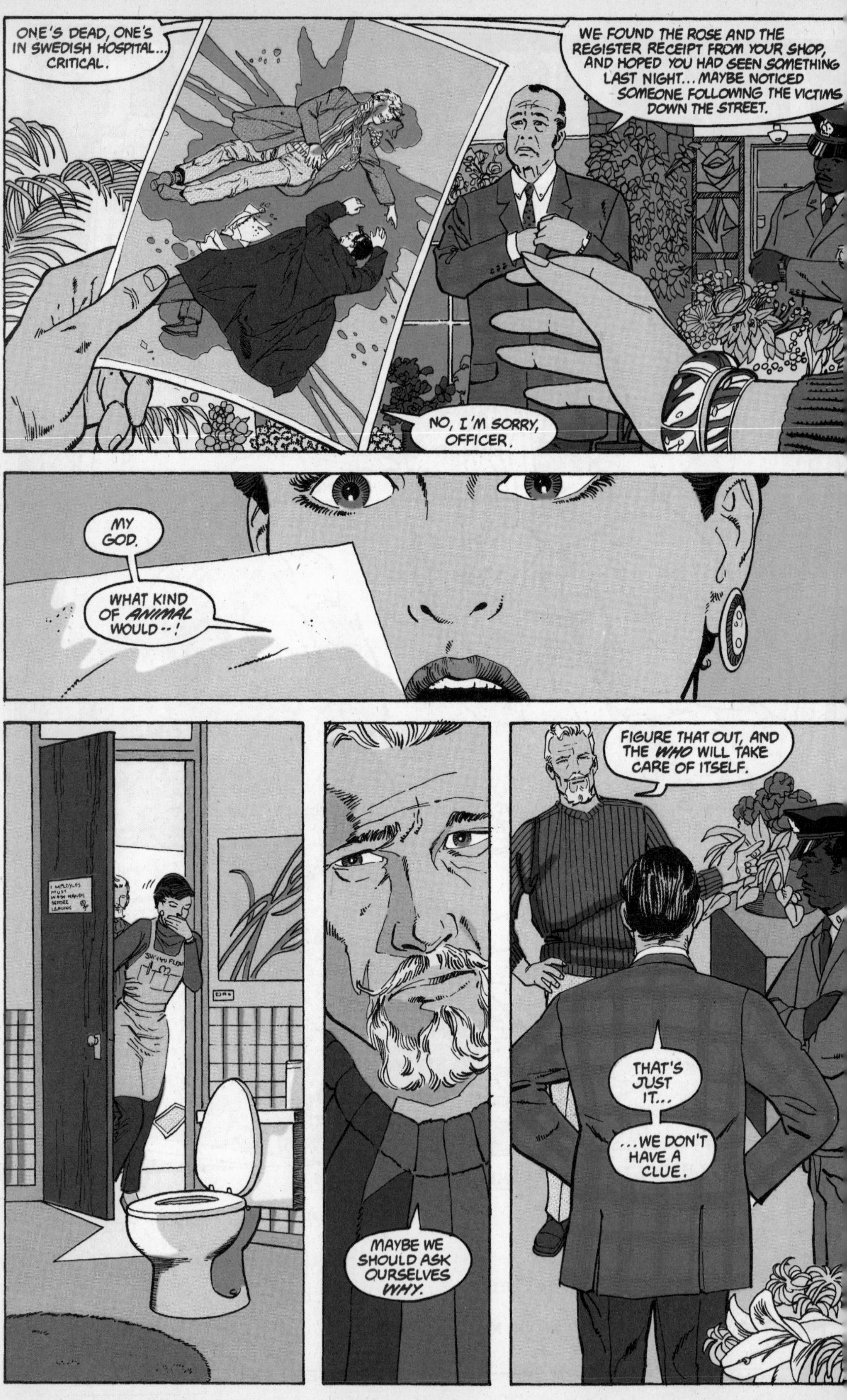
ONE'S DEAD, ONE'S IN SWEDISH HOSPITAL... CRITICAL.
WE FOUND THE ROSE AND THE REGISTER RECEIPT FROM YOUR SHOP, AND HOPED YOU HAD SEEN SOMETHING LAST NIGHT... MAYBE NOTICED SOMEONE FOLLOWING THE VICTIMS DOWN THE STREET.
NO, I'M SORRY, OFFICER.
MY GOD.
WHAT KIND OF ANIMAL WOULD--!
MAYBE WE SHOULD ASK OURSELVES WHY.
FIGURE THAT OUT, AND THE WHO WILL TAKE CARE OF ITSELF.
THAT'S JUST IT...
...WE DON'T HAVE A CLUE.

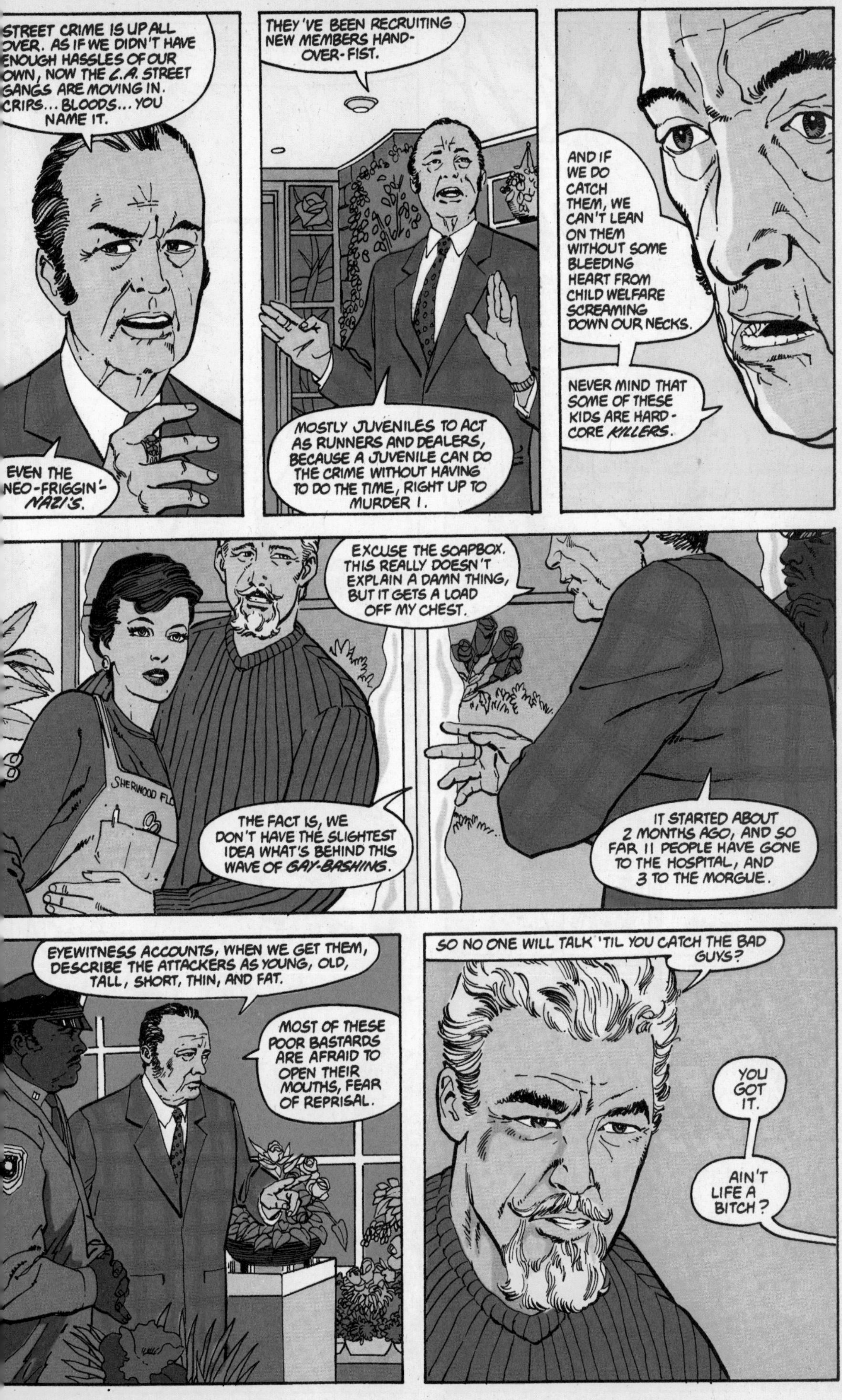
STREET CRIME IS UP ALL OVER. AS IF WE DIDN'T HAVE ENOUGH HASSLES OF OUR OWN, NOW THE L.A. STREET GANGS ARE MOVING IN. CRIPS... BLOODS... YOU NAME IT.
EVEN THE NEO-FRIGGIN'-NAZI'S.
THEY'VE BEEN RECRUITING NEW MEMBERS HAND-OVER-FIST.
MOSTLY JUVENILES TO ACT AS RUNNERS AND DEALERS, BECAUSE A JUVENILE CAN DO THE CRIME WITHOUT HAVING TO DO THE TIME, RIGHT UP TO MURDER 1.
AND IF WE DO CATCH THEM, WE CAN'T LEAN ON THEM WITHOUT SOME BLEEDING HEART FROM CHILD WELFARE SCREAMING DOWN OUR NECKS.
NEVER MIND THAT SOME OF THESE KIDS ARE HARD-CORE KILLERS.
EXCUSE THE SOAPBOX. THIS REALLY DOESN'T EXPLAIN A DAMN THING, BUT IT GETS A LOAD OFF MY CHEST.
SHERWOOD FL
THE FACT IS, WE DON'T HAVE THE SLIGHTEST IDEA WHAT'S BEHIND THIS WAVE OF GAY-BASHING.
IT STARTED ABOUT 2 MONTHS AGO, AND SO FAR 11 PEOPLE HAVE GONE TO THE HOSPITAL, AND 3 TO THE MORGUE.
EYEWITNESS ACCOUNTS, WHEN WE GET THEM, DESCRIBE THE ATTACKERS AS YOUNG, OLD, TALL, SHORT, THIN, AND FAT.
MOST OF THESE POOR BASTARDS ARE AFRAID TO OPEN THEIR MOUTHS, FEAR OF REPRISAL.
SO NO ONE WILL TALK 'TIL YOU CATCH THE BAD GUYS?
YOU GOT IT.
AIN'T LIFE A BITCH?

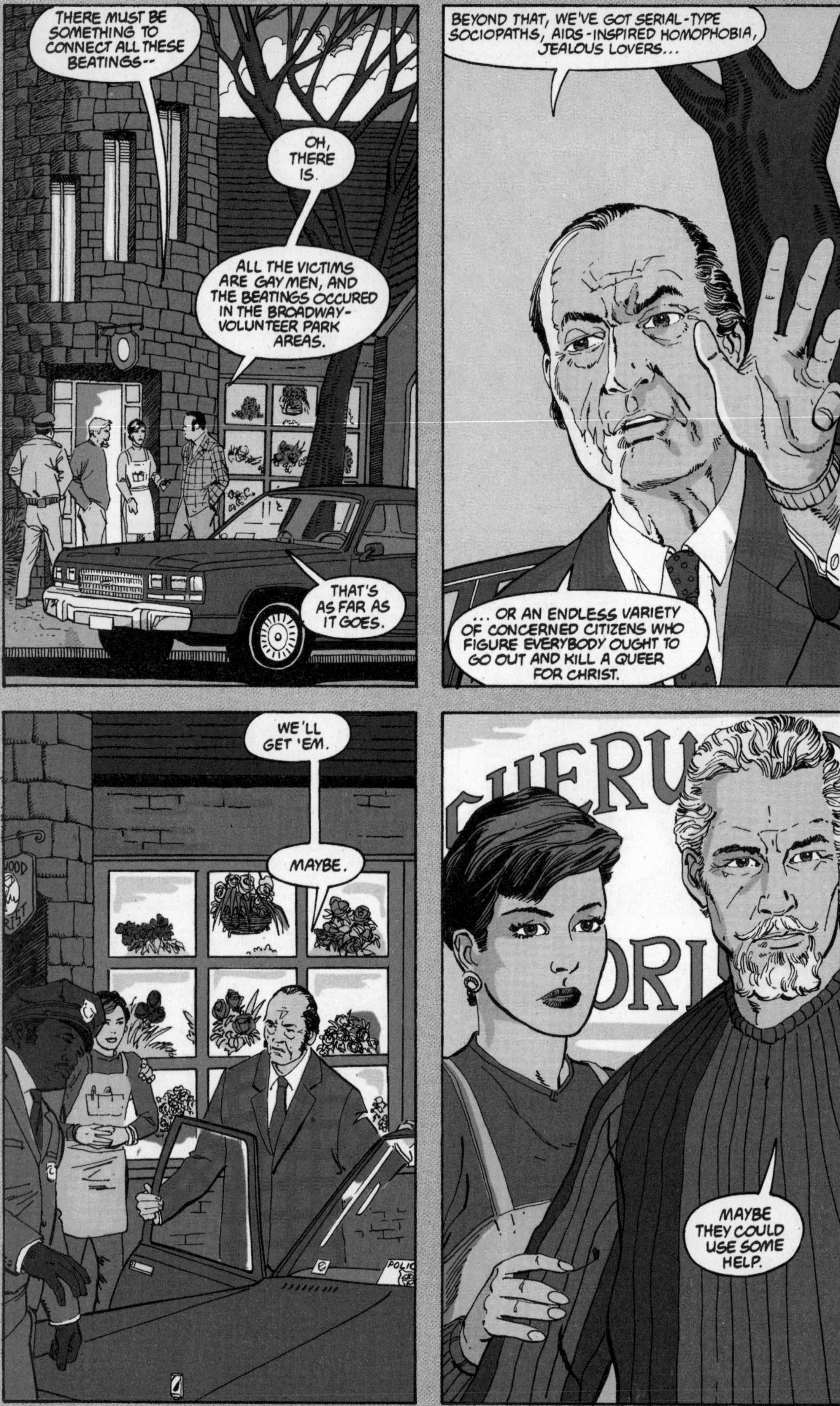
THERE MUST BE SOMETHING TO CONNECT ALL THESE BEATINGS--
OH, THERE IS.
ALL THE VICTIMS ARE GAY MEN, AND THE BEATINGS OCCURED IN THE BROADWAY-VOLUNTEER PARK AREAS.
THAT'S AS FAR AS IT GOES.
BEYOND THAT, WE'VE GOT SERIAL-TYPE SOCIOPATHS, AIDS-INSPIRED HOMOPHOBIA, JEALOUS LOVERS...
... OR AN ENDLESS VARIETY OF CONCERNED CITIZENS WHO FIGURE EVERYBODY OUGHT TO GO OUT AND KILL A QUEER FOR CHRIST.
WE'LL GET 'EM.
MAYBE.
MAYBE THEY COULD USE SOME HELP.

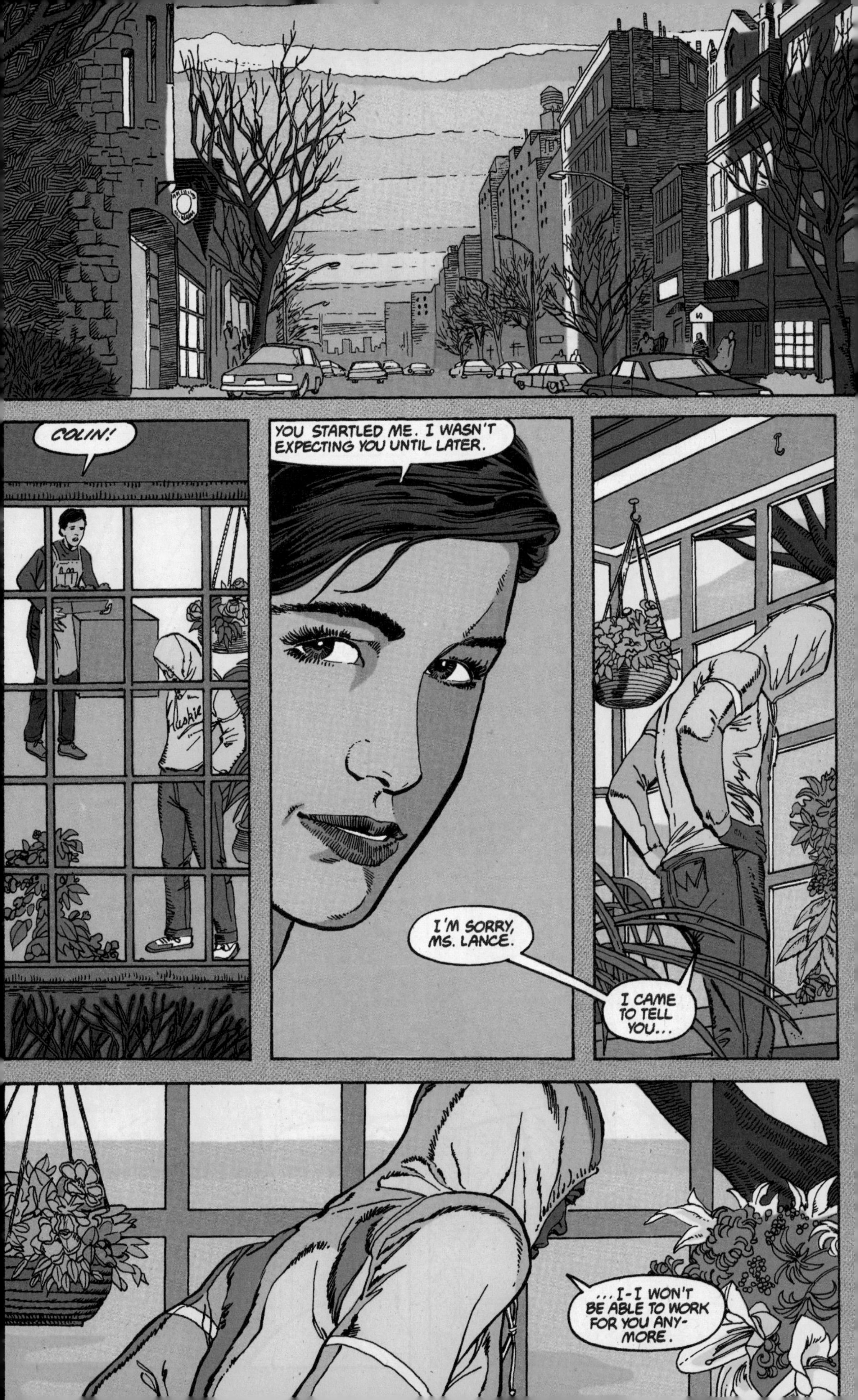
COLIN!
YOU STARTLED ME. I WASN'T EXPECTING YOU UNTIL LATER.
I'M SORRY, MS. LANCE.
I CAME TO TELL YOU...
...I-I WON'T BE ABLE TO WORK FOR YOU ANY-MORE.

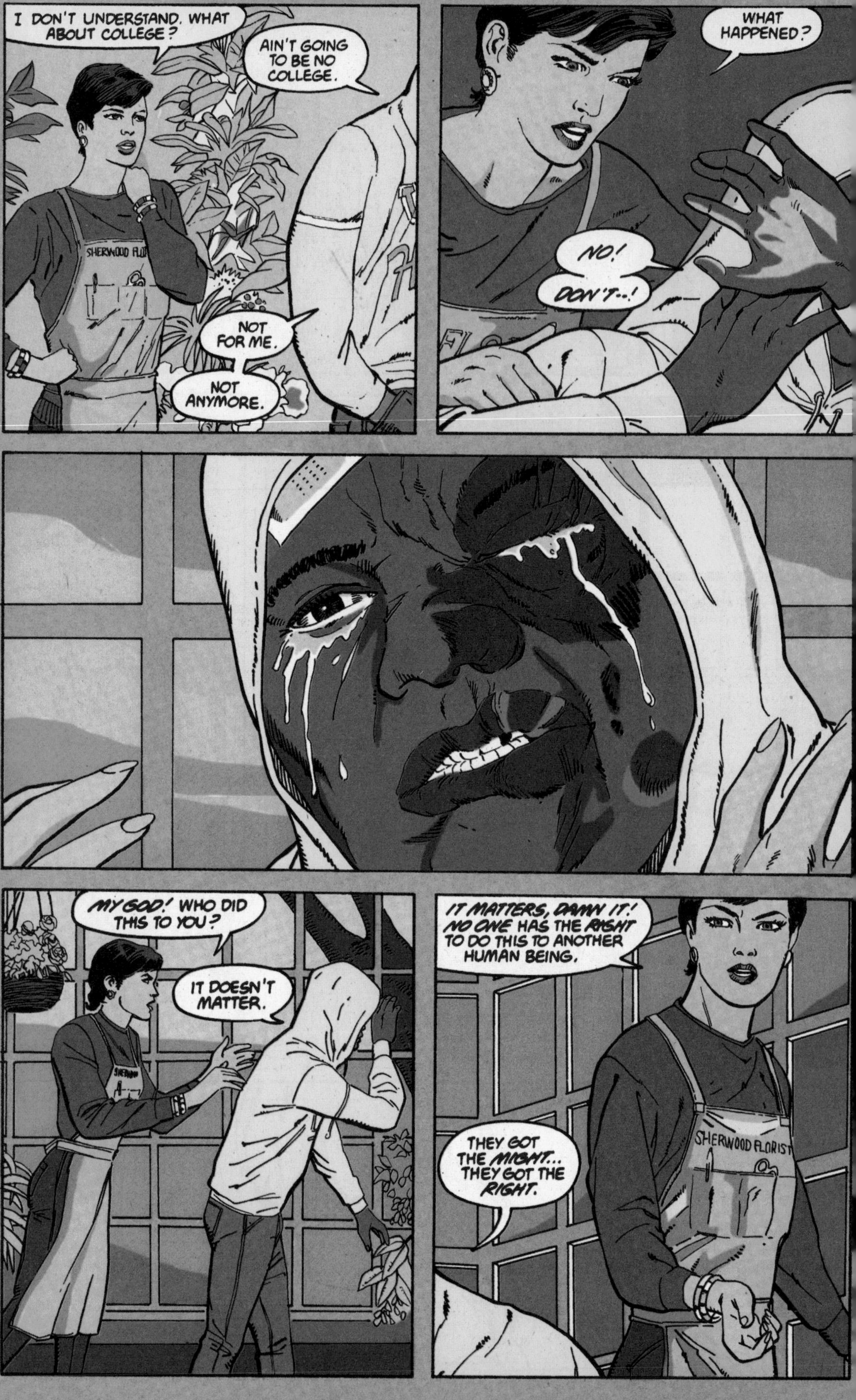
I DON'T UNDERSTAND. WHAT ABOUT COLLEGE?
AIN'T GOING TO BE NO COLLEGE.
NOT FOR ME.
NOT ANYMORE.
WHAT HAPPENED?
NO!
DON'T--!
MY GOD! WHO DID THIS TO YOU?
IT DOESN'T MATTER.
IT MATTERS, DAMN IT! NO ONE HAS THE RIGHT TO DO THIS TO ANOTHER HUMAN BEING.
THEY GOT THE MIGHT... THEY GOT THE RIGHT.

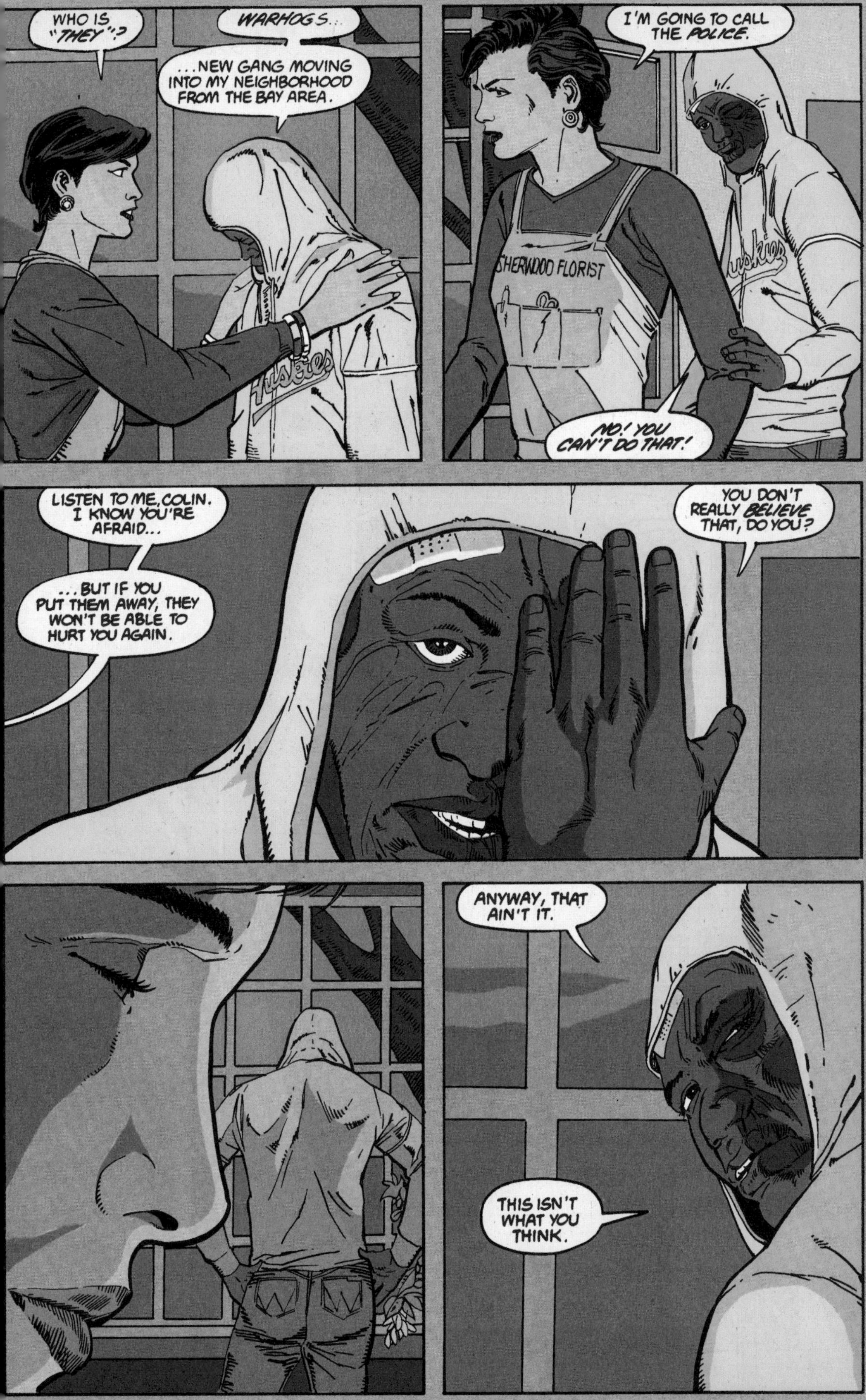
WHO IS "THEY"?
WARHOGS...
...NEW GANG MOVING INTO MY NEIGHBORHOOD FROM THE BAY AREA.
I'M GOING TO CALL THE POLICE.
SHERWOOD FLORIST
NO! YOU CAN'T DO THAT!
LISTEN TO ME, COLIN. I KNOW YOU'RE AFRAID...
...BUT IF YOU PUT THEM AWAY, THEY WON'T BE ABLE TO HURT YOU AGAIN.
YOU DON'T REALLY BELIEVE THAT, DO YOU?
ANYWAY, THAT AIN'T IT.
THIS ISN'T WHAT YOU THINK.

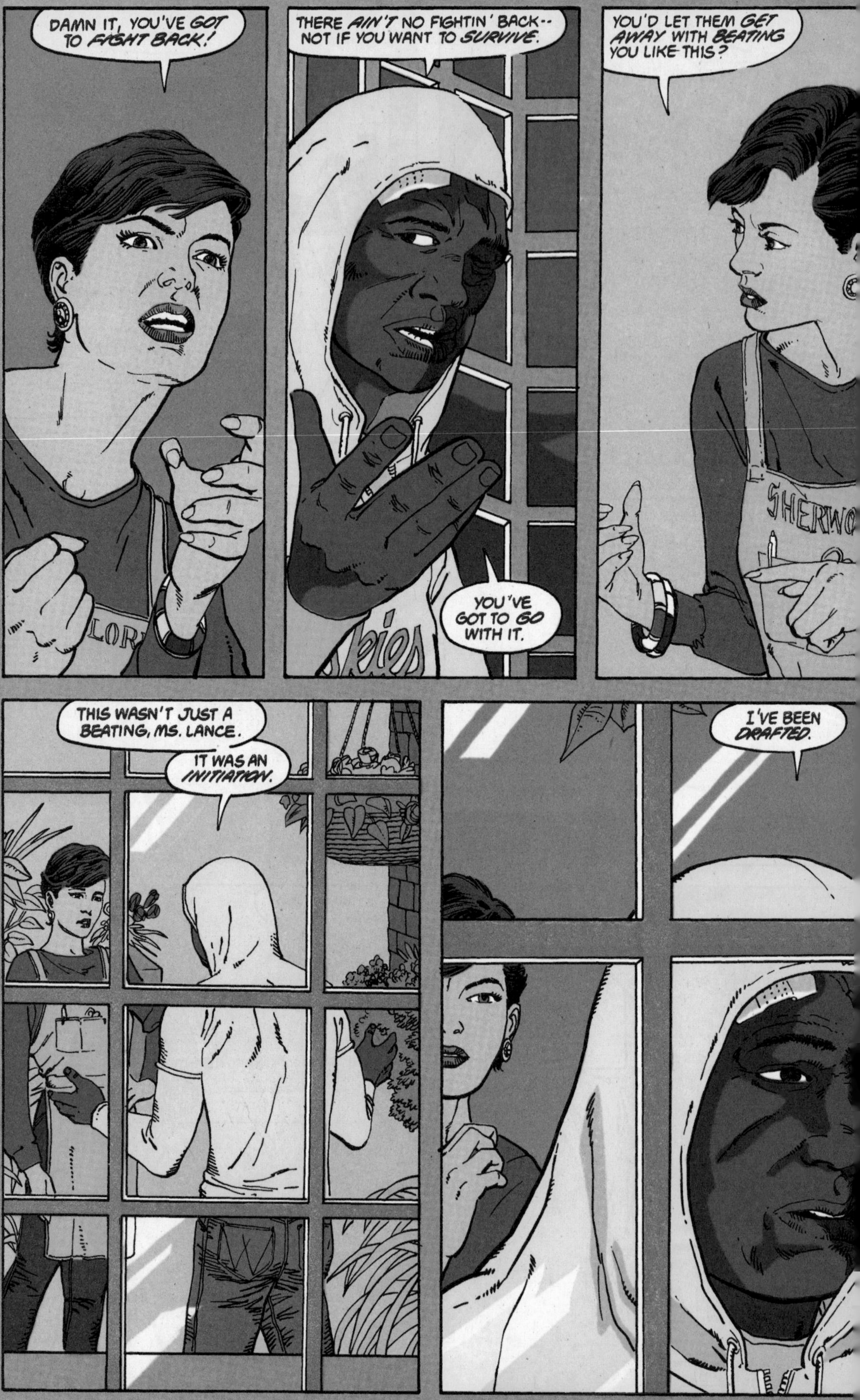
DAMN IT, YOU'VE GOT TO FIGHT BACK!
THERE AIN'T NO FIGHTIN' BACK-- NOT IF YOU WANT TO SURVIVE.
YOU'VE GOT TO GO WITH IT.
YOU'D LET THEM GET AWAY WITH BEATING YOU LIKE THIS?
SHERWO
THIS WASN'T JUST A BEATING, MS. LANCE.
IT WAS AN INITIATION.
I'VE BEEN DRAFTED.

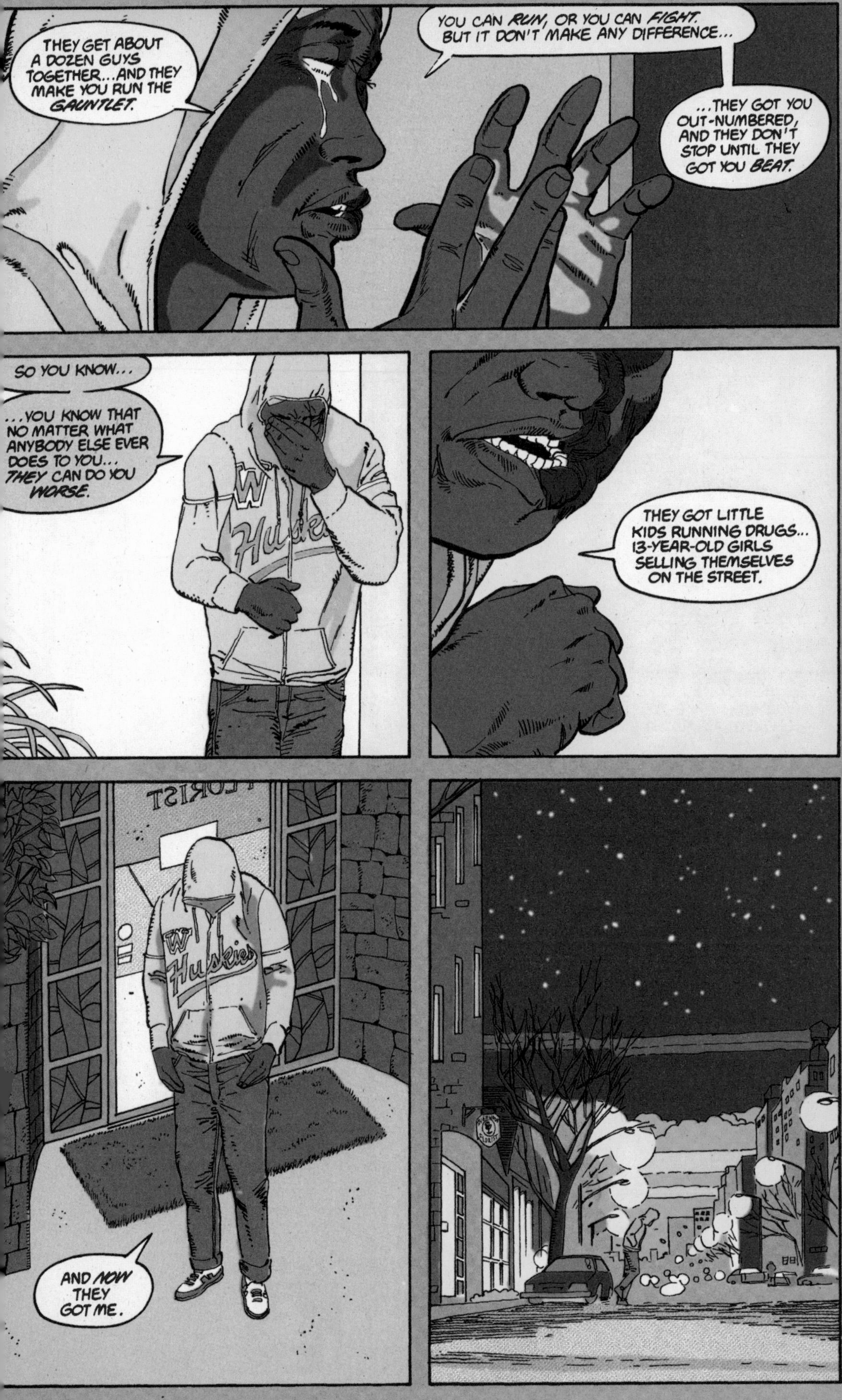
THEY GET ABOUT A DOZEN GUYS TOGETHER...AND THEY MAKE YOU RUN THE GAUNTLET.
YOU CAN RUN, OR YOU CAN FIGHT. BUT IT DON'T MAKE ANY DIFFERENCE...
...THEY GOT YOU OUT-NUMBERED, AND THEY DON'T STOP UNTIL THEY GOT YOU BEAT.
SO YOU KNOW...
...YOU KNOW THAT NO MATTER WHAT ANYBODY ELSE EVER DOES TO YOU... THEY CAN DO YOU WORSE.
THEY GOT LITTLE KIDS RUNNING DRUGS... 13-YEAR-OLD GIRLS SELLING THEMSELVES ON THE STREET.
AND NOW THEY GOT ME.

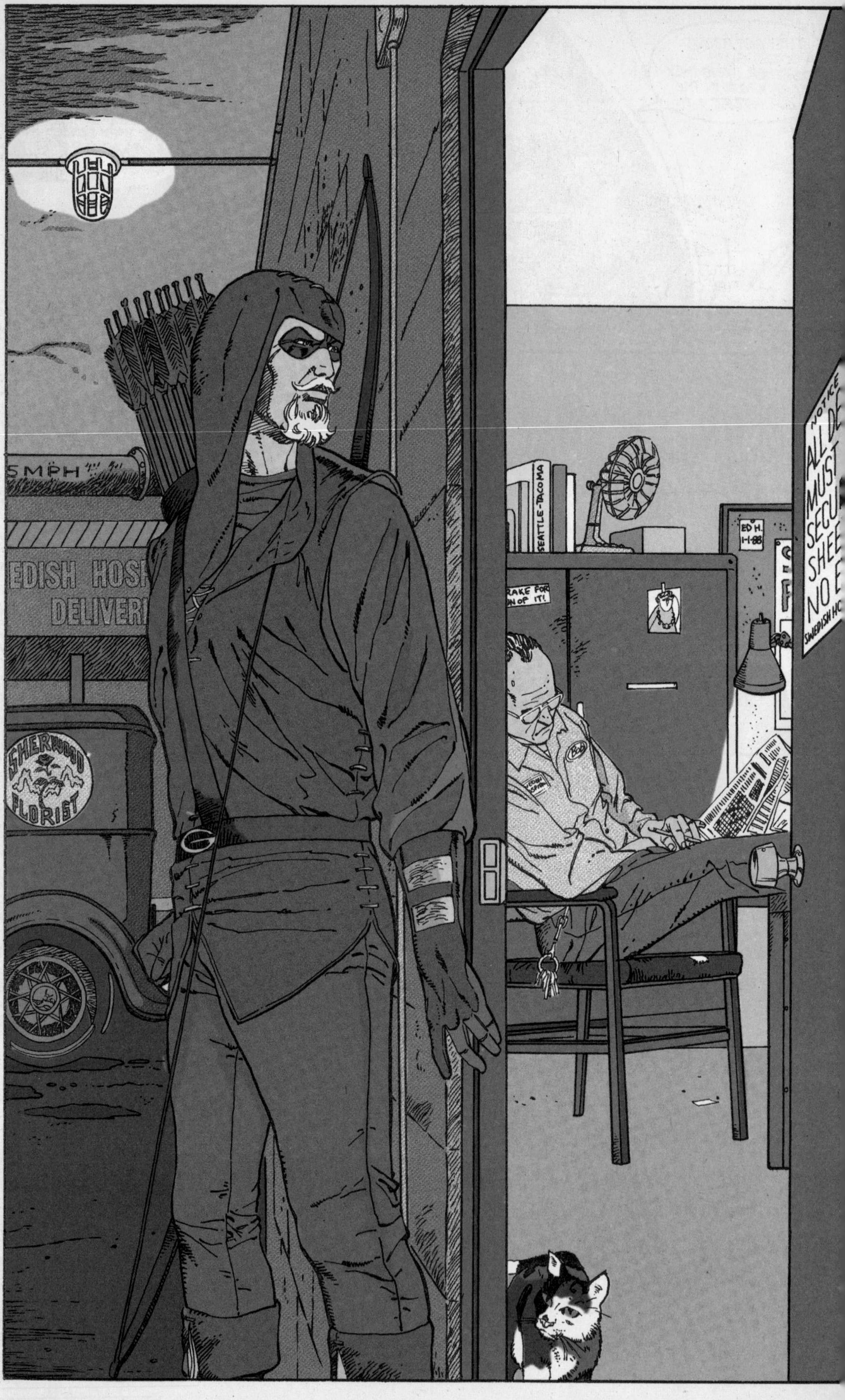
5MPH
SHERWOOD
FLORIST
SEATTLE-TACOMA
ED H.
1-1-88
NOTICE

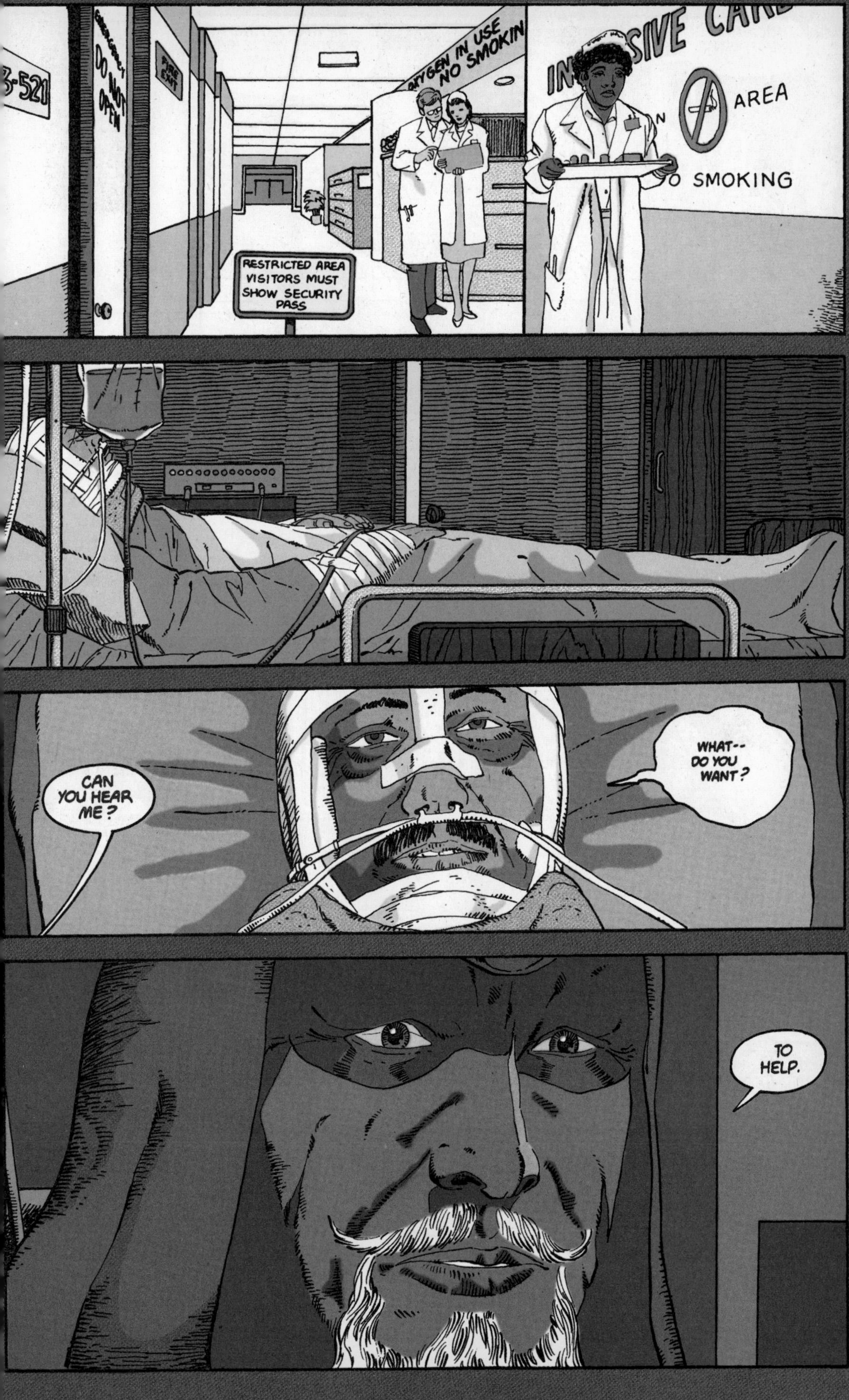
DO NOT OPEN
FIRE EXIT
OXYGEN IN USE
NO SMOKIN
AREA
O SMOKING
RESTRICTED AREA
VISITORS MUST
SHOW SECURITY
PASS
CAN YOU HEAR ME?
WHAT-- DO YOU WANT?
TO HELP.

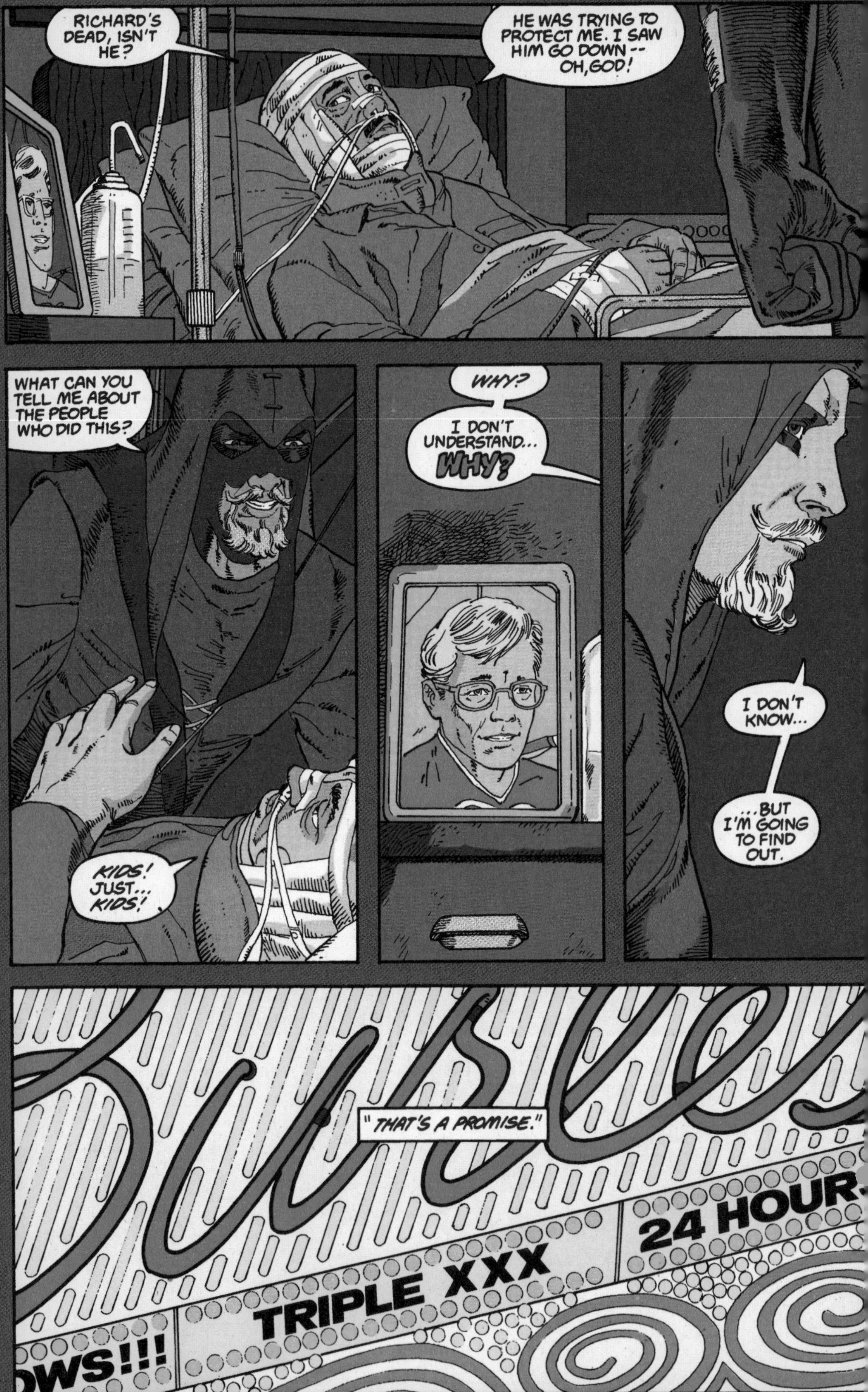
RICHARD'S DEAD, ISN'T HE?
HE WAS TRYING TO PROTECT ME. I SAW HIM GO DOWN -- OH, GOD!
WHAT CAN YOU TELL ME ABOUT THE PEOPLE WHO DID THIS?
KIDS! JUST... KIDS!
WHY?
I DON'T UNDERSTAND... WHY?
I DON'T KNOW...
...BUT I'M GOING TO FIND OUT.
"THAT'S A PROMISE."
24 HOUR
TRIPLE XXX
OWS!!!

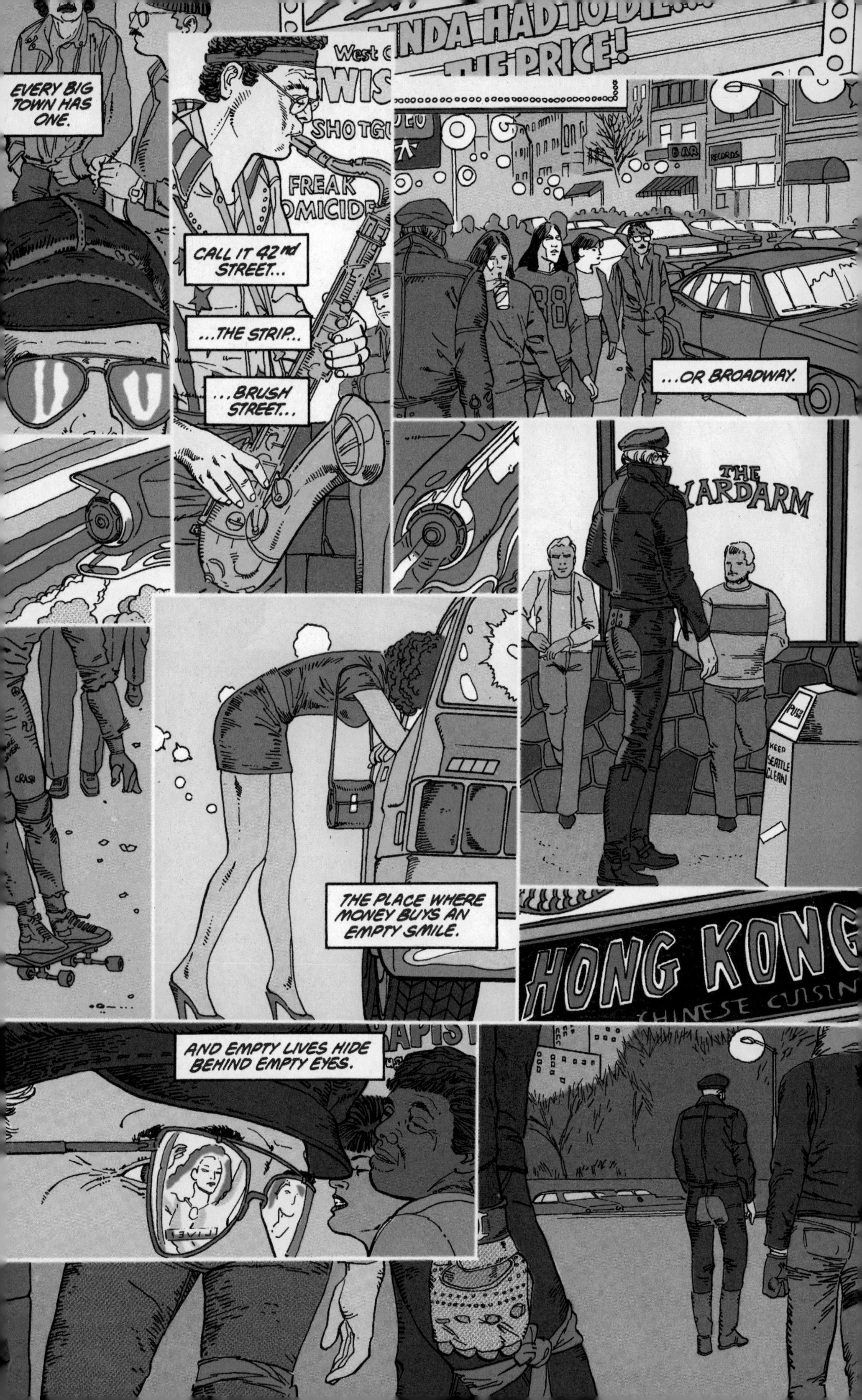
EVERY BIG TOWN HAS ONE.
CALL IT 42nd STREET...
...THE STRIP...
...BRUSH STREET...
...OR BROADWAY.
THE PLACE WHERE MONEY BUYS AN EMPTY SMILE.
AND EMPTY LIVES HIDE BEHIND EMPTY EYES.

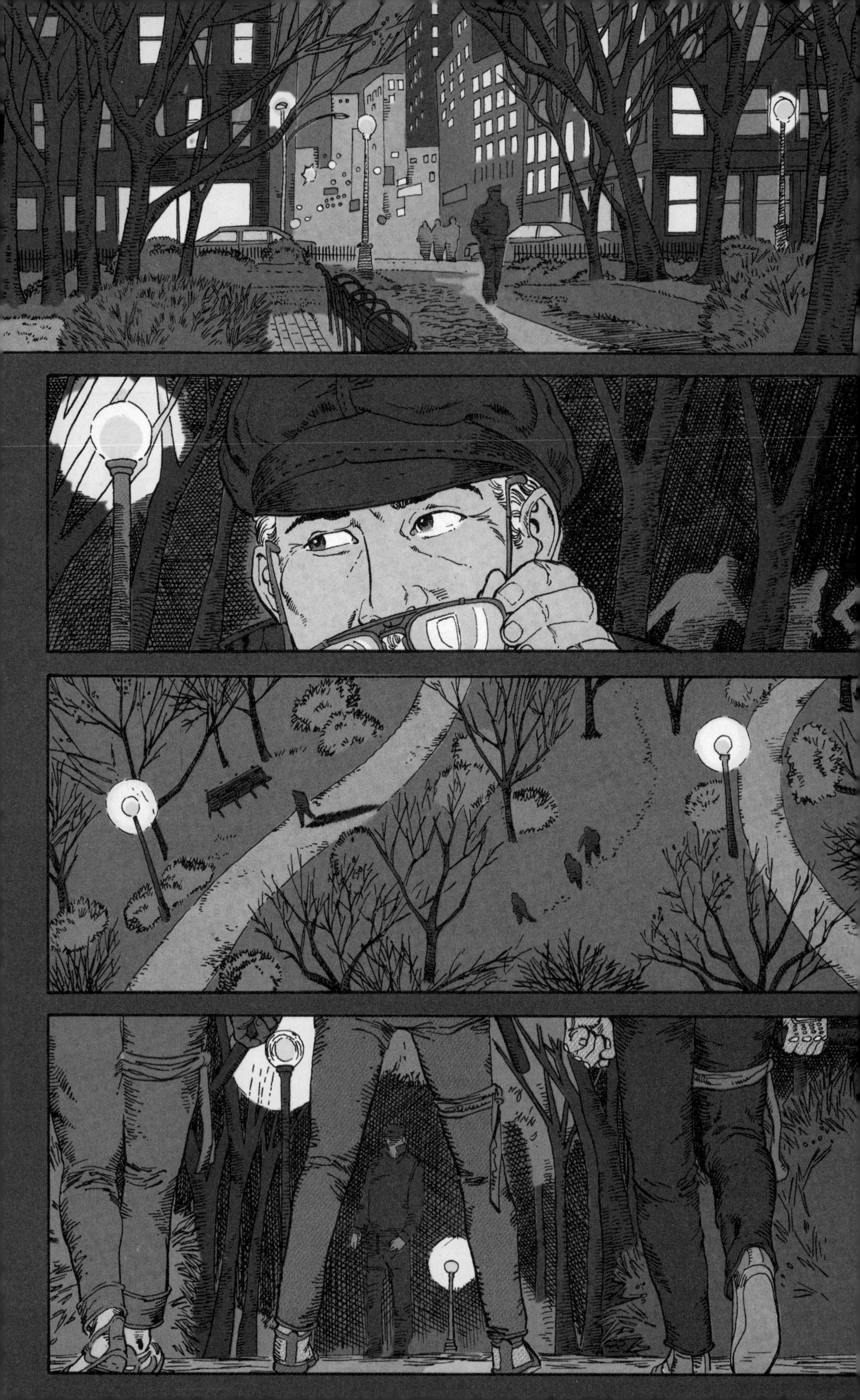

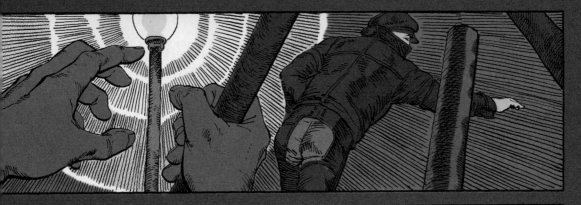

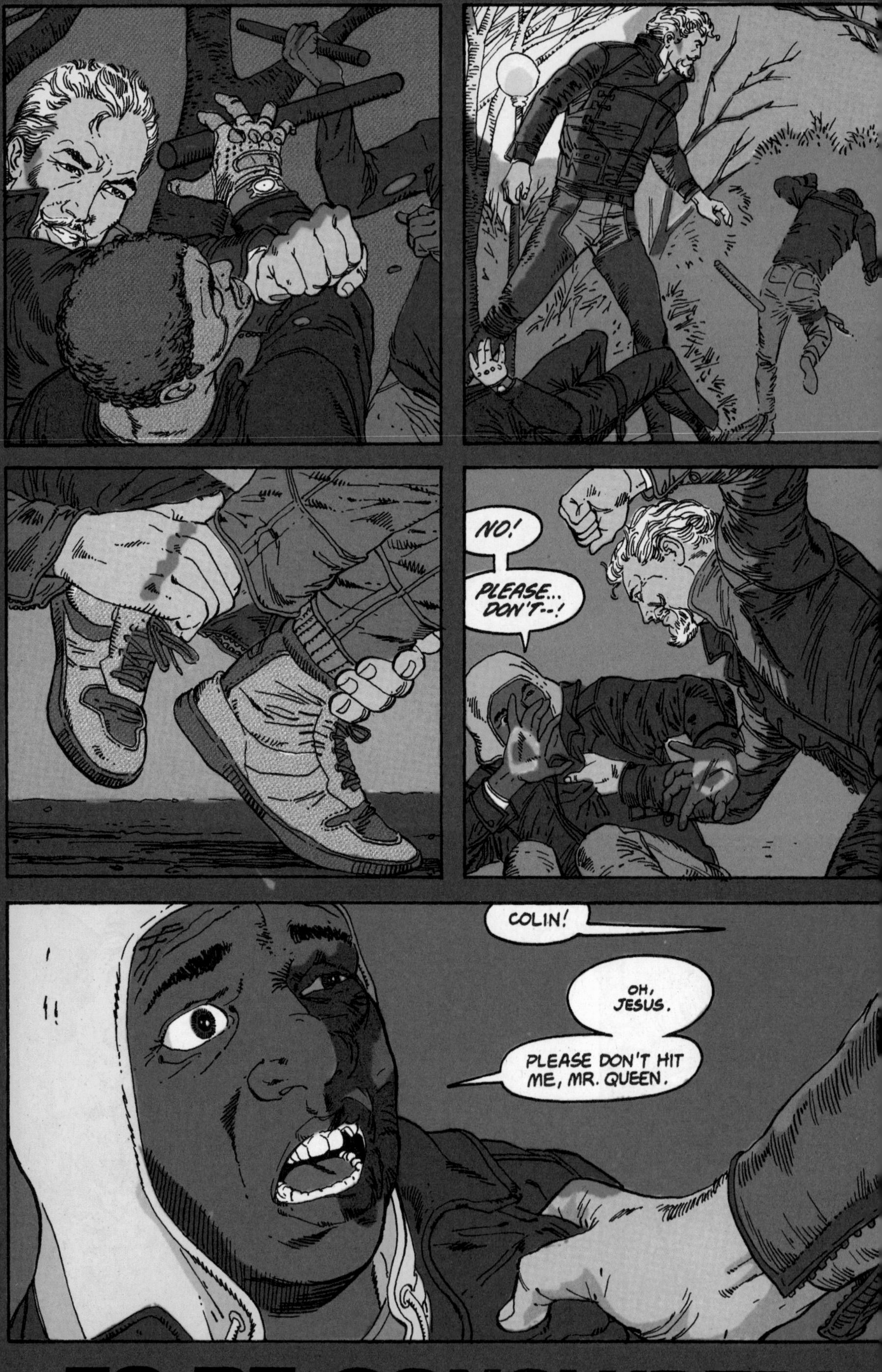
NO!
PLEASE... DON'T--!
COLIN!
OH, JESUS.
PLEASE DON'T HIT ME, MR. QUEEN.

TO BE CONCLUDED!

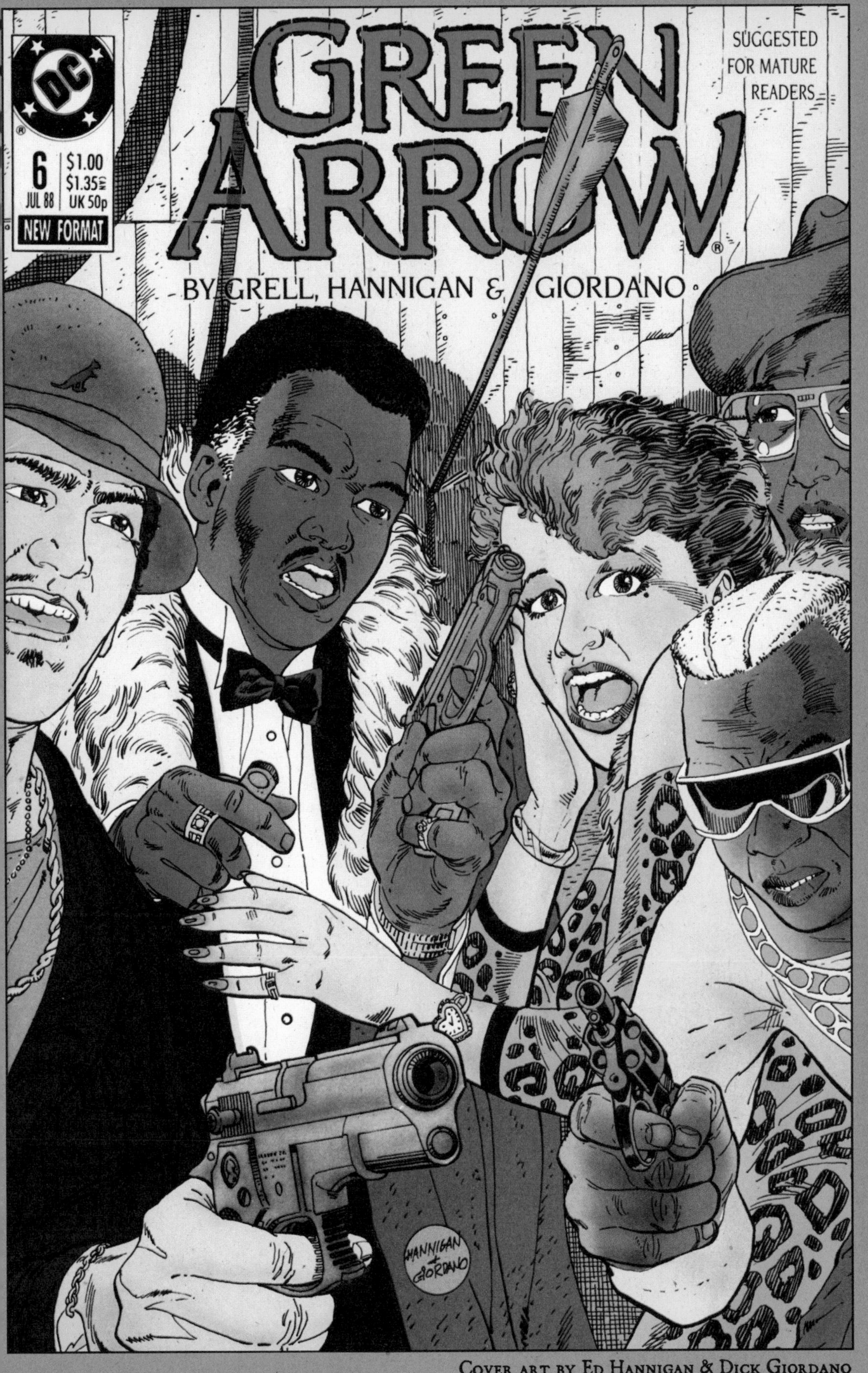
GREEN ARROW
SUGGESTED FOR MATURE READERS
DC
6
JUL 88
$1.00
$1.35
UK 50p
NEW FORMAT
BY GRELL, HANNIGAN & GIORDANO
HANNIGAN + GIORDANO

Cover art by Ed Hannigan & Dick Giordano

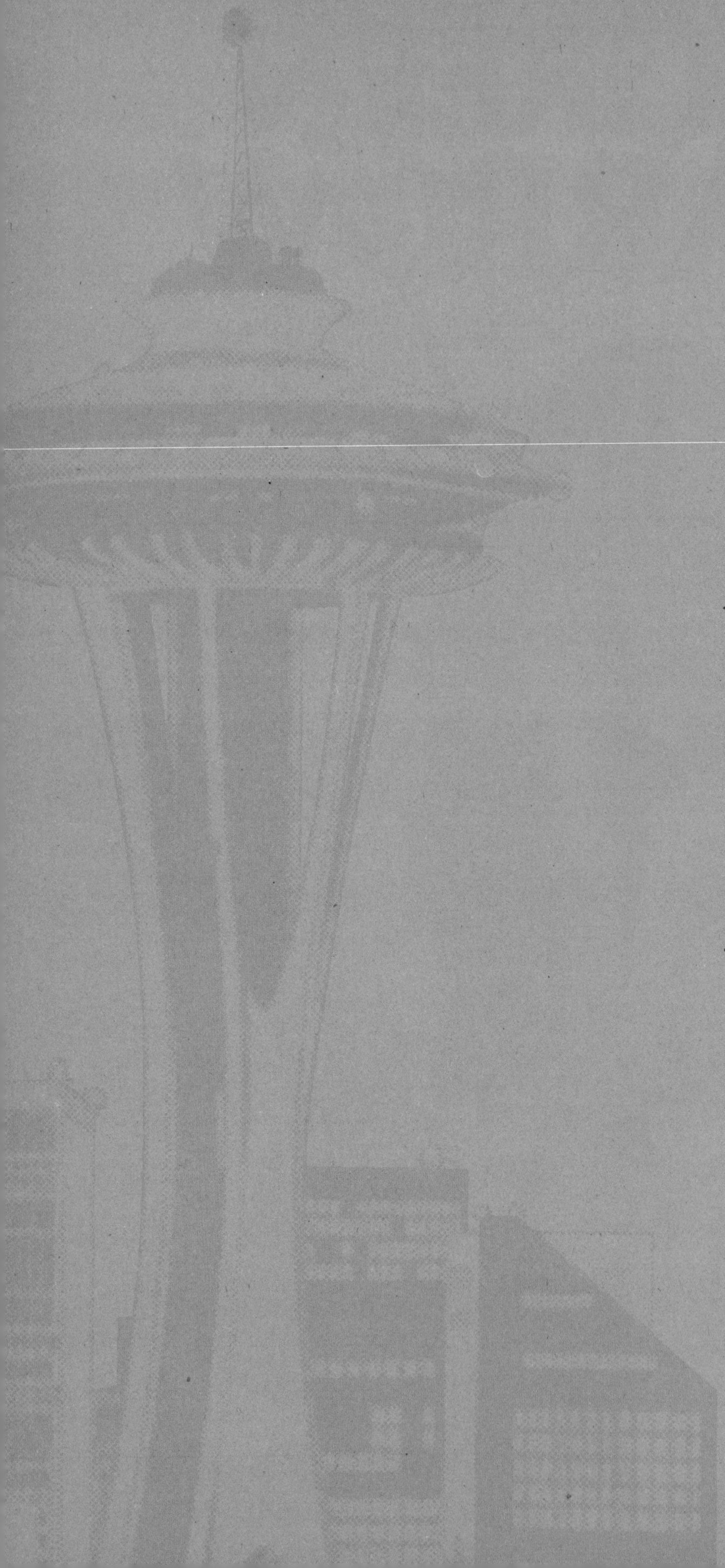

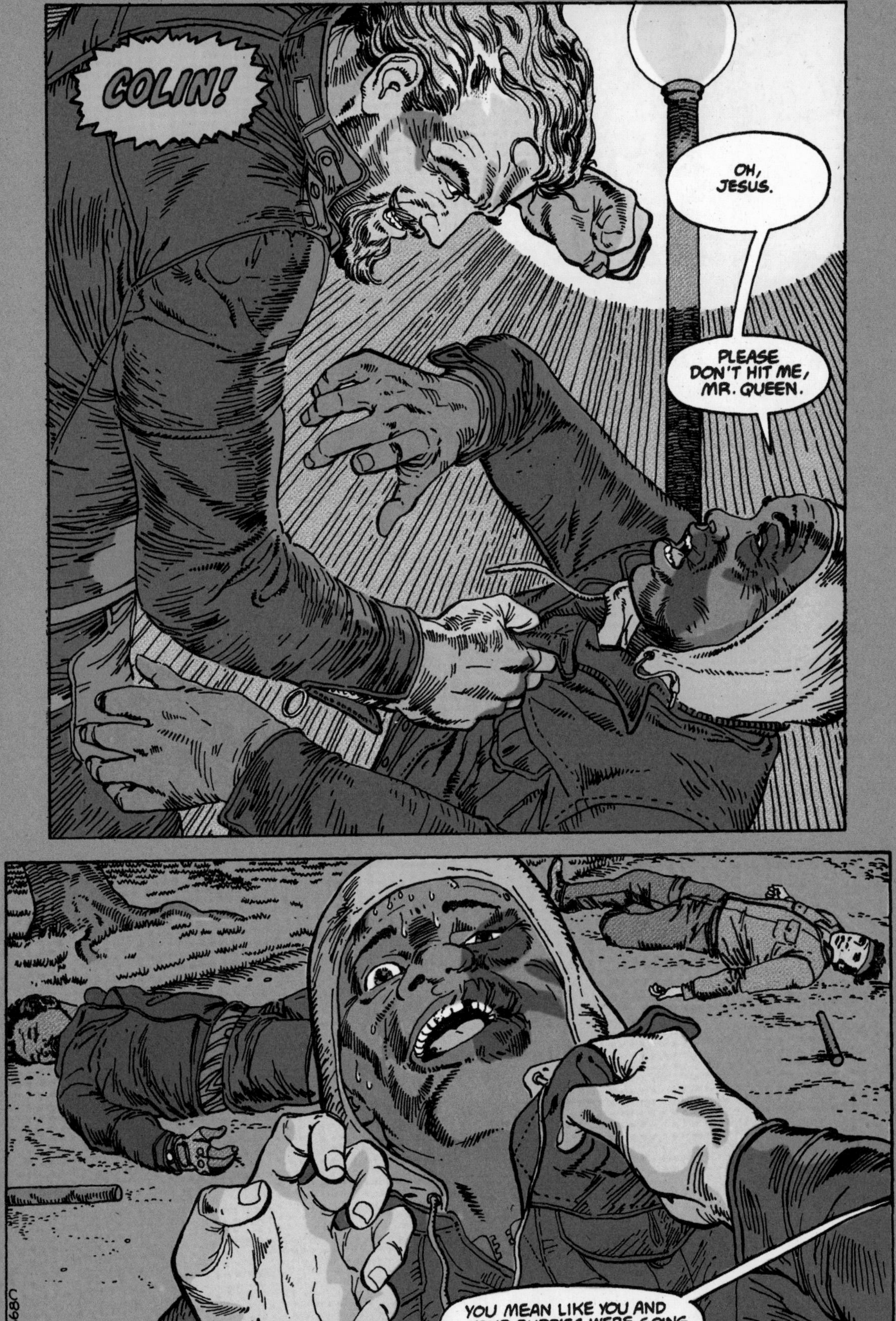
COLIN!
OH, JESUS.
PLEASE DON'T HIT ME, MR. QUEEN.
YOU MEAN LIKE YOU AND YOUR BUDDIES WERE GOING TO DO TO *ME*?

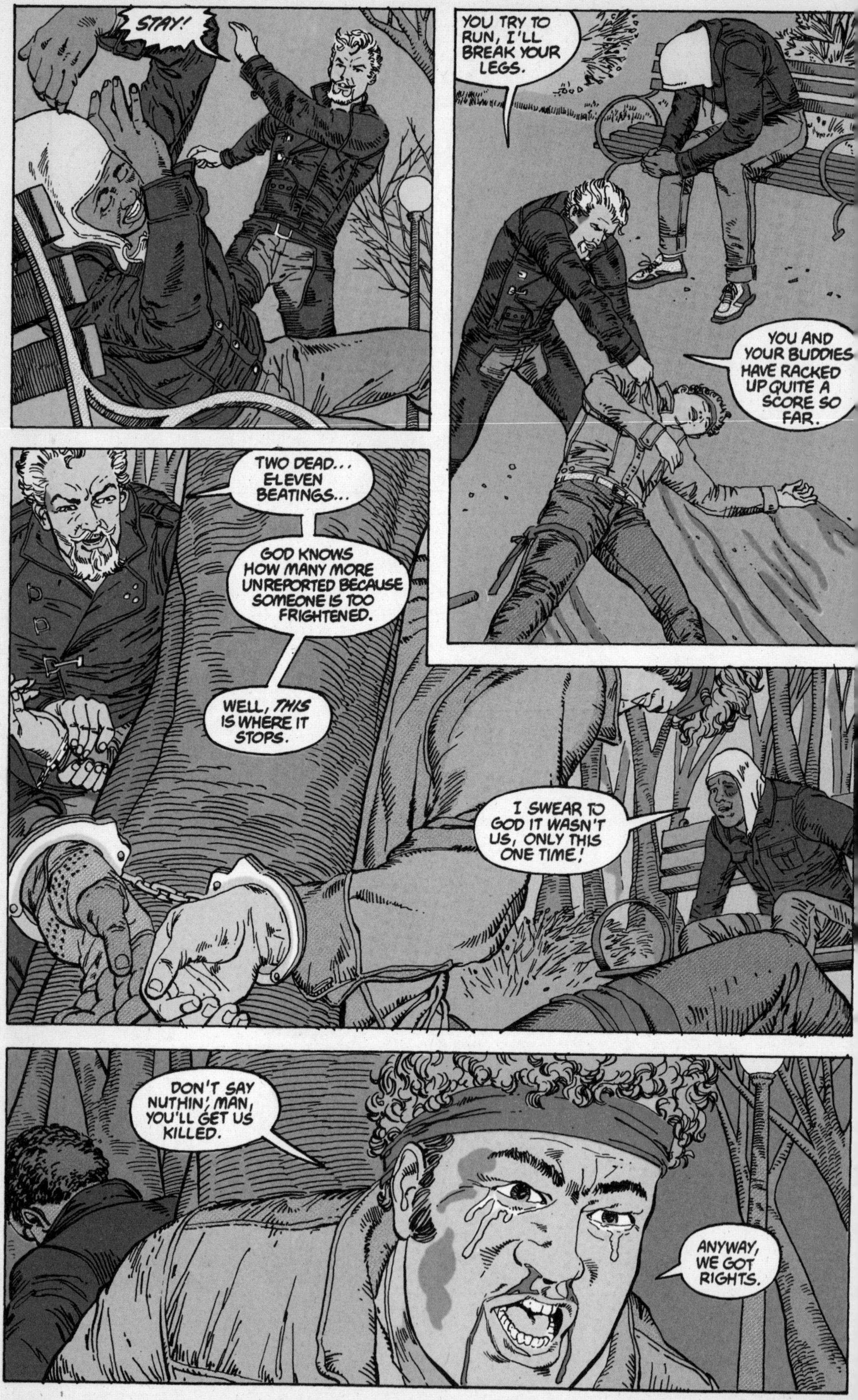
STAY!
YOU TRY TO RUN, I'LL BREAK YOUR LEGS.
YOU AND YOUR BUDDIES HAVE RACKED UP QUITE A SCORE SO FAR.
TWO DEAD... ELEVEN BEATINGS...
GOD KNOWS HOW MANY MORE UNREPORTED BECAUSE SOMEONE IS TOO FRIGHTENED.
WELL, *THIS* IS WHERE IT STOPS.
I SWEAR TO GOD IT WASN'T US, ONLY THIS ONE TIME!
DON'T SAY NUTHIN', MAN, YOU'LL GET US KILLED.
ANYWAY, WE GOT RIGHTS.

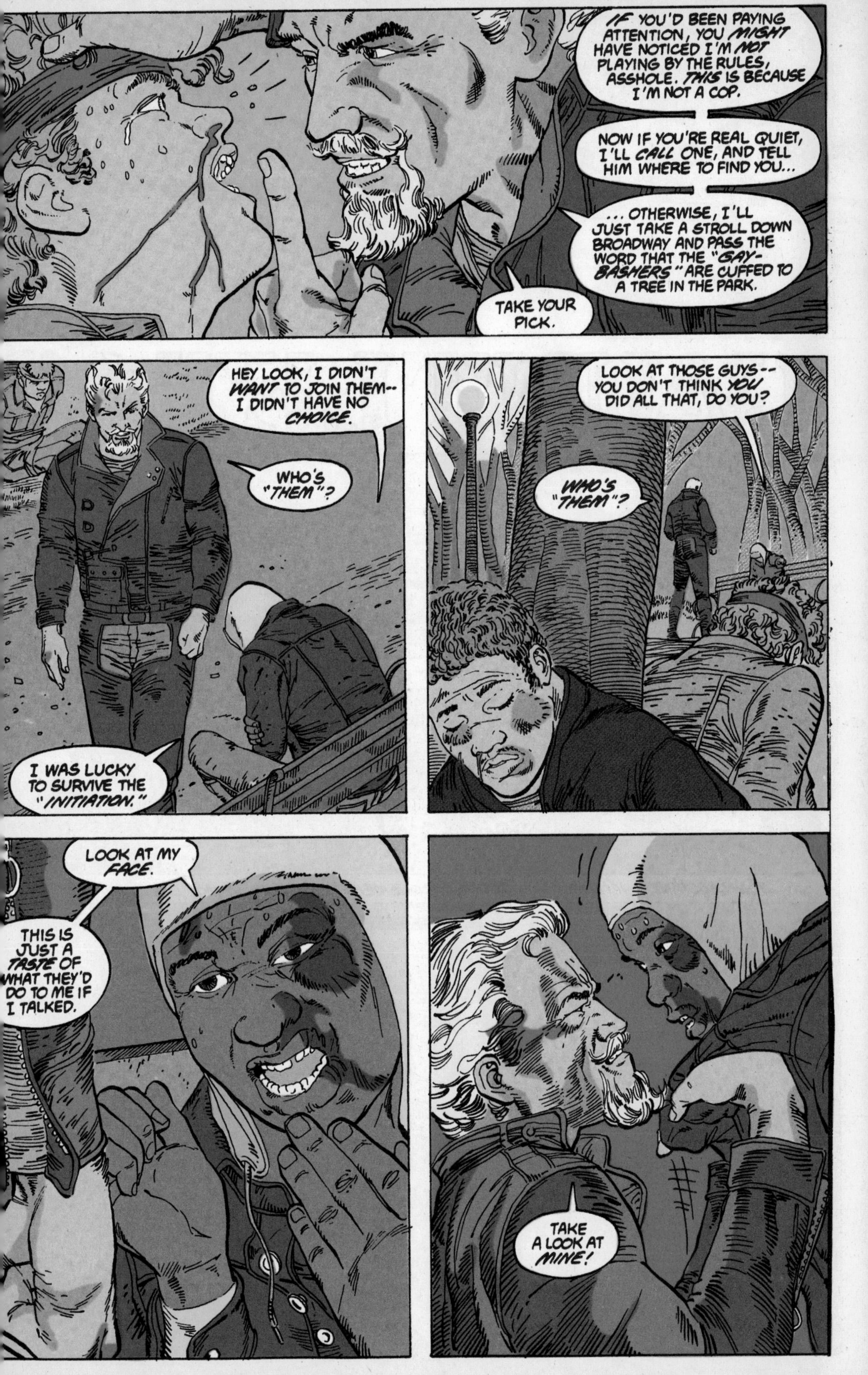
IF YOU'D BEEN PAYING ATTENTION, YOU MIGHT HAVE NOTICED I'M NOT PLAYING BY THE RULES, ASSHOLE. THIS IS BECAUSE I'M NOT A COP.
NOW IF YOU'RE REAL QUIET, I'LL CALL ONE, AND TELL HIM WHERE TO FIND YOU...
... OTHERWISE, I'LL JUST TAKE A STROLL DOWN BROADWAY AND PASS THE WORD THAT THE "GAY-BASHERS" ARE CUFFED TO A TREE IN THE PARK.
TAKE YOUR PICK.
HEY LOOK, I DIDN'T WANT TO JOIN THEM-- I DIDN'T HAVE NO CHOICE.
WHO'S "THEM"?
I WAS LUCKY TO SURVIVE THE "INITIATION."
LOOK AT THOSE GUYS-- YOU DON'T THINK YOU DID ALL THAT, DO YOU?
WHO'S "THEM"?
LOOK AT MY FACE.
THIS IS JUST A TASTE OF WHAT THEY'D DO TO ME IF I TALKED.
TAKE A LOOK AT MINE!

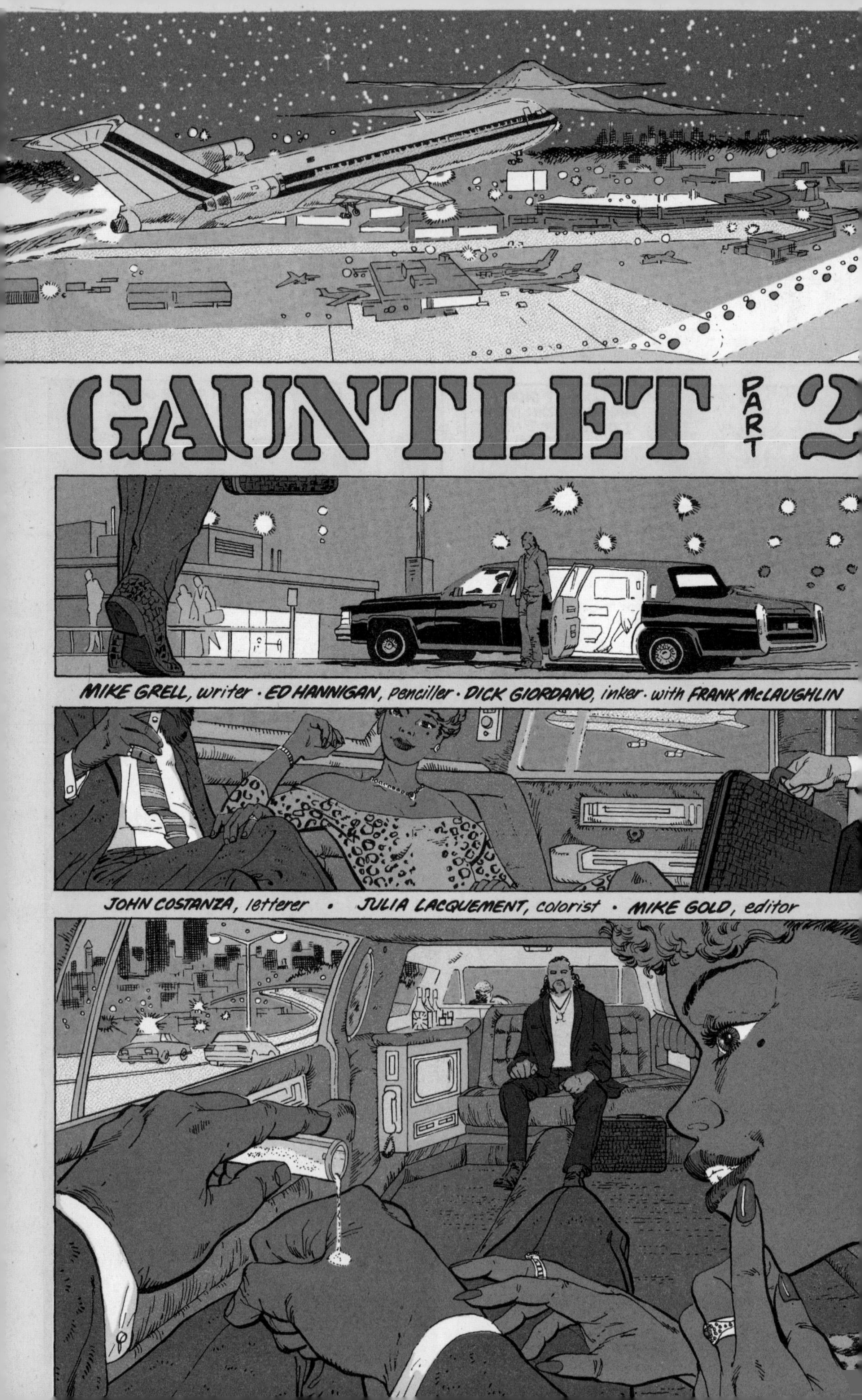
GAUNTLET PART 2
MIKE GRELL, writer · ED HANNIGAN, penciller · DICK GIORDANO, inker · with FRANK McLAUGHLIN
JOHN COSTANZA, letterer · JULIA LACQUEMENT, colorist · MIKE GOLD, editor

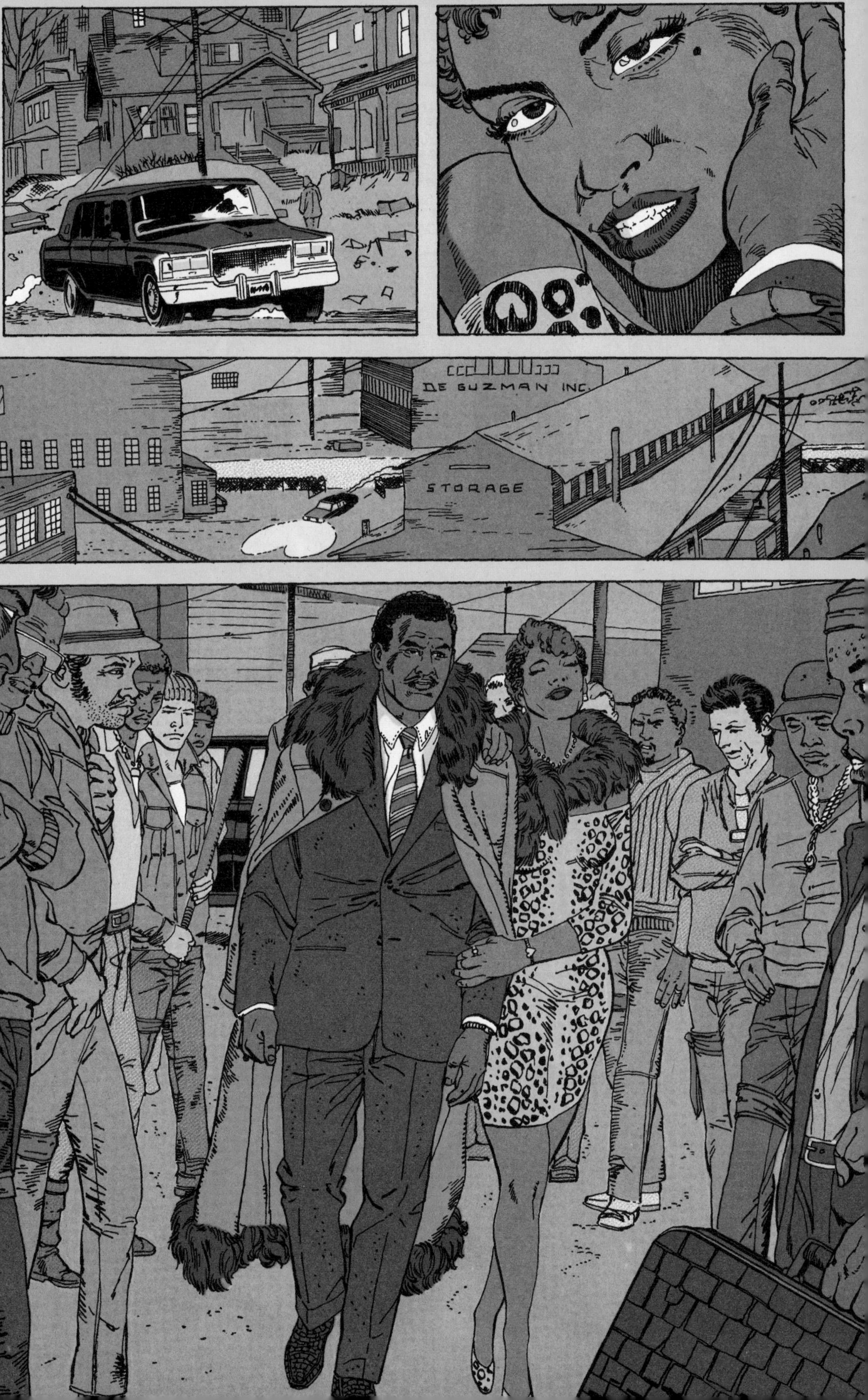
DE GUZMAN INC.
STORAGE

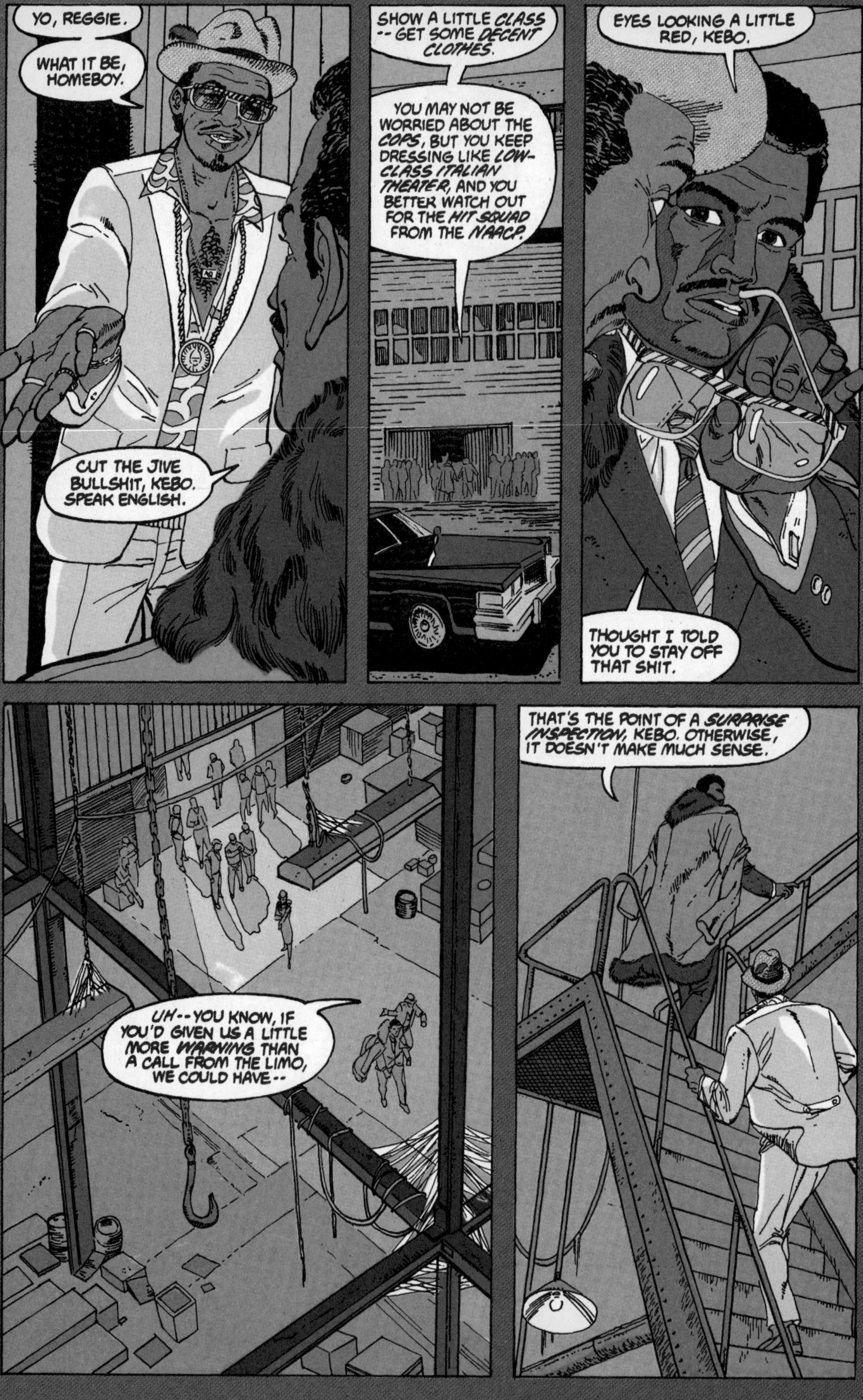
YO, REGGIE.
WHAT IT BE, HOMEBOY.
CUT THE JIVE BULLSHIT, KEBO. SPEAK ENGLISH.
SHOW A LITTLE CLASS -- GET SOME DECENT CLOTHES.
YOU MAY NOT BE WORRIED ABOUT THE COPS, BUT YOU KEEP DRESSING LIKE LOW-CLASS ITALIAN THEATER, AND YOU BETTER WATCH OUT FOR THE HIT SQUAD FROM THE NAACP.
EYES LOOKING A LITTLE RED, KEBO.
THOUGHT I TOLD YOU TO STAY OFF THAT SHIT.
UH--YOU KNOW, IF YOU'D GIVEN US A LITTLE MORE WARNING THAN A CALL FROM THE LIMO, WE COULD HAVE--
THAT'S THE POINT OF A SURPRISE INSPECTION, KEBO. OTHERWISE, IT DOESN'T MAKE MUCH SENSE.

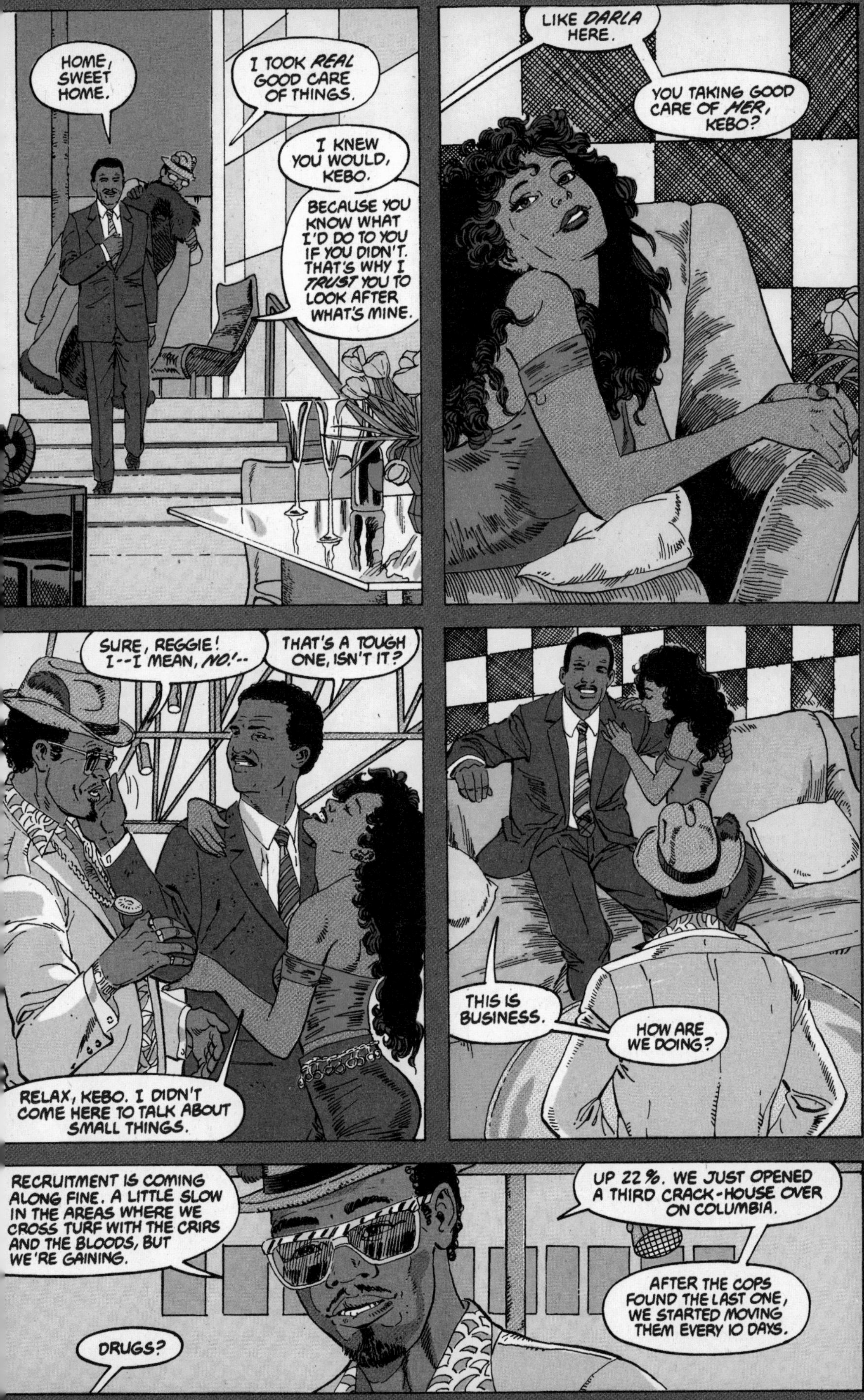
HOME, SWEET HOME.
I TOOK REAL GOOD CARE OF THINGS.
I KNEW YOU WOULD, KEBO.
BECAUSE YOU KNOW WHAT I'D DO TO YOU IF YOU DIDN'T. THAT'S WHY I TRUST YOU TO LOOK AFTER WHAT'S MINE.
LIKE DARLA HERE.
YOU TAKING GOOD CARE OF HER, KEBO?
SURE, REGGIE! I--I MEAN, NO!--
THAT'S A TOUGH ONE, ISN'T IT?
RELAX, KEBO. I DIDN'T COME HERE TO TALK ABOUT SMALL THINGS.
THIS IS BUSINESS.
HOW ARE WE DOING?
RECRUITMENT IS COMING ALONG FINE. A LITTLE SLOW IN THE AREAS WHERE WE CROSS TURF WITH THE CRIPS AND THE BLOODS, BUT WE'RE GAINING.
DRUGS?
UP 22%. WE JUST OPENED A THIRD CRACK-HOUSE OVER ON COLUMBIA.
AFTER THE COPS FOUND THE LAST ONE, WE STARTED MOVING THEM EVERY 10 DAYS.

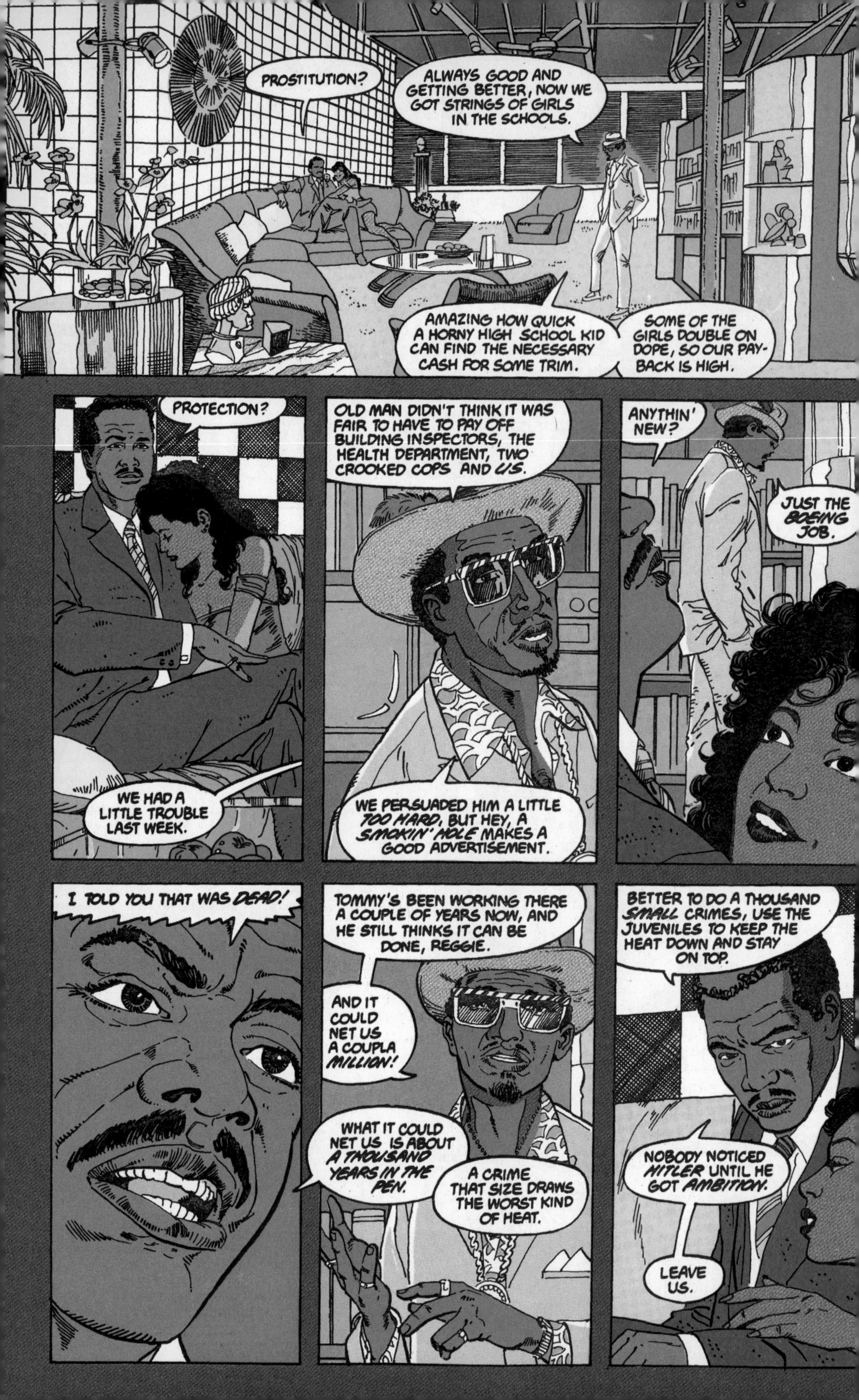
PROSTITUTION?
ALWAYS GOOD AND GETTING BETTER, NOW WE GOT STRINGS OF GIRLS IN THE SCHOOLS.
AMAZING HOW QUICK A HORNY HIGH SCHOOL KID CAN FIND THE NECESSARY CASH FOR SOME TRIM.
SOME OF THE GIRLS DOUBLE ON DOPE, SO OUR PAY-BACK IS HIGH.
PROTECTION?
WE HAD A LITTLE TROUBLE LAST WEEK.
OLD MAN DIDN'T THINK IT WAS FAIR TO HAVE TO PAY OFF BUILDING INSPECTORS, THE HEALTH DEPARTMENT, TWO CROOKED COPS AND US.
WE PERSUADED HIM A LITTLE TOO HARD, BUT HEY, A SMOKIN' HOLE MAKES A GOOD ADVERTISEMENT.
ANYTHIN' NEW?
JUST THE BOEING JOB.
I TOLD YOU THAT WAS DEAD!
TOMMY'S BEEN WORKING THERE A COUPLE OF YEARS NOW, AND HE STILL THINKS IT CAN BE DONE, REGGIE.
AND IT COULD NET US A COUPLA MILLION!
WHAT IT COULD NET US IS ABOUT A THOUSAND YEARS IN THE PEN.
A CRIME THAT SIZE DRAWS THE WORST KIND OF HEAT.
BETTER TO DO A THOUSAND SMALL CRIMES, USE THE JUVENILES TO KEEP THE HEAT DOWN AND STAY ON TOP.
NOBODY NOTICED HITLER UNTIL HE GOT AMBITION.
LEAVE US.

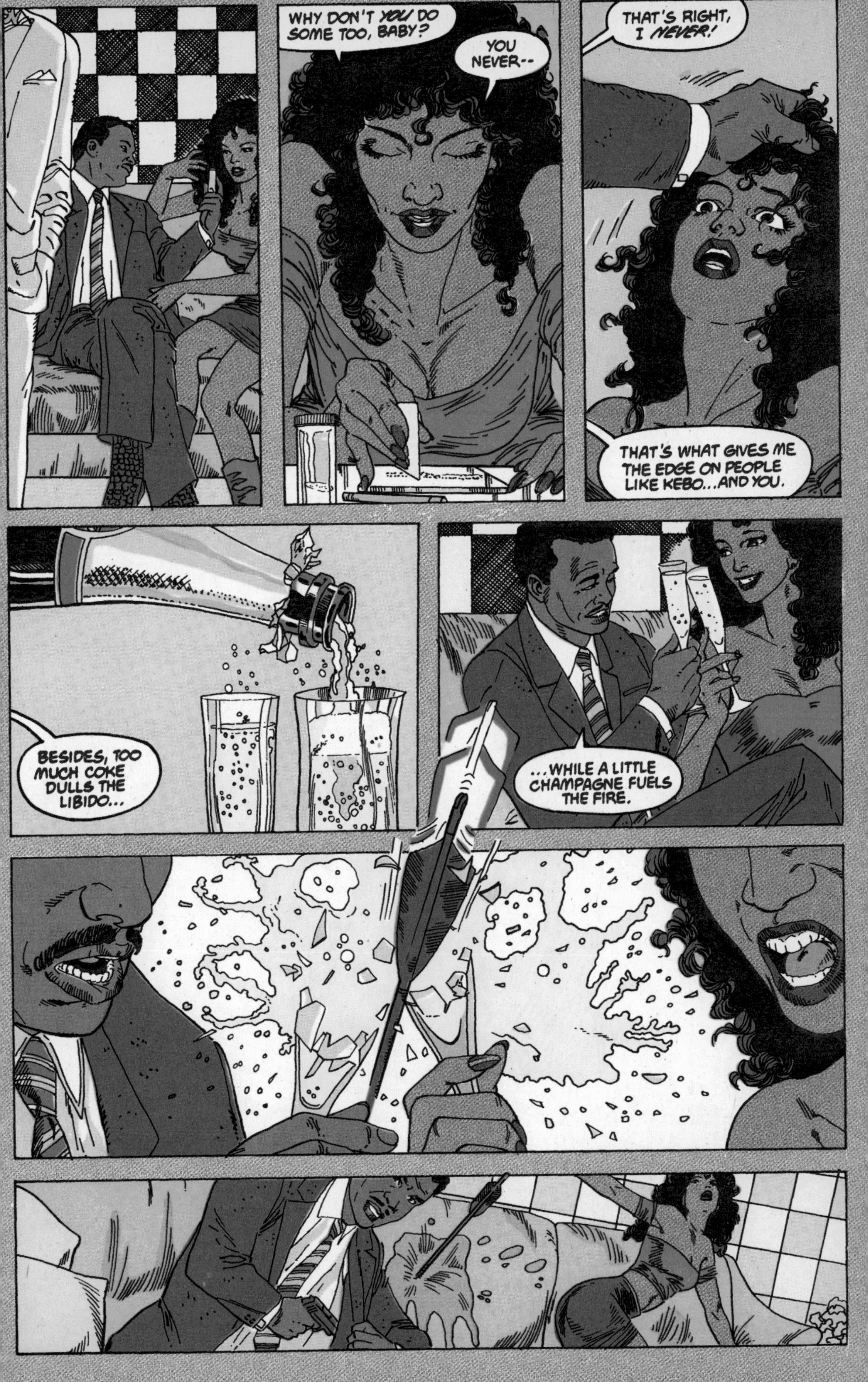
WHY DON'T YOU DO SOME TOO, BABY?
YOU NEVER--
THAT'S RIGHT, I NEVER!
THAT'S WHAT GIVES ME THE EDGE ON PEOPLE LIKE KEBO...AND YOU.
BESIDES, TOO MUCH COKE DULLS THE LIBIDO...
...WHILE A LITTLE CHAMPAGNE FUELS THE FIRE.

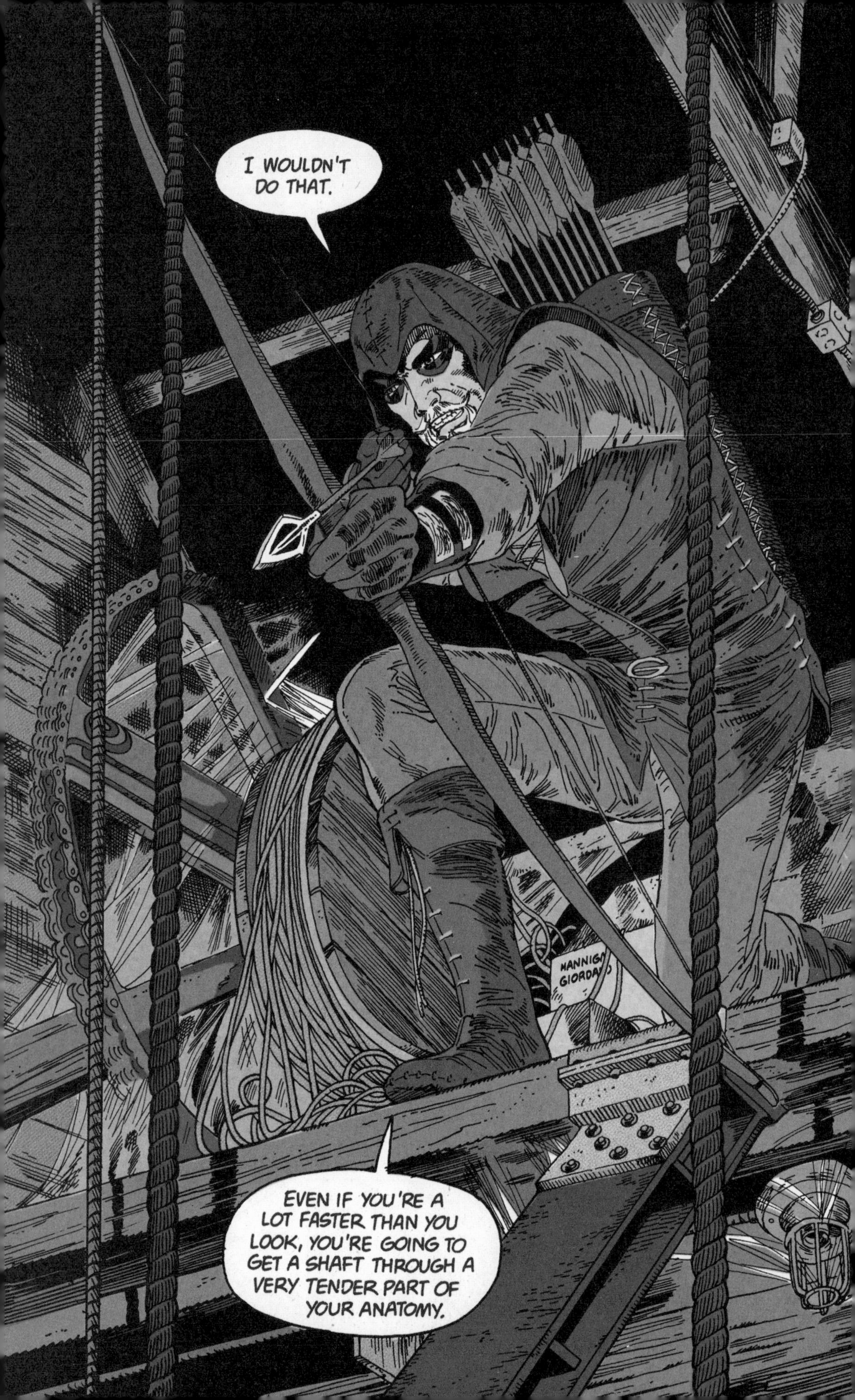
I WOULDN'T DO THAT.
EVEN IF YOU'RE A LOT FASTER THAN YOU LOOK, YOU'RE GOING TO GET A SHAFT THROUGH A VERY TENDER PART OF YOUR ANATOMY.

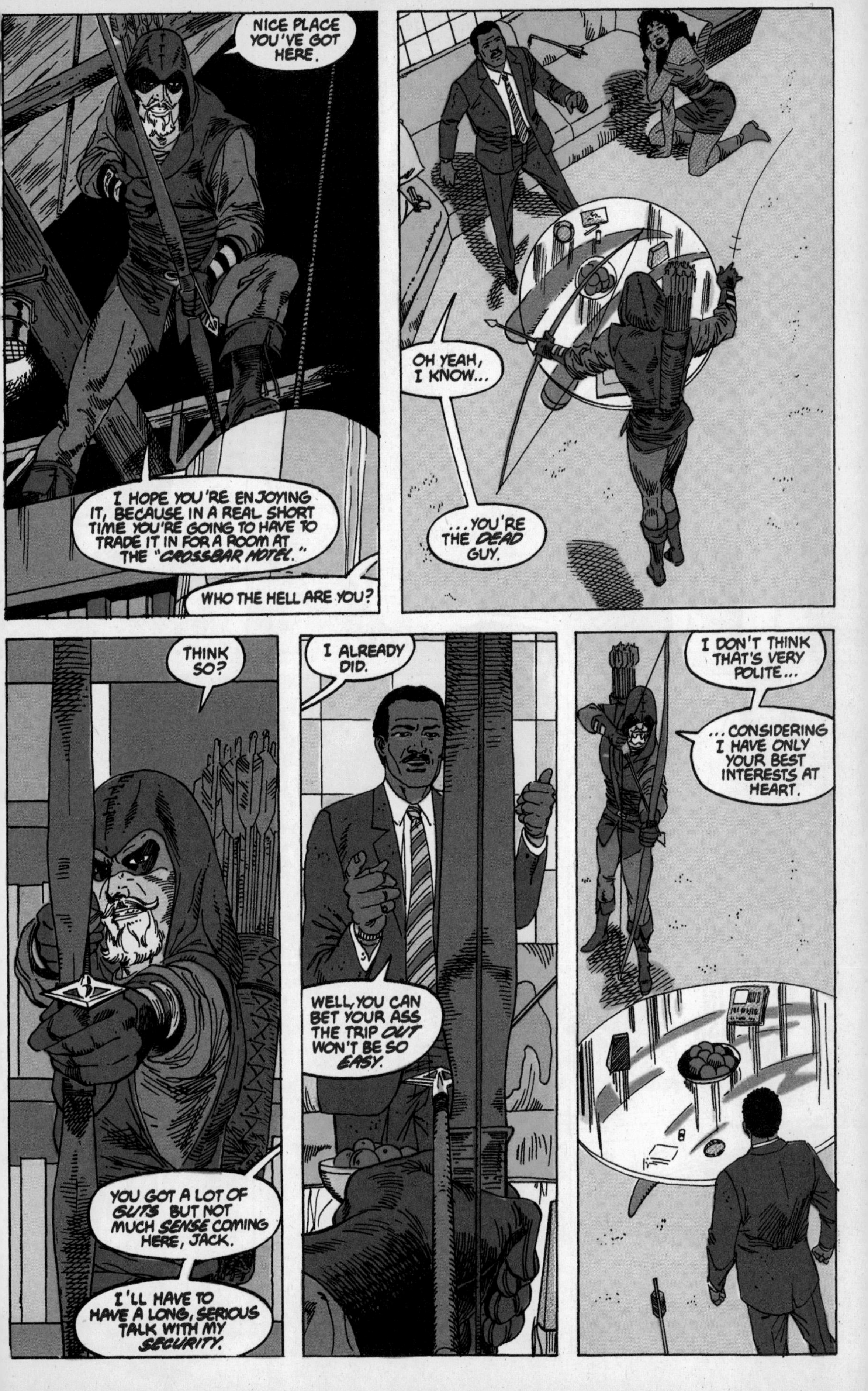
NICE PLACE YOU'VE GOT HERE.
I HOPE YOU'RE ENJOYING IT, BECAUSE IN A REAL SHORT TIME YOU'RE GOING TO HAVE TO TRADE IT IN FOR A ROOM AT THE "CROSSBAR HOTEL."
WHO THE HELL ARE YOU?
OH YEAH, I KNOW...
...YOU'RE THE DEAD GUY.
THINK SO?
YOU GOT A LOT OF GUTS BUT NOT MUCH SENSE COMING HERE, JACK.
I'LL HAVE TO HAVE A LONG, SERIOUS TALK WITH MY SECURITY.
I ALREADY DID.
WELL, YOU CAN BET YOUR ASS THE TRIP OUT WON'T BE SO EASY.
I DON'T THINK THAT'S VERY POLITE...
...CONSIDERING I HAVE ONLY YOUR BEST INTERESTS AT HEART.

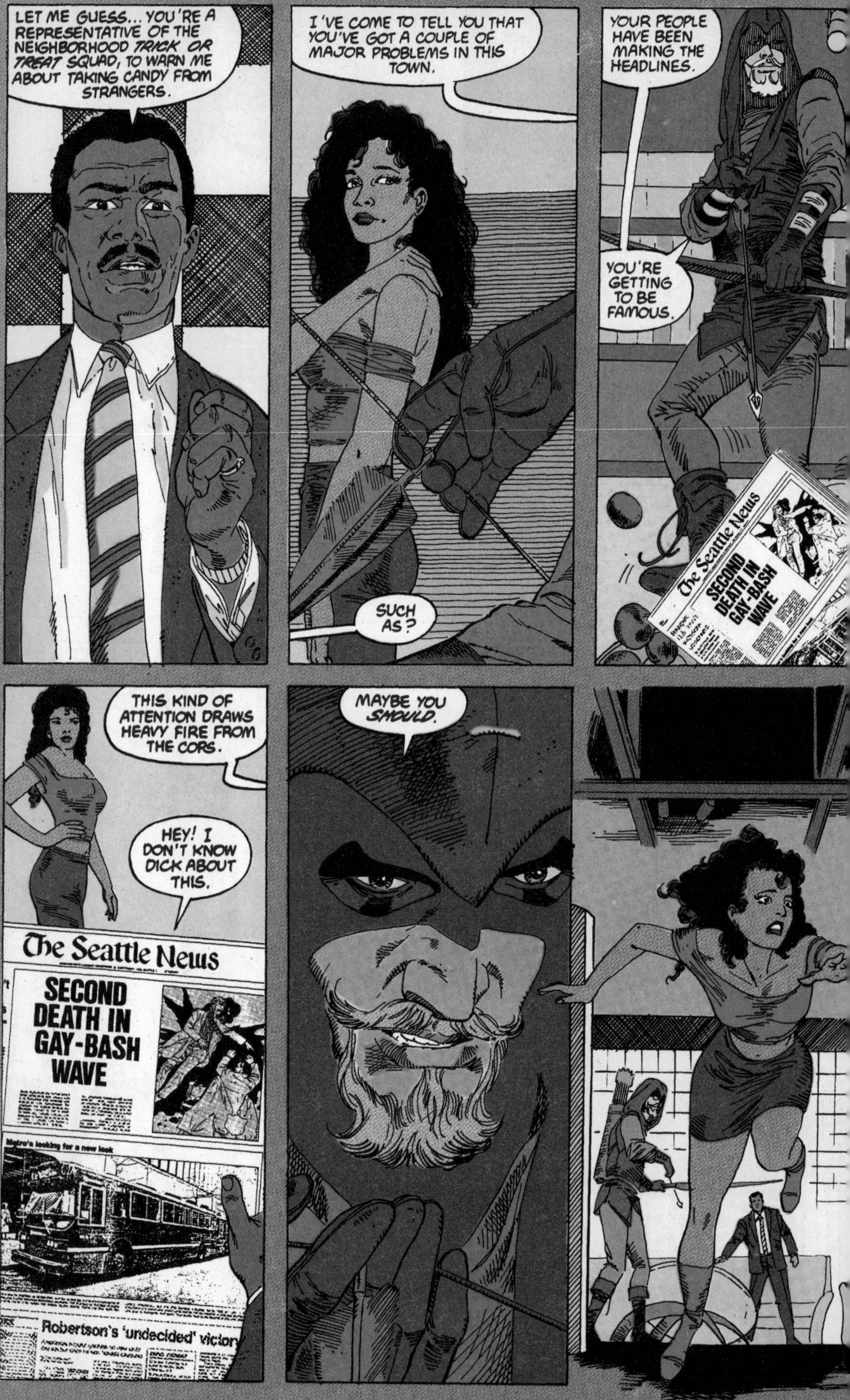
LET ME GUESS... YOU'RE A REPRESENTATIVE OF THE NEIGHBORHOOD TRICK OR TREAT SQUAD, TO WARN ME ABOUT TAKING CANDY FROM STRANGERS.
I'VE COME TO TELL YOU THAT YOU'VE GOT A COUPLE OF MAJOR PROBLEMS IN THIS TOWN.
SUCH AS?
YOUR PEOPLE HAVE BEEN MAKING THE HEADLINES.
YOU'RE GETTING TO BE FAMOUS.
The Seattle News
SECOND DEATH IN GAY-BASH WAVE
THIS KIND OF ATTENTION DRAWS HEAVY FIRE FROM THE CORS.
HEY! I DON'T KNOW DICK ABOUT THIS.
The Seattle News
SECOND DEATH IN GAY-BASH WAVE
Metro's looking for a new look
Robertson's 'undecided' victor
MAYBE YOU SHOULD.

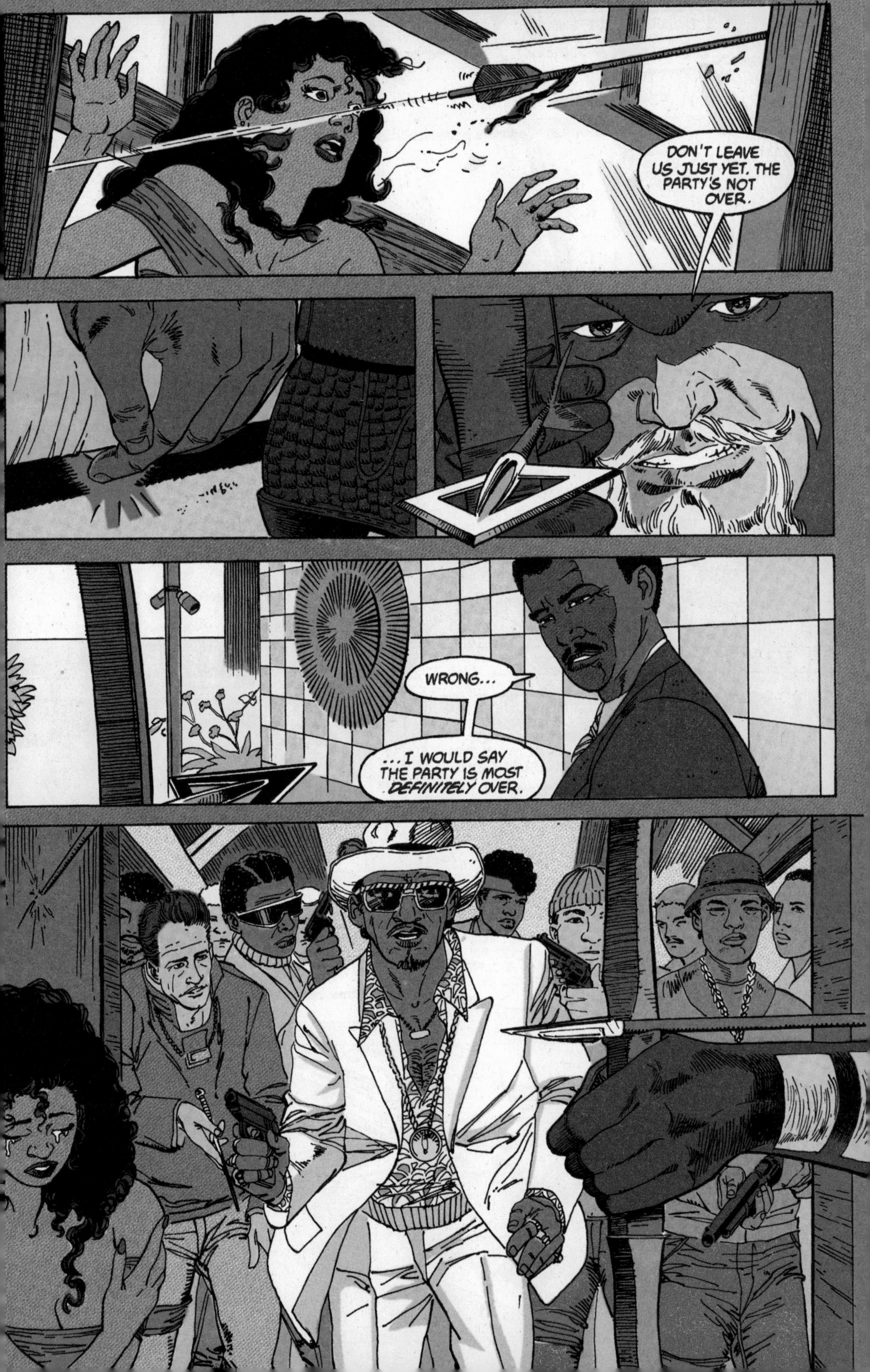
DON'T LEAVE US JUST YET. THE PARTY'S NOT OVER.
WRONG...
...I WOULD SAY THE PARTY IS MOST DEFINITELY OVER.

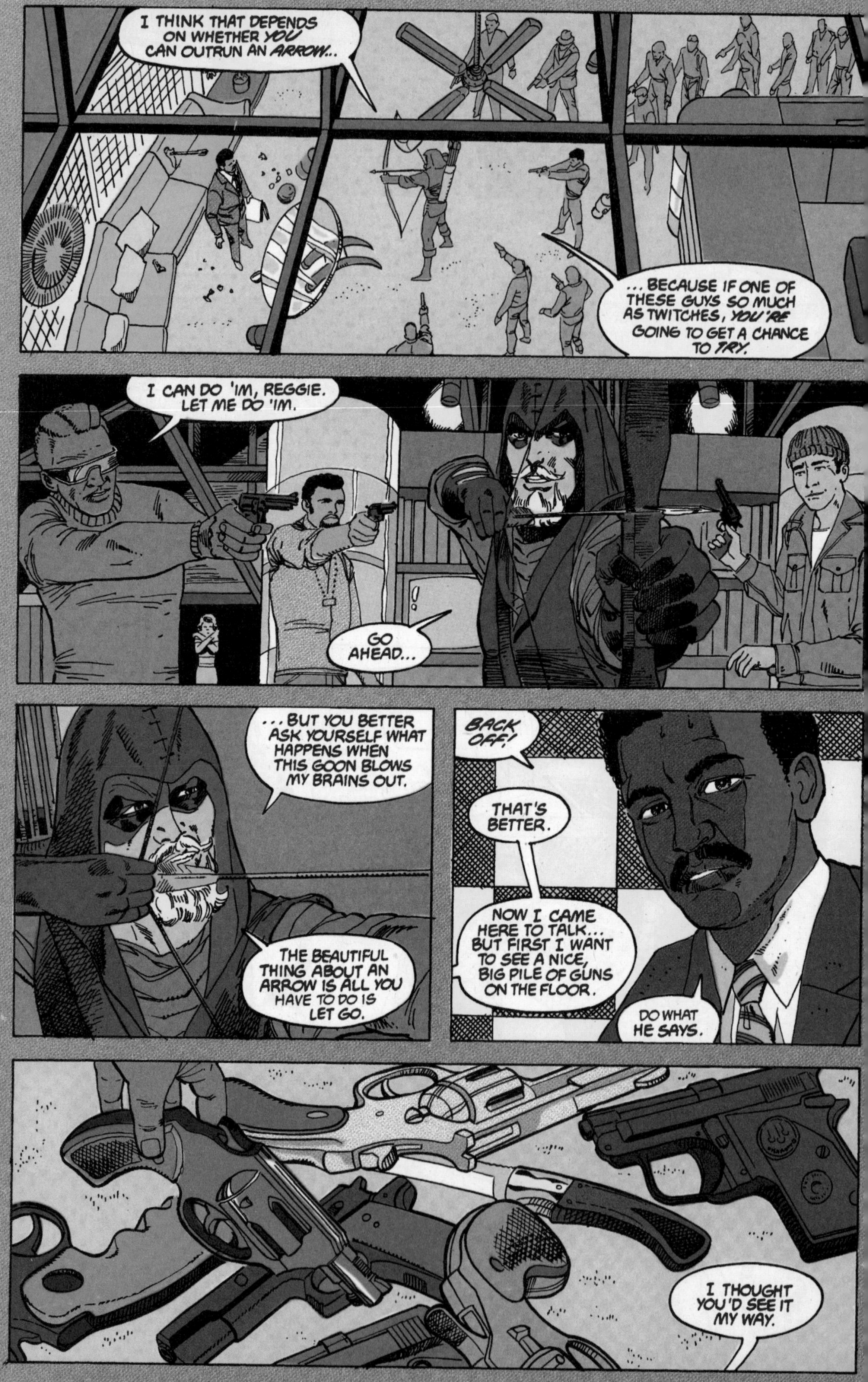
I THINK THAT DEPENDS ON WHETHER YOU CAN OUTRUN AN ARROW...
... BECAUSE IF ONE OF THESE GUYS SO MUCH AS TWITCHES, YOU'RE GOING TO GET A CHANCE TO TRY.
I CAN DO 'IM, REGGIE. LET ME DO 'IM.
GO AHEAD...
... BUT YOU BETTER ASK YOURSELF WHAT HAPPENS WHEN THIS GOON BLOWS MY BRAINS OUT.
THE BEAUTIFUL THING ABOUT AN ARROW IS ALL YOU HAVE TO DO IS LET GO.
BACK OFF!
THAT'S BETTER.
NOW I CAME HERE TO TALK... BUT FIRST I WANT TO SEE A NICE, BIG PILE OF GUNS ON THE FLOOR.
DO WHAT HE SAYS.
I THOUGHT YOU'D SEE IT MY WAY.

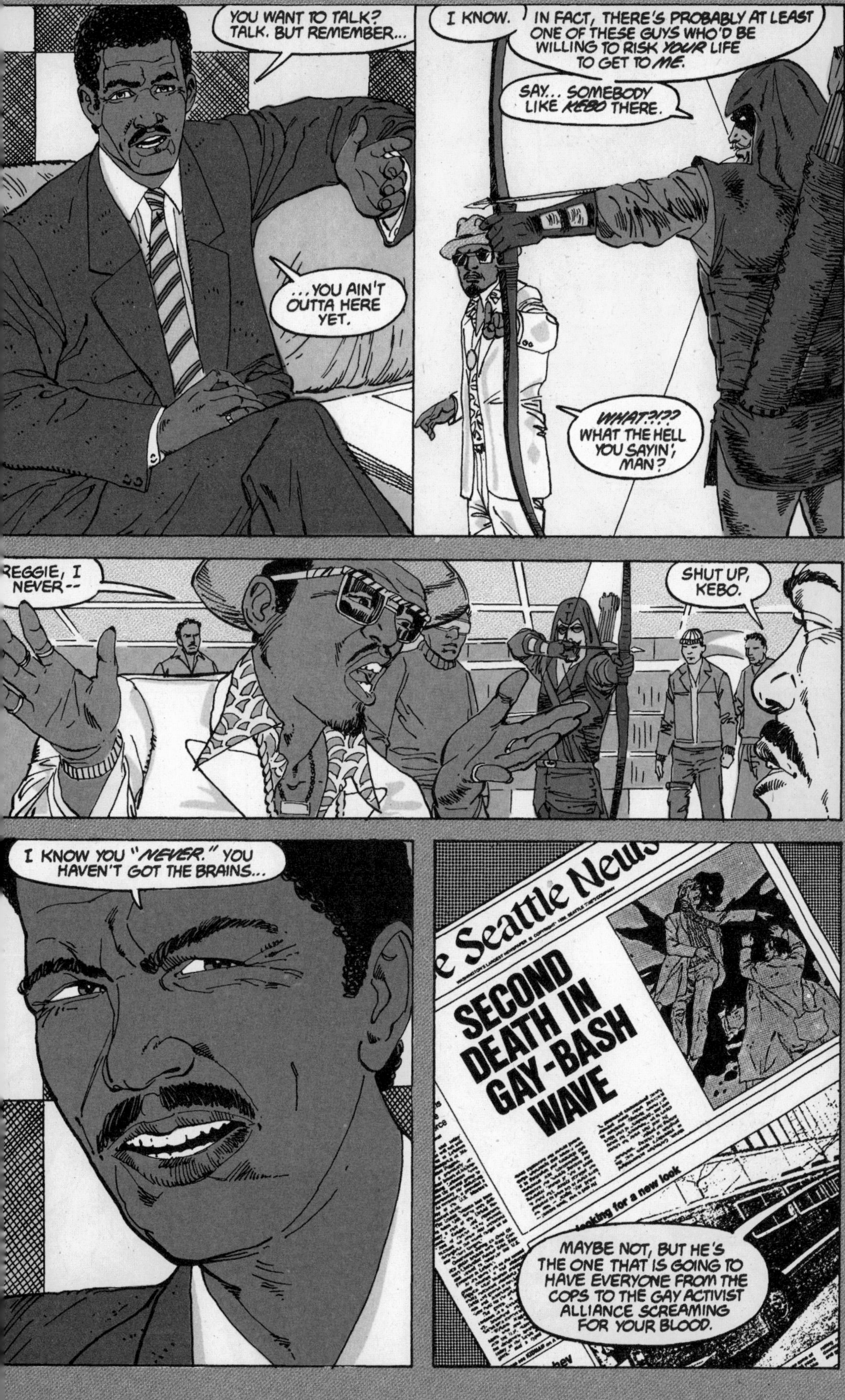

YOU WANT TO TALK? TALK. BUT REMEMBER...
...YOU AIN'T OUTTA HERE YET.
I KNOW.
IN FACT, THERE'S PROBABLY AT LEAST ONE OF THESE GUYS WHO'D BE WILLING TO RISK *YOUR* LIFE TO GET TO *ME*.
SAY... SOMEBODY LIKE *KEBO* THERE.
WHAT?!?? WHAT THE HELL YOU SAYIN', MAN?
REGGIE, I NEVER--
SHUT UP, KEBO.
I KNOW YOU "*NEVER*." YOU HAVEN'T GOT THE BRAINS...
SECOND DEATH IN GAY-BASH WAVE
looking for a new look
MAYBE NOT, BUT HE'S THE ONE THAT IS GOING TO HAVE EVERYONE FROM THE COPS TO THE GAY ACTIVIST ALLIANCE SCREAMING FOR YOUR BLOOD.

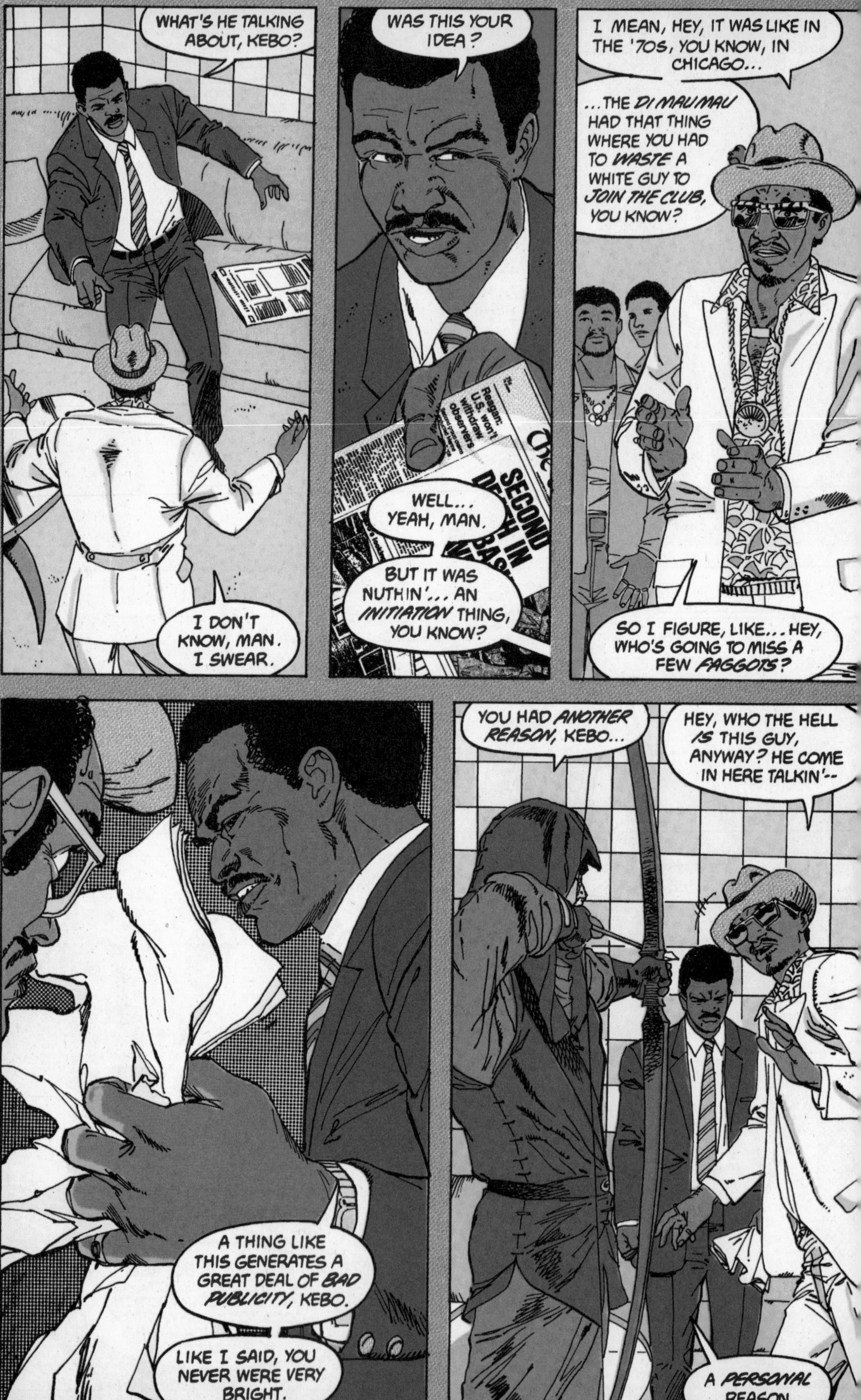
WHAT'S HE TALKING ABOUT, KEBO?
I DON'T KNOW, MAN. I SWEAR.
WAS THIS YOUR IDEA?
Reagan: U.S. won't withdraw observers
WELL... YEAH, MAN.
BUT IT WAS NUTHIN'... AN *INITIATION* THING, YOU KNOW?
I MEAN, HEY, IT WAS LIKE IN THE '70S, YOU KNOW, IN CHICAGO...
...THE *DI MAU MAU* HAD THAT THING WHERE YOU HAD TO *WASTE* A WHITE GUY TO *JOIN THE CLUB,* YOU KNOW?
SO I FIGURE, LIKE... HEY, WHO'S GOING TO MISS A FEW *FAGGOTS?*
A THING LIKE THIS GENERATES A GREAT DEAL OF *BAD PUBLICITY,* KEBO.
LIKE I SAID, YOU NEVER WERE VERY BRIGHT.
YOU HAD *ANOTHER REASON,* KEBO...
HEY, WHO THE HELL *IS* THIS GUY, ANYWAY? HE COME IN HERE TALKIN'--
A *PERSONAL* REASON.

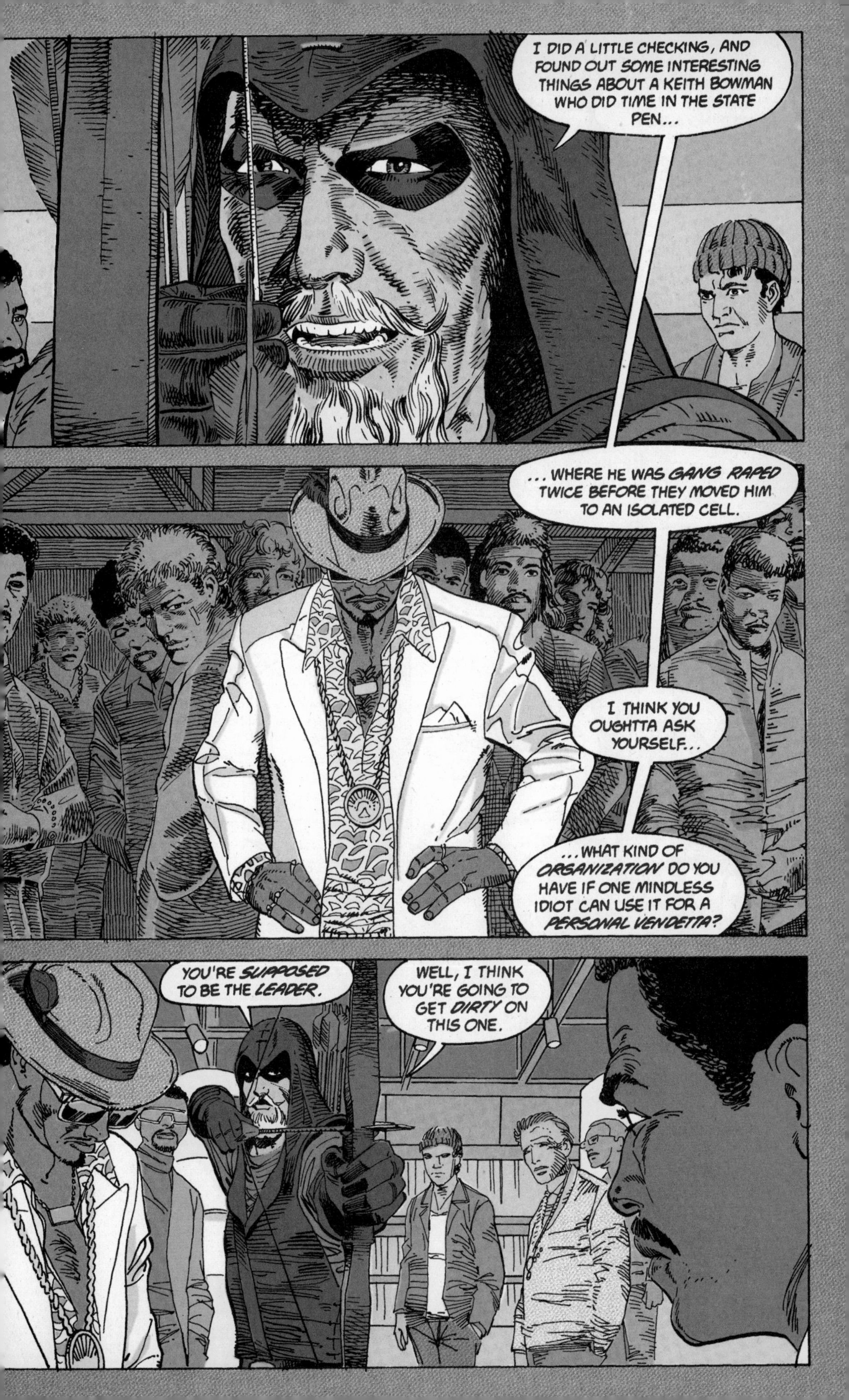
I DID A LITTLE CHECKING, AND FOUND OUT SOME INTERESTING THINGS ABOUT A KEITH BOWMAN WHO DID TIME IN THE STATE PEN...
...WHERE HE WAS GANG RAPED TWICE BEFORE THEY MOVED HIM TO AN ISOLATED CELL.
I THINK YOU OUGHTTA ASK YOURSELF...
...WHAT KIND OF ORGANIZATION DO YOU HAVE IF ONE MINDLESS IDIOT CAN USE IT FOR A PERSONAL VENDETTA?
YOU'RE SUPPOSED TO BE THE LEADER.
WELL, I THINK YOU'RE GOING TO GET DIRTY ON THIS ONE.

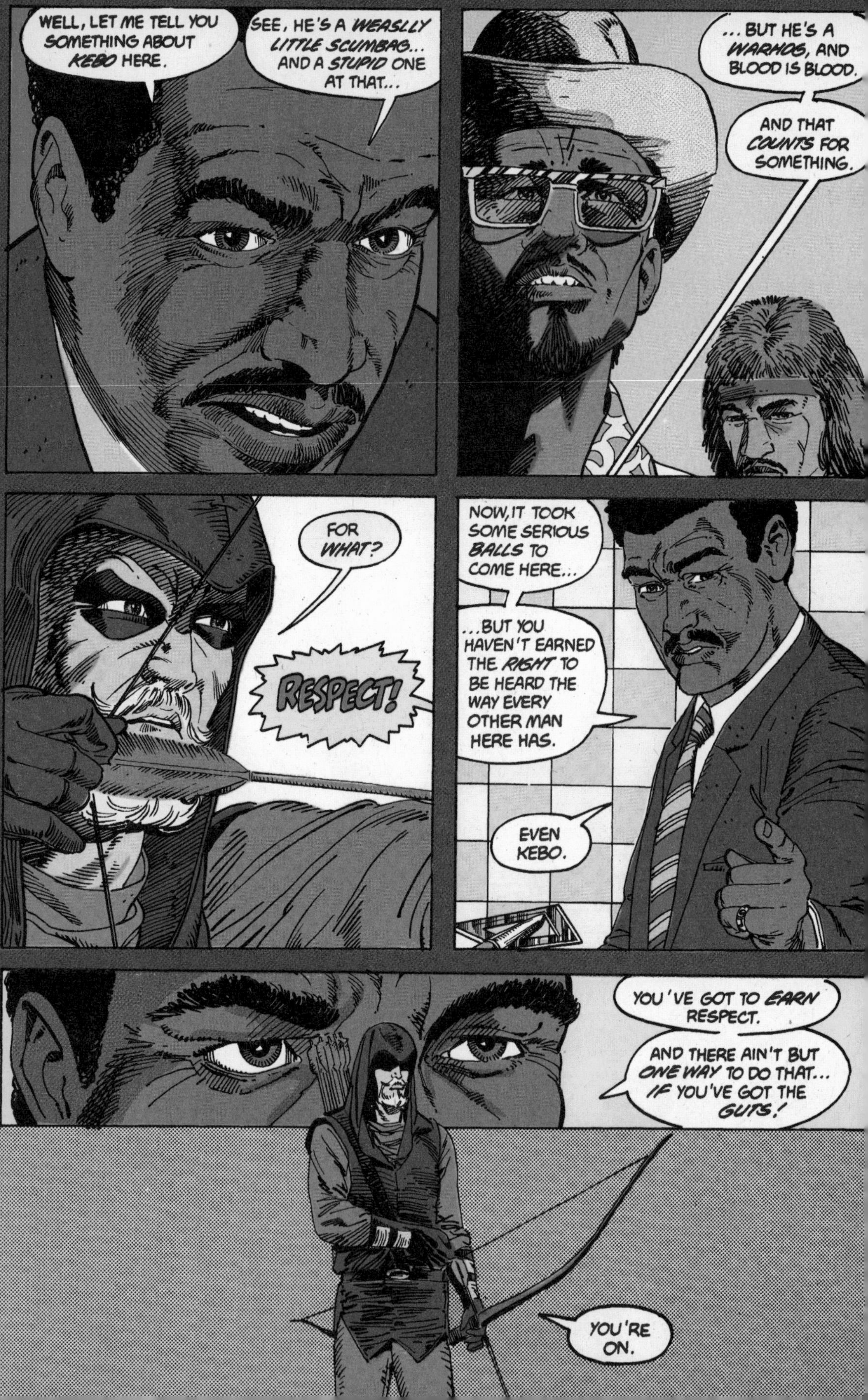
WELL, LET ME TELL YOU SOMETHING ABOUT KEBO HERE.
SEE, HE'S A WEASLLY LITTLE SCUMBAG... AND A STUPID ONE AT THAT...
...BUT HE'S A WARHOG, AND BLOOD IS BLOOD.
AND THAT COUNTS FOR SOMETHING.
FOR WHAT?
RESPECT!
NOW, IT TOOK SOME SERIOUS BALLS TO COME HERE...
...BUT YOU HAVEN'T EARNED THE RIGHT TO BE HEARD THE WAY EVERY OTHER MAN HERE HAS.
EVEN KEBO.
YOU'VE GOT TO EARN RESPECT.
AND THERE AIN'T BUT ONE WAY TO DO THAT... IF YOU'VE GOT THE GUTS!
YOU'RE ON.

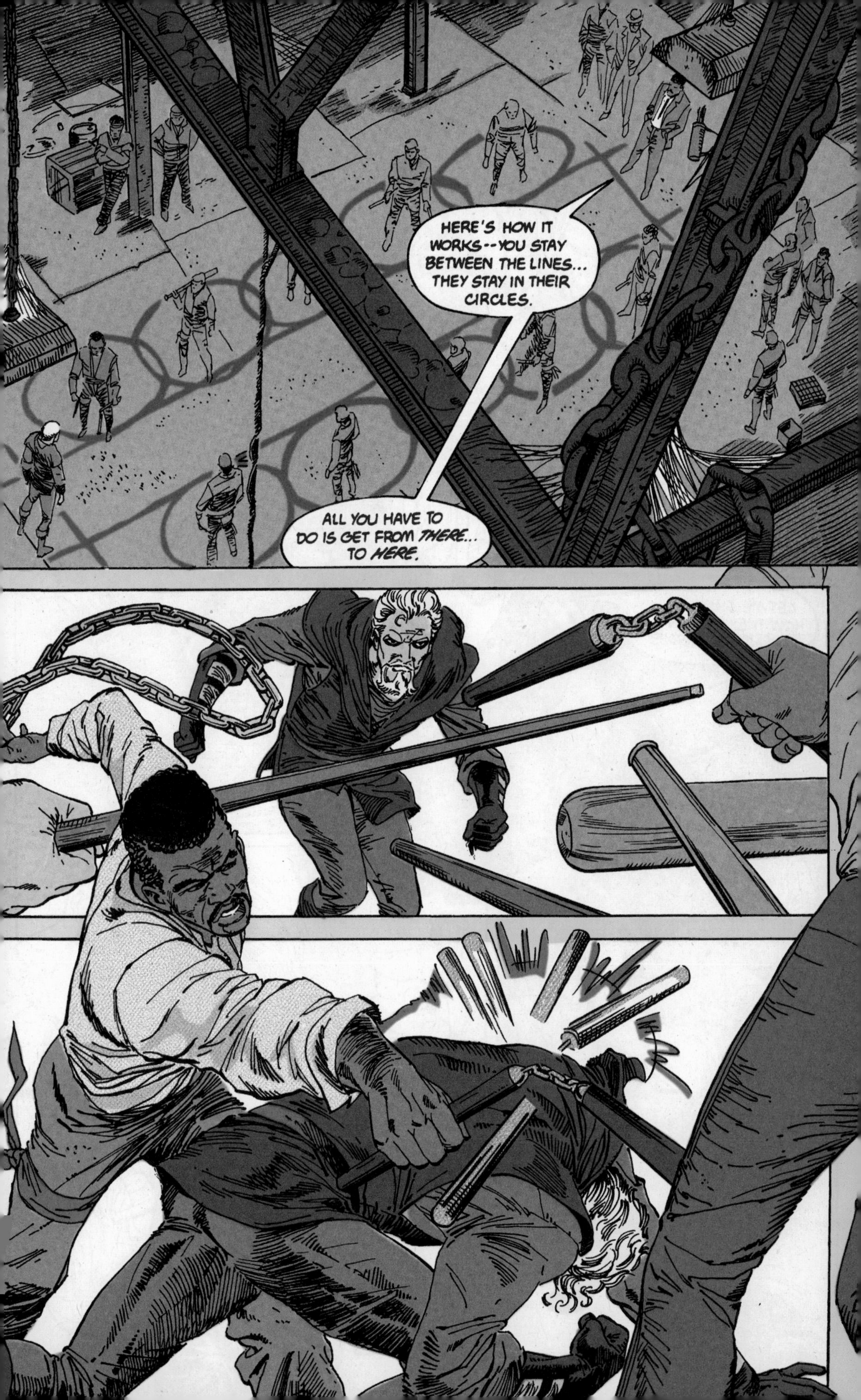
HERE'S HOW IT WORKS--YOU STAY BETWEEN THE LINES... THEY STAY IN THEIR CIRCLES.
ALL YOU HAVE TO DO IS GET FROM *THERE*... TO *HERE*.

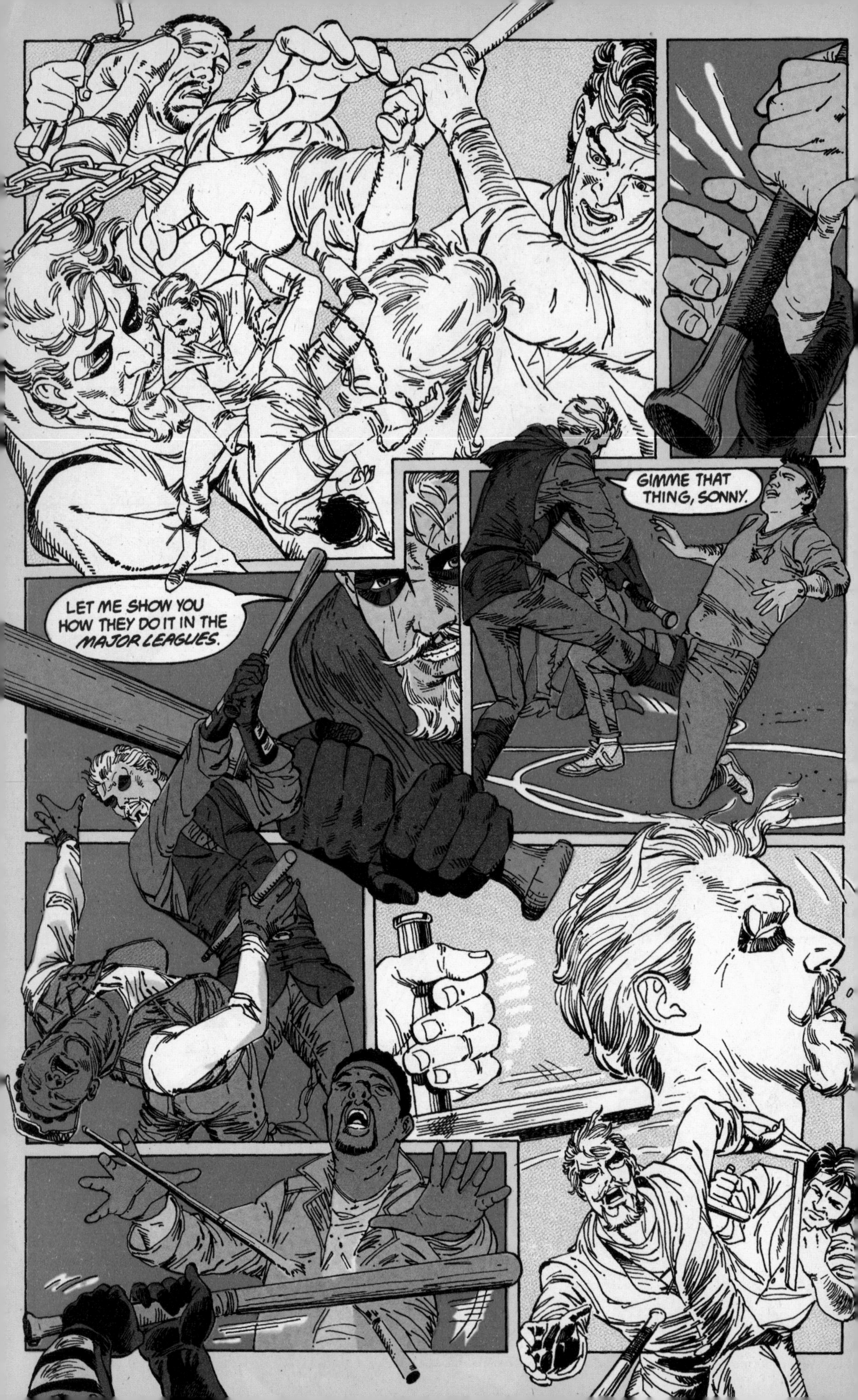
GIMME THAT THING, SONNY.
LET ME SHOW YOU HOW THEY DO IT IN THE MAJOR LEAGUES.

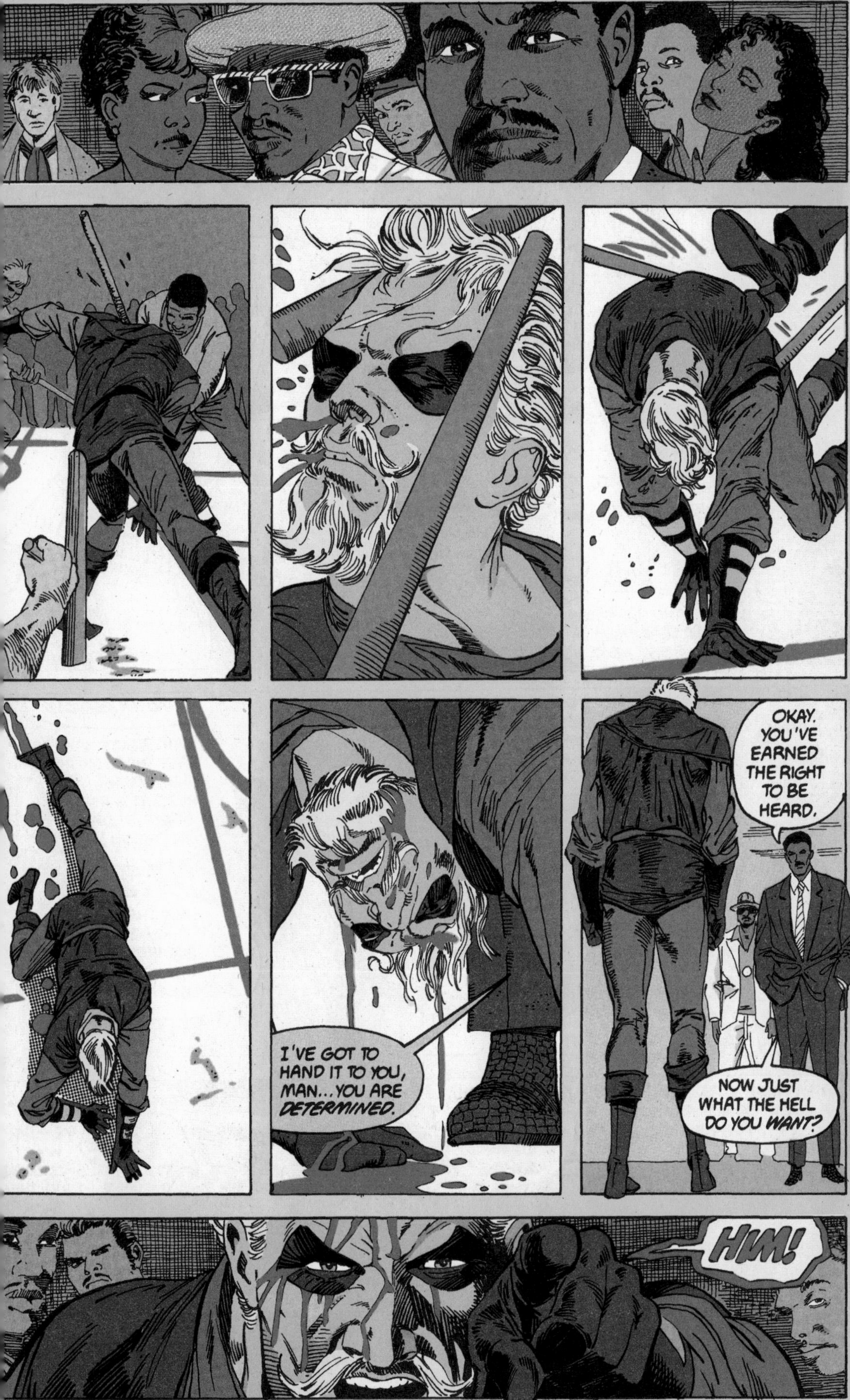
I'VE GOT TO HAND IT TO YOU, MAN... YOU ARE DETERMINED.
OKAY. YOU'VE EARNED THE RIGHT TO BE HEARD.
NOW JUST WHAT THE HELL DO YOU WANT?
HIM!

HEY! REGGIE, MAN. WHAT IS THIS SHIT?

IT'S ONLY A MATTER OF TIME BEFORE THE *COPS* FOLLOW THE SAME TRAIL I DID...

...AND IT'S GOING TO LEAD THEM *RIGHT HERE.*

LOOK, REGGIE, DON'T BE LISTENING TO THIS JIVE-ASS HONKY!

I SAY WE *WASTE* HIM.

I DON'T KNOW, KEBO. HE'S GOT A *POINT.*

WHAT?!! WHAT YOU SAYIN', MAN?

YOU SCREWED UP.

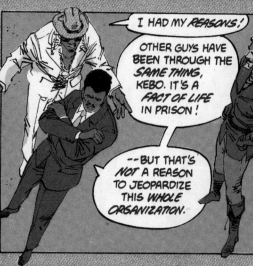

I HAD MY *REASONS!*

OTHER GUYS HAVE BEEN THROUGH THE *SAME THING,* KEBO. IT'S A *FACT OF LIFE* IN PRISON!

--BUT THAT'S *NOT* A REASON TO JEOPARDIZE THIS *WHOLE* ORGANIZATION.

HOW 'BOUT *AIDS,* MAN? *THAT* A GOOD ENOUGH *REASON* FOR YOU?

THAT'S RIGHT, MAN. THEY GIMME THEIR DAMN *DISEASE!*

THEY KILLED ME--SO WHY SHOULDN' I KILL THEM BACK?

YOU AIN'T GOIN' TO TURN ME OVER, REGGIE!

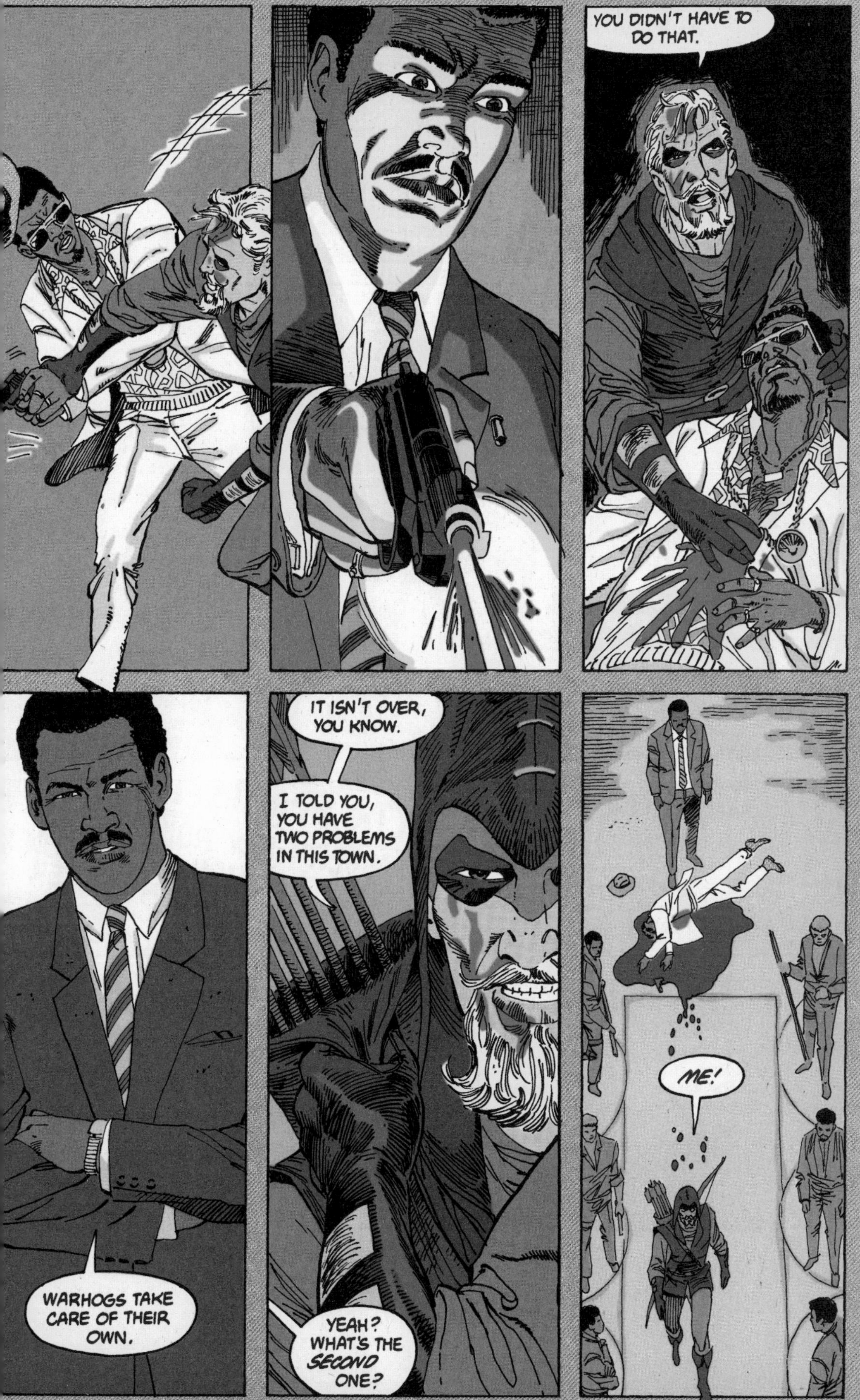
YOU DIDN'T HAVE TO DO THAT.
WARHOGS TAKE CARE OF THEIR OWN.
IT ISN'T OVER, YOU KNOW.
I TOLD YOU, YOU HAVE TWO PROBLEMS IN THIS TOWN.
YEAH? WHAT'S THE SECOND ONE?
ME!

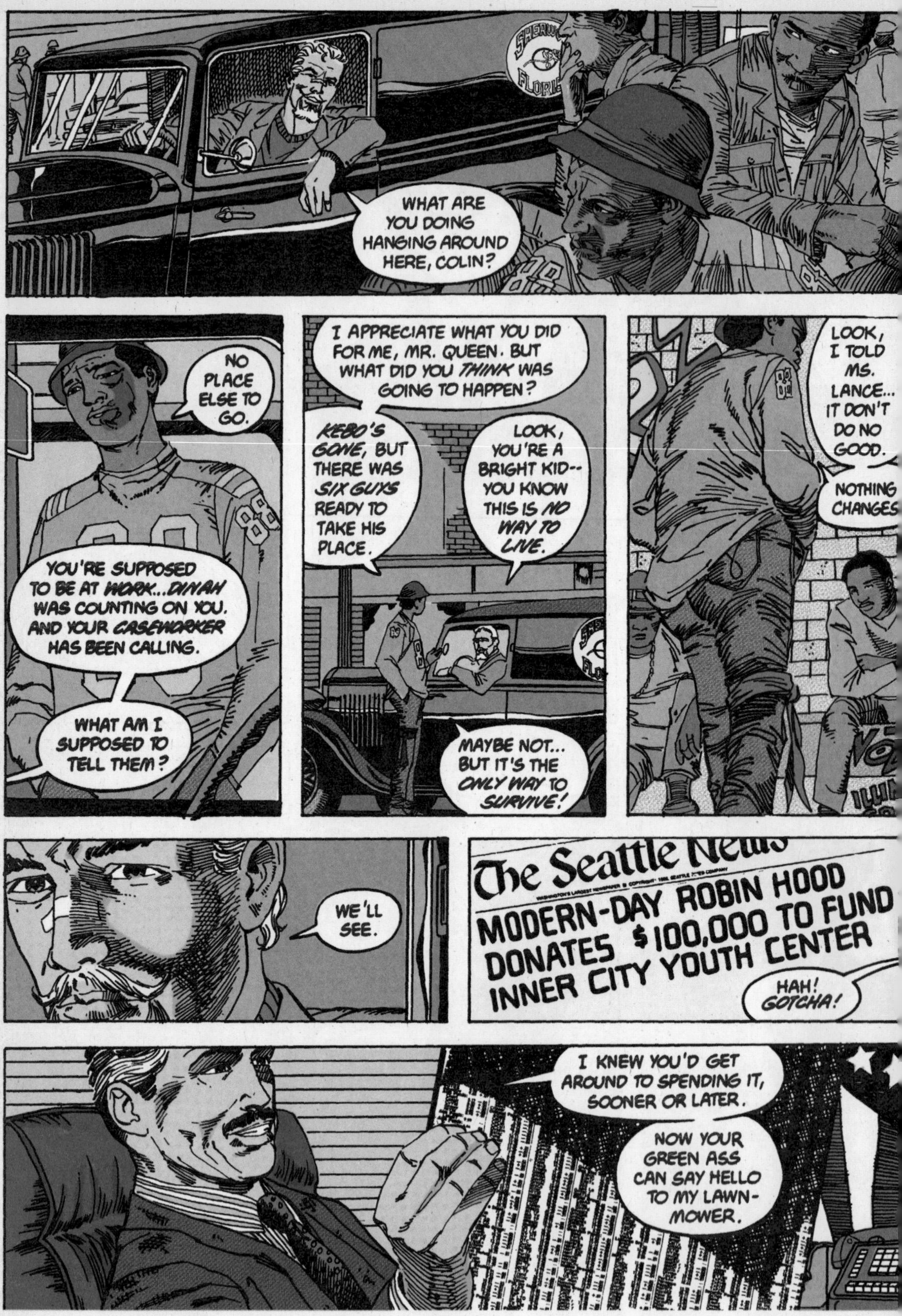
WHAT ARE YOU DOING HANGING AROUND HERE, COLIN?
NO PLACE ELSE TO GO.
YOU'RE SUPPOSED TO BE AT WORK...DINAH WAS COUNTING ON YOU. AND YOUR CASEWORKER HAS BEEN CALLING.
WHAT AM I SUPPOSED TO TELL THEM?
I APPRECIATE WHAT YOU DID FOR ME, MR. QUEEN. BUT WHAT DID YOU THINK WAS GOING TO HAPPEN?
KEBO'S GONE, BUT THERE WAS SIX GUYS READY TO TAKE HIS PLACE.
LOOK, YOU'RE A BRIGHT KID-- YOU KNOW THIS IS NO WAY TO LIVE.
MAYBE NOT... BUT IT'S THE ONLY WAY TO SURVIVE!
LOOK, I TOLD MS. LANCE... IT DON'T DO NO GOOD.
NOTHING CHANGES
WE'LL SEE.
The Seattle News
MODERN-DAY ROBIN HOOD DONATES $100,000 TO FUND INNER CITY YOUTH CENTER
HAH! GOTCHA!
I KNEW YOU'D GET AROUND TO SPENDING IT, SOONER OR LATER.
NOW YOUR GREEN ASS CAN SAY HELLO TO MY LAWN-MOWER.